TIBET

Perspectives and Prospects

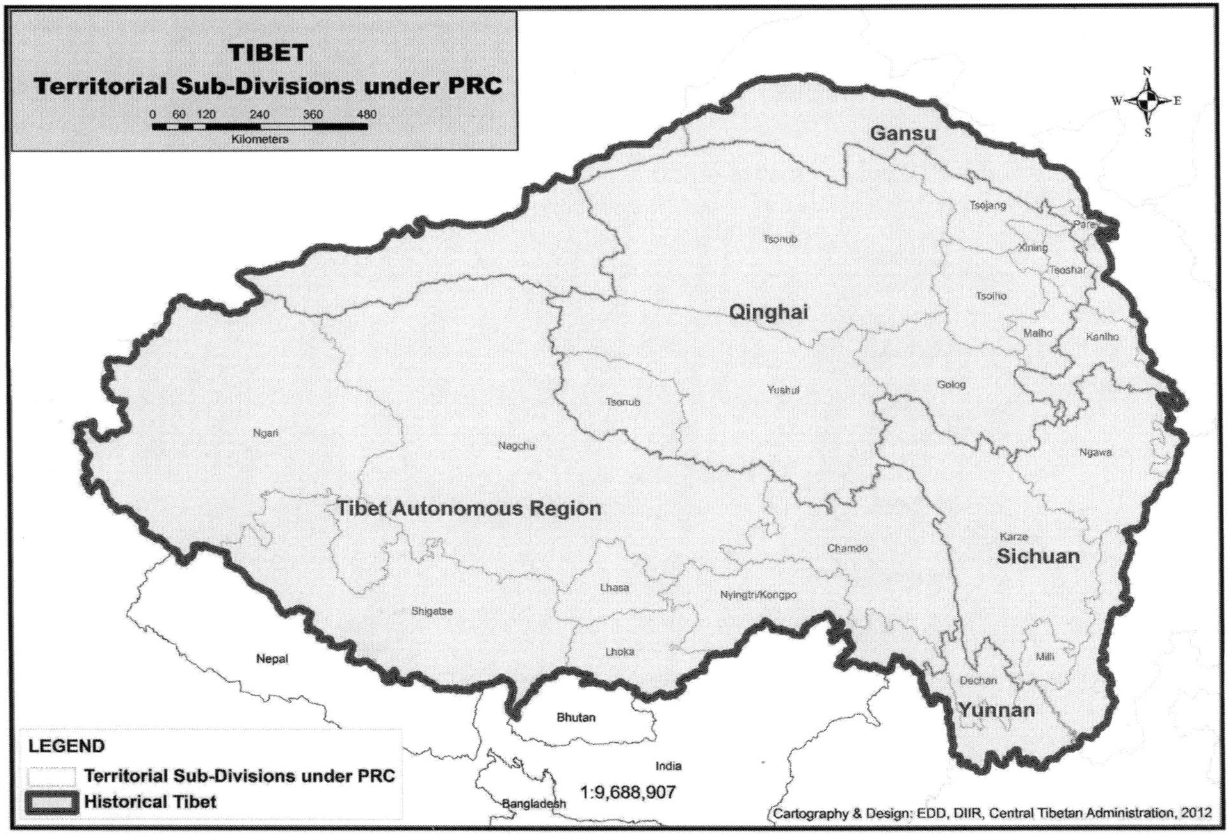
TIBET
Territorial Sub-Divisions under PRC
0 60 120 240 360 480
Kilometers
N
W
E
S
Gansu
Qinghai
Tsonub
Tsojang
Parey
Xining
Tsoshar
Tsolho
Malho
Kanlho
Golog
Yushul
Tsonub
Ngari
Nagchu
Ngawa
Tibet Autonomous Region
Karze
Sichuan
Chamdo
Lhasa
Nyingtri/Kongpo
Shigatse
Lhoka
Milli
Dechan
Yunnan
Nepal
Bhutan
India
Bangladesh
1:9,688,907
LEGEND
Territorial Sub-Divisions under PRC
Historical Tibet
Cartography & Design: EDD, DIIR, Central Tibetan Administration, 2012

TIBET

Perspectives and Prospects

Edited by

Prabhat P. Shukla

Vivekananda International Foundation
New Delhi

Aryan Books International
New Delhi

Cataloging in Publication Data—DK
[Courtesy: D.K. Agencies (P) Ltd. <docinfo@dkagencies.com>]

Tibet: perspectives and prospects / edited by Prabhat P. Shukla.
p. cm.
Contributed articles.
Includes bibliographical references and index.
ISBN 9788173054723

1. Tibet Autonomous Region (China)—Politics and government. 2. Tibet Autonomous Region (China)—Foreign relations—India. 3. India—Foreign relations—Tibet Autonomous Region. 4. Tibet Autonomous Region (China)—Social conditions. 5. Tibet Autonomous Region (China)—Economic conditions. I. Shukla, Prabhat P. (Prabhat Prakash), 1951- II. Vivekananda International Foundation.

DDC 951.5 23

ISBN: 978-81-7305-472-3

Published in **2013** by

Vivekananda International Foundation
3, San Martin Marg, Chanakyapuri, New Delhi - 110 021
www.vifindia.org

in association with

Aryan Books International
Pooja Apartments, 4B, Ansari Road, New Delhi - 110 002 (India)
Tel.: 23287589, 23255799; Fax: 91-11-23270385
E-mail: aryanbooks@gmail.com
www.aryanbooks.co.in

Designed and Printed in India at
ABI Prints & Publishing Co., New Delhi

Contents

Section II
CURRENT SITUATION AND TRENDS

Section III
HUMANITARIAN AND SOCIO-ECONOMIC ASPECTS

Abbreviations

ASEAN	:	Association of Southeast Asian Nations
BASIC	:	Brazil, South Africa, India, China (grouping on climate change negotiations)
BCE	:	Before the Common Era
CE	:	Common Era
CPPCC	:	Chinese People's Political Conservative Conference
CTA	:	Central Tibetan Administration
CTBT	:	Comprehensive Test Ban Treaty
CTSA	:	Central Tibetan School Administration
DIIR	:	Department of Information and International Relations
DMC	:	Democratic Management Committee (Supervisory bodies in Tibet established by the Communist Party)
EDD COP	:	Environment and Development Desk Conferences of the Parties (UNFCCC)
ETIM	:	East Turkestan Islamic Movement

GAN	:	Gansu
GDP	:	Gross Domestic Product
IC	:	Identity Certificate
ICIMOD	:	International Centre for Integrated Mountain Department
J&K	:	Jammu and Kashmir
MTAP	:	Mongol and Tibetan Autonomous Prefecture
NCBCD	:	National Committee on Border and Coastal Defence
NGO	:	Non Governmental Organisation
NRSC	:	National Remote Sensing Centre
OADM	:	Optimal Add Drop Multiplexer
OECD	:	Organisation of Economic Cooperation and Development
OXC	:	Optical Cross Connect
PLA	:	Peoples Liberation Army
PLAAF	:	Peoples Liberation Army Air Force
PLAN	:	Peoples Liberation Army Navy
PRC	:	Peoples Republic of China
PSB	:	Public Security Bureau (of Peoples Republic of China)
QIN	:	Qinghai
QTR	:	Qinghai Tibet Railway
RC	:	Registration Certificate
SAARC	:	South Asian Association for Regional Cooperation
SEP	:	Special Entry Permit
SIC	:	Sichuan

TAP	:	Tibetan Autonomous Prefecture
TAR	:	Tibet Autonomous Region
TCiE	:	Tibetan Community in Exile
TEK	:	Traditional Ecological Knowledge
TGiE	:	Tibetan Government in Exile
TWA	:	Tibetan Woman's Association
TYC	:	Tibetan Youth Congress
UNGA	:	United Nations General Assembly
UNSC	:	United Nations Security Council
VIF	:	Vivekananda International Foundation

Foreword

Is Tibet a closed chapter of history? Many who take a short-term view of history and mistake the present for perpetuity think so. For them, what exists is final. History in its march has, however, always proved the status quoists wrong—from the expansion and subsequent disintegration of the Roman Empire to the balkanisation of the USSR. The old Tibetan saying that "The clouds of summer float by but the sky stays where it is forever", underlines the ancient wisdom of the East, that anything that has changed in the past will change in the future as well. The long-term strategic view of history often gets obfuscated in the dissonance of the immediate—the marching troops, political melodrama, shrill cacophony of the media, and the silence of expediency. Muted but unmistakable changes in Tibet are discernible, and that makes revisiting the issue in the contemporary context relevant.

There was an air of melancholy in the Dalai Lama's lament that,

> When Tibet was free, we took our freedom for granted. Our physical isolation lulled us into a sense of complacency. In former times, Tibetans were a war-like nation whose

> influence spread far and wide. With the advent of Buddhism our military prowess declined.

But more than the melancholy, it was reiteration of the harsh reality of human experience that goodness, unless fortified by strength to assert it, is meaningless and the verdict of the world is always in favour of the strong and not the right.

The developments that took place from the invasion of Tibet's eastern province of Kham by the Chinese army in 1949 to its total subjugation in 1959, leading to the exodus of over one hundred thousand Tibetans led by the Dalai Lama is a sordid chapter of history. It was all the more so as it came close on the heels of the post-War UN Charter that asserted that the world was determined to uphold, "The dignity and worth of the human persons, in the equal rights of men and women and of nations large and small and to establish conditions under which justice and respect for the obligations arising from treaties and other sources of international law can be maintained." It appeared that the world was ushering in a new era—but in reality it was not. The tragedy was not only what the Chinese army did but more so what the rest of the world failed to do.

For centuries, these distinct people inhabiting the roof of the world had a common civilisation, a unique priestly governmental system, flag, currency and the sovereign right to enter into treaties. There is a long and continuous recorded history of Tibet from the time of King Songtsen Gompo from the sixth century AD till date, underlining its separate identity. However, as is true of most ancient states, Tibet too had its ups and downs during its long history and there were times when its freedom in varying degrees was buried under some Chinese empires. It is, however, also true that there had been periods when strong Tibetan regimes exercised control over Chinese territories. One of the landmark treaties was signed between Tibetans and the Chinese as early as 821 AD evident by the text on the stone pillar close to Jokhang temple in Lhasa which states that "Great Tibet" and "Great China" would "act towards each other with respect, friendship and equality." As an independent nation, Tibet entered into treaties with Bushair (1681), Laddakh (1683 and 1842), Nepal (1856), Mongolia (1913), etc. Signing of the Simla treaty in 1914 with the British where it delineated its frontier with India is a historic landmark.

In recent history, Tibet enjoyed all the characteristics of a sovereign nation following the expulsion of the Chinese forces from the Tibetan territory by the 13th Dalai Lama in 1911. All pre-1950 maps, globes and atlases show Tibet as an independent nation. There was an independently functioning government in Tibet when on the dawn of October 6, 1950, the 52nd, 53rd and 54th divisions of the 18th Army of the Chinese military attacked the Tibetan frontier, guarded by 3,500 soldiers and by 2,000 Khampa militiamen. Though heavily outnumbered, the Tibetean forces fought to the last man on the banks of Drichu River and at the river crossing near Markham in the South.

The fact that Tibet was an independent country that was invaded by China was upheld by the Legal Enquiry Committee of the International Commission of Jurists. It asserted in its report that,

> Tibet demonstrated from 1913 to 1950 the conditions of statehood as generally accepted under international law. In 1950, there was a people and a territory, and a government that functioned in that territory, conducting its own domestic affairs free from any outside authority. From 1913-1950, foreign relations of Tibet were conducted exclusively by the Government of Tibet, and countries with whom Tibet had foreign relations are shown by official documents to have treated Tibet as an independent State.

Historical realities are hard to wish away and like the buried seeds assert themselves when the time is ripe.

The relevance of the Tibet issue is, however, not only political. Much beyond politics, there lies a threatened civilisation, cultural heritage, spiritual order and way of life nurtured over the centuries. The struggle in Tibet is more than political; it is for its cultural and spiritual survival. In the march of history the identities rooted in these enduring human attainments prove to be indissoluble; often unfolding the future in most unpredictable ways.

As often misconstrued, the civilisational identity of Tibet is not limited to the geographical confines of the Tibetan Autonomous Region (TAR), drawn up by the Chinese. It extends far beyond and includes areas inhabited by the people who identify themselves as 'Bodpas' and consider the Dalai Lama as their temporal and spiritual head. Often referred as 'historical' or 'cultural' Tibet, besides TAR, includes the provinces of Qinghai, Gansu, Sichuan and Yunnan; together accounting for roughly one fourth the area of present-day China. These areas, with an average altitude of 3,000 metres, are topographically clearly distinguishable with non-Tibetan low lands and are marked by a sparse density of population, ethnically different from people of mainland China.

The other aspect that lends the Tibetan issue a sense of urgency is its human rights dimension. The deeply religious people, unable to defend themselves, have fallen victim to rapacious expansionism and religious suppression of a power, that subscribes to the Marxian prototype that, "Religion is the sigh of the oppressed creature." The post-2008 spate of protests and suicides that have rocked Tibet are as much against Sinification and cultural degradation as for political freedom. The gruesome trail of self-immolations over the years has become more intense, widespread and frequent; the year 2012 alone recording over 82 incidents. Significantly, the incidents were not only confined to Tibet

Autonomous Region (TAR) but also to historical Tibet; which includes several areas that have now been declared as non-Tibetan provinces of China. For the last six decades, the people of Tibet have been facing grave violations of human rights, denial of religious freedom and restrictions to pursue their way of life. Ample evidence of gross human rights violations have been placed before the UN Human Rights Council (UNHRC) and other international bodies by the Tibetans living in exile and their supporters. In March 2012, four international NGOs deposed before the UNHRC on gross violation of human rights, abuse of power and denial of religious freedom. Faith in the pacifist philosophy of Buddhism, small and scattered population, economic poverty and lack of international support make the hapless population an easy target for the Chinese army to suppress and subjugate. Dubbing the Dalai Lama a conspirator, the Chinese consider these self-immolations as part of his crafty machinations. The Chinese Embassy in New Delhi in its website reproduced a December 11, 2012, report from the *People's Daily* insinuating that self-immolations in China's ethnic Tibetan areas were "among the latest tactics that the Dalai clique has taken in recent years to achieve their political purposes". This, however, has failed to obfuscate the harsh reality that the resentment in Tibet against repression and violation of human rights is assuming serious proportions. There is a need for realistic and meaningful initiatives by all stakeholders, including the international community to establish peace and normalcy in Tibet. It is unfortunate that the talks between Dalai Lama and the Chinese did not yield any fruitful results. There exists a sort of stalemate which needs to be broken through bold political initiatives.

The problem of over one million Tibetan exiles, living in different parts of the world, is another important dimension of the Tibetan issue. These exiles, most of them living in India, in terms of their legal status, being neither citizens of any country, nor refugees, illegal immigrants or stateless persons are non-existent. Uprooted from their homeland for over half a century, their economic and social life is in shambles. The only hope that sustains them is their abiding faith in the Dalai Lama's leadership, their religious and temporal head, who heads the Tibetan government in exile and takes care of their basic survival needs. This, however, is undergoing a change following the Dalai Lama's historic step to give up his political power.

The Dalai Lama's voluntary abdication of his political power in March 2011 and its devolution to an elected democratic leadership is a watershed. In April 2011, Dr. Lobsang Sangay was elected to the high office of Kalon Tripa (Prime Minister) of the government in exile. This step has long term implications. First, of course, is that hereafter the political and administrative powers which were earlier vested in the Dalai Lama would be exercised by a democratically elected body. Secondly, it brings about a separation of religious authority from the political authority which had been the hallmark of the priestly arrangement in Tibet for centuries. Lastly, and most importantly, this brings to an end the reliance of the movement on the life of an individual. It will prove those wrong who thought that the life of the Tibetan movement was co-terminus with that of the Dalai Lama. Through this transfer of political power, the Dalai Lama has made every Tibetan—in and out of Tibet—a stakeholder in the Tibetan struggle.

From the Indian perspective, Tibet has a special security import. India shares nearly a 4,000 kms. of border with Tibet, which is now the Sino-Indian border. Despite India's best efforts and sixteen rounds of talks to settle the border dispute, little progress has been made in this direction. China's development of military infrastructure in Tibet, assistance to Pakistan in developing strategic weapon systems, new assertions in the Indian Ocean, claiming

Tawang in Arunachal Pradesh as 'Southern Tibet', etc. have raised security concerns in India. Seen in the backdrop of China's rise as a major military and economic power and its comprehensive military modernisation programme, that is more aggressive than defensive, serious security concerns have been raised in India. India's security interests are thus intricately linked to developments in Tibet and need detailed study and analysis.

In recent years, there has been considerable interest among the scholars, human right activists, strategic thinkers and the wider public about Tibet. I am happy that the Vivekananda International Foundation (VIF) is bringing out a publication focussing on different aspects of the Tibet imbroglio. Some noted experts and professionals with long experience have contributed to this work. The articles cover a wide range of issues providing comprehensive perspectives as also an analysis of contemporary developments.

I am grateful to Ambassador Prabhat Shukla for his painstaking efforts to bring out this book. I am sure the readers will find the publication useful.

New Delhi
February 1, 2013

Ajit Doval
Director, VIF

Editor's Introduction

This book reflects the views of an institution, and individuals, who are deeply concerned about Tibet. This concern ranges from the past, especially the recent tragic past, to the future. As to the past, there is a sense of concern that India and, before 1947, British India, did not play fair by that unfortunate country. More specifically, the contributions reflect the anguish felt by a growing number of people around the world that the history and the current reality of Tibet are not adequately known, and hence the tragedy continues—away from the glare of publicity.

For starters, it is important for Indians to understand, and internalize, that Tibet was an independent country at least by the first half of the twentieth century. Without this, the McMahon Line, which so many of our soldiers died defending, is illegal, as the Chinese claim it is. For, if Tibet was not competent to sign the Simla Conference documents, the McMahon Line which resulted from the discussions, has no legal validity. This, the question of whether Tibet was independent prior to its occupation in 1950, is also one of the main issues that is holding up forward movement in the dialogue between His Holiness the Dalai Lama and the

Government of the People's Republic of China. They want the former to acknowledge that Tibet was always part of China, whereas His Holiness says that such an acceptance would be contrary to historical fact. He is willing, under clear duress, to accept that Tibet is part of China today, but it was not in the past.

While the British had their reasons for treating Tibet the way they did, and imposing the suzerainty of China on the country, independent India had no such reasons. The oddity here is that independent India did, in fact, treat Tibet as an independent country at the very beginning—in the 1947 Asian Relations Conference, which Nehru called on the eve of the formal independence of India. The Chinese delegation—then representing the Nationalist [Kuomintang] Government of Chiang Kai-shek—there had objected to the participation of Tibet and to its flag being displayed. However, these objections were ignored by India and Tibet did participate as an independent country. For some inexplicable reason, Nehru changed his position when the Communist Party seized power and proclaimed the People's Republic. What made this doubly odd was that the Nationalists had been staunch supporters of Indian independence at a time when the Chinese Communist Party had been dismissive and derogatory towards the freedom movement. Chiang was personally known to Nehru, and had spoken publicly in support of Indian independence.

Nehru's noting in 1949 on the absence of any possibility of a military threat to India from Tibet is a classic of why leaders must possess intellectual humility. It was, in a way, this error of judgement that was to prove fatal to him, for the rude awakening in 1962 did really hasten his death in 1964. Unfortunately, it also burdened Indian thinking, planning, as well as diplomatic and military action for decades afterwards. It continues to be a burden on the country even today.

The other aspect that bears emphasising is the role that India played after the Chinese forces occupied Tibet. The country that had willingly, if with more enthusiasm than good sense, referred the Jammu & Kashmir dispute to the UN, effectively blocked any discussion of Tibet in the UN. After many twists and turns, when the issue finally came before the Security Council in November 1950, it was the Indian Permanent Representative who assured the Council that a peaceful settlement was being worked out, and therefore the Council need not consider the matter for now. This complete lack of statecraft informs all subsequent developments relating to Tibet and to India-China relations more broadly. Why this was so—and remains so—is an enduring mystery that the historical record does not clear up.

Given this history, it is clear that there is a very serious challenge facing Tibet and the international community in addressing it. Fortunately, there are some issues that do admit of international involvement. These have also been dealt with at some length in the book. There is, first, the environmental question. The way the waters of Tibet have been diverted and dams built, or plans to that effect, are a clear environmental threat to Tibet itself; they are also a serious threat to the lower riparian states, including India, Bangladesh, and several of the South-East Asian countries. It is to be hoped that these countries, and their partners, will be able to work together to persuade the Beijing authorities of the need to re-examine these projects.

There is, secondly, the issue of Human Rights. The violation of the human and other rights of the Tibetans rank among the worst and most egregious. They do not get the attention in the media that they deserve, but the situation there is nothing short of what His Holiness has called it—cultural genocide. Self-immolations are also a continuing part of the tragic narrative. To their credit, some of the Human Rights agencies have called it correctly, and some countries, like the US, have appointed Special Envoys for Tibet, but the results have not been encouraging. Further efforts are called for, and India, above all, has to stop being so apologetic in respect of what it does with, and for, His Holiness.

Third, and perhaps most important, there are the UNGA Resolutions on self-determination for Tibet. The first of these was adopted in 1961—the first explicitly to call for self-determination—and repeated, in modified form, in 1965. The latter becomes important because India voted in favour for the first time. It can surely not be a coincidence that this was after Nehru was no more. There are those who argue that a UNGA Resolution does not have the legal backing that a Security Council Resolution has. They are right, of course, but the vote on the partition of Palestine, and hence the establishment of the state of Israel, was held in the UNGA. Similarly, many other actions—in Korea, in Afghanistan—were sanctioned by the UNGA because the Security Council would not approve certain resolutions because the interests of a Veto Power were involved.

Of course, it is only realistic to acknowledge that movement in any of these directions will require a Government in Beijing that will pay heed to these concerns of the Tibetans and the international community. It must be clear beyond peradventure that the present regime will not countenance any such change. However, there are winds of change blowing in China too. Whether one looks at the politics of the country, or its economy, or societal movements, this fact cannot be denied. The kind of disclosures on the wealth amassed by the relatives and friends of leaders like Xi Jinping [disclosed in Bloomberg] or Wen Jiabao [disclosed by the *New York Times*] or the story of Bo Xilai are all indicative of divisions in the political elite in China. Equally, the economy is showing signs not just of slowing down, though that would be bad enough; structural issues are emerging that could seriously impact the future growth of the economy, and the prospects of a soft landing. There is the overreliance on investments and exports, both of which are nearing the end of their utility. There is also the large monetary overhang, reflected in the fact that money supply [M2] in the economy is close to 200 per cent of the GDP.

All of this, in turn, is feeding social unrest on an ever-increasing scale. Most students of Chinese politics are familiar with Wukan, where popular pressure forced policy and personnel changes. A similar process has also taken place in Ningbo, where the driver of popular concern was the environment. From all accounts, this is a pervasive problem—social unrest, that is—and is only getting aggravated with the passing years. Collectively, these instances of unrest are calling into question the legitimacy of the system that has ruled China for the last six decades. The system has run on a complex social contract, consisting of high growth delivered by the government, in return for the people's acquiescence in the rigid system they are compelled to live under.

In fine, the saga of Tibet is still ongoing. It is a negative reflection on the policies of India—British and post-Independence—that Mongolia and Tibet both started from the same spot historically in 1912-13. Today, Mongolia is an independent country, thanks to the hard-headed stewardship of the Russians. For it was they who demanded, both from the Nationalists and later from the Communists, an unequivocal recognition of the independence of Mongolia. India did less well in the statecraft involving Tibet, and we are all witness to the trauma of the people of that country. There was a fear, at the dawn of the twentieth century, that the 13th Dalai Lama was too close to the Russians, and favoured taking Tibet under their tutelage. Perhaps he simply showed good sense, and was the loser for having failed to do what he wished to do.

With these remarks, the book is commended to the reader. It is a collection of articles contributed by individuals with their own views and analyses. The idea of the book emerged from a seminar that was held some time back, at which the new Kalon Tripa of Tibet, Dr. Lobsang Sangay, and other leaders, participated. Their remarks have been presented in the form in which they were delivered—as speeches. The others have been adapted as essays. The book makes no attempt to harmonise these views, except insofar as the factual accuracy of the references is concerned. The alert reader will notice the individual variations, and is free to pursue the facts further.

What the Vivekananda International Foundation stands by is the right of these views to be heard and publicised, and debated, where required. It is also my pleasant task to express my thanks to my junior colleagues, Neha Mehta and Arka Biswas, for helping me with the editing of the book.

In this spirit the book is commended to the reader.

Prabhat P. Shukla
Joint Director, VIF

Vision for Tibet

Lobsang Sangay

...We are fighting for Tibetan Dignity, Tibetan Identity, Tibetan Freedom. What we are seeking is Equality...

Often when journalists ask me what do I feel about India, I say that I grew up in a Tibetan refugee camp subsidised by the Indian government, I went to a refugee school subsidised by the Indian government, I went to Delhi University again subsidised by the Indian government and nowadays I travel around on trains and cars whose gas is subsidised by the Indian government. In short, I am a proud product of subsidies provided by the Indian government! Hence it is very appropriate that I come here to share my thoughts with very prominent Indians in the centre of the capital city Delhi.

When I was first asked to come here, I was a bit hesitant. As you know, during the elections I was labeled the youngest and least experienced of the candidates; therefore, I thought perhaps it is better that I spend much of my time preparing for the

---

Text of remarks made at a VIF Seminar in September 2011 [updated].

parliamentary session which will begin from September 16 and continue till October 1, 2011. As you know, it is a grueling session between the executive and legislative branches because it is not a parliamentary system where the majority of the parliament runs the executive branch. Ours is somewhat like the presidential system. Our Speaker is also here today. So I thought of spending most of my time preparing for the parliamentary session. Because when I took oath on August 8, and from then to September 16 I had to face a challenge which is a sort of one-man-rule, that is, I have to take up the reins of the government alone till the parliament confirmed my cabinet. I have to run the whole administration myself—all seven departments, hundreds of monasteries and so on. On a daily basis, files pile up before me, I keep giving executive orders, signing so many documents. But then I thought I don't mind being grilled by the parliament and because I owe much to this effort of the VIF I should come down and share my thoughts here. It's a great privilege and honour.

People misunderstand when you talk of Tibet. I shall discuss the political, environmental and cultural maps of Tibet, followed by briefly narrating history and then the current political environment and situation. I will also discuss what the devolution of political authority by His Holiness means in general, but I will limit it to myself, to me as a person. So in short I have to cover two thousand years of Tibetan history and the current situation in the next 20 some minutes; I will spend a minute for a hundred years [of history], so please bear with me. So I hope when you go through it you will not suffer from headaches but rather get some clarity on the situation of and in Tibet.

When we talk about Tibet, the Chinese definition of Tibet constitutes only the Tibet Autonomous Region (TAR) whereas the Tibetan definition of Tibet includes three traditional provinces of Tibet called U-Tsang, Kham and Amdo, more than half of which is incorporated into Chinese Provinces of Yunnan, Sichuan, Qinghai and Gansu. In a sense, geographically Tibet is almost 1/4th the territory of China. So territory-wise the area is 2 million sq kms, which is as big as the whole of Western Europe or Texas and California combined; so it is a huge tract of land. When China says Tibet is just the TAR, we refuse it by saying Tibet includes parts of Qinghai and Sichuan, where my father was born. The Tibetan uprising in 2008 occurred in hundred or so counties of the Tibetan areas, so I think the Tibetan voice has made it very clear as to what really constitutes Tibet. Our definition of TAR is mainly U-tsang province, but Amdo is the region where His Holiness the Dalai Lama was born. Linguistically also, both the political and traditional maps also reflect that Sichuan and Qinghai provinces features Tibetan speaking areas and it overlaps. And you can see from the geography itself that the Tibetan Plateau is Tibet. So it is very clear that when we say Tibet it is the Tibetan Plateau—so then geographically also it is different from China.

There is a lot of environmental destruction happening because of climate change. In Delhi also we have heavy rains now in September which is unusual. The melting of glaciers and permafrost in Tibet directly affects the monsoon and the climate of Asia. There are the ten major rivers flowing from Tibet. So this is one answer to the question, why India or Asia should care about or support Tibet—the environmental impact on the countries of Asia is very clear. Fresh water from Tibet provides drinking water to all people living in the continent of Asia and around. The rivers flow all the way to Mekong, to Thailand, to Burma, Bangladesh and Pakistan. In India also you see the Brahmaputra River which comes from Tibet. Tibet has been a steward, a guardian of Tibetan water and environment in general and we have maintained the spiritual and natural way of dealing with the environment, in the sense that we have allowed the natural flow of rivers, we have respected that. Now with the Chinese coming in, what has happened is that they have dammed the major rivers—not just one but up to dozen dams in some rivers.

As has been mentioned in the Indian media, the Brahmaputra is dammed quite heavily which affects India and her neighbouring countries. If nothing else, the Chinese will have control over the flow of water to India and other regions of the subcontinent. Millions of people in Bangladesh and all over survive on fishery and agriculture and when you dam rivers, you have control over them and thus it will affect millions of people's livelihood.

And you know rare earths are now becoming very famous; without these one cannot produce many of the technological gadgets; China has a monopoly over these. Almost 80-90% of rare earths come from China, actually from Inner Mongolia, and the major source of water is from Tibet, so China controls both these resources. Recently they have announced that the largest gold reserve in Asia is in Tibet and the gold price is shooting sky high nowadays. So, as you can see, Tibet was neither a small territory nor a small power. Historically during 7th and 8th centuries it was a major power and its influence extended all the way up to the Chinese capital, Chang'an. Once the Tibetan army marched all the way to the Chinese capital and captured it including the emperor and reportedly appointed a puppet Chinese emperor. The Tibetan King Songtsän Gampo had two wives. One of them was the Chinese princess named Wencheng and the other was Nepalese princess named Bhrikuti Devi. At that time, Tibet was such a power that even the Chinese and Nepalese kings gave their nieces and daughters in marriage to buy peace with Tibet.

And then we move straight to 1910, when the 13th Dalai Lama fled to India after the Chinese invasion. The challenge Tibetans face now is how to restore freedom in Tibet and ensure the return of H.H. the 14th Dalai Lama to Lhasa. This was the same challenge faced by the 13th Dalai Lama. With the Chinese invasion, the 13th Dalai Lama fled to India and the Tibetans successfully managed his rightful return to Lhasa. So the challenge remains the same, and we have done it before, and we believe we can do it again. The Tibet-Mongolia treaty was signed in 1913, which declared both countries as independent countries. All of you know about the Simla Agreement in 1914. On the left of the document you will see a stamp of the British Indian and Tibetan representative. The treaty demarcated the McMahon line as the border between India and Tibet. Then came the 17-point agreement which was signed between Tibetan and Chinese representatives in Beijing in 1951, the year we lost our sovereignty. The agreement essentially surrendered our sovereignty but it was under duress because our representatives were told that if they did not sign, the Chinese would move forward with their invasion and occupy our land. Having said that, and as mentioned earlier, His Holiness seeks genuine autonomy within the framework of the Chinese constitution.

If you read Article 1 of the 17-point agreement it says that Tibet shall return to the motherland. China claims Tibet has always been part of China but as you can see, the history of Tibet's empire, the 1913 treaty with Mongolia and even the 17-point agreement, all show that Tibet was not always part of China; otherwise there would be no question of Tibet returning to the 'motherland' if it was not out of China or always part of it. Similary, Article 4 says that the power and status of His Holiness and the Tibetan government will be kept intact, something along the line of the one country and two systems formula. Therefore, the present system implemented in Hong Kong and Macao by the Chinese government was very much enshrined in the 17-point agreement that we signed in 1951. However, by 1959, it was very clear that the Chinese government had other ideas. They wanted to occupy and colonise Tibet rather than grant what was agreed to in the 17-point agreement.

On March 10, 1959, there was a major uprising in Lhasa and then after the occupation of Tibet around 80,000 Tibetans fled to India. With the kind effort of the Indian government, Tibetans were provided land in various parts of India to start refugee camps and many of them were given jobs as road construction workers. So from Sikkim to Manali to Dalhousie, the highways were built by Tibetans. And then during the Cultural Revolution in China the second most popular Tibetan leader Panchen Lama went through a very harrowing time. Then the present times, and you read for example in the *Frontline* magazine and the *Hindu* newspaper, Mr. N. Ram saying that he went to Tibet and found everything there fine, that Tibetans are satisfied with the situation, that they are happy.

But the actual picture is otherwise.

For example, there is a picture that shows a small Chinese shop in Lhasa displaying a job advertisement. It said 'if you are Tibetan we will give you 30 Renminbi, if you are Chinese we will give you 50 Renminbi.' So in Lhasa, the capital city of Tibet - Lhasa means land of God for Tibetans, it is sacred - a Chinese shop has the audacity to put a job placement that says Chinese will be paid more than a Tibetan.

How would you feel if there is a signboard in a Chinese shop in Delhi which says if you are Indian we give you Rs. 30 a day and if Chinese we give you Rs. 50 a day? So these are signboards of Chinese economic development—the socialist paradise that they promised. Initially, when they came they promised a socialist paradise and told the Tibetan people that they would be happy to remain within the Chinese domain. I am again reminding you that this situation of deprivation is prevalent in all parts of Tibet; hence there was protest all over Tibet.

You can see from recent pictures in newspapers of monks committing self-immolation, given the unbearable situation, given the repression that is going on in Tibet. Tibetans find it so unbearable that they are willing to give up their lives. You can see the monks, they are healthy, and then self-immolating themselves; all this has happened recently. It is not unusual. This is going on; Tibetans are being pushed to the brink by the Chinese occupation. The Tibetan spirit still remains however. It has been 60 years of occupation since 1951 and a whole generation of Tibetans has changed, in the sense that the majority in Tibet have never seen or met with His Holiness the Dalai Lama. Most of us have not been to Tibet as well and the interaction between us is quite limited. Having said that, the Tibetan spirit inside and outside is still strong. The evidence of this spirit could be seen in 1987, 1988, 1989 when there were a series of protests in Tibet most of which were led by monks around the Jokhang temple—Tibet's holiest shrine.

The Chinese government thought that they could find a solution to these kinds of protests by replacing all the monks in Jokhang temple with loyalists. They removed all the monks from the temple and recruited new monks, the only ones in the whole of Tibet who are paid salaries. Even the Tibetans have a little bit of suspicion towards these monks and believed that they had leanings towards the Communist Party. In 2008, when protests happened all over Tibet, the Chinese government thought perhaps they could have some propaganda by inviting 20 odd journalists to Lhasa to show that peace has returned to the city. They showed them around some Tibetan Communist Party offices and obviously the Tibetan Communist Party members will parrot the party line; the group was then taken to the Jokhang monastery, where the Chinese thought the monks would authenticate the Chinese version.

When the group reached the monastery, these paid monks came out and said "no, His Holiness is not responsible for the uprising in 2008 and it's a lie, Tibet is not free". In short, the Tibetan spirit is so strong that even though you are paid and fed by the Communist Party, your loyalty to your leader and to your cause and to the Tibetan people and Tibet is so deeply embedded that they will come forward and speak the truth.

This slide shows that we have no freedom of speech, this is in Amdo area, and all of them are young and leading the protest. So if anyone has any doubt as to what has happened to the Tibetan spirit, you can see that the essence of loyalty, of patriotism, the essence of urgency for the cause is very strong and very deep. What the Chinese government did at that point of time is that they rolled out tanks in the streets of Lhasa and other places.

Now I will come to the final part. What does the devolution of political authority to the Tibetan people mean? The August 8 was the inauguration of the newly elected Kalon Tripa, and if you read newspapers it was widely covered by the international media, which indicates that the Tibetan issue is very much alive and strong in the mind of the international community.

I remember when I was in Delhi University I used to be the president of regional Tibetan Youth Congress. We organised protests in front of the Chinese embassy and made sure they were covered. We had press releases prepared in advance, and we would go and drop them into all the press boxes and scan the newspapers the next day for some news. Sometimes a small caption gave us a great thrill. Today media coverage is on the rise, and on an almost daily basis I get media requests from various parts of the world. So it has changed, as media interest, sympathy and support of the international community is strong.

I also want to make it very clear what Tibet means and how Tibet looks, its huge area, its serious issues as well as its major ramifications. Two, when people hear the words 'after the devolution', they feel as though there is some disconnect between the period before and after the devolution of power. But what has happened is the continuation of the same political leadership. What His Holiness said on that day is this: 'When I was young, an elderly regent Takdrag Rinpoche handed over Sikyong (political leadership) to me, and today I am handing over Sikyong to young Lobsang Sangay…in doing this I have fulfilled my long-cherished goal". That is a very important historical statement because since 1642 till August 8, 2011 the political authority rested with the institution of the Dalai Lamas. From the Great Fifth Dalai Lama onwards and through the 6th, 7th, and 8th Dalai Lamas, the transition continued till 8 August. Therefore, when he said I am handing over political leadership to young Lobsang Sangay he was handing over the political authority of the institution of the Dalai Lama to the Kalon Tripa; it is the continuation of history, the continuation of the same political authority of the 369-year-old institution of the Dalai Lamas and most importantly after he made the statement he said that this has been his 'long-cherished goal' which is again very important.

Another thing that the former Kalon Tripa did was to hand over a seal of the 7th Dalai Lama to me. The seal was established in 1751 in Tibet and the same seal was brought out to India in 1959. The same seal was handed over to me, this means that the same political authority established by the 7th Dalai Lama continued with me, the same legitimacy that the institution of the Dalai Lama had continued with me, the same political leadership that the institution of the Dalai Lama had continued with me. So devolution of authority means separation of the spiritual and the political authority of the institution of the Dalai Lamas—the spiritual authority continues with the Dalai Lama but the political authority continues with the Central Tibetan Administration (CTA) and the political leadership, so it's a continuation and not the end.

Sometimes they say His Holiness has given up power, everything has changed, I want to clarify that nothing has changed, my role is not to do something different, rather my role is to live up to the expectation of His Holiness and that I can provide the leadership whereby the Tibetan people can stand on their feet and take the Tibetan movement forward. My role is to fulfill the vision of a secular democratic society that His Holiness has and also to remember the hard work of elder Tibetans, including those who are dying in Tibet and those who were construction workers—who built roads for India. They have worked very hard and built the CTA and the freedom movement is strong only because of the past hard work of the older generations. My duty is to remember that and to build on their legacy to move the Tibetan freedom struggle forward.

When I was in Harvard, I spent sixteen years meeting hundreds and hundreds of Chinese students and scholars. I organised seven major conferences involving Chinese scholars who had come all the way from Beijing University or the Chinese Academy of Social Sciences and even the Communist Party School. I have a sixteen years' record of having held dialogues with Chinese intellectuals, now the Chinese government and media label me as illegal and so on. I wasn't 'illegal' when I was in Harvard as I used to meet with them on a daily basis. But now suddenly when I got elected they are labeling me. But that label is not going to change me and my belief in dialogue had been established when I was in Harvard. This means when His Holiness says that we are sincere in having a dialogue with the Chinese government to resolve issues peacefully, he means it, when I say it I also mean it.

When you meet with Chinese it is not that easy, some Chinese are nice, some are nasty, some are ignorant, so I tolerated their ignorance and nastiness for sixteen years. That means I believe in His Holiness's idea that we have to solve the issue peacefully through dialogue. I have also organised two conferences between His Holiness and Chinese scholars in 2003 and 2009 when more than a hundred Chinese scholars and students met with His

Holiness. We have a proven record of believing in and organising conferences to solve the issue peacefully through dialogue. That's why there are many Chinese intellectuals in China and outside China who are really interested on the issue of Tibet, including the Nobel Peace Laureate Liu Xiaobo and others.

What does Tibet mean for India and the Indian people? We recognize Tibet is a core issue between India and China. We are not against there being a better relationship between India and China or a business relationship, but the truth is that most of the countries have not profited from doing business with People's Republic of China. But it is also true that we are not against it, we are for doing business with the Chinese people. Once I was asked to give talk to the Nepalese students and scholars at Harvard Kennedy School and they said we want railway lines all the way from Lhasa to Kathmandu. I asked why. They said we want to do business with the Chinese, but I said no one in the world has profited by doing business with the Chinese. In the end you will be cumulatively in the loss column. I wished them good luck and said that initially we also thought that when the Chinese first came we would profit from their business, as they started building roads, giving us silver coins, etc. Initially they were polite, but once the roads were built, overnight they changed their personality, for they became rude, overbearing, and started shooting, and finally occupied us. Their roads surrounded the strategic areas, they went to the mountains and destroyed our pristine forests, our woods went to China, and our minerals were mined and continue to be mined. They took away all kinds of mineral resources, I am not surprised that the Chinese are staying longer than guests are expected to stay and they have valid reasons, it seems! So the idea that they are there to help us is absolutely not true.

Now why should India and the Indian people take interest in the issue of Tibet? Obviously, Buddhism we borrowed from

India, we say Tibetan civilisation but it is very much Buddhist and borrowed from India. Our literature is very similar to the Indian; it is adapted from the Indian script. And there is also the issue of security, on a daily basis, there is incursion in the border areas. The Chinese presence is also strong in the seas, building ports in Burma to the ones in Sri Lanka and Pakistan. Then there are the airfields, so many airfields in Tibet, some say five major airfields, and railway lines coming up to the Nathu La, may be up to Nepal and Bangladesh soon. It is a fact that India is surrounded by Chinese presence; so when we talk about the Chinese, it's not that you have to go to Nathu La to see Chinese, even in Kanyakumari now you will feel the presence of the Chinese. These facts are all based on the Indian media reports; I am not saying anything new here.

His Holiness said that the act of devolving his political authority to the Tibetan people means that he is a true democrat, he believes in democracy and it was his vision to establish secular democracy in exile so he took steps every ten years to devolve authority and the completion occurred on August 8, 2011. And if you look at the Tibetan charter or Constitution it is very much based on the Indian Constitution. Dr. Rajendra Prasad helped edit the first Tibetan Constitution. Trikamdas was another lawyer who helped to draft it. You will witness that our parliament is very much akin to the Indian parliamentary system, there is zero hour, and in it I will be grilled without any forewarning.

In short, what we have built in Dharamsala is a kind of system modeled after the Indian democratic principles, Indian democratic values and system. And what we are, the basis of our struggle is non-violence, *ahimsa*, we borrowed that from India, His Holiness says that he is a *chela* of Mahatma Gandhi. In some sense, what we are losing today, i.e. the Buddhist civilisation, and Tibetan literature, is very much connected with India. And what we are fighting back with is also based on Indian values of democracy and *ahimsa*, so in some sense if we succeed Indian values will succeed, India's borders will be secured. If we fail, Buddhism and the literature we borrowed from India will also disappear and the Tibetan people might become a museum piece and Tibet might disappear altogether from the map of the world. Hence for India Tibet is a core issue. I appeal to all of you who are here to take interest in the issue and thank VIF for organising this conference and hopefully we will have it on a yearly basis and I shall be happy to come and send more scholars.

I conclude my remarks by referring to the verses of the *Bhagavad Gita* recited at the beginning. It was said that dignity, freedom and equality are three principles mentioned in the *Gita*. These are the principles we are fighting for, *we are fighting for Tibetan dignity, Tibetan identity, Tibetan freedom, and what we are seeking is equality.* These are also enshrined in the Indian Constitution, this is what we are aspiring for, these are what all human beings should have, and we are denied these while we ought to have them too. I also believe as another verse said, *'rise up rise up with determination'.*

The Tibetan spirit is strong and Tibetans inside and outside Tibet have the determination to strive for what is ours, i.e. our homeland, our identity and our dignity. With the help of India and the Indian people our freedom will be restored and His Holiness will return to Tibet one day!

Devolution of Power by HH the Dalai Lama: Implications

Penpa Tsering

As someone who has seen the whole process of devolution of power by His Holiness, I am proud to have been re-elected again as the Speaker of the Tibetan Parliament. I was Speaker of the previous House for two and a half years, and it is my privilege to share His Holiness's vision for the future.

In fact, it was a very emotional moment for Tibetans all over the world, particularly for Tibetans inside Tibet, when we had to face the inevitability of the firm determination of His Holiness to devolve power. And in the Parliament when we convened in March 2011 to discuss this devolution as suggested by His Holiness, for the first five days, we had many rounds of discussion but then we came to the conclusion that we should request His Holiness to continue with his political and administrative responsibilities. But

---

Text of remarks made at a VIF Seminar in September 2011 [updated].

ultimately on 18th of March, 2011 which also happens to be the fifteenth day of Tibetan first lunar month when we have an official function at the main temple, His Holiness again stressed his decision and explained why he devolved his power at this time.

I think His Holiness' vision has two parts; one of course is the devolution of His Holiness's political authority that was basically aimed at strengthening and securing the Central Tibetan Administration (CTA) within and beyond the lifetime of the 14th Dalai Lama. And the second one is obviously the religious role of the Dalai Lamas. Recently, Dr. Sangay referred to this, when we celebrated the 51st anniversary of the founding of Tibetan democracy in exile and when His Holiness met the Chief Minister of Himachal Pradesh, he explained the reasons and the religious angle in his decision to devolve political power. He said it will be much easier for the coming Dalai Lamas to maintain just a religious role. The first four Dalai Lamas had a purely spiritual role, confined to the boundaries of Tibet. But the 3rd Dalai Lama had a very successful religious role, not just in Tibet but also in Mongolia and now His Holiness wants to revert to the role of the Dalai Lamas back to the first four Dalai Lamas. Because His Holiness feels that by the Dalai Lamas getting involved in a political role, it is always in some ways, however capable the Dalai Lamas are, as particularly the 5th and 13th Dalai Lamas were, they become controversial in some way or the other. So His Holiness is very clear about the role of the coming Dalai Lamas to assume mainly religious roles, but this will have a lot of ramifications including on the reincarnation of the 15th Dalai Lama and the 16th Dalai Lama and so on, because China has already made its intentions very clear regarding the recognition and reincarnation of the next Dalai Lama. So this is perhaps another way of thwarting China's move to recognise the future Dalai Lamas.

Dr. Sangay also mentioned this morning that His Holiness is a democrat, a true democrat at heart. Even way back in 1952, just after signing the 17-point agreement, His Holiness wanted to introduce land and taxation reforms inside Tibet but it could not be implemented because of the political situation at that time. But then immediately coming into exile in 1959 when His Holiness stayed in Mussourie for one year, we got to hear from one of the former ministers of that time, speaking on 2 September 1960, when the first Parliament took oath of office, that immediately after coming into exile His Holiness said that we *have* to adopt a democratic polity. In February 1960, when most of the Tibetans who were working on road construction having few skills and were unused to the ways of India, unused too, to the heat and other constraints, many Tibetans met in Bodh Gaya and there His Holiness said for the first time that we would have to elect our representatives. By the 2nd of September 1960, as mentioned, we had elected the first Parliament and the members took the oath of office. Dr. Sangay also mentioned that His Holiness had by that time started working on a broad outline of a Constitution for Tibet and by 10 October 1961 the outline was ready. It was based on a lot of inputs from Indian friends and experts on constitutional law to further develop it. The whole structure that was developed at that time, the outline of it was distributed to the Tibetan public for their views and by 10 March 1962 His Holiness had promulgated a Constitution for Tibet. So it is the vision of His Holiness that goes back to those times when he was very young, at a very vulnerable age, and in a very difficult situation. But since then I think the Tibetan people have tried their best to give expression to the vision of His Holiness.

By 1987 and 1988, His Holiness again started talking to the public saying that we need to democratize further and he also proposed several topics like whether we should have a Prime Ministerial post or whether we should have a bicameral House, whether we should have political parties, or whether we should increase the strength of the Parliament and so on. And then there was the Parliament and Cabinet, both dissolved in May 1990 and he set up the Constitution Drafting Committee. For one year they worked hard, and by 1991, the number of Members of Parliament was increased, and the Parliament was completely empowered as a legislative body, a Charter was enacted, which we follow even today, one that could best be implemented in the circumstances of exile. Then after one decade in 2000 His Holiness again started talking about reforming the elections of the Cabinet members and finally by 2001 we made amendments to the Charter and by 2001 we had a directly elected Kalon Tripa—or the chief of the Cabinet for the CTA.

Now some years later His Holiness, in my memory about three years back, when we were to make a small DVD on the functions of the Parliament and the development of Tibetan democracy, we had a short interview with His Holiness and His Holiness at that time, mentioned that one person governing a country or a Labrang, i.e. a management committee of Lamas to rule over a nation, is completely outdated. So, as one can see, any discerning person who has been following His Holiness, who understands His Holiness' thinking will see that the process has been set in motion fifty-one years back and today we have reached this stage.

And this time also, since August 2010 when we had the first national general meeting of Tibetans in the settlement in south India, His Holiness talked about his complete retirement but at that time we did not feel that he would completely retire from both administrative and political responsibilities. Then again in October 2010 in Toronto, when His Holiness met a group of Chinese people, one Chinese asked him, 'you have been talking about semi-retirement what about your complete retirement' and then His Holiness said wait for a few months, you will hear an announcement. And coming back to India in November 2010 His Holiness was interviewed on TV, the whole thing was blown up, and there was a lot of misrepresentation and one reason why I thought the whole process got a little bit expedited was because some people thought that as soon as His Holiness consults his Parliament in the upcoming session, he will relinquish all his responsibilities. But if you carefully read what His Holiness had said in the TV interview, at that time there was no time limit.

And then the recent elections where the candidates were also very active, Lobsang Sangay was the most active campaigner and the enthusiasm that was shown by the electorate of Tibetans all over the world was a huge encouragement for His Holiness to decide on the time frame. Then His Holiness talked about his real intentions on the 10th of March 2011 and then again in his statement to the Parliament on 14 March. It was a very emotional moment for us. As Parliamentarians, we are supposed to represent the people. As soon as the news broke, of His Holiness wanting to devolve all his powers, we received a large number of communications from inside Tibet and from Tibetans all over the world requesting His Holiness to continue with his leadership. And the Parliament also took a lot of time to take a decision, but ultimately we had to make the changes in deference to the wishes of His Holiness as we were sandwiched between the aspirations of the people and the firm determination of His Holiness.

Following that, we set in motion a democratic process. We formed a Charter Amendment Committee and convened a second national general meeting in the 3rd week of May which was followed by a special session of the 14th house that was just coming to an end. In that special session we made all the changes and on the 29th of May at 8:30 in the morning, His Holiness signed for the last time the amendment to the Charter. So even then, it was very emotional because the former Kalon Tripa, myself and the Deputy Speaker, went to present the papers to His Holiness. On behalf of the Parliament, I felt that we did manage to fulfil the long cherished dream of His Holiness to devolve all his powers and today His

Holiness argues that it would have been hypocritical of him if he had not made the changes, talking about separation of church and state and all that. His Holiness now feels much relieved that he is not being a hypocrite.

When we had the national general meeting, we had requested His Holiness to continue as a titular head, something similar to the British monarchy but His Holiness jokingly told us, 'if I have to be a king, bring me a queen then I will be the head of the state'. So even during those very tense moments for us, His Holiness always brought a lot of cheer to the whole process. Even though it was very difficult, we did manage to fulfil a part of his vision. Now of course he can spend more of his time speaking about world peace, universal responsibilities, teaching secular moral ethics, inter-religious harmony, etc. all over the world. His Holiness said 'the day I decided this [to devolve power] I slept peacefully'. Of course, he will continue to guide the Tibetans—that is one important thing we need to understand.

In the amendments that we made to the Charter, we included a preamble to prove the historical legitimacy of the government that has been handed over to the elected leadership and also included Article Number 1 in the new Charter which was to serve the purpose of not severing ties between His Holiness the Dalai Lama, Tibet and the Tibetan people. So we have also managed to partly fulfil the aspiration of the Tibetan people.

So that is where we stand today. Of course, we face many challenges with respect to the devolution of power. His Holiness has been very generous. Dr. Sangay showed a photograph of the meeting with the Speaker of the US House of Representatives. At that meeting, His Holiness took us both by the hand and said, 'Today we have brought two new people', and started introducing us to the Congressional leadership. At other meetings, he introduced Dr. Sangay, saying, 'He is my political boss'. So that is where things stand. Of course, it will have major ramifications, but we have gone through a historical change.

In terms of relations with China, in terms of dialogue with China, this change will have significant ramifications on the dialogue. It will also have lot of implications for the response of the international community which His Holiness has been trying to shoulder by taking us with him and introducing—since I sensed that His Holiness was going to do something very serious this time, because since April-May 2010 he started taking the Kalon Tripa and the Speaker with him on a majority of his visits abroad so that not only the international community but also the diasporic Tibetan community get accustomed to the new leadership. And with the role and time that His Holiness could spend on his most important vision of international harmony, inter-religious harmony and making a world a better place to live, Tibetans and all other people will also find a place under that broad vision and we in turn would find dignity, freedom and justice.

By proposing the golden mean approach, we have made lot of compromises. His Holiness had always been very realistic and he always makes decisions based on reality and we hope that the efforts of our Indian friends will be a major contributing factor in advancing the Tibetan cause in India and worldwide. At one time we had to really struggle to meet people. I worked in Delhi for seven years as the director of the Tibetan Parliamentary Policy Research Centre and today I see a lot of old friends here, but at that time we had to make lot of effort to meet even one former foreign secretary. Now many people have become accessible and we feel that the continued spirit of the Tibetans inside Tibet, especially the one that we saw in 2008 all across Tibet, was an inspiration for not only the younger generation inside Tibet but also the younger generation of the Tibetans in India and elsewhere in the world. So we need your continued support.

SECTION I

Historical and Civilisational Setting

1

Tibet in World Politics

Abanti Bhattacharya

The question of Tibet has been a subject of deep concern and controversy in Asian geo-politics. Its status has remained unresolved since the mid 19th century and continues to haunt international politics and India-China bilateral relations in the 21st century. For China, however, the status of Tibet is a settled issue and is not open to negotiation. But the India-China border dispute and China's persistent claims over Arunachal Pradesh clearly indicate the unresolved status of the Tibetan issue. The 2008 Tibetan uprising and the recent incidents of Tibetan self-immolation have further demonstrated that the Tibetan issue is far from over and the question of Tibetan identity would remain a challenge for China.

This chapter attempts to look into the status of Tibet from the colonial period to the present times. The aim of the chapter is to explore the possible future of the Tibetan question given the current Chinese preparation towards crafting a post-Dalai Lama period vis-à-vis the Dalai Lama's own efforts at evolving plausible guidelines to ensure the continuity of the Tibetan movement in his absence.

Looking at the history of Tibet from the colonial period to the present times, this study suggests that in the absence of the Dalai Lama, the Tibetan question would be relatively weak but it would continue to be a sticking factor in China's domestic and foreign policies. Further, given Tibet's geo-political and historical entanglement with India and China, a meaningful and lasting solution to the Tibet problem could only be achieved by accepting Tibet as a factor in China's relations with India.

TIBET IN THE COLONIAL ERA

The question of Tibet goes back to the high period of imperialism in Asia when Tibet and Qing China got embroiled in the 'Great Game' between Britain and Tsarist Russia through the second half of the 19th century.[1] When the imperial powers were knocking at the door, Tibet and the Qing imperial state were bound together in a kind of patron-priest relationship which rendered high degrees of autonomy to Tibet and kept its socio-political structures largely intact.[2] Fearing Tsarist expansion in Asia, the British colonial power in India for the first time realized the need to define the status of Tibet. In fact the Tibetan skirmish with the British over Sikkim exposed the limited nature of Chinese authority in Tibet and led the British power in India to directly establish contact with the Dalai Lama. The British power interpreted the existing patron-priest relationship between Tibet and China as some kind of 'loose reign' over Tibet and consequently devised the strategy of conferring China suzerain rights over Tibet. In fact, a recent study on the status of Tibet vis-à-vis China indicates that the arrangement of suzerainty was not an original idea of the British but that they derived it from the existing priest-patron relationship that had defined the relationship between Tibet and China under the Mongols and the Manchu rulers.[3]

The British strategy of suzerainty was essentially devised to keep the Russians out from the region bordering India. More than that, it meant to engage a weak China and encourage it to play a role so as to avoid a power vacuum in the region and thereby prevent the penetration of Russian influence in Tibet. Eventually, this meant turning Tibet into a buffer zone between British India and Tsarist Russia. This arrangement, while eliminating Russian influence on Tibet, preventing China's sovereignty and ensuring Tibetan autonomy, ultimately guaranteed security of British Indian frontiers and ensured British commercial rights in China.[4] Keeping these imperatives in context, the British government repudiated its own gains achieved through the Younghusband expedition of 1904 and signed the Anglo-Russian Agreement of 1907 whereby the British India government and Russia agreed to keep Tibet under Chinese suzerainty. The Younghusband expedition, however, exposed the prospect of British threat to the Qing frontier and the subsequent period thus saw the Chinese expansion into the areas adjacent to China proper, the so-called Inner Tibet or the Kham region. In fact, a new twist to Tibetan history was added when Tibet under the 13th Dalai Lama bid for Tibetan independence which in effect further embroiled Tibet in the Great Game. Tibetan independence greatly concerned the Manchus and what followed then was subjugation and sinicisation of Kham (not the Central Tibet or the U-Tsang region). Tibetan expert Sam Van Schaik argues that the 13th Dalai Lama regarded this Qing expansion as colonization of Eastern Tibet and thus also forfeiture of the age-old priest patron relationship.[5] In 1911, the Manchu power collapsed and the 13th Dalai Lama declared Tibet's independence.

While Tibetan nationalism marched ahead to consolidate the newly gained independence under the 13th Dalai Lama, Republican government rose from the ashes of the Manchus and laid claim to all the Qing imperial territories based on the union of five races. As the Chinese expansion posed a renewed threat to the British power in India, it was deemed necessary for the British to delineate the Indo-Tibetan border. The British devised the strategy to break Tibet into Inner and Outer Tibet and called for a tripartite meeting of British India represented by Sir Henry McMahon, China by Chen Yifan and Tibet by Lonchen Shatra in Simla in October 1913. Here again, it needs to be pointed out that the idea of dividing Tibet into Outer and Inner was not entirely a British innovation. Rather out of the heated debates between Tibet and China on where the border should lie, the British decided to agree on the border close to the old Manchu line.[6] Tibet lost its territory and accepted Lhasa's control only on Outer Tibet and admitted Chinese suzerainty on Inner Tibet. Under the British pressure the Chinese side was forced to initial the pact. But it was not approved by the Chinese Republican government. Nevertheless, the 1914 Agreement set the India-Tibet frontier east of Bhutan, along the crest of the Himalayas, which came to be called the McMahon Line. In addition, Britain obtained exclusive trading rights, extraterritoriality and the right to station a resident in Lhasa. Though the Chinese side did not ratify the treaty, Tibet became a British protectorate, forcing the Russians and the Chinese out of the region. However, China's acceptance of the British delineated McMahon line was contingent upon Chinese acceptance of the Tibet- China border as delineated in the 1914 settlement.[7] The 1914 arrangement was workable only under a powerful British power in India and a weak Chinese government. When the People's Republic of China (PRC) was established in the Mainland China after three years of civil war between the Communist and the Nationalist forces, the first thing the new Communist government did was to invade Tibet and settle the Tibet question in its favour, reflected in the 1951 17-Point Agreement.

TIBET IN THE POST-COLONIAL ERA

In the post-1949 period, when the PRC came into being, India urged China to let Tibet be a buffer, as this would be in line with its historical status, its religious, cultural and political identity, and minimise China's military presence in the region. But China determined to restore its imperial order articulated its security and national interest in terms of establishing sovereignty over Tibet. It refused to recognise the Simla Agreement between Tibet and British India. In 1950-51, the entry of 20,000 PLA (People's Liberation Army) troops into Tibet ended the buffer status and for the first time in history brought India and China face to face sharing a common boundary. On 23 May 1951, Tibet was forced to sign the '17-Point Agreement on Measures for the Peaceful Liberation of Tibet', which affirmed Chinese sovereignty over Tibet. The Dalai Lama accepted to abide by the agreement in order to save his people from genocide. Also, as Sam Van Schaik succinctly argued, the 17-Point Agreement was supported by many Tibetans because they saw the agreement as a continuation of the arrangement the Tibetans had with the Mongols and the Manchus. As such, Schaik says Mao was not any different.[8]

The 17- Point Agreement was initially put into effect in Outer Tibet (U-tsang). The Inner Tibet, which under the Communist was reconstituted as Gansu, Qinghai, Sichuan and Yunnan provinces came under the impact of the Chinese collectivization programme that eventually caused widespread resentment among the Tibetans. The resentment coalesced into large-scale uprisings in the Gelug monasteries first in Sampeling, and then in Litang in 1956. The monasteries were bombed, which led the Khampas to perceive the Chinese as enemies of Buddhism. The rebellion soon engulfed Outer Tibet. By 1959, the unrest was brutally crushed and tens of thousands of Tibetans were killed. In the wake of the Communist onslaught the Dalai Lama and many Tibetans fled to

India in 1959. When the Dalai Lama touched Indian soil in Tejpur he issued a statement on April 18, 1959 that since the Chinese government had violated the terms of the 17-Point Agreement, Tibet was no longer bound by it. And that from then on he would strive for the restoration of Tibetan independence. Since then, the Tibetan Government-in-Exile (TGIE), based in Dharamsala in the state of Himachal Pradesh in India, and the Tibetan people adopted a policy of seeking independence for Tibet.

At this juncture, it is important to understand the role of the United States towards Tibet.[9] The 1950s is the beginning of the bipolar politics and Tibet got entangled in it as it was the nest of Asia. When in 1951 the Chinese People's Liberation Army (PLA) invaded Tibet, the Dalai Lama did try to seek the US support against Communist invasion. But the US support did not come. Failing to get any support, the Dalai Lama agreed to sign the 17-Point Agreement. When the Dalai Lama had reconciled to stay back in Lhasa under the terms of the new agreement, the US again sent another message asking him to disavow publicly the 17-Point Agreement in return for the US recognition of the Dalai Lama's position as the 'head of the autonomous Tibet'. This time too the US was unwilling to accommodate the Dalai Lama's demand for Tibet's independent statehood.[10] During the Lhasa uprising, there were instances of the CIA's covert operations in Tibet. But the CIA's operations in Tibet were only intended to create some "tactical difficulties" for China;[11] the US did not principally oppose China's sovereignty in Tibet. After the Dalai Lama fled into exile he had again asked the US for international recognition of Free Tibetan Government. But the Eisenhower administration restrained the Tibetans from presenting a political case to the United Nations that would have accused the PRC of aggression against an independent country.[12] Thus, the US, in effect, diverted the Tibetan independence cause to the human rights problem and pressurized the Dalai Lama to project Tibetan suffering as a case of

China's violation of human rights. Therefore, more than the Dalai Lama's call for the Middle Way, it was the US suggestion of projecting the Tibetan question as a human rights issue that really harmed the Tibetan cause and muddled the status of Tibet further.

Not surprising thus that in the post-War era the status of Tibet got enmeshed with the notions of self-determination and the wider human rights debate.[13] The two United Nations covenants on human rights—Civil and Political Rights and Economic, Social and Cultural Rights—contained in their first article a guarantee of the right of self-determination.[14] However, the Covenants did not mention the procedure for realization of self-determination. Then again, the right of self-determination had little practical validity since, in technical terms, this principle did not qualify as a human right, because human rights are rights of the individual, not of the collectives.[15] Further quite significantly, while adopting the Declaration on the granting of independence to colonial countries and peoples in 1960, the UN General Assembly in the same resolution also recognized the principle of national unity that conflicted with the principles of self-determination.[16] It stated, 'any attempt aimed at the partial or total disruption of national unity and the territorial integrity of a country is incompatible with the purposes and principles of the charter of the United Nations.'[17] Therefore, though the Tibetans demand for the right to self-determination on the basis of the 1960 UN General Assembly and the two Covenants stood, the principle of national unity nullified their demand. In effect, a kind of ambiguity prevailed between the notions of individual and collective human rights which, in turn, problematised the Tibetan issue.

Furthermore, Tibetan nationalism, having latched on to the Western human rights debate, came into conflict with the Chinese definition of human rights.[18] It may be noted that human rights in China are different from the Western idea of human rights in three aspects.[19] First, human rights are considered as culturally relative rather than universal. Second, China prioritizes subsistence rights over political and civil rights. Therefore, 'developmentalism' has acquired a principal focus in China's conceptualization of human rights. Third, China accords priority to collective rights. By appropriating the culturalist view of human rights, China not only deflected the Western criticism but also effectively laid out its own discourse on human rights. The economic development and prosperity of the minority were thus viewed to be important to improve the human rights condition of Tibetans. This notion of economic development of the backward minority regions was argued to solve the national question. In Chinese understanding, neither the self-determination of the Tibetans nor the Western perspective of human rights had any place.

Thus broadly in the post-Colonial era, the Tibetan question got embroiled in the Cold War politics and the human rights debates in China and the West. Eventually, after the US-China rapprochement of 1971, Tibet turned into an obscure issue in US foreign policy. In fact, the US concerns about Tibet remained confined to the rhetoric of human rights abuses in China. Though the US used human rights as a tool for manoeuvreing its relations with China, it never used it to the extent of jeopardizing its economic relations with the latter.

TIBET IN THE POST-COLD WAR ERA

With the beginning of economic reforms in China, new efforts were made under the post-Mao leadership to resolve the Tibet question. These efforts culminated in extending invitations to four fact-finding delegations from Dharamsala to Tibet between 1979 and 1980 to actually project improved conditions of the Tibetans under the Communist rule. These efforts were also geared towards inducing the Dalai Lama to return to China since his return would legitimize China's sovereignty over Tibet. However, the reconciliation talks between the Dalai Lama's representatives and China foundered on the Dalai Lama's refusal to accept Tibet as historically part of China and also on China's rejection of Dalai Lama's proposal for self-rule under the 'one-country, two systems' format.

The failure spurred the Dalai Lama to turn to the West and launch a fresh attempt to promote the cause of Tibetan independence. Thus began his international campaign to attract worldwide attention to the Tibetan problem. In 1987, his international campaign bore huge results. In June 1987, the US House of Representatives adopted a bill that condemned human rights abuses in Tibet, instructed the US President to express sympathy for Tibet, and urged China to establish a constructive dialogue with the Dalai Lama. In September 1987, the Dalai Lama was invited to speak to the Congressional Human Rights Caucus in Washington, where he for the first time called on China to resolve the Tibet issue on the basis of his formulation of a five-point peace plan. After the Cold War ended, the Congressional support for Tibet further grew.[20] In 1990, Congress authorized the creation of a Tibetan-language broadcast unit at the Voice of America, and in 1991 Congress "included a number of tough, though non-binding provisions on Tibet in a State Department Authorization Act that was signed into law by President George H.W. Bush later that year."[21] The provisions described "Tibet, including those areas incorporated into the Chinese provinces of Sichuan, Yunnan, Gansu and Qinghai," as an "occupied country" and declared that the Dalai Lama and the government-in-exile were "Tibet's true representatives." Although the pro-Tibet statements in the legislation were only a non-binding "sense of Congress" resolution, they were seen in Dharamsala as a major victory.[22]

In September 1988, the Dalai Lama came up with a fresh proposal in Strasbourg that for the first time indicated his acceptance of the Chinese sovereignty over Tibet in exchange for 'genuine autonomy'. This proposal came on the heels of Chinese government's announcement of allowing the Dalia Lama's return to Tibet on condition of his giving up the demand for full independence. Under the Strasbourg Proposal, the Tibetan political autonomy would include all affairs concerning the Tibetans, except defence and foreign relations, and the Tibetan political system would be democratic. But the Dalai Lama did not accept what the PRC wanted him to admit, that is, Tibet had always been and would always be a part of China. Consequently, the PRC rejected the Strasbourg Proposal and condemned it as 'disguised independence'. The Dalai Lama on his part by giving up the demand for full independence made a major concession to the Chinese. His call for 'genuine autonomy' and not independence has seemingly weakened the movement from 1988 onwards, when also officially in the Strasbourg Proposal autonomy replaced independence as the goal of the Tibetan movement. The Dalai Lama's conciliatory stand has decidedly emboldened China's Tibet policy, which is based on the idea of Han nationalism and submergence of all minority identities into the larger Han identity.

In 1996, China initiated the "strike hard" campaign in Tibet and in 2000 in order to consolidate its grip on Tibet further the PRC launched the Western Development Strategy—a multi-pronged strategy of repression, economic development, resource extraction, strategic infrastructure development and Hanization. Beijing also began a vigorous disparagement of the Dalai Lama in the 1990s under the Patriotic Education programme.

China's repressive measures eventually created the context for a Tibetan uprising in 2008. What made the Tibetan protests, the biggest in twenty years, quite startling was first that it could be organised under the repressive communist regime with its well-established coercive mechanisms to curb resistance, or what it calls anti-China activities. Second, the protests indeed indicated the failure of China's economic policy in Tibet, which focused primarily on creating prosperity in minority areas to mitigate separatism. In other words, the protest exposed the 'colonising' nature of China's Westward Development Project and validated the Tibetan claim that economic policies and projects introduced in Tibet were not meant for the development of the 85 per cent of rural Tibetans but to facilitate China's strategic and defence requirements. Third, the uprising indicated that the identity issues are hard to counter.

THE FUTURE OF TIBET

The 2008 Tibetan uprising did not pose any significant challenge to China, not only because of Beijing's enormous economic and military strength, but more so because over the years the Tibetan movement has weakened. The Tibetan movement, which started in the 1950s with the goal of independence and self-determination, got diverted to human rights issue under the US pressure in the 1950s, and further got diluted under the Dalai Lama's call for 'genuine autonomy' in the 1980s.[23]

While the Dalai Lama has been advocating 'genuine autonomy', there is quite a large section of Tibetans, particularly Tibetan non-governmental organizations (NGOs) who are clearly dismayed with his conciliatory stand and instead advocate the goal of complete independence for Tibet. Among the NGOs, the only exception in this regard is the Tibetan Women Association (TWA), which supports the 'middle path approach'. The rest, including the most radical and the largest among the Tibetan diaspora—the Tibetan Youth Congress (TYC)—has laid down clear aims, with the primary objective being total independence of Tibet even at the cost of one's life.

Tibetans themselves are thus divided in the goal they seek. If the goal of independence had remained steadfast, it would have remained a formidable challenge to China's might. But today's Tibetan resistance movement is merely a matter of internal dissent for authoritarian China, and it has adequate coercive structures to muzzle the movement.

More worrying for the Tibetan cause was the 29 October 2008 parliamentary statement by the UK Foreign Secretary David Miliband which articulated a U-turn in the British government's position on the status of Tibet. After 94 years, the British government stated for the first time that "Tibet is a part of the People's Republic of China".[24] This was a complete negation of the earlier long-held position which acknowledged Chinese interest in Tibet but asserted that Tibet had never been fully part of China. Also, this U-turn meant to disregard earlier British position that its recognition of Chinese 'suzerainty' was dependent on China's granting of political autonomy to Tibet.[25] Britain's U-turn has undeniably and decisively weakened the status of Tibet further.

Analyzing the future of the Tibetan question, it is apparent that the Tibetan movement has weakened over the years and China is leaving no stone unturned to completely remove the Tibetan question from affecting Beijing's domestic and international politics.

CHINA'S PREPARATION FOR THE POST-DALAI LAMA ERA

The PRC while has a well-defined Western Development Strategy to consolidate its grip over Tibet, it is also steadfastly preparing for a post-Dalai Lama era.[26] China's latest move towards incremental preparation for the post-Dalai Lama era came on February 28, 2010, when it nominated its designated Panchen Lama, Gyaincain Norbu, to the Parliamentary advisory body, the National Committee of the Chinese People's Political Consultative Conference (CPPCC) as one of the 13 new members. Prior to this, on October 18, 2008, the Chinese government formulated plans to set up the first-ever academy of Tibetan Buddhism in southwestern China. The construction for the $11.7 million project began in October 2008. The purpose is to train "patriotic and devotional religious personnel". In other words, the attempt is to build an officially approved cadre of monks in order to dilute the influence of defiant monks in Tibet, who have faith in the Dalai Lama. In fact, the signs for the creation of a new monkhood subservient to Beijing was witnessed in July 2007 when in a major diplomatic move, the government in China passed a law on reincarnation—Order No. 5 of China's State Administration of Religious Affairs, Management Measures for the Reincarnation of 'Living Buddhas' in Tibetan Buddhism—which required all reincarnate Lamas to be approved by the state. Through this major tactical step, China asserted its right to manage and select all reincarnate Lamas of Tibetan Buddhism and thereby sought to choose its own Dalai Lama after the present one passes away. This is based on the assumption that with the exit of the present Dalai Lama, the Tibetan problem would inevitably end.

Earlier from April 13 to 16, 2006, China organised for the first time a World Buddhist Forum in Hangzhou to espouse its leadership of the Buddhist world. It also provided an international platform to China's own Panchen Lama to bolster his legitimacy both internally and globally. It may be recalled that in 1995 China had hand-picked Gyaincain Norbu as the 11th Panchen Lama rejecting Gedhun Choekyi Nyima selected by the Dalai Lama. Since then, China has been steadily raising his profile. The Dalai Lama was not invited for this international forum in which over 1,000 monks and experts from thirty-seven countries gathered to participate in the discussion on building a harmonious world, because he was seen as "splitting the motherland and sabotaging the unity of ethnic groups." As such, his participation would have caused "disharmony", as reported by Xinhua.

More importantly, the Fifth National Conference on the Work Report on Tibet held in Beijing in January 18-20, 2010 indicates China's policy direction on Tibet. It was convened especially to consider a post-Dalai Lama scenario. Evidently, the 2010 Work Report on Tibet came after the March 2008 Tibetan uprisings. The last Conference was held in 2001. Therefore, the then President Hu Jintao identified Tibet as a "special contradiction between people of all ethnic groups and the separatist forces led by the Dalai clique" and called for "leapfrog development" and "lasting stability" as primary aspects of the Tibet Work Conference. Another crucial aspect of this conference was Hu's emphasis on ensuring establishment of "a normal order of Tibetan Buddhism". He did not elaborate what normal order meant but Beijing's policies towards Tibet indicate China's avowed policy to isolate the Dalai Lama and create an interpretation of Buddhism with Chinese characteristics as evident in the reincarnation law, the establishment of first-ever Buddhist academy and holding the World Buddhist Forum in Hangzhou.

Externally, China has re-cast its Nepal policy seemingly keeping an eye on the post-Dalai Lama politics.[27] With growing tensions in Tibet, particularly after the March 2008 uprising, China's conception of Nepal as a new buffer has indeed acquired special significance. Its policy towards Nepal came to be driven essentially by the need to curb the clandestine activities of some 20,000 Tibetan refugees (the second largest Tibetan refugee community in the world) in Nepal. The very presence of the Tibetan refugees in Nepal and their arrival each year in their hundreds to the Himalayan state attest to the human rights violations rampant in Tibet. More than that, their periodic staging of protests draws international attention to the Tibetan issue that in effect, exacerbates China's vulnerability in Tibet. By far the predominant concern for China at the moment is how to handle a post-Dalai Lama scenario. China does not rule out a turbulent movement of the Tibetans in the post-Dalai Lama era and hence its Nepal policy is to a large extent geared towards preparing a post-Dalai Lama Tibet. Consequently, China has been increasingly playing a proactive role in determining the future shape of Nepal's politics. During each of the high-level meetings China has extracted assurances from Nepal that it adheres to the one-China principle, acknowledging Tibet as an inalienable part of China, and ensures that no anti-China activity is allowed on its soil. The most glaring of all steps recently undertaken by the Nepalese government was to ban the Tibetans in Nepal from celebrating the Dalai Lama's birthday on 6 July 2011. While China has certainly started to prepare for the post-Dalai Lama period, the Tibetans under the Dalai Lama are also not far behind.

THE TIBETAN PREPARATION FOR THE POST-DALAI LAMA ERA

The Dalai Lama's devolution of power is an important step towards preparing the Tibetans for a post-Dalai Lama scenario. The Dalai Lama says, "My intention to devolve political authority derives neither from a wish to shirk responsibility nor because I am disheartened. On the contrary, I wish to devolve authority solely for the benefit of the Tibetan people in the long run. It is extremely important that we ensure the continuity of our exile Tibetan administration and our struggle until the issue of Tibet has been successfully resolved."

The devolution of power to the democratically elected leader is a momentous decision and geared to achieve three significant objectives. One is to settle the question of the reincarnation issue, while the second is to stabilize and legitimize the democratic ethos of the Tibetans; and three, to create a possibility of the Dalai Lama's pilgrimage to Wu-tai Shan.

With regard to the reincarnation issue, in the post-Dalai Lama era the Chinese leadership armed with Order No. 5 of China's State Administration of Religious Affairs are planning to implant a second Dalai Lama as they had done in the case of Panchen Lama. But the recent Dalai Lama's renunciation of political power has made reincarnation inconsequential for the political future of the Tibetan movement. Further, this step is likely to arrest the possibility of violence within the Tibetan community after the Dalai Lama passes away. There are fears that once the Dalai Lama departs, the Tibetan movement would turn violent and fall into disarray.

The election of the new Tibetan Prime Minister by the Tibetans from 30 countries around the globe, while it gives political legitimacy to the exiled Tibetan government, also greatly strengthens the democratic roots of the Tibetans. This would also pose a challenge to the authoritarian Chinese Communist regime that invaded Tibet in the 1950s on the ground of rescuing the Tibetans from the backward regime of the Dalai Lama. In fact, over time the intensification of the democratic process would lend a de-facto character to the Tibetan power outside of China that might motivate the Tibetans within China for genuine autonomy envisaged by the Dalai Lama. It would also strengthen the Tibetan movement to stand on its feet in the Dalai Lama's absence.

The Dalai Lama's renunciation of political power may create the possibility of his pilgrimage to China's Wu-tai Shan. The Dalai Lama on several occasions expressed his desire to visit Mount Wu-tai Shan in China for a pilgrimage. Wu-tai Shan is regarded as one of the four sacred Buddhist sites and is the abode of Manjushri, Bodhisattva of wisdom. The Chinese leadership may now be more receptive to the Dalai Lama's visit as he has renounced political power. This might put the Dalai Lama in a more favourable light as well.

ASSESSING THE FUTURE OF TIBET

For the Chinese, the Tibetan question is a matter of sovereignty and not a question of identity. So the Chinese talks with the Tibetan task force groups are "not about the status of Tibet but about the future of the Dalai Lama and the people around him." In their eyes, the status of Tibet as a sovereign part of China is a settled issue. Evidently, China's Tibet policy forms the linchpin of its nationalist project. Its sovereignty over Tibet has significant ramifications not only for its national integrity but also for stability in its other minority areas, particularly Xinjiang. If Tibet falls from China's grip, Xinjiang would follow suit. The bottom line of China's Tibet policy thus has been the maintenance of its sovereignty over Tibet through military and economic means, whereby the region is fully integrated with the mainland and Tibetans are reduced to a minority in their own province. Beijing's long-term strategy is to simply bide its time as long as the Dalai Lama is alive, after which it believes that the Tibetan resistance would suffer without the stature of, and the respect commanded by, the Dalai Lama. And it would further hamper the movement by planting its own Dalai Lama, as it has done in the case of the Panchen Lama. Thus, Hu Jintao's reconfigured Tibet policy based on promotion of Buddhism and creation of a new monkhood is aimed at confronting the security situation in the post-Dalai Lama era. It is also geared towards weakening India's manoeuvrability on the Tibet issue and bilateral border negotiations.

For the Tibetans spread all over the world, the Dalai Lama is the face of the Tibetan movement. After he passes away, the movement would definitely lose some shine. His absence is also likely to disillusion many Tibetans and that might push them to opt for violent methods. But a lot depends on how the new Prime Minister gives shape to the Tibetan movement and keeps up the momentum. His presence is likely to check the movement from falling into disarray.

With regard to dialogue between the Tibetan task force and the Chinese, it is highly unlikely that China would continue the process. In fact, the Chinese sources have already indicated that the Tibetan Exile Government under the new Prime Minister is 'illegitimate' hence is 'disqualified' to hold talks with the Chinese government on the Tibet question. Indeed, agreeing for talks with the new Prime Minister would bestow legitimacy to the Tibetan Government-in-Exile which China would never want.

With regard to the role of the US, in the post-2008 international financial crisis, the American power is seen to be declining. It would under no circumstances support the Tibetan movement at the cost of jeopardising its economic relations with China. From time to time, the US does use the Tibetan human rights issue and the US leadership meets the Dalai Lama. However, the US own policy on Tibet suffers from ambiguity and is unlikely to change in the future. With China's growing might in the international arena, the Western powers are likely to accommodate rather than confront it.

As for India, in the post-War era it has failed to fathom the strategic security environment in the context of the victory of the Communist power whose sole strategic goal was determined by not only regaining the Qing territories but also adhering to the Westphalian sovereign notions of boundaries that are immutable, inviolable and non-negotiable. Quite naturally, it lost Tibet as buffer. Thereafter, India's policy towards Tibet is fraught with many dilemmas. In the 1950s, though India opposed China's invasion of Tibet, it refused to sponsor a Tibetan appeal to the United Nations, turned down US proposals for co-operation in support of the Tibetan resistance and persuaded the young Dalai Lama not to flee abroad but to reach an agreement with the Chinese government. Subsequently, under the spell of 'Hindi-Chini Bhai Bhai', India signed the 1954 agreement with China on Tibet and unilaterally surrendered its Tibetan card to the Chinese without reciprocal gains. The 1956 uprising in Tibet exposed the insincerity of the Chinese towards granting autonomy to Tibet and in an effort to retrieve the lost ground India granted asylum to the Dalai Lama in 1959. But Beijing saw the granting of asylum to the Dalai Lama and enabling him to mobilize international support as an anti-China policy. Consequently, in all subsequent India-China joint statements, Beijing ensured the insertion of a clause on India's acceptance of Tibet as a part of China. India never realized the implications of this except during the 2010 Joint statement where for the first time Tibet was not mentioned. But in reality it did not indicate a major policy change as the 2010 statement also added that it upheld all the previous joint statements between India and China.

By repeatedly reiterating over the years that Tibet is a part of China, India diluted its leverage not only in shoring up the Tibetan cause but also in its border negotiations with China. At the same time, China continues to fear that India might use the Tibetan card at some point in the future. Despite these Chinese fears, India has steadfastly avoided using the Tibetan card as a bargaining strategy. Given the present dynamics of India-China relations with greater synergy as the goal, New Delhi is not likely to take up the Tibetan cause actively. Further, though the presence of the Dalai Lama and the Tibetans in India naturally strengthens India's Tibetan card, questions remain about the viability of this card in the post-Dalai Lama era. India would certainly lose some leverage that it still enjoys vis-à-vis China by the mere presence of the Dalai Lama.

On the whole, the status of Tibet is far from settled. The current spate of self-immolation among the Tibetans suggests the resilience of the Tibet factor and the associated identity issues in the face of increased repression of the Chinese government. It clearly demonstrates that the questions of identity cannot be resolved by flooding the region with money. In fact, it demonstrates the failure of China's minority policy carved out to deal with the ethnic nationality question in the 1950s. This failure is specifically striking as it comes on the heels of the so-called revised policy decision on Tibet in 2010 underscored in the Tibet Work Report that called for harmonious development in Tibet. Since, for China, Tibet is a matter of sovereignty, not an issue of identity, the 2010 Work

Report does not seek to address the core problem of identity of the Tibetans and hence the renewal of unrest and self-immolation in China. Arguably, under the increasing Chinese repression the Tibetan movement is finding new ways of upholding its identity. Self-immolation suggests Tibetans are increasingly relying on their own strength to consolidate their movement instead of relying upon outside support. It can be thus inferred that in the post-Dalai Lama era, in the absence of the Dalai Lama the movement may lose some of its force and China may then try to control the Tibetan movement through its repressive machinery but the Tibetan identity will remain a burning issue in China's foreign and domestic policy.

It is also evident that so long as China treats the Tibetan nationality question as a strategic issue instead of an identity issue, the Tibetan question will remain unresolved. Howsoever the Chinese may put it, the Tibet question is not a settled issue. The entanglement of the India-China border dispute with the Tibet issue and the presence of the Dalai Lama in India along with 120,000 Tibetan refugees spread across 39 settlements make the Tibet issue not a question of internal politics of China. Tibet's history and geo-politics deeply entangles both India and China which the British imperial powers had clearly realized in the 19th century. Therefore, the Tibet issue would require a co-ordinated solution. In fact, an effective solution to the India-China border dispute would depend on recognizing the Tibet question as the central question between India and China. Particularly, China needs to treat Tibet not simply as a strategic issue but an identity issue and open up dialogue with the Dalai Lama. A meaningful and lasting solution to the Tibet question can only be had in negotiation with the Dalai Lama.

ENDNOTES

1. See, Dibyesh Anand, "Strategic Hypocrisy: The British Imperial Scripting of Tibet's Geo-political Identity", *The Journal of Asian Studies*, Vol. 68, no. 1 (February 2009), pp. 227-52.
2. See, Dawa Norbu, *China's Tibet Policy* (Curzon Press, Surrey, UK, 2001).
3. See, Sam Van Schaik, *Tibet: A History* (New Delhi: Amaryllis, 2012).
4. Dawa Norbu, *China's Tibet Policy.*
5. Sam Van Schaik, *Tibet: A History*, p. 232.
6. Ibid., p. 237.
7. Steven A. Hoffmann, "Rethinking the Linkage between Tibet and the China-India Border Conflict", *Journal of Cold War Studies*, Vol. 8, Issue 3 (Summer 2006), pp. 165-94.
8. Sam Van Schaik, *Tibet: A History*, p. 263.
9. Melvyn C. Goldstein, "The United States, Tibet and the Cold War", *Journal of Cold War Studies*, Vol. 8, no. 3 (Summer 2006), pp. 145-64.
10. Ibid., p. 149.
11. Xiaoyuan Liu, *Recast All Under Heaven: Revolution, War, Diplomacy, and Frontier China in the 20th Century* (New York: The Continuum International Publishing House, 2010), p. 215
12. Melvyn C. Goldstein, *The United States, Tibet and the Cold War*, p. 151.
13. Abanti Bhattacharya, "Chinese Nationalism and the Fate of Tibet: Implications for India and Future Scenarios", *Strategic Analysis*, Vol. 31, no. 2 (March 2007), p. 246.
14. David Robertson, *A Dictionary of Human Rights*, Europa Publishers Ltd., London, 1997.
15. See Athena S. Leoussi, *Encyclopedia of Nationalism*, Transaction Publishers, London, 2001. Also see Warren W. Smith, Jr., no. 3, who discusses in detail the question of Tibetan self-determination and shows how international law is deaf to Tibet's appeal for right to self-determination.
16. Athena S. Leoussi, no. 40, p. 272.
17. Ibid.

18. Abanti Bhattacharya, *Chinese Nationalism and the Fate of Tibet: Implications for India and Future Scenarios*, p. 246.
19. Robert Weatherly, *The Discourse of Human Rights in China: Historical and Ideological Perspectives* (Macmillan Press, London, 1999). Maria Svensson, "The Chinese Debate on Asian Values and Human Rights: Some Reflections on Relativism, Nationalism and Orientalism", in Michael Jacobson and Ole Bruun (eds.), *Human Rights and Asian Values*, (Curzon Press, Surrey, UK, 2000).
20. Melvyn C. Goldstein, *The United States, Tibet and the Cold War*, p. 158.
21. Ibid.
22. Ibid.
23. Genuine autonomy, according to the Dalai Lama, is the 'Middle-Way Approach' and it actually meant accepting Tibet to be a part of China. The Middle-Way Approach, as defined by the Dalai Lama, is "a non-partisan and moderate position that safeguards the vital interests of all concerned parties— for Tibetans: the protection and preservation of their culture, religion and national identity; for the Chinese: the security and territorial integrity of the motherland; and for neighbours and other third parties: peaceful borders and international relations."
24. Richard Spencer, "UK recognises China's direct rule over Tibet", *The Telegraph*, November 05, 2008, http://www.telegraph.co.uk/news/worldnews/asia/tibet/3385803/UK-recognises-Chinas-direct-rule-over-Tibet.html
25. Ibid.
26. Abanti Bhattacharya, "As China Prepares for post-Dalai Lama Tibet, What is India to do with the Tibetan Exiles?" *IDSA Strategic Comment*. March 25, 2010. http://www.idsa.in/
27. Abanti Bhattacharya, Contextualizing China's Nepal Policy: From Non-interference to Pro-activism, International Seminar on India-Nepal Relations, Centre for the Study of Nepal, Banaras Hindu University, March 28-30, 2011.

2

The Dalai Lama's Reincarnation and the Institution Post-Devolution

Chok Tsering

ABSTRACT

The institution of the Dalai Lama has undergone significant changes since its inception in the fifteenth century. The reincarnation debate is very crucial in Sino-Tibetan relations as it reflects the struggle over legitimacy and control of Tibetan Buddhism. It also reflects the future status of Tibet and the Tibetans. This paper gives a brief introduction to the origin of the institution of the Dalai Lama and analyzes the present controversies surrounding the fourteenth Dalai Lama's reincarnation. It also attempts to throw light on the future possibilities of Sino - Tibetan relations in a post-Dalai Lama scenario.

GENESIS OF THE DALAI LAMA'S INSTITUTION

The debate on the Dalai Lama's reincarnation has become more and more vibrant in recent times as it created a furor in the media as well as in public discussions. The Dalai Lama represents the highest religious authority for the Tibetans and the institution of the Dalai Lama has existed for over 600 years. The Dalai Lama is venerated by Tibetans all over the world. In view of his increasing age, China has become conscious of the need to control the process of selecting his reincarnation, and has enacted new laws in the selection of tulkus.[1]

In order to trace the origin of the Dalai Lamas and their emergence to power, it is necessary to go back to the fifteenth century to the inception of the institution of the Dalai Lama. The formation of this institution was initiated by Gedun Drupa, the first Dalai Lama (1391–1475) and his lineage eventually became identified with the patron and protector of Tibet. Gedun Drupa met Jhe Tsongkhapa, the founder of the Gelugpa Sect, in 1415 and emerged as one of his foremost disciples.[2] He was the founder of the Tashi Lhunpo monastery in 1447[3] based in the city of Shigatse in Tsang region of Tibet, which later became the official residence of the Panchen Lamas. Posthumously, the first Dalai Lama became one of the most important in the history of Tibet as he set the stage for future Dalai Lamas to continue his rule.

Gedun Gyatso was recognized as the immediate successor and confirmed as the reincarnation of Gedun Drupa. The institution of the Dalai Lama was established then and successive reincarnations have been recognized. However, the first two Dalai Lamas were primarily religious personalities and were mainly engaged in establishing new monasteries and teaching the Buddhist scriptures. The third Dalai Lama, Sonam Gyatso, was enthroned at the age of four and he emerged as one of the leading teachers of his day. Due to his great intellectual power, he was invited by the Mongolian king, Altan Khan, in 1578[4] and the relations between Tibet and Mongolia developed eventually after his Buddhist teaching there. In return for the third Dalai Lama's teaching, he received a number of presents, together with the title of the Dalai Lama. Altan Khan conferred the title "Dalai Lama" to Sonam Gyatso which in Mongolian means "ocean of wisdom." This title connotes that the Lama's learning was as deep and as broad as an ocean. The title of Dalai Lama was retroactively awarded to his two predecessors as well. Therefore, the origin of the concept of the Dalai Lama is mainly derived from the fifteenth century after developing cordial relations with Mongolia. Sonam Gyatso died on his way from Mongolia to Tibet in 1588.[5]

Surprisingly, the fourth Dalai Lama, Yonten Gyatso was born in Mongolia and the relations between the two countries developed significantly due to his predecessor's religious ties, cultural affinity as well as his birth there. During the reign of the fourth Dalai Lama, Mongol monks and scholars assumed roles of authority among the Tibetan Buddhist leadership. Unfortunately, he died at the very tender age of 27.

The fifth Dalai Lama, Lobsang Gyatso (1617–1682) became one of the most important Dalai Lamas of Tibet as he made the institution of the Dalai Lama the central figure of the country. He established the Tibetan government as the "Gaden Phodrang Chogley Namgyal,"[6] in 1642 and organized his government on the basis of "Choesi Sungdrel," the combination of both religion and politics. In this government, both the monks and laymen shared the responsibility of the governance of the country. He also formulated laws of public conduct, instituted a number of changes in the religious sphere with the aim of lessening the conflict between the different religious traditions and appointed governors to different districts. Politically, Tibetans considered the fifth Dalai Lama as very successful in unifying the country and he was called the "Great Fifth" in Tibetan history.[7]

Tsangyang Gyatso, the sixth Dalai Lama was born in Tawang, present Arunachal Pradesh and unlike any other Dalai Lamas, he was unique in his own way. He rebelled against the principles of the Buddhist traditions and negated the institution of the Dalai Lama. He did not take the political responsibility of the country seriously instead he composed excellent, romantic verses and songs which became popular and still are very famous among Tibetans.[8] He wanted to demolish the century old Tibetan religious traditions and wanted to change the role of Dalai Lama and his institution. His birth in Tawang is one of the major reasons for China to claim Monyul (Tawang Region) as part of Tibet, now under the PRC, which has resulted in border disputes between China and India in the Northeast region.[9]

The seventh and the eighth Dalai Lamas restricted themselves mainly to spiritual matters. In the eighteenth century, the Manchu officials proposed a Golden Urn system to decide on the recognition of the reincarnations of the Dalai Lamas and Panchen Lamas.[10] However, this procedure of golden urn system (lottery system) was followed only once for recognition of the eleventh Dalai Lama.

The ninth to the twelfth Dalai Lamas did not play a notable role in Tibetan history as all of them died at early stages of their lives and could not rule the country. Therefore, the role of the Dalai Lama as the ruler of the country declined significantly after the death of the fifth Dalai Lama. This remained the case till the Twelfth, due to their weak personal health as well as numerous domestic conflicts in Tibet.

The shattered institution of the Dalai Lama was revived by the thirteenth Dalai Lama, Thupten Gyatso (1876–1933). Tibet at that time was going through great pressure from different directions as seen in the interference from the Manchu Dynasty in China as well as the British in India. The latter had been interested in trade relations with Tibet and had sent their expedition to Tibet to negotiate with the Dalai Lama. But on the eve of the advance of the British expeditionary force to Lhasa, the Dalai Lama left and took asylum in Mongolia where he sought assistance from Russia.

In 1910, a considerable amount of Tibetan territory was included into the Chinese Qing Dynasty's control and they attacked Lhasa, forcing the Dalai Lama to seek shelter in India for a short period of time. During this period, the Ambans[11] marched through Lhasa, firing on members of the Lhasa police, and killing many of them. The Tibetans in response took up arms and besieged the Chinese in Lhasa; eventually they expelled the Chinese troops from Tibet in 1912, by which time the Qing Dynasty had collapsed.

This was followed by internal disturbances in the Chinese polity. The Manchu Dynasty collapsed in late 1911 and eventually the Chinese troops left Lhasa. In 1912, the Dalai Lama returned to Tibet and soon declared Tibet's independence.[12] Due to the invasions of Tibet (1904–1912) and the extensive travels of the thirteenth Dalai Lama, he acquired experience and familiarized himself with the complexities of power politics in other countries. These experiences instilled in him a realisation of the need for modernization. Accordingly, he tried to modernize Tibet by introducing updated civil and military methods, new teaching methods and curricula in the schools, unlike the traditional Buddhist culture.

But his modernization policies were greatly criticized by other religious leaders and monasteries, since they were perceived as an attack on the traditional monastery education and thus a loss of power for the religious leaders.

The Simla Convention between British India, China and Tibet was also finalised during his reign in 1914 which drew the famous McMahon Line. His dream of modernizing Tibet could not be fulfilled as he died in 1933. But Thupten Gyatso had revitalized the institution of Dalai Lama and maintained his power throughout his regime.

Traditionally, most of the Dalai Lamas are enthroned at the age of four to seven and they are taught the Buddhist culture and education by their tutors till they reach the age of eighteen, when they take up the responsibility of the nation at the age of 16-21 except the present Dalai Lama as he was forced by events to take up executive power fairly early. After the death of each Dalai Lama, a regent is appointed, and a search is conducted throughout the country for the rebirth of the deceased. The regent rules the country until the succeeding Dalai Lama assumes the responsibility of country. The regents have similar powers as the Dalai Lamas.

However, throughout much of the nineteenth century, the Dalai Lamas were without any power. Four of the Dalai Lamas (ninth-twelfth) passed away while still quite young. Therefore, most of the crises in Tibetan history occurred during the interim period of the absence of the Dalai Lama or when they were young. Thus, the history of the reincarnation shows both peaceful and turbulent experiences of transfer of power.

THE FOURTEENTH DALAI LAMA AND THE DEVOLUTION OF POLITICAL POWER

The fourteenth Dalai Lama, Tenzin Gyatso was born in 1935 at Taktser in Amdo region of Tibet. At the age of four, he was enthroned and moved to Lhasa with his family members. Unlike other Dalai Lamas, his reign faced a strong threat from one of the most powerful communist countries in 1949 and he assumed both the spiritual and temporal responsibility of the country a year later at the age of fifteen. This leader was inexperienced in administration and which was a great setback to the Tibetan government in Lhasa. With subsequent attacks from China, the Dalai Lama sought asylum in India and established his own government in exile. After the fourteenth Dalai Lama's successful running of the Tibetan Government-in-Exile (TGiE) for more than a half century, he handed over his political powers earlier in 2011.

The Central Tibetan Administration (CTA) in Dharamsala has recently undergone a democratic transition. Unlike other democratic nations where they struggled for democratic transition from "below", this democracy was first introduced among the Tibetans in early 1960s; and it was interpreted as a "gift" from the exiled leader which implied the Tibetans have achieved democracy without having to struggle for it. From its initial stage half a century back, the Tibetan movement has emerged as a successful case of activism from exile especially the democratic transition in the exile government. The democratic transition includes their structure of governance, use of the popular vote, increments in the number of Members of Parliament and most importantly, devolution of political power by the Dalai Lama. The Tibetans, both in exile and in Tibet, have viewed such changes in a positive manner as the reforms gave them increased incentives to participate in exile politics, reflected through the increased voter turnouts.

By giving the baton of responsibility to the new generation, the Dalai Lama has shown immense faith in the ability of the new leadership to carry forward the Tibetan people towards their long-cherished goal. One of the reasons for the devolution of political power is for the benefit of the Tibetan people in the long run, especially in a post-Dalai Lama scenario. In his March 14, 2011 statement to the Assembly of Tibetan People's Deputies (ATPD), he has clearly mentioned that it is extremely important that we ensure the continuity of our exile Tibetan administration and our struggle until the issue of Tibet has been successfully resolved.[13] He also stated that such a step was meant to fully democratize the Tibetan system of governance.

However the Dalai Lama's announcement of devolution of political authority got a negative response from the TGiE in the initial stages. In the March 10 2011 Statement of the Kashag (Cabinet) of the TGiE,

> a great number of Tibetans in exile from the various organizations, settlements, monastic institutions and

> individuals and particularly many Tibetans from inside Tibet collectively and individually have been ardently supplicating His Holiness the Dalai Lama not to take such a step. We the Kashag would like to make the same request in the strongest terms.[14]

But the Dalai Lama with his unwavering vision urged the TGiE to have a directly elected Kalon Tripa (Prime Minister) who is answerable for political questions concerning Tibet.

But, the changes in the CTA and the Dalai Lama's devolution of political power left many questions unanswered which have made the matter more complex. For instance, after his resignation from temporal power, the negotiations between the Dalai Lama's representatives and Chinese government have remained stalemated because the talks, as seen by the Chinese, are between the Chinese government (the United Front Work Department) and the representatives of the Dalai Lama. Thus, legitimacy was never given to the CTA, located in Dharamsala. So this issue becomes problematic since the political responsibility has come on to the elected Kalon Tripa, Lobsang Sangay. These issues have made the condition of Tibetans more critical and the Tibetans will face more problems in future regarding the Dalai Lama's representatives in foreign countries on the question of whether they will be recognized by any other country or not.

In the same way, the question of the Dalai Lama's reincarnation became murkier. China has always mentioned that the Dalai Lama is the sole reason for trouble in Tibet and it has warned other countries to stop giving support to the Dalai Lama and his people. But as a matter of fact, his charismatic leadership and non-violent means have received huge attention worldwide and it has automatically attracted world leaders. However, after the devolution of his power, China has shown more seriousness in the matter of the Dalai Lama's reincarnation and selection of his successors. They dubbed the political transition as a deceptive trick to betray the motherland.[15] This reaction of China makes the issue of Tibet more complicated in the post-Dalai Lama scenario.

CHINA'S POLICIES TOWARDS TIBETAN BUDDHISM

Mao Zedong once said "religion is poison" when the Dalai and former Panchen Lama visited Peking in 1954. The Chinese maintained that "*to believe in religion is fruitless. Religion is the instrument of autocratic feudal lords and religious works have no benefits whatsoever to the people.*"[16] With the ascendance of the Communists and the Cultural Revolution, Tibetan Buddhism along with the other religions in China suffered severe setbacks. According to the exile document, the Chinese have demolished almost 6,000 Tibetan religious institutions and monasteries.[17] This move was partly facilitated by commercial interests and the tourist potential that the monasteries drew from Western travellers.

Numerous restrictions have been imposed and religious activities recognising, or drawing inspiration from, the Dalai Lama are strictly banned in Tibet. For many years, they have destroyed all these institutions and now claim rights over the Dalai Lama's reincarnation. Such brazenly contradictory ideas make China's stand more complicated. On the one hand, they have demolished the religious institutions in Tibet; on the other they have also started to interfere in the rebirth of numerous high Lamas, including the Dalai Lama.

China reviles the present Dalai Lama and calls him a "splittist", "demon" and also "a wolf in monk's robes." The basic principle behind reincarnate Lamas is that the rebirth occurs to continue the work of the previous embodiment. If the fourteenth Dalai Lama is a "splittist", what power does the People's Republic of China (PRC) possess to transform the separatist soul into a patriotic soul while it transmits from one body to another?[18] Beijing blamed the Dalai Lama for 'splitting the motherland' and accused him of being the mastermind behind all anti-Chinese protests inside as well as outside China. This accusation was especially highlighted in the context of the 2008 Tibetan uprising which occurred just prior to the Beijing Olympics and was aimed at garnering international attention on the Tibetan issue.

Again the Chinese government banned all public displays of the Dalai Lama's image in Tibet Autonomous Region (TAR) since 1994, and prayers for his longevity are not offered in monasteries. Instead, they compelled the monks to criticize the Dalai Lama's image.[19]

Despite verbally abusing him and blaming him for instigating all anti-China protests inside and outside Tibet, the Chinese are still keen to influence the Dalai Lama's reincarnation. So the major reasons for China's interest in his successor are:

First, the aim of Chinese government to install its own Dalai Lama is to try and manipulate the mindsets of the Tibetan people. It is an attempt to show the Tibetans that the Communists are serious about religious matters and to preserve the traditional heritage of the Buddhist lineage. China adopts a policy of fake religious freedom, which includes respecting and protecting Tibetan Buddhism. After the 1987 demonstration, they followed the "strike hard" and "patriotic re-education" campaign against the Tibetans, during which they emphasized on the importance of the study of communist ideology and the benefits of economic development.

However, the regular periods of unrest and self-immolation in recent times reflect the frustration amongst Tibetans resulting from the sustained violation of their rights. Almost a hundred Tibetans have set themselves on fire since February 2009 to protest Beijing's rule over Tibetan areas. Economic development and modernization has not led to social peace, but rather periodic eruptions of unrest. Economic development alone is insufficient for creating political stability or lessening ethnic tensions. It is the identity and dignity of the Tibetan people which led them to take the extreme step of self-immolation.

Second, the Chinese authorities fear and mistrust any institution that is not completely under their control. According to Wang Lixiong, the religious leaders have greater say over the changes in the moral values and development in the public life of Tibetans in Tibet.[20] For instance, Tulku Tenzin Delek opened a school for orphans without permission from the government, which was much appreciated by the local people for his charitable activities. However, the Chinese leaders fear his work, as it might weaken the government's authority. Later Tulku Tenzin Delek was arrested and sentenced.[21] Due to these reasons, China keeps close track of the reincarnations of all religious leaders, and now is paying special attention to the institution of the Dalai Lama.

Third, with the growing image of the Dalai Lama in the international arena, China feels insecure and uncomfortable with his growing stature amongst international audiences. Beijing strongly believes that the issue of the Dalai Lama is the issue of Tibet and once the Dalai Lama leaves the scene, it is possible that a faction amongst the exiled leadership might call for Tibetan independence through violent means, and then the issue will be solved. Or they will not have a single leadership to lead the Tibetan movement further after the passing of the Dalai Lama. Therefore, we can also say that China is waiting for the Dalai Lama's death.

FUTURE POSSIBILITIES OF THE 15TH DALAI LAMA AND ITS IMPACT ON TIBETANS

The Dalai Lama's succession issue has gained prominence after the talks between the Dalai Lama's representatives and the Chinese government broke down in January 2010. China has asserted equal claims over the choice of his successor. The Dalai Lama has also given some clues regarding his reincarnation; certain possibilities were laid out: there could be a female Dalai Lama; there might not be a Dalai Lama and the institution of the Dalai Lama could end after him; a leader of another Tibetan Buddhist lineage inheriting his spiritual role; or he may appoint his own successor, who may be elected.

However, the Chinese have made his reincarnation issue more problematic as the government has passed a series of laws stipulating that it has ultimate authority over the "management of living Buddha reincarnation." In 2007, China enacted a law that asserted the Central government to be the final authority in the process that recognizes a reincarnated Lama and even the Dalai Lama's reincarnation must be approved by the Chinese Central Government.[22] They declared the so called "Order No. Five" concerning the control and recognition of reincarnations, which came into force on September 1, 2007. The enforcement of such laws and methods in religious issues damage the unique cultural traditions of Tibet. According to Padma Choeling, Chairman of the TAR government,

> we must respect the historical institutions and religious rituals of Tibetan Buddhism. I am afraid it is not up to anyone to abolish the reincarnation institution or not.[23]

But as a practical matter, the traditional practice of identifying a young Tibetan boy by the search committee as his reincarnation may not make sense in the present world. Because, firstly the present Dalai Lama lives in exile and he has already given a clue that this successor will be found outside Tibet or they might not have a fifteenth Dalai Lama.[24] Secondly, the times have changed and the next Dalai Lama need not necessarily be a boy. After giving all these clues, if still China recognizes its own Dalai Lama, then the obvious question is can there be any legitimacy behind "China's Dalai Lama?" The answer is no.

Despite China's continuous claim on the reincarnation of the Dalai Lama, the Dalai Lama himself clarified in the 11th Buddhist Religious meeting in September 2011, where he said that he would give clear written instructions of his reincarnation at the age of ninety if it is decided that the reincarnation of the Dalai Lama should continue,[25] and at that time he would ask the religious leaders of all sects and also consult the Tibetan public. His statement shocked both Tibetans and the Chinese government. Most probably the whole world is waiting for 2025 when the Dalai Lama reaches ninety years and he might spring another surprise on the world. He even once said that,

> the institution of the Dalai Lama... that will come and go depends on the actual circumstances. If people feel that there should be another Dalai Lama then I will be there. As long as suffering of the sentient being is there, I will serve as much as I can, this is my determination.[26]

He said that he has the "sole legitimate authority"[27] over his reincarnation.

The dialogue conducted between the Dalai Lama's special envoys and the Chinese leadership in the previous decade was never officially recognized by the Chinese government, which often described them as private interactions with the representatives of the Dalai Lama. The Chinese government has never accepted the TGiE. They called it an illegitimate and illegal government and even the host country, India, has not recognized it. Even after almost two years of Lobsang Sangay's rule, nothing concrete has emerged regarding the prospects of negotiations between the Chinese and the exiles. So with the devolution of authority, the first and foremost issue is the lack of any channel for dialogue.

Many believe that the reincarnation conundrum of the Panchen Lama might be repeated, if the institution of the Dalai Lama continues. The Panchen Lama is the second highest in the religious hierarchy of Tibetan history, next to Dalai Lama. In 1995, the Dalai Lama recognized a six year old boy as the reincarnation of Panchen Lama. Soon after the recognition, the Chinese placed him under house arrest and his whereabouts are still not known.

Instead, they appointed their own candidate as the Panchen Lama. In the same way, this might happen again for the Dalai Lama's reincarnation; one recognized by the exile Tibetan community and the other by the Chinese. But what the Tibetans believe is that the reincarnated Lamas are mainly for the continuation of work unfinished by his predecessors, so the Dalai Lama recognized by the Chinese will not have legitimacy.

The Beijing government is aware that Buddhism is central to the Tibetans, and has tried to select and prop up Lamas who will support the government while still retaining legitimacy among the people.

CONCLUSION

Wang Lixiong has rightly said

> while the Dalai Lama is still alive, Tibetans harbor hope. But once the Dalai Lama dies, grief will give rise to frenzy.[28]

Of all his predecessors, the Tibetans consider the present Dalai Lama as the most powerful in unifying the whole country under one roof overcoming sectarian differences, with His Holiness following all major as well as minor traditions of Tibetan Buddhism. The Tibetans face a strong threat from Communist China's presence and policies in Tibet, but are still united in exile as well as in the roof of the world under his guidance. Like any other exiled people across the world, even after five decades of exile, the struggle for existence and identity is still a daunting challenge for the Tibetan community and the issue of Tibet becomes murkier with the ageing Dalai Lama.

This is further complicated by Communist China's machinations and desire to control the process of reincarnation of the Dalai Lama as well as other Lamas in Tibet. Much of this emerges from the fact that the *tulkus* are a centre of informal power and authority, which they have wielded to control the masses; this forms a major bone of contention between Beijing and Tibetan Buddhism, as the former had a terrible past with religious movements, seen most recently with the Falun Gong and many others during earlier Imperial rule. With the devolution of the political authority of the Dalai Lama, China gained more opportunity to tighten its control over Tibet by expanding its economy. In conclusion, the reincarnation of the Dalai Lama becomes highly important and a fresh zone of tension and instability will be created in the Tibetan Plateau.

ENDNOTES

1. Tulkus are Tibetan honorific term denoting a reincarnate Lama, called a "Living Buddha" and they are highly respected by the Buddhists.
2. Rahul Ram, *The Dalai Lama: The Institution*, Vikas Publishing House Pvt Ltd., 1995, p. 16.
3. Kapstein T. Matthew, *The Tibetans*, Blackwell Publishing Ltd., UK, 2006, p. 129.
4. Rahul Ram, p. 23.
5. Kapstein T. Matthew, p. 134.
6. Gaden Phodrang Government remained the government of Tibet till the recent changes in the Central Tibetan Administration in Exile in which His Holiness the Dalai Lama relinquished from the political power of the exile community.
7. Kapstein T. Matthew, p. 136.
8. Ibid., p. 130.
9. The focus on Tawang reflected Beijing's belief that it had a strong historical case. Following the Chinese invasion of Tibet, New Delhi decided in February 1951 to bring Tawang under its administrative hold. China's current claim to Tawang rests largely on the fact that it came under Indian control in 1951. So the problems have still not resolved and it became murkier two years back when New Delhi allowed Dalai Lama to visit Tawang in response to which China provided stapled visas to Arunachal residents to visit China. Therefore the border dispute over Arunachal Pradesh is closely attached with the sixth Dalai Lama.

10. The Golden Urn system was actually used only in the cases of the eleventh and twelfth Dalai Lamas. However, the twelfth Dalai Lama had already been recognized before the procedure was employed.
11. The word 'amban' is derived from an English word Ambassador where the Manchu government stationed their representatives in Lhasa during the Qing dynasty.
12. Kapstein T. Matthew, p. 171.
13. Message of the His Holiness the Dalai Lama to the Fourteenth Assembly of the Tibetan People's Deputies, March 14 2011.
14. The Kashag's Statement on March 10 2011.
15. Dalai Lama to hand over Political Leader Role, *The Wall Street Journal*, March 11, 2011. http://online.wsj.com/article/SB10001424052748703453804576191542646350586.html
16. Patterson N.George, China and Tibet: Background to the Revolt, *The China Quarterly*, no. 1, Jan-March, 1960, p. 94.
17. *The Tibet Museum, Tibet's Journey in Exile*, Department of Information and International Relations, 2008, p. 71.
18. Dibyesh Anand, "The Next Dalai Lama: China has a Choice", *The Guardian*, December 15, 2010. http://www.guardian.co.uk/commentisfree/belief/2010/dec/15/china-dalai-lama-exile-tibetans
19. Barry Sautman, "Tibet and the (Mis-) Representation of Cultural Genocide", in Barry Sautman (ed.), *Cultural Genocide and Asian State Peripheries*, Palgrave Macmillan, New York, 2006, p. 185.
20. Wang Lixiong, "The End of Tibetan Buddhism", in Wang Lixiong and Tsering Shakya (eds.), *The Struggle for Tibet*, Verso, London, 2009, p. 148.
21. Tulku Tenzin Delek is a reincarnated Gelugpa Lama, who is highly respected by the locals in the regions and the authorities accused him of carrying out a series of terrorist explosions.
22. "Will a Dalai Lama Succeed the Dalai Lama?", *Sunday Times of India*, New Delhi, March 13 2011.
23. "Dalai Lama to Step Down", *The Hindu*, Chennai, March 11 2011, Friday.
24. "After the Dalai Lama Dies and Choosing a New Dalai Lama", http://factsanddetails.com china. php?itemid=1691&catid=6 &subcatid=33

25. Statement of His Holiness the Fourteenth Dalai Lama, Tenzin Gyatso, on the Issue of His Reincarnation, translated from the Tibetan, September 24, 2011.
26. Sana Hashmi, "Dalai Lama and the Devolution of Political Authority in Tibet", *World Focus*, 32 (11-12), November-December 2011, p. 878.
27. Statement of His Holiness the Fourteenth Dalai Lama, September 24 2011.
28. "After the Dalai Lama Dies and Choosing a New Dalai Lama", http://factsanddetails.com china.php?itemid=1691&catid=6 &subcatid=33

REFERENCES

Abraham, Thomas, "Little Can be Achieved through Negotiations on Tibet", *Economic & Political Weekly*, April 5 2008, pp. 8-11.

Anand, Dibyesh, "The Next Dalai Lama: China has a Choice", *The Guardian*, December 15, 2010. At 90, will decide on Institution of Dalai Lama, *The Sunday Express*, New Delhi, September 25, 2011.

Bell, Charles, *Portrait of a Dalai Lama—The Life and Times of the Great Thirteenth*, Munshiram Manoharlal Publishers Pvt. Ltd., 2000.

Burke, J. Denis, "Tibetans in Exile in a Changing Global Political Climate", *Economic & Political Weekly*, April 12, 2008, pp. 79-85.

"Dalai Lama to Step Down", *The Hindu*, Chennai, March 11, 2011, Friday.

"Dalai Lama to Hand Over Political Leader Role", *The Wall Street Journal*, March 11, 2011.

Frachette, Ann, "Democracy and Democratisation among Tibetans in Exile", *The Journal of Asian Studies*, 66(1), Feb 2007, pp. 97-127.

Hashmi, Sana, "Dalai Lama and the Devolution of Political Authority in Tibet", *World Focus*, 32(11-12), November-December 2011, pp. 875-79.

Kapstein, T. Matthew, *The Tibetans*, Blackwell Publishing Ltd., UK, 2006.

Lixiong, Wang, "The End of Tibetan Buddhism", Tsering Shakya and Wang Lixiong (eds.), *The Struggle for Tibet*, Verso, London, 2009.

Message of the His Holiness the Dalai Lama to the Fourteenth Assembly of the Tibetan People's Deputies, March 14, 2011.

Norbu, Dawa, "China's Dialogue with the Dalai Lama 1978-1990: Prenegotiation Stage of Dead End?", *Pacific Affairs*, 64(3), Autumn 1991, pp. 351-72.

Patterson, N. George, "China and Tibet: Background to the Revolt", *The China Quarterly*, no. 1, Jan-March, 1960, pp. 87-102.

Raghavan, Srinath, "The Chinese Puzzle", *Economic and Political Weekly*, 45(3), January 16 2010, pp. 22-25.

Rahul, Ram, *The Dalai Lama: The Institution*, Vikas Publishing House Pvt Ltd., 1995.

Sautman, Barry, "Tibet and the (Mis-) Representation of Cultural Genocide", in Barry Sautman (ed.), *Cultural Genocide and Asian State Peripheries*, Palgrave Macmillan, New York, 2006.

Shakabpa, W.D. Tsepon, *Tibet: A Political History*, Potala Publications, New York, 1967.

Statement of His Holiness the Fourteenth Dalai Lama on the Issue of his Reincarnation, September 24, 2011.

The Tibet Museum, Tibet's Journey in Exile, Department of Information and International Relations, 2008.

Verma, S. Virendra, "Post Dalai Lama Situation and the Middle Path: Discussions with Chinese Scholars", *China Report*, 45(1), 2009, pp. 75-87.

"Will a Dalai Lama succeed the Dalai Lama?", *Sunday Times of India*, New Delhi, March 13 2011.

Xiaowen, Ye, "China's Religions: Retrospect and Prospect", *Chinese Journal of International Law*, 4(2), 2005, pp. 441-53.

3

Tibet in International Law and Practice

P.P. Shukla

> Since Tibet is not the same as China, it should ultimately be the wishes of the people of Tibet that should prevail and not any legal or constitutional arguments. That, I think, is a valid point. Whether the people of Tibet are strong enough to assert their rights or not is another matter. Whether we are strong enough to see that is done is also another matter. But it is a right and proper thing to say and I see no difficulty in saying to the Chinese government that whether they have suzerainty or sovereignty over Tibet, surely, according to any principles, the principle they proclaim and the principles I uphold, the last voice in regard to Tibet should be the voice of the people of Tibet and nobody else.
>
> *Jawaharlal Nehru, 7 December, 1950, Lok Sabha*

The plan of study is to divide Tibetan history into three parts: one, prior to the 19th Century, the second from the 19th century to the beginning of the 20th century, and finally, the

20th century itself, including and bringing the study up to the current period of the 21st century.

The period before the 19th century is important, of course, but so much happened in the subsequent years that the relevance of the evidence from further back becomes debatable. Much of the evidence from the Chinese side is also sketchy over this period and consists of tokens of control which are not relevant to the current practice of diplomacy or international law. For instance, the claim that they appointed representatives [who were considered as Ambassadors by the Tibetans] or awarded titles is unconvincing. Britain still awards titles to countries like Australia and even appoints the Governor-General. But no one would accept any claim of British sovereignty over Australia. Besides, China itself was ruled during this period by the Manchus, who were themselves non-[Han] Chinese, so it is questionable whether their territories may logically be considered Chinese. It would be akin to India claiming Afghanistan because the Mughals controlled that territory or Burma because the British did.

The 19th century however, saw some important events, and these are important indications of the nature of the relationship between Tibet and China. Two events stand out. The first was the relationship between Tibet and Nepal. Nepal invaded Tibet [its second invasion in the 19th Century] in 1854 and the Chinese central authorities did nothing to help Tibet, which was forced to conclude a Treaty in 1856 with Nepal which provided for a tribute—the sum of Rs.10,000 annually, a large sum those days—to be paid by Tibet. Although the Treaty paid obeisance to the Emperor of China, the fact is that Beijing neither helped in the war, not did it play any role in the Treaty signing. This is not the attribute of a sovereign. Nonetheless, the Beijing authorities use this Treaty, among others, to lay claim over both Tibet and even Nepal. The latter is dormant now, but the potential for trouble exists and needs to be recognised.

This particular aspect of Tibetan sovereignty was brought out by the Indian officials in their negotiations with China which took place in the late 1950s and is reflected in the following extract from the Officials' Report.

EXCERPT FROM THE OFFICIALS' REPORT (1960)

...during the 300 years prior to 1950, Tibet, whatever her status, had enjoyed the right to sign treaties and have direct dealings with her neighbours on boundary questions, was clearly established by history. The Indian side had already drawn attention to the treaties of 1684 and 1842 signed by Tibet with Ladakh. In 1856, she signed a treaty with Nepal, and the People's Government of China themselves recognised the validity of this treaty, because they felt it necessary to abrogate it in their treaty, signed exactly a hundred years later, in 1956 with the Nepal government. It was asserted by the Chinese side that the Chinese Amban in Tibet had assisted in the conclusion of the 1856 treaty. This, too, was an incorrect statement of facts; but even if true, it would only corroborate the Indian position that China recognised the treaty-making powers of Tibet. For it would mean that China assisted Tibet in directly negotiating a treaty which, among other things, granted extra-territorial rights to Nepal.

If the Chinese felt the need to abrogate the Treaty in 1956, it means that they acknowledged its validity till the time of abrogation.

For the second event, the clock needs to be turned back a little further. A few years earlier, starting in 1841, a war broke out between Tibet and the Dogra rulers of Kashmir. This resulted in Letters of Agreement being signed between the warring parties, under which the boundaries between Ladakh and Tibet were clarified and recognised and trade relations were regularised. Ladakh also agreed to pay an annual tribute to Tibet. Again the central authorities played no role in the entire episode. The importance of this agreement between Ladakh and Tibet in further establishing Tibetan sovereignty is also brought out in the Officials' Report, as quoted above.

Another aspect worth mentioning is the attempt at about this time by Beijing to regulate the selection of the Dalai Lama. This happened in 1793, and the central part of the regulations introduced by Beijing read as follows:

> When the reincarnate boy has been found, his name will be written on a lot, which shall be put into a golden urn bestowed by the central government. The high commissioners will bring together appropriate high-ranking Living Buddhas to determine the authenticity of the reincarnate boy by drawing lots from the golden urn.

However, the Tibetan authorities ignored this and in 1804, the Ninth Dalai Lama was selected in the usual way by the Regent.

The final piece of evidence dates to the last three decades of the 19th Century, and involves British attempts to establish direct relations with Tibet. A bit of background would be helpful here. The strategic setting was the rapid expansion of two major Empires—the British and the Russian—towards the heart of Asia. The British Empire expanded west and north from Calcutta, the Russian south and east from St Petersburg. They met, or drew close, along the Central Asian redoubts. Tibet at this time was playing host to the famous historical figure Agvan Dorjiev, a Buryat monk who arrived in Lhasa in 1880, and soon became a debating partner of the Dalai Lama. The contemporary British media were replete with articles about the Russian advance into Tibet through the agency of Dorjiev. For long afterwards, it was doubted whether the Russians and Dorjiev were indeed playing any political role, but recent disclosures make it clear that there were indeed strategic and military matters under consideration between Russia and Tibet, through the mediation of Dorjiev. However, the British had their own plans and fears, and turned to the Chinese Empire in order to use its supposed suzerain status to work their strategy in Tibet.

The British had been trying to open relations with Tibet at this time, mainly to counter the Russian moves described briefly above, and were doing this by attempting to involve the Chinese on their side. With this aim they signed an agreement in 1876 [the Chefoo Agreement the main objective of which was to let the British missionaries enter China, only one paragraph was about Tibet], but the Tibetans refused to accept the validity of this agreement as far as they were concerned and refused to be bound by its terms. A decade and a half later, they tried again through a second agreement with China, the Convention of March 1890, this time in order to regulate the boundaries between Sikkim and Tibet, as well as [through the Annex] to regulate trade between British India and Tibet. However, this agreement, like the previous effort by the British to work through the Chinese, did not succeed either, and for the same reason. The Tibetans refused to acknowledge the validity of any treaty or arrangement that did not directly involve them. Meanwhile, they were steadily moving to accept Russian protection, under the guidance of Dorjiev. The Russians were already emerging as perhaps the major strategic adversary to the British in Asia. Accordingly, after having waited for the Beijing connection to deliver, the British were forced to conclude that this was not going to work, and they had to move independently and directly on Tibet. This was the genesis of the Younghusband expedition in 1903-04. The spur was the failure of Beijing to deliver on its part of the agreements signed in the late 19th Century, and the real reason was the success of the Russians in dealing directly with Tibet. The Russians did not entirely ignore Beijing, and did sign a separate agreement with China, but it was clear that they were focusing on working directly with Tibet, which was responding positively.

This was the situation the British faced at the dawn of the 20th Century, and decided that they had to take direct action, since China was unable to deliver on the commitments undertaken over the past twenty years. The result was the Younghusband expedition. Lord Curzon was the Viceroy and he declared that "the so-called suzerainty of China over Tibet [is] a constitutional fiction, a political affectation which has been maintained because of its convenience to both parties". At the end of the expedition, the two sides signed the Anglo-Tibetan Convention on 7 September 1904. Thus, the Tibetans were once more left to fend for themselves in the face of a military attack, without any aid from China. And once again, Tibet entered into a treaty with a foreign power without any role for Beijing. The provisions of the Convention of 1904 also make revealing reading; the preamble admitted that "doubts and difficulties about the meaning *and validity*" [emphasis added] had arisen over the 1890 agreement with China [a polite way of recording the fact that Tibet was refusing to recognise and therefore to implement that agreement]; the rest of the Treaty essentially ratified the substance of the earlier agreements between Britain and China on the border between Sikkim and Tibet, and allowed for trade rights for British India. Finally, another important outcome was to check Russian influence in Tibet and Tibet was required not to cede or lease any part of its territory to any foreign power, and to remove all foreign representatives, and to extend no economic concessions to any foreign power. Russian influence was thus also blocked, though Dorjiev remained active in Tibet for some time longer.

[In the 1940's the British repeatedly told the Tibetan Foreign Bureau that they signed the Convention and then left after a few weeks. They never acted as an invading power which remains in the invaded territories. They wanted to show the difference of attitude between China and HMG]

What this episode shows again is that China played no role in defending Tibet, and no role in treaty-making by Tibet. What is more, it also showed that treaties and agreements entered into by China on behalf of Tibet could not be implemented because Tibet would not acknowledge China's right to make any commitments on its behalf. And it demonstrated that such commitments would remain unimplemented.

The 20th century thus opened with Tibet becoming an active focus of the power play between the Great Powers, and with China having played no role that a sovereign or suzerain would be required to play, though for completeness, it may be mentioned that Manchu China did help Tibet in 1792 during the war with the Gorkhas.

But more was to come. Not for the last time, differences arose between the Viceroy in India and London over policy in Asia. In London, the view was that Britain had to work diplomatically with both China and Russia, the former to block the Russians in Tibet, the latter to prepare for the looming challenge from Germany. Thus, the Lhasa Convention between Britain and Tibet was reaffirmed by China in the British-Chinese Convention of 1906. This "confirmed" the 1904 Convention and stated that the trade concessions granted under the 1904 agreement would not be available to any state, other than China, thus addressing the fear of Russian influence in Tibet, by co-opting China for the purpose. Unfortunately for Tibet, the British further confirmed the dilution of the 1904 Convention by signing the Anglo-Russian Convention in 1907 which covered Afghanistan, Iran and Tibet. According to this, Tibet was once again, inter alia, deemed to be under the suzerainty of China. All this was the result of London over-ruling Calcutta in the larger interests of co-opting Russia over the growing differences with Imperial Germany, in the face of which London wished to settle as many issues with the other major powers as it could. Tibet needed to be sacrificed for this purpose. [An interesting sidelight on the diplomacy of those days is that when the Kaiser Wilhelm examined the text of the Anglo-Russian Convention, he minuted on the text that this was clearly aimed against Germany.]

This was the tangled situation in the early 1900s, when the Chinese Empire collapsed in 1911, and was replaced by a republican government. One of the early developments following this was the Tibet-Mongolia Treaty of 1913, under which each recognised the other as an independent country. Although there have been some efforts to deny the existence of any such agreement, the Government of Mongolia made this Treaty public in 1982, at a time when relations between the Soviet bloc and China were extremely hostile. The Thirteenth Dalai Lama had also formally declared Tibet an independent country in 1912 and all Chinese officials, including all armed personnel, had been expelled. Representatives of Nepal had witnessed the agreement and its implementation. The Chinese were again expelled from Tibet in July 1949.

This was the setting for the Simla conference in 1914. The conference began early in the year, and representatives from Britain, Tibet and China were all present. They examined and accepted each others' credentials, thus indicating that all three were participating as equals. The major result for India was the boundary between British India and Tibet—the McMahon Line. It also divided Tibet into an Inner and Outer Tibet [with the latter being autonomous, the former not], an issue that still rankles among Tibetans, for it left many Tibetans under direct Chinese administration [interestingly it is these populations who today oppose the Chinese rule on the Tibetan Plateau]. The Chinese withdrew their representative, Chen I-fan [Ivan Chen], in protest because they did not approve of the line dividing Outer Tibet from China. This was the only reason, and had nothing to do with either Tibet signing an agreement with the British as a sovereign country, or with the delineation of the McMahon Line. This fact was highlighted in the Eden Memorandum addressed to TV Soong, the Foreign Minister of China many years later, in 1943. By then, the Second World War was coming to a successful end—the

Germans had already surrendered at Stalingrad—and the civil war in China was causing concern as to the eventual outcome. This was why Eden communicated to the Nationalist Government that Britain had, since 1921, been regarding Tibet as an autonomous country under Chinese suzerainty, but with treaty-making powers. A brief quote from the Eden Memorandum will bring this out.

EXCERPT FROM THE EDEN MEMORANDUM 1943

> Since the Chinese Revolution of 1911, when Chinese forces were withdrawn from Tibet, Tibet has enjoyed de facto independence. She has ever since regarded herself as in practice completely autonomous and has opposed Chinese attempts to reassert control. This was reiterated in the House of Commons in December 1949.
>
> Since 1911, repeated attempts have been made to bring about an accord between China and Tibet. It seemed likely that agreement could be found on the basis that Tibet should be autonomous under the nominal suzerainty of China, and this was the basis of the draft tripartite (Chinese-Tibetan-British) convention of 1914 which was initialled by the Chinese representative by was not ratified by the Chinese Government. The rock on which the convention and subsequent attempts to reach an understanding were wrecked was not the question of autonomy (which was expressly accepted by China) but was the question of the boundary between China and Tibet, since the Chinese Government claimed sovereignty over areas which the Tibetan Government claimed belonged to their autonomous jurisdiction. [Emphasis added].

The American archives show a similar disposition in the US Administration which also made recognition of Chinese suzerainty conditional on autonomy for Tibet. And this was the situation that independent India inherited in 1947. Leaving aside the early period, by 1949, it was clear to most observers that the Communists were heading for victory in the civil war. The British resident in Tibet warned the Government in Delhi of the dangers for India through Tibet in such a development. Prime Minister Nehru's assessment of this caution was typical in its combination of ignorance and intellectual arrogance, as he discounted any possibility of any such security threat. Writing an internal Note on 9 July 1949, he observed:

EXCERPT FROM NEHRU'S NOTING 1949

> Whatever may be the ultimate fate of Tibet in relation to China, I think there is practically no chance of any military danger to India arising from any possible change in Tibet. Geographically, this is very difficult and practically it would be a foolish adventure. If India is to be influenced or an attempt made to bring pressure on her, Tibet is not the route for it.
>
> I do not think there is any necessity at present for our Defence Ministry, or any part of it, to consider possible military repercussions on the India-Tibetan frontier. The event is remote and may not arise at all.

This was the strategic appreciation that seemed to guide Nehru through the early traumatic years after the Chinese invaded and occupied Tibet in 1950. He seemed to be deeply committed to working with the Chinese in order to bring about a grand Asian revival, and Tibet for him was a hindrance in this grand scheme. But in the process, he made blunders on Tibet which that unfortunate country, and India too, is still paying for. It is noteworthy that Nehru had overridden Nationalist Chinese objections during the 1947 Asian Relations Conference which he hosted in April, and allowed Tibet to take part as an independent country, and to travel on Tibetan passports, but he did not show anything like the same firmness in approaching the Communists. What made this even more inexplicable is the fact that the Nationalists had been active supporters of the Indian freedom movement, whereas the Communists had had choice things to say about Nehru and Indian freedom.

In time-honoured and indeed, treaty-bound tradition, the Dalai Lama, now already the [current] Fourteenth, then a teenager, turned to India when the Chinese troops occupied to seek refuge and support in 1950-51. He was preparing to go to the UN to lay out his case [he took refuge in Chumbi Valley a few months after sending his appeal to the UN GA], when the Indian government decided that it would not sponsor any discussion on Tibet in the UN. As a non-member, Tibet could not bring up the matter in the UN itself. The reasoning of the Indian government was that there was nothing anyone could do in military terms to help Tibet; further, any discussion in the UN would only antagonise the Chinese, and make the situation worse for the Tibetans. Of course, this quite disregarded the fact that Tibet itself wanted the matter discussed at the UN. Further, it emphasised the irony that while India took the Jammu & Kashmir question to the UN, it would not support a reference on Tibet at the UN.

Finally, [tiny] El Salvador agreed to sponsor the discussion. But just as the matter was coming up for discussion at Lake Success at the end of November 1950, the Indian delegation informed the UN that they had received word that China was willing to settle the matter peacefully. Hence, said the Indian representative, the matter should be withdrawn from consideration. The British and the Americans accepted the primacy of the Indian role in Tibetan, matters and went along. The US archives show that the Americans did try several times to persuade Nehru to do more to help Tibet, including at the UN, but it was not to be—Nehru was more concerned about his role in the Korea conflict.

It was not until 1956 that things began to change, as the ground situation continued to worsen and Tibetan resistance to Chinese occupation grew. For the purposes of this paper, however, it is important to emphasise that the matter did finally come up in the UN General Assembly in later years—in 1959, 1961, and 1965. The first of these was confined to the violation of the rights of the Tibetan people, but the second, in 1961, carried a call for the right of self determination of the Tibetan people. It was a short Resolution, but the operative part is worth quoting from:

EXCERPT FROM UNGA RESOLUTION 1723 OF 20 DECEMBER 1961

THE GENERAL ASSEMBLY

> ...
>
> *Considering* that these events violate fundamental human rights and freedoms set out in the Charter of the United Nations and the Universal Declaration of Human Rights, including the principle of self-determination of peoples and nations, and have the deplorable effect of increasing international tension and embittering relations between peoples,
>
> 1. *Reaffirms its conviction* that respect for the principles of the Charter of the United Nations and of the Universal Declaration of Human Rights is essential for the evolution of a peaceful world order based on the rule of law;
>
> 2. *Solemnly renews its call* for the cessation of practices which deprive the Tibetan people of their fundamental human rights and freedoms, including the right to self-determination; [Emphasis added].

India did not sponsor or support either of the Resolutions, and the explanation must be Nehru's continuing commitment to seeking peace at any price with China. It did not work, and the war of 1962 brought such humiliation and hurt upon Nehru that it would not be wrong to say that it destroyed his standing in the country, and hastened his death in 1964. Notably, however, India did speak and support the next UN Resolution, in 1965, symptomatically, under a new Prime Minister. The 1965

Resolution did not specifically reiterate the call for self-determination, but it reaffirmed the earlier Resolutions, and had the support of India, among other major powers. Thus, the UN is committed to giving the Tibetans the right of self-determination, but this will obviously not happen as long as China remains willing to use its veto power in the UN Security Council. Nevertheless, the legal position is clear and worth recording.

There is one other issue that needs to be addressed. This concerns the two legal agreements entered into by the People's Republic of China with Tibet in 1951 and with India in 1954. As to the first, it was always under a cloud because the Tibetan delegation that signed it in Beijing was coerced into doing so, and moreover, the seals were forged in Beijing itself. This had to be done because the delegation was not empowered by the Dalai Lama to enter into any agreement on the status of Tibet [the Dalai Lama got the information through radio when he was in Chumbi Valley], but only to negotiate the withdrawal of the Chinese troops. Furthermore, even though the Dalai Lama was persuaded in the end to accept the 17-point Agreement as it has come to be known in history, it cannot be considered binding any more. It was denounced by the Dalai Lama in 1959 after he fled from Lhasa in Lhuntse Dzong, on his way to the Indian border. The International Commission of Jurists examined this denunciation and found in 1960, after the Dalai Lama had been forced into exile, that the denunciation was legally valid and tenable.

ICJ REPORT ON TIBET AND CHINA (EXCERPT) (1960) [P. 346]

> The view of the [Legal Inquiry] COMMITTEE was that Tibet was at the very least a de facto independent State when the Agreement of Peaceful Measures in Tibet was signed in 1951, and the repudiation of this agreement by the Tibetan Government in 1959 was found to be fully justified.

As to the India-China agreement of 1954, it was valid for eight years to begin with, and lapsed in 1962. This happened in the month of April 1962, when relations between the two countries were extremely tense and war was to break out a few months later, in October. However, since the agreement has lapsed, there is no legal validity to this commitment. Legally, it means that Tibet and India revert to the previous Agreement, i.e. the Simla Convention of 1914, which can be considered as a valid Treaty once the regulations of the 1954 Panchsheel Agreement have lapsed. What is noteworthy is that China used to insist on an inclusion in all the Joint documents with India that it should carry a reiteration of Tibet as a part of China. However, since the last two years, this reference is missing.

There is, of course, a question mark on all this in light of the Dalai Lama's own stated position that he no longer seeks independence from China but only a wide degree of genuine autonomy. This, however, is only a proposal and does not alter the legal status of Tibet. That will happen only when and if a new agreement is reached along the lines suggested by the Dalai Lama among the countries concerned. The Dalai Lama's quest for genuine autonomy is different from the traditional British definition of 'autonomy' in this context, because London wanted responsibility for Foreign Affairs to remain with Lhasa.

This is also the appropriate place to mention that the Dalai Lama is getting on in years, and the Chinese have made it clear that they are preparing for a struggle over the succession and his reincarnation. In a reprise of the 1793 effort, they have again laid down their perspective on the reincarnation—something strange for an avowed socialist and atheist state to do. Nonetheless, they have the Panchen Lama under their control, and it would be unwise to underestimate their determination to ensure their control over the choice of the next Dalai Lama. His Holiness is, of course, well-versed in the ways of the Chinese, and is clearly preparing for the succession. However, the unambiguous status of the current Dalai Lama is a unique asset for Tibet, and every effort needs to be made to settle matters with a reasonably short period of time.

In closing, it is worthwhile reflecting upon the Tibet-Mongolia Treaty of January 1913. Both countries recognised each other's independence. The Mongolians turned to Russia for guidance and protection, the Tibetans to Britain and later India for the same. Mongolia is today an independent country—a condition extracted by the Soviet leaders from Nationalist China and then the People's Republic, regardless of the fraternal ties between them. Tibet is a country and culture on the verge of extinction, a sorry reflection on the Indian leadership.

4

India-Tibet Relation in Intellectual, Spiritual and Cultural Domains

Geshe Ngawang Samten

I

There are two points that that are worth highlighting by way of opening ideas. There has been since time immemorial a living faith among the Sadhus in India that Tibet at the foot of the Mount Kailash is an auspicious and holy land, that it is inhabited by yogis of marvellous spiritual achievement, and every Sadhu cherishes the wish to undertake a pilgrim's journey not only to the Himalayan shrines, but to the trans-Himalayan abode of deities as well. There are numerous accounts written by Sadhus who had visited Tibet. Swami Akhandananda, a fellow monk of Swami Vivekananda, had been to Tibet twice in the course of his wanderings to the Himalayan and trans-Himalayan regions. He took his abode in Tibetan monasteries, and has written about the rich spiritual atmosphere there, the modes of worship, and the impeccable chaste character of the Lamas. In accordance with the Tibetan term "Gelong", he was named *akhandananda*, meaning the one whose celibacy was never broken. He was inspired greatly by the bodhisattva ideal, and spent his life in the service of the poor, the dispossessed and the sick.

Swami Vivekananda was thrilled when he heard from Akhandananda about the latter's experiences in Tibet's Buddhist monasteries, and as homage to Tibetan monasticism he suggested that his fellow monk should be called *akhandananda.*

The second idea is momentous. Swami Vivekananda's formative years were spent in Kolkata, where there was a renaissance of Buddhist studies, manuscripts were being discovered and published by the Asiatic Society. There was great intellectual enthusiasm about Buddhism in the air. Vivekananda had visions of the Buddha even when he was a young boy, and later he told one of his disciples that he was terrified. But the memory of the vision remained with him. More often than not, he mentioned and referred to the Buddha with great devotional admiration. In his address to the Chicago session of the Parliament of Religions in 1893, he declared that Buddhism was "the fulfilment of Hinduism". In the closing paragraph of *Karma yoga,* Vivekananda relates in high rhetoric that no one other than the Buddha was the ideal of ethics, that he had no trace of ego in him, absolutely pure and transparent, dispensing with gods and rituals he walked the length and breadth of the land, teaching how to live a worthy moral life, dispassionately for the good of others. "The Buddha's heart", he said, was the seat of all that is noble, great and divine.

When Vivekananda along with Swami Shivananda went to Bodh Gaya, he was moved to ecstasy and wept in rapture at encountering the beatific vision of the Buddha. On return, he told his guru, Ramakrishna, that no one equalled the Buddha in the practice of austerities, purity of character, and nobility of the moral ideal. Vivekananda's adoration of the Buddha was so great that when once asked whether he was a Buddhist (Nivedita tells it in her *My Master as I saw him*) he said, that was a tall claim to make.

He regarded himself "a servant of the servant of the servant of the Buddha".

Vivekananda was one illustrious example of modern Indian intellectuals who recognized the inalienable bond of Hinduism with Buddhism, and declared it in unmistakable terms, even though the whirligig of time has brought in changes vast and deep on the externals of the culture and outlook of the Indians. There flows an undercurrent of adoration of the Buddha and the bodhisattva ideal that fertilizes the subsoil of the Indian psyche.

II

What could be the reasons for it? There existed Indo-Tibetan or Tibetan-Indian spiritual relations spanning the millennia. It was the age when the Buddhist monastic universities were flourishing in India. Nalanda, Odantapuri, Vikramshila, Taxila were great centres of spiritual learning and *sadhana,* alongside of the study of the Abhidharma, Sutra and Vinaya. Nalanda was the ace university and globally celebrated, and drew students from all over Asia. There are accounts of Chinese travellers that depict how vibrant academic activities went on at these universities. A wide range of disciplines like philosophy, logic, epistemology, grammar, language, psychology, medicine, astronomy, metallurgy, arts and poetry were taught. There were interactions with the positions of non-Buddhist traditions as well. Buddhist influences are now traced in non-Buddhist philosophical works of Vaisesika, Advaita, Nyaya and Hindu Tantra. Some of the great names in Indian thought, Nagarjuna, Shantideva, Asanga, etc. were associated with Nalanda.

It was at such an auspicious and propitious time, i.e. in the 7th century CE that Tibet embraced Buddhism, and the entire Knowledge System of the time was taken over to Tibet in the form of monumental enterprise of translations from Sanskrit, Pali and other languages of learning. The decision to adopt Indian Buddhism as the state religion was, on Tibet's part, a matter of great moment.

Buddhism was there in China since two centuries earlier and China was geographically more accessible to Tibet. But the idea of adopting Buddhism from India in a direct manner was historically a matter of immense significance. The hazards of crossing the Himalayan heights and snow were real, yet student pilgrims traversed the inhospitable mountainous terrain to reach Nalanda and study. Had Tibet adopted Buddhism from China, Tibetan Buddhism would have had a different sheen and the rich tradition of Nalanda could have passed into oblivion and disappeared without leaving a trace anywhere.

When Tibet decided to go Buddhist following the Nalanda School, it was a formidable military power in Central Asia. In spite of its mighty political authority it decided to welcome Indian Buddhism and thereby brought about great transformations in various aspects of its life, viz. political, social, educational and cultural. The Tibetan emperor, Songtsan Gampo (617–649 CE), sent brilliant students under the leadership of one of his young ministers, Thonmi Sambhot, to India and learn at the feet of the great Indian masters. Sambhot returned to Tibet, while others succumbed to the hardship of the journey. However, Sambhot devised the script modelled on Gupta Lipi—a later developed version of Brahmi script—prevalent in India at that time and formulated the grammar of the Tibetan language. He also pioneered the great and momentous project of translating the teachings of the Buddha into Tibetan language. Building of monasteries and translation of sacred texts went on through the patronage of succeeding emperors. A later emperor Trisong Detsan (742–797 CE) undertook methodically rigorous steps to enshrine Buddhism in the heart of Tibet, in both spiritual and scholarly modes. He invited Acharya Shantarakshita (725–790 CE), the abbot of Nalanda to visit Tibet, countering local resistance from indigenous orthodoxy. On Shantarakshita's instance the great yogi, Padmasambhava, was invited from India. He subdued anti-Buddhist forces, and in time the Samye Monastery came up. During Shantarakshita's second visit to Tibet, a group of Tibetans were ordained as monks, and this paved the way for establishing the Bhiksu Sangha, the first one of its kind. Had there been no Sangha, Buddhism in Tibet would not have flourished.

The emperor Trisong Detsen supervised the entire project by laying down guidelines for authentic rendering of the teachings of the Buddha and related sacred texts in an authentic manner. Each work was translated in collaboration with an Indian master and a Tibetan *lotsawa* or translator. There was an editorial board to look into the authenticity of the rendering and approve it. The Samye monastery was the centre of the translation project. Young Tibetans were also being sent to India for study, and there continued the trend of inviting Indian masters to Tibet.

As for the authenticity of the translated texts, it was not only the lexical meaning or the thematic sense that was taken care of, but also the spirit and intention. This important feature is not easy to convey in modern renderings. It is a unique instance of maintaining a high standard of authenticity, a rare one indeed anywhere and anytime. The decision to translate the canonical literature into Tibet's indigenous language made the entire corpus of the teachings and works of commentary accessible to the Tibetans, and this helped Buddhism permeate into the everyday life of the common people, their very life came to be nourished by the religion.

As time rolled on, it was felt that a fresh look at the translations already made was needed. And the third Dharma emperor, Ralpachen, saw to it that revisions were made. He patronized the project of comparing various renderings of Indian texts and consulting recensions from Bengal, Kashmir, Magadh and Gandhara. There Tibetan translators, namely Kawa Paltseg, Chogro Loyi Gyaltsan and Shang Yeshe-De are outstanding for their performance in the monumental task.

However, matters did not move in the expected way. There were regicides and the prospect of Buddhism in Tibet looked bleak. But the religion had already struck root deep enough to sustain the monastic way of life in the country along with intellectual, spiritual and cultural activities. And the programme of receiving Buddhism from India was resumed again. This time from the western region of Tibet, where the descendants of Tibetan royal family had settled and ruled, they resumed the older practice of sending Tibetan boys as students to India and welcoming Indian masters. Rinchen Sangpo returned to Tibet in 988 CE as a scholar and spiritual master. A great scholar, he rendered several Sanskrit texts into Tibetan. Besides, he commissioned many monasteries to be built, and with the King's efforts he succeeded in inviting the great Indian master, Atisha Dipankara Srijnana, the abbot of Vikramshila University to visit Tibet in 1042 CE. Atisha, as he was known in Tibet, composed the *Bodhipathapradipa*, a classic Mahayana work incorporating the quintessence of Tantra along with teachings on compassion, the awakening of boddhicitta and selflessness—*anatma*. This fusion marked a great advance in the spiritual practice of Mahayana ideals prevalent in the great learning centres of India. Atisha's disciple, Domtonpa founded the Kadampa school or lineage, which influenced all the later lineages. The earlier lineage came to be known as Nyingma or the Old school. Thus Buddhism in Tibet manifested itself in two forms: the one in Central Tibet hosting the Earlier Dissemination and the establishment of monasticism, and the other in Western Tibet from the late 10th century CE onwards, the later Dissemination of Dharma.

Before the 11th century CE, Tibetan scholars had engaged themselves primarily with translation of the Buddha's teachings and the treatises of the Indian masters. This was the main focus, even though independent commentarial works were written at intervals. But a new trend set in with the latter half of the 11th century CE. Patsab Nyimadag, a most influential scholar, studied in India for 24 years and promoted the philosophical school of Prasangika Madhyamika, later to become the most influential Tibetan Buddhist philosophical school.

Marpa (1012–1097 CE) was a great scholar, translator and a spiritually-realized person. He visited India thrice, and studied with such great siddhas as Naropa and Maitripa. On his return to Tibet, Marpa translated many a work and passed on a rare level of spiritual realization and transmission to his disciples. The one among them was Milarepa, the celebrated yogi of Tibet who attained enlightenment. Marpa's lineage came to be known as the Kagyu tradition of Tibetan Buddhism. It developed subsequently under various spiritual masters into a number of branches.

The 11th century CE scholar Drogmi Lotsawa Shakya Yeshe (993–1074) who studied in India for several years as a disciple of the Indian master Viravajra, one of the lineage holders of Mahasiddha Virupa, attained the status of a spiritual master. After his return to Tibet he received the teachings of Lamdre, a Tantra text, from Gayadhara, an Indian master, and passed on the transmission to Khon Konchog Gyalpo (1034–1102 CE), who later founded the Sakya monastery in Tsang region of Central Tibet. This tradition emerged eventually as a major tradition of Tibetan Buddhism and is known as the Sakya tradition. The foremost thinker of this school of thought, Sachen Kunga Nyingpo (1092–1158 CE) is reverentially referred to as Sakya Pandit in recognition of his exceptional intellectual power and spiritual mastery.

Historically speaking, well before Buddhism disappeared from the Indian scene, it had struck deep root in Tibet. The motivation was kept alive by academic expertise and spiritual realization of the Tibetan monks on the one hand and the availability of extensive literature in the monasteries on the other. There had also been a constant flow of Indian scholars and Tibetan scholars between India and Tibet. Between the 11th and the 12th centuries, Tibet witnessed an incredible growth and development of Tibetan culture in the areas of intellectual achievement, art and spirituality.

When in the 13th century Buddhist monastic universities in India declined as a result of being razed by Turkish invasion, quite a number of Buddhist scholars and masters went over to Tibet. The one such great scholar was the abbot of Vikramshila, Shakyashribhadra. While in Tibet, he continued his academic activities, writing, teaching and giving spiritual guidance to the Tibetans around. There is much sense in saying that Tibet was by that time second only to India in terms of intellectual pursuits and spiritual practice in the domain of Mahayana Buddhism. The last major school of Buddhism was founded by Je Tsongkhapa (1357–1419 CE). As the founder of the Gedenpa School he was both a path breaker and path finder. His 18 volumes of works shed light on the multiple spectra of Buddhist thought and practice, and more importantly, the philosophical views of Nagarjuna and Chandrakirti, the Prasangika Madhyamika masters of India.

It may also be mentioned that it is the Mulasarvastivada line of Vinaya that is followed in Tibetan monasticism. It is one of the three existing Vinaya traditions of ancient Indian monasticism; the two other are the Theravada and the Dharmaguptika traditions followed in South Asian countries and Chinese Buddhist areas respectively.

Tibetan traditions are inclined towards Madhyamika views, yet Vijnanavada, Sautantrika and Vaibhasika are accorded due importance. The insights of these views are valued and incorporated into the body of thought of Tibetan Buddhism. The Tantric tradition, which came from Nalanda and others, is practised by advanced learners, and it is distinguished as Buddhist Tantra that had its roots in India.

The Chinese occupation of Tibet in 1950, and subsequent repression compelled His Holiness the Dalai Lama to flee to India in 1959 and seek political asylum. It was but natural since the two countries had profound relations for more than a thousand years. Following His Holiness to India, there came spiritual masters and eminent scholars. The burning issue in the state of exile was that of preserving the unique culture of Tibet, its philosophical traditions, arts and crafts and language. Under the great leadership of His Holiness the Dalai Lama, Tibetans-in-exile have resumed their academic and spiritual activities, re-established many of the monasteries and opened academic Institutions. In the meantime, His Holiness has emerged as a global icon of peace, and drawn the attention of intellectuals, scientists and philosophers across the world and there has come about almost a resurgence of interest in Buddhism in its Tibetan incarnations. This has impacted on India as well, and many Indian universities have opened courses on Buddhism and the Tibetan language. International attention to Tibetan Buddhism has engaged academicians in new translations of Buddhist texts from Tibetan into Indian and European languages.

His Holiness' vision was to establish an Institute of higher Tibetan studies in India in the early 1960s to provide an opportunity for students from Tibet and from Indian Himalayan regions to pursue their studies further, especially those who had been forced to discontinue their studies. It was established in 1967, following discussion between His Holiness the Dalai Lama and Pandit Jawaharlal Nehru earlier, while he was still alive. Among the academic exercises the University has undertaken has been to publish rare texts, extant only in Tibetan renderings, while the originals are lost, in a systematic manner. An important feature of the University publications is the restoration of the works of Indian masters into Sanskrit and the translation of the works of both the Indian and Tibetan Buddhist masters into Hindi and other languages from Tibetan sources. The University has a distinguished group to carry out research on Buddhist manuscripts, compilation of dictionaries and allied works. More than 60 books have been restored into Sanskrit and more than 80 works have been rendered into Hindi language. There are around 50 volumes of a research journal named *Dhih*.

Buddhism has been the bridge across the Himalayas between Tibet and India. Tibet has treasured and preserved the priceless heritage of Indian wisdom during the days of Nalanda and other Buddhist monasteries. Yoga and Tantra were taken from India, and the Tibetans even perfected them in practice. But for the Tibetan monks the of medieval Indian heritage of learning would have been altogether lost to mankind. This is preserved in Tibetan translations with living traditions.

The *Kangyur* and the *Tengyur* are the only depository of the immense wealth of Indian intellectual heritage, both sacerdotal and secular with about five thousand titles. One can hardly ignore the fact that Tibet owes to India its religion and religious culture, while India owes to Tibet the preservation of the riches of its own past. This mutuality is crucially important for the cultural history of the two countries.

SECTION II

Current Situation and Trends

5

Tibetan Refugees in India

Ajit Doval

When in 1959, China forced the Dalai Lama and more than 80,000 of his followers out of their peaceful abode in Tibet, the exiles must have believed that the world would stand by their just cause, and they would soon return home. They still believe in this but the rest of the world is not so sanguine. From the early eighties to the mid-nineties, another 25,000 joined the exodus. The trickle of Tibetan refugees continues even today, albeit at a slower pace owing to the restrictions imposed by the Chinese. These exiled Tibetans, most of them living in India for over half a century now, who had lived in isolation in the hallowed lands of the Himalayas, remain isolated still. In terms of their legal status, they are neither citizens of any country, nor refugees, illegal immigrants or stateless persons. When the preamble of the UN Charter had envisaged saving "succeeding generations" from such privations, and reaffirmed its faith "in the dignity and worth of human persons", the world had thought such human tragedies would never occur again. More importantly, if it did, the world would not remain a silent spectator.

Much has been written about Tibet's rich history, culture, its mystic Lamaism, its militarization by China, agitations and self-immolations, but not many have cared to know more about the uprooted people of Tibet. The question of their survival, economic conditions, how they administer themselves and what they think about their future remain less documented. Since India is home to more than 1,20,000 displaced Tibetans, it is a natural stakeholder in the restoration of peace and normalcy in Tibet, that could lead to their eventual return in dignity and honour.

It is true that India did accept Tibet as an integral part of China in 1954. However, it needs to be emphasised that the decision was taken consequent to a 17- point agreement that China entered with Tibet in 1951, albeit under duress. Whatever little legal sanctity the Agreement had became untenable with the ouster of the Dalai Lama, one of the high contracting parties, and his subsequent repudiation of the Agreement. The repeated violation of the provisions of the Agreement by China has further undermined its validity. The following commitments and their violations by the Chinese are illustrative of this fact:

a) The central authorities will not alter the existing political system in Tibet. The central authorities also will not alter the established status, functions and powers of the Dalai Lama. Officials of various ranks shall hold office as usual.
b) The policy of freedom of religious belief laid down in the common programme of the CPPCC shall be carried out. The religious beliefs, customs and habits of the Tibetan people shall be respected, and Lama Monasteries shall be protected. The central authorities will not effect a change in the income of the monasteries.
c) The spoken and written language and school education of Tibetan nationality shall be developed step by step, in accordance with the actual conditions in Tibet.

d) In matters relating to various reforms in Tibet, there will be no compulsion on the part of the central authorities. The local government of Tibet shall carry out reforms of its own accord, and, when people raise demands for reform, it shall be settled by means of consultation with the leaders of the Tibet.

e) The PLA entering Tibet shall abide by all the above-mentioned policies and shall also be fair in all buying and selling, and shall not arbitrarily take a needle or thread from the people.

DIASPORA

Since 1959, the Dalai Lama and thousands of his followers who entered India have been living as exiles. During the first wave of the flight of Tibetans in 1959, termed by the 1961 UN General Assembly as an "exodus", the Indian government had set up transit camps for these entrants and provided basic amenities like shelter, medical treatment and food. It was after the opening of Tibet to trade and tourism by China that the second wave of exodus to India began. There were approximately 25,000 Tibetans in the period 1986–1996 itself.

A demographic survey conducted by a commission of the Central Tibetan Administration (CTA) had held that by 2009 total populace outside China had increased to 127,935 from 111, 020 in 1998. In countries other than India, their numbers approximately stood at 13,514 in Nepal, 1298 in Bhutan, 9000 in the US, 4275 in Canada and 4000 in Switzerland.

LEGAL AND POLITICAL STATUS

It is ironic that India, which in six decades of its independence, had to cope with nearly 2 million refugees of various kinds (other than illegal immigration of over 20 million people from Bangladesh), has no laws or definitive policy to deal with refugees.

Besides Tibet, there has been sizeable refugee problem from East Pakistan (1971), Chakma influx (1963), Sri Lanka Tamils (1983, 1989 and 1995), Afghanistan (1980 onwards), and Myanmar.

The Foreigners Act of 1946 and the Registration of Foreigners Act (1939) provide the legal rubric to govern issues pertaining to the foreigners in India. Tibetan entrants fall under the ambit of these laws. As foreigners, they cannot own property, hold government jobs, exercise the right to vote or enjoy other privileges available to the Indian citizens. As, in India, there are no laws pertaining to the refugees, they are also not entitled to any privileges available to the refugees in most countries of the world. It is noteworthy that India is not a signatory to the UN Convention of July 28, 1951 on the status of Refugees, or the Jan. 31, 1967 UN Protocol. Interestingly, in 1953, India's Foreign Ministry through R.K. Nehru had conveyed to the United Nations Commissioner for Refugees that the global refugee policy was essentially part of the Cold War strategy of the West and hence India wanted to keep itself out of it.

Contrary to what is commonly perceived, India did not grant the Dalai Lama or other Tibetan entrants refugee status in India. They are foreigners, defined more by their cultural and ethnic rather than political identity, and granted temporary shelter in India. In this paper, the term refugees for Tibetans have been used in a generic, rather than legal sense.

India has restricted its assistance to humanitarian support, scrupulously avoiding any overt or covert political support. The Dalai Lama was initially provided shelter in Mussoorie, a hill resort in UP and later, in 1960, relocated to McLeodganj, Dharamsala in Himachal Pradesh. To administer his people, he constituted the Central Tibetan Administration (CTA) operating from Dharamsala, which continues to be his current headquarters. As with the passage of time, it became clear that the stay of the Tibetan exiles would be a long one, India helped initiate a few programmes to provide some means of sustenance to them. Thus, a few settlements were created where the CTA relocated the refugees and sought to provide some basic jobs and facilities.

To maintain a record of the Tibetans, the Indian government in consultation with the Central Tibetan Administration (CTA), issues Registration Certificates (RCs) to them. While RCs do not grant any formal legal status or rights to its holders, the Indian government allows only the RC holders to live in the designated settlements. These certificates also serve as documents of identity and have to be renewed periodically. Tibetans are also issued another document known as Identity Certificate (IC), which enables them to travel to countries that accept them in lieu of a passport. Presently, the countries that extend this facility include the United States, Switzerland and some in West Europe, and most of the OECD area.

For a Tibetan refugee possessing an IC to be able to re-enter India legally, the IC must bear a stamp that reads "No Objection to Return to India." Recent policy changes have foreclosed other options for international travel, such as exit permits that were in vogue in the past. Only Special Entry Permits (SEPs) are being granted to the new entrants who are classified into three categories, viz. pilgrimage, education and "other". The pilgrimage SEP allows the bearer to stay in India for up to three months, with the possibility of an extension up to six months. They are, however, ineligible to acquire an RC or any other Indian document. Tibetans entering India with an SEP for "education" purposes may, however, be allowed to stay for a longer period. The category "other" is reserved mostly for special cases, like former political prisoners. On an average 3000-4500 Tibetans have been landing in India since the late 1990s. Most of them come as pilgrims via Nepal and return after their stay of 3-6 months.

In very exceptional cases, Tibetan refugees can acquire Indian citizenship in accordance with the provisions of the Indian Constitution, the Indian Citizenship Act and the Citizenship Rules,

1956, as amended from time to time. In a historic judgement of the Delhi High Court in 2009 in the Namgyal Dolkar vs. Ministry of External Affairs, Tibetans born in India between January 26, 1950 and July 1, 1987, were made eligible for seeking Indian citizenship. The apparent consequence of this decision is that some 30,000 Tibetans in India, that is, those born in India within this specified time can enjoy what is often called *right of citizenship through birth*. The decision does not change the status of Tibetans who fled to India following the 1959 Lhasa Uprising, or those born in India to Tibetan parents after July 1, 1987. However, very few Tibetans have shown any inclination to acquire Indian citizenship.

POLITICAL STRUCTURE

Tibetan exiles have a unique political structure wherein the Dalai Lama holds a pivotal position in all matters—political, spiritual, social and cultural. In spite of the overarching authority of the Dalai Lama, political affairs are conducted through a well-structured democratic process. Significantly, in July 2011, the Dalai Lama voluntarily surrendered his political power in favour of a newly elected Kalon Tripa (Prime Minister), Lobsang Sangay. Even so, it has not diluted his position of pre-eminence and leader of the Tibetan community. The daily affairs of the Tibetan refugees are administered by a Central Tibetan Administration (CTA) that has its headquarters in Dharamsala in Himachal Pradesh. It lays claim to represent what it calls "Historic Tibet", that includes the Tibet Autonomous Region, Qinghai province, two Tibetan Autonomous Prefectures, Tibetan Autonomous County in Sichuan, Tibetan Autonomous County in Gansu and Tibetan Autonomous Prefecture in Yunnan.

The Tibetan Parliament

It serves as the highest legislative body of the Tibetan refugees in exile comprising 44 members, directly elected by the people. The representation in the Tibetan parliament is unique in that it is marked by an equal representation from all provinces and religious sub-sects. The parliamentarians are elected on the basis of their affiliation to the traditional three Tibetan provinces (Cholka Sum) of *U-Tsang, Dotoe and Domey.* Each province has 10 members in Parliament while the five religious sects, viz. *Sakya, Gelug, Bon, Nyingma* and *Kagyu* have two members each. The remaining four members are elected from the Tibetans living in other countries. Two seats are reserved for women.

The representation to religious sub-sects is an issue of debate in Tibetan politics. Other than the case for keeping mutually contesting religious leaders out of the political arena, it is argued that since monks and nuns can contest from their geographically delineated provincial constituencies, there is no need to make them doubly privileged by providing separate representation. A survey conducted in November 2011 by the Vivekananda International Foundation (VIF), brought out that out of 150 respondents 47% felt that representation to the monks was justified, while 51% were opposed to it and 2% had no views on the subject. In fact, some smaller sects like the Bodong and Jonang are critical of the practice as they do not find any representation in the parliament. Nevertheless, since the sub-sects play an important role in the Tibetan politics, this practice has come to stay and their representatives have a significant role in political decision-making. The major sub-sects and their current representatives in the 15th parliament are as under:

Sakya	Norbu Tsering and Choedak Gyatso
Gelug	Rongpo Lobsang Nyangdak and Atrug Tsetan
Bon	Geshe Monlam Tharchin and Geshe Namdak Tsukphue
Nyingma	Sonam Tenphel and Gyari Bhutruk
Kagyu	Karma Choephel and Tenpa Yarphel

The Cabinet (Kashag)

Kashag is the apex executive body comprising seven departments, viz. religion and culture, education, health, home, finance, security and information and international relations. The Kalon Tripa (Prime Minister) leads the Kashag and is the executive head of Central Tibetan Administration (CTA). Each department is headed by a Kalon (Minister). The CTA also has three autonomous bodies, namely the Election Commission, the Public Service Commission and Controller of Accounts. The Election Commission conducts elections for the parliament and the local bodies. The Public Service Commission looks after the recruitment, training and appointment of the civil servants of the CTA. The Controller of Accounts is responsible for auditing the accounts of all the CTA departments and its subsidiaries. The CTA has its representative offices in 12 countries that practically function as their embassies. These offices are functioning in Geneva, New York, Tokyo, London, Kathmandu, Budapest, Moscow, Paris, Canberra, Pretoria, Taipei and Brussels.

Over the years, a strong democratic ethos has become entrenched within the exiled Tibetan community. The Dalai Lama, from the early days in India was a convert to the Indian democratic model, and was keen to inculcate and promote democratic traditions. Thus, in a calibrated manner, he surrendered his absolute authority and delegated it to the elected representatives. As a measure of reform, in 2001, the election for 12th Kalon Tripa (Prime Minister), was held on the basis of direct voting that led to the victory of Samdong Rinpoche. During his term, the 12th Kashag (Parliament) considerably enhanced its power and greater accountability and transparency was brought in the functioning of the Tibetan parliament. This helped streamline parliamentary practices, financial transactions of the CTA were made public and the ministers were made accountable to the parliament.

The significance of the Dalai Lama's divesting of power in July 2011 and transferring it to the newly elected Kalon Tripa, created serious consternation within the Tibetan community. Given his great emotional appeal, a majority of the Tibetans did not want him to abdicate political power. However, with the passage of time, this change was taken in its stride and the community accepted it. Commenting on the development, Thubten Samphel, the former Information Secretary of the CTA averred, "the devolution of political power shows the fulfilment of the vision of His Holiness the Dalai Lama for a fully democratic and totally transparent system of administration. His Holiness felt the need for change within the administration by bringing new generations in the Administration." The prominent Tibetan leader and Secretary of the Department of Education, Karma Gelek Yuthok, also echoed popular sentiment, "I did not believe it when he initially announced the resignation from political power, but it was only due to my emotional attachment and faith in him that I accepted it. In the long term, he took this important decision through which he has covered hundred questions in one answer."

Clearly, the divestment of power by the Dalai Lama was a major political initiative aimed at opening opportunities for the common Tibetans to continue their struggle even beyond his lifetime. The changed political dispensation has provided them with a new sense of political equality and becoming equal stakeholders in their political struggle for liberation.

SOCIO-ECONOMIC CONDITIONS

The Government of India accorded high priority to the resettlement and rehabilitation of exiled Tibetans who had sought refuge in India in 1959. Prime Minister Nehru promised assistance to the refugees and sent letters to the Chief Ministers of States asking them to make available land to enable them to start a new life. The Government of Mysore (present Karnataka) was the first to grant a large forest area for the settlement of Tibetans. In the early 1960s the Tibetan refugees had, with the help of local administration, cleared the thick forests and developed unused land in Bylakuppe to build houses and commence agriculture. This settlement was later named 'Lugsum Samdupling', and became the model for subsequent settlements. The rationale behind the establishment of separate settlements was to insulate them from the local populace and keep them away from meddling in local political affairs. Besides, it helped Tibetans to maintain their distinct identity, preserve their culture and traditions, and promote their arts and crafts.

Since a vast majority of the refugees were farmers, the establishment of agricultural settlements was accorded high priority. There are presently 35 settlements classified into three categories viz. i) agricultural settlements (14); ii) handicraft based Centers (9); and iii) agro-industrial and cottage industries (12). The handicraft industry focuses on production of Tibetan artefacts, woollen garments, wood carving, etc. This provides a valuable secondary source of income to many refugees. The Tibetans are also engaged in small-scale enterprises like operating restaurants, trading in hill produce, and construction work. The home-knitted woollen sweaters made by Tibetan women are very popular and can be seen being sold during winter months in most parts of India.

Tibetan settlements are administered by the Gyapon who is appointed by the CTA. He is responsible for the development, administration and addressing local grievances of the people. He also manages community facilities like health and education in the settlements.

In brief, the economic support provided by the Government of India in the early years had served to meet their basic survival requirements. However, the income-generating programmes initiated in subsequent years, combined with the hard labour, put in by the Tibetans, improved their economic conditions. A study conducted in Dharamsala indicated that out of 10,900, settlers about 40% are engaged in small business selling artefacts, artificial ornaments, religious items and running food stalls.

The first generation refugees are economically better off and own hotels, restaurants, personal shops and such-like. Their children are better educated and engaged in the jobs provided by the CTA and some cultural organisations. Many from the younger generation have gone abroad and regularly remit money to their families, and that has improved their economic situation. The survey of refugees in Dharamsala indicated that 16% were engaged in business, 35% were working for the CTA, 25% were students, 9% were working for the NGOs, 13% were monks and nuns, and only 2% were unemployed. Since most of the refugees do not possess their own homes, a substantial portion of their income (sometimes as high as 30%) goes towards house rent, and in many cases, a small room is shared by 2 to 3 persons. Only about 10% people were found to be in the higher income brackets, owning a house, cars and sending children to private schools. The VIF survey indicated that, by and large, there was no glaring disparity in the incomes. Only 3% each earned less than Rs. 5,000 or over Rs. 15,000 a month. The remaining 94% earned between Rs. 5,000 to Rs. 15,000 per month; 41% Rs. 5,000-10,000, and 53% Rs. 10,000-15,000 per month. It is worth noting that in the wake on the prevailing price index in India, a majority of Tibetans are living just above the subsistence level. It was, however, found that there was no resentment amongst Tibetans over economic hardships or economic inequality. The CTA is able to provide adequate schooling and medical facilities to the refugees and they were found to be quite satisfied with the administration.

The literacy rate among the Tibetan refugees has considerably risen through the decades and stands at 82% today. The CTA and the Government of India had accorded a high priority to education. Prime Minister Nehru had offered to the Dalai Lama reservation of seats for Tibetan children in Indian educational institutions in

1959. Dalai Lama, however, preferred to establish Tibetan institutions to preserve the culture and traditions which, in hindsight, was a very wise decision as it helped the younger generation preserve their distinct identity. The first Tibetan school was set up in Mussoorie in 1960, and they stand at a strong 60 in number currently. Of them, 28 are run by the Central Tibetan School Administration (CTSA), which is an autonomous body of the Government of India's Ministry of Human Resource Development; 12 schools are administered by Sambhota Tibetan School Administration (STSA), an autonomous body of the CTA's Education Department. The remaining 20 schools are autonomous and funded and administered by 2 NGOs—the Tibetan Children's Village and Tibetan Homes Foundation. All secondary and senior secondary Tibetan schools in India are affiliated to the Central Board of Secondary Education, which is the apex board for examination at an all India level.

HOW DO TIBETAN EXILES VIEW THEIR FUTURE?

The survey conducted by Vivekananda International Foundation (VIF) in 2011 also revealed some startling facts. Contrary to what most analysts would believe, they are neither overawed by China's rising economic and military strength, nor pessimistic about their future. In a sample of about 300 respondents, 96% were confident that Tibet's political situation will change and they will be able to return to their homeland. Only 3% felt that they had lost their political cause for ever, while 1% held no view. On the question of the possible future political status of Tibet, 60% felt genuine autonomy was an achievable objective. Only 40% were hopeful of complete independence. Significantly, a majority of the pro-independence respondents belonged to the younger age group.

On the advisability and utility of holding talks with the present Chinese rulers, the opinions were sharply divided. While 40% felt that the process of engagement should continue, 59%

felt that nothing worthwhile would be served by continuing the talks. Anger and resentment against the Chinese rulers for violation of human rights in Tibet was total, and the exiles asserted that the situation in Tibet had sharply deteriorated over the years. No one felt that as a result of the claimed economic and infrastructural development in TAR, the conditions of Tibetans in Tibet had improved and that they were a happier lot. The development of infrastructure like roads, railways, airfields, communication network were seen on the one hand as instruments of military subjugation and on the other, an attempt to destroy Tibet's unique civilization, religion and identity. Concerns were also expressed over the ecological and environmental degradation of the world's highest snow bound plateau; often referred as the third arctic pole by the Tibetans.

The perceptions of the Tibetan refugees on the prevailing situation in Tibet are based on accounts of new arrivals, mostly the Tibetans pilgrims. Limited news items emanating from the Chinese and global media is another source. Of late, the messages exchanged in cyber media are emerging as a powerful communication tool, despite the Chinese making concerted efforts to counter it both through technical means and taking stringent action against anti-integrationists. The Chinese stridency has particularly increased after the 2008 Olympic Games and there have been large-scale human rights violations. The frequent incidents of self-immolations seriously disturb the Tibetans and evoke sharp anger and resentment.

The Tibetan refugees do not hold a very positive view of the world and its response to the Tibetan cause, though they are careful and hesitant to articulate it openly. They believe that if world opinion had strongly pressurised China, it could have prevented persecution of Tibetans in Tibet, helped in achieving autonomy, and ensuring the success of the dialogue process initiated by the Dalai Lama. Though generally supportive of Western democracies, particularly the US, for their understanding and sympathy to their cause, they think that politically not much has been done to mitigate their miseries. They are also beholden to some international NGOs for the moral and material support extended by them. Some of the senior Tibetan leaders feel that in the long term, democratic countries will have to stand up to the autocratic regime in China and then the Tibet issue will get resurrected at that time. They also hold the view that internal power struggles in China will lead to far-reaching political changes at some point as even the Han majority was getting increasingly restive under the present one party rule. Further, large sections of Chinese are getting inclined to freedom and democracy with an empathy and better understanding of the Tibetan cause, they contend.

The perception of Tibetan exiles regarding India was found to be positive at the religio-civilisational level; it was in fact almost reverential—providing shelter to them in 1959 and thereafter has earned their gratitude for India. Politically, there was an understanding that India had limited options vis-à-vis China and, because of its own national security interests, it could not go beyond a point. However, the younger Tibetans felt that India has failed to play the Tibet card to its best advantage. There was also resentment on the denial of democratic freedoms to Tibetans to peacefully agitate and organise protests against the Chinese repression. They considered India to be unjustifiably cautious to Chinese sensitivities, which the Chinese interpreted as a sign of India's weakness.

The faith and loyalty of Tibetans, both in the institution of Dalai Lama and its present incumbent is absolute and unflinching. However, some hot-headed youth occasionally argue that he is 'too good and soft'. Cutting across the denominational and geographical divide, most of the Tibetans are highly appreciative of his long-term vision and political judgement, international stature and acceptability, gentle persuasiveness and practical realism. They accredit him with providing political and spiritual leadership to Tibetans in difficult times and single handedly creating global awareness about the Tibetan cause. The Dalai Lama's divestment of power in favour of the Kalon Tripa is viewed pragmatically, enabling the Tibetan cause not to become co-terminus with his life span. With the realisation that it may be a long struggle, this act has transformed the Tibetan issue into a people's movement and left it to the common Tibetans and their elected representatives to carry it forward. In Lobsang Sangay, the new Kalon Tripa, he has found a leader who is young, articulate, well educated, with international linkages and acceptable to the younger generation. His leadership qualities inspire hope and confidence among struggling Tibetans. Finally, the numbers of Tibetans in exile may not be large but they can be powerful catalyst of change in Tibet.

6

Beijing-Dharamsala Dialogue: Post-Devolution Prospects

C.D. Sahay and Bhavna Singh

A dialogue between two contending parties is traditionally understood to be a process through which an exchange of ideas and positions in a constructive manner with a view to achieving mutual understanding of the issues involved in a spirit of tolerance. The process should be devoid of rigidity of mindsets on both sides and carried out with seriousness of intent and purpose. And if it is carried out in this manner, dialogue becomes the most effective tool for conflict management and indeed conflict resolution. But for this to happen, both the contending parties must also essentially have clarity of ideas on what they want and how far are they willing to move to accommodate the views and aspirations of the other side. Most importantly, there should be genuine sincerity of purpose in the search for a mutually acceptable resolution of the dispute in a non-adversarial approach.

The moot question, therefore, is whether the process of 'engagement' between Beijing and Dharamsala, that started more than three decades back, really meets the basic criteria of a serious and genuine process of 'dialogue' as mentioned above. To start with, it is absolutely clear that a dispute does exist between Beijing and Dharamsala and that two contending parties to the dispute are also clearly defined. Thus the basic pre-requisites for initiating a process of 'dialogue' between the two parties do clearly exist. It is also a given that the dispute can only be resolved through a process of dialogue. However, a look at the history of the talks between the two sides does not give the impression the other essential elements for a dialogue process to succeed, are present in full measure. The required level of intensity and constructive/co-operative approach seem to be missing. One also gets the impression that at least from the Beijing side, the process of engagement is not designed towards conflict resolution but is only being pursued for the limited purpose of conflict management. This leads to the most serious flaw in the long pursued exercise that the objective of the two parties, stated or otherwise, are not coincident.

Therefore, it came as no surprise that the announcement by HH the Dalai Lama to relinquish his political authority foxed the Chinese government and the Tibetan Community-in-Exile (TCiE) alike. While China immediately declared that the talk of "Dalai Lama's retirement is a trick to deceive the international community", the reactions from the TCiE were restrained and pensive; ranging from disappointment, anguish to taciturn acceptance. Nonetheless, undeniably a formal authority structure has been put in place for the Tibetan Government-in-Exile (TGiE) through the 15th Parliamentary election and nomination of the third Kalon Tripa (Prime Minister) amid much speculation and debate. Though largely accepted by different sections of Tibetan émigrés, the development has not augured well for the future of the Sino-Tibetan Dialogue which concluded its tenth round in January 2010.

THE INITIAL YEARS

In the context of Tibet, the most significant development in the post-Mao era was the decision of Deng Xiaoping to initiate contact with the Dalai Lama in 1978. By then, Deng had already initiated his historic programme of 'Four Modernisations' and the process of Sino-US rapprochement had also taken off, leading to a natural dilution in the US/Western support and commitment to the Tibetan cause. Cognizant of this, the Dalai Lama, on his part, softened his stand on the issue of 'Tibetan Independence' keeping in view the economic welfare of the six million Tibetans in the Tibetan Autonomous Region (TAR). In his address on 10 March 1978 at Dharamsala, he declared, "if the six million Tibetans in Tibet are really happy and prosperous as never before (as claimed by the People's Republic of China), there is no reason to argue otherwise."[1] This was indeed a positive message of intent on the part of the Dalai Lama and a gesture of goodwill that resulted in the visit of Gyalo Thondup[2] to Beijing in March 1979.[3]

This meeting paved the way for serious negotiations between Beijing and Dharamsala after 20 years of no contact. Deng Xiaoping also in a seemingly accommodating gesture said, 'apart from the question of total independence, all other issues could be discussed and all other problems could be solved.'[4] He also agreed to allow the Dalai Lama to send his fact-finding delegations to Tibet to observe the socio-economic conditions there.[5]

A positive beginning was thus made for classical negotiations to begin. In Beijing's perception, the invitation to the Dalai Lama to send a fact-finding delegation was made on the assumption that the delegations of the TCiE will be impressed with the reforms and the economic progress made by TAR under the communist regime since 1959 and in the hope the Dalai Lama would return to China. However, the Dalai Lama was circumspect and only sent his representatives instead of going himself in August 1979 under the leadership of Kalon Juchen Thupten Namgyal accompanied by some other members from the Central Tibetan Administration.[6] When the delegation arrived in Tibet, it received an enthusiastic welcome from the Tibetans. The reportedly huge turnout among the local Tibetan population of Lhasa to welcome the representatives of the Dalai Lama surprised the delegates and possibly disappointed the Chinese authorities. The delegates could discern a degree of nervousness amongst the Chinese leaders. One of the Chinese officials reportedly mentioned to his colleague that, 'the efforts of the last 20 years have been wasted in a single day.'[7] In the assessment of the Dalai Lama setup, the visit of the fact-finding delegation became a 'serious embarrassment' for the Chinese leaders since the designed objective of overwhelming the delegates with the economic development achieved in Tibet under the communist rule could not be met.

Notwithstanding the initial disappointment, China agreed to receive the second and third delegations of the Dalai Lama's representatives subsequently in 1980. The second delegation comprised of younger members from Dharamsala and the third delegation was led by the Dalai Lama's younger sister, Jetsun Pema[8]. Both these moves were significant in that involvement of the youth in the process in the early stage would ensure their support to the process and the presence of the Dalai Lama's sister was bound to add a personal and emotional touch to the visit which was to look at the educational conditions obtaining for the Tibetans in Lhasa and beyond. Both the delegations again received warm welcomes in all parts of Tibet and led to revival of ethnic associations. Their visit was followed by several anti-Chinese protests by the Tibetans in support of the Dalai Lama's return and independence of Tibet. Apparently and expectedly these developments pushed the Chinese to adopt a rather defensive position.

At the same time, the third delegation conveyed to the Chinese leaders Dalai Lama's willingness to send some teachers from Dharamsala to Lhasa to teach the Tibetan language. This generated an awkward response from the Chinese authorities who waved off the suggestion by stating that the exiles had been brought up in India amongst good facilities and would find it difficult to live in Tibet where the facilities were lacking at the moment, obviously a rather lame excuse than a serious or valid reason. One thing that emerged very clearly is that despite the Chinese propaganda over the previous two decades, the Tibetans still harboured strong faith in the Dalai Lama and a strong sense of the unique Tibetan identity. The huge support for the Dalai Lama amongst the Tibetan community in Tibet even after twenty years of massive indoctrination under communist ideologies also brought a strong sense of confidence to the exiled leader.

As the talks progressed, Hu Yaobang[9] conveyed a "five-point proposal" for the Dalai Lama through Gyalo Thondup on 28 July 1981. Hu's five-point policy's primary motive was to pursuade the Dalai Lama to return to China (necessary to note here that his return was intended for China and not Tibet). The Tibetans were disappointed by his proposal and the Dalai Lama rejected it based on the objection that the Chinese had tried to reduce the question of Tibet into a personal question about the status and personality of the Dalai Lama and were inconsiderate about the rest of Tibetans in TAR.

Subsequently, two delegations of senior Tibetan leaders were sent in 1982 and 1985 to Beijing for discussions on the future of Tibet.[10] During the meetings, the Tibetan delegations presented their demands including demilitarization of the whole of Tibet and making it into a 'zone of peace'. They also asked for the unification of the three provinces of Tibet.[11] These visits were closely followed by the fourth fact-finding delegation which flew into Tibet in 1985 itself. However, by June 1986, the Chinese government was already transiting to a hardened position on the Sino-Tibetan dialogue process. They refused to receive the fifth delegation on the ground that the delegates should travel only on overseas Chinese passports. The earlier four delegations and the two exploratory missions between 1979 and 1985, it may be recalled, had all travelled on 'identity certificates' issued to them by the Indian Government. The Tibetans refused to comply with this new demand made by the Chinese government.

The idea behind the visit of the TCiE delegation was based on the dictum that—"it is better to see once than to hear a hundred times"[12] and was also the primary way of achieving the Dalai Lama's goal through dialogue and peaceful contact. However, Beijing's experience with the Tibetan delegations in terms of the massive support it received from the locals every time led the Chinese authorities to close this window of opportunity for settlement through dialogue. It had not only based its strategy on several political miscalculations about the TCiE but also demonstrated its own ignorance about the state of affairs inside Tibet (TAR).[13] The change of the leadership along with the expulsion of Hu Yaobang, who advocated in favour of resolution of this issue at the earliest through dialogue, also played a significant role in the breakdown of this phase of attempted negotiations.

INTERNATIONALIZATION AND STALEMATE

With the decision of the Chinese leadership to terminate engagements with the Dalai Lama's representatives or other leaders from the TCiE, the Dalai Lama was compelled to turn towards the international community for support for the Tibetan cause. It was in this context that the Dalai Lama spelt out his five-point peace plan for Tibet at the US Congressional Human Rights Caucus in Washington on 21 September 1987. Under this plan, he emphasised the following:[14]

1. Transformation of the whole of Tibet into a zone of peace;
2. Abandonment of Chinese programme of population transfer in Tibet;
3. Respect for the Tibetan people's fundamental human rights and democratic freedoms;
4. Restoration and protection of Tibet's natural environment and
5. Beginning earnest negotiations on the future status of Tibet.

The proposal was well received in both US and other European countries, but met with summary rejection by Beijing. On the other hand, the proposal had a spin-off effect on the Tibetan population in TAR. Within six days of its enunciation, a violent demonstration erupted in Lhasa. It was reportedly the biggest since the 1959 uprising. Beijing blamed the Dalai Lama for instigating these protests and responded with mass arrest and imprisonment of the protestors.

A year later, on 15 June 1988, the Dalai Lama in his address to the European Parliament in Strasbourg, further elaborated on his five-point peace plan which came to be known as the "Strasbourg Proposal." In this, the Dalai Lama clarified that he was seeking "genuine autonomy" for Tibet within the ambit of the Chinese state and not independence.[15] China was not convinced and continued to oppose the demand for 'genuine autonomy', dubbing the Dalai Lama as being insincere in his talks. The Tibetan community felt let down by this proposal of the Dalai Lama as it amounted to granting a major concession to the Chinese, climbing down from the demand for independence for TAR to 'genuine autonomy' without any corresponding reconciliatory move by China in return.

Nonetheless, on 23 September 1988, Beijing conveyed to its embassy in New Delhi its willingness to hold talks with the Dalai

Lama any time. The talks, it added, could be held in Beijing, Hong Kong or at any of the Chinese embassies or consulates abroad as chosen by the Dalai Lama. They, however, placed one condition that no foreigners should be involved with these talks. "We are ready to designate one official with certain rank to have direct dialogue with the Dalai Lama"—Beijing clarified.[16] In response, the Dalai Lama chose Geneva as the venue and announced it publicly. He also spelt out the names of the Tibetan negotiating team along with a Dutch lawyer who was to act as an advisor to them. The Chinese government rejected the suggestion on the earlier stated ground of no involvement of any foreigner.

Shortly thereafter, some significant developments followed that impacted the dialogue process. These included the removal of the liberal-minded Wu Jinghua from his post of First Party Secretary of the Tibet Autonomous Region (TAR) in late 1988 [to be replaced by Hu Jintao, the former Party General Secretary and Presedent, the reshuffle in the Communist Party in late 1989 and more importantly, the unexpected death of the Panchen Lama on 28 January 1989, the second highest figure in the Tibetan spiritual structure based on the principle of reincarnation. In addition, Hu introduced martial law in Tibet in March 1989, and this was followed by the Tiananmen Square demonstrations by the students in June that year, which further aggravated the situation. This led to massive crack down by the authorities inside Tibet and in areas inhabited by ethnic Tibetans. The year 1989, however, marked another dramatic international setback for Beijing as the Dalai Lama was awarded the Nobel Peace Prize which not only further enhanced his international visibility, stature and prestige, but also brought the Tibet question back on the international agenda. The state of the Beijing-Dharamsala dialogue continued to deteriorate further as the global scenario changed.[17] These understandably disturbed the Chinese political system, both internally and externally and impacted the dialogue process[18] and Beijing yet again lost interest in renewing negotiations with Dharamsala.

In July 1993, two senior delegates from Dharamsala including Sonam Topgyal, the senior minister in cabinet and Gyalo Thondup, went to Beijing for almost a week. They observed that the hardened Chinese attitude towards the Dalai Lama had still not diluted. They continued to reiterate that the Dalai Lama was still not serious about making any kind of compromise that would be acceptable to China. Coincidentally, as the Sino-Tibetan relations deteriorated on one side, the US government began to take more keen interest in the issue. President Bill Clinton urged his counterpart Jiang Zemin in their first meeting in 1993 that the Chinese leaders should open direct talks with the Dalai Lama. Notwithstanding, all contacts between Dharamsala and Beijing ended in August 1993 despite strong pressure from the West. Beijing began to construe this increased attention as part of a larger 'western conspiracy'. Chinese attempts at integration of the TAR internally became more and more embedded as the Chinese authorities began to meddle with religious affairs of Tibetans, especially with regard to appointments of higher religious figures like the Panchen Lama.

RENEWED INITIATIVES AND THE LAST DECADE

The post-1995 attitude of the Chinese government towards interaction with the Dalai Lama setup have been guided by the dynamics of global and regional developments including India's growing stature in the South Asian region and constant pressure from the US which had designated the Tibetan issue as the 'top-most priority for the Sino-American relations'. During Bill Clinton's live televised press conference with Jiang Zemin on 27 June1998, he urged the leaders at Beijing to open dialogue with the Dalai Lama. To this Jiang replied, "as long as the Dalai Lama makes a public commitment that Tibet is an inalienable part of

China and Taiwan is a province of China, then, the door to dialogue and negotiation is open."[19] The Chinese had cleverly intertwined the Taiwanese and Tibetan questions to suit their international posturing.

The dramatic flight of Karmapa to Dharamsala in December 1999 became yet another matter of embarrassment for China. The Karmapa was recognized by both the Chinese and Tibetan authorities as the legitimate leader of one of the most powerful sects of Tibetan Buddhism. His escape from China exposed the lack of religious freedom in Tibet; China's efforts to exercise total control over the religious leaders had been unsuccessful.

China could hardly afford to be seen as a rising power with global and regional aspirations and yet allow the world to continually use the Tibet issue to puncture its credentials to that status. Perhaps, it was also driven by a sense of greater self-confidence. A combination of all these, led the Chinese authorities to re-evaluate their Tibet policy subsequently. Accordingly, they re-established direct contact with the Dalai Lama's representatives in June 2001. Gyalo Thondup was re-invited to Tibet in 2002 and the dialogue process re-commenced in September 2002. Lodi Gyari, the Dalai Lama's special envoy led a delegation comprising Kelsang Gyaltsen, envoy of the Dalai Lama and two senior assistants, Sonam N. Dagpo and Bhuchung K. Tsering.[20] The visits were primarily aimed at confidence-building and re-establishing direct contact with the leadership in Beijing. Lodi Gyari, the head of the delegation, after returning from the trip, expressed amazement on the dedication and competence of the Tibetan officials they met, as also with the progress and development in the Chinese cities.[21]

However, as far as the progress achieved in the negotiations, in 2006, the then Prime Minister of the TGiE, Samdhong Rinpoche frankly opined, "We don't have any definite idea where the negotiations are going. We are roaming in the dark. To have contacts and to talk is much better than having no contact and not talking. In a nutshell, I can only say that we have direct contact and we have a dialogue."[22] Nine rounds of talks took place between the representatives of the Dalai Lama and the Chinese between September 2002 and 2009. But the negotiations broke down in January 2010 when the Dalai Lama publicly voiced his intent to relinquish his political role as head of the Tibetan movement and only continue to guide fellow Tibetans as their religious and spiritual leader.

THE DIALOGUE PROCESS: GEO-POLITICAL CONSTRAINTS

Despite the nine rounds of negotiations, no substantive progress was achieved in terms of narrowing down the differences between the two sides. The main focus during these negotiations from the Tibetan perspective remained the demand for reunification of all Tibetan areas within the PRC and acceptance of the Dalai Lama's Middle-Way approach for the resolution of the Tibet issue. Beijing, on the other hand, maintained that the Dalai Lama's movement was designed towards 'splitting the motherland' and also accused him of masterminding all anti-Chinese protests within and outside China. This accusation was especially highlighted in context of the March 2008 Tibetan uprising [to mark the anniversary of the 1959 revolt] which occurred just prior to the Beijing Olympics and was aimed at garnering international attention on the Tibetan issue.

As the two continued to have fundamental disagreements on virtually all issues on the agenda for the dialogue, Dharamsala remained convinced that Tibetans inside China were facing severe repression at the hands of the state authorities. Despite China's claims on *regional autonomy for ethnic minorities* as spelt out in its 2005 White Paper, the Tibetan delegations observed severe religious subjugation and Han chauvinism particularly in the nomination of all-powerful Party chiefs, thereby undermining political autonomy.

Dharamsala also suspects, perhaps not with much justification that the lack of positive movement in the Sino-Tibetan dialogue could be due to growing engagement between India and China in repairing their bilateral relations. The diplomatic thaw between India and China in 2003 with Prime Minister Atal Bihari Vajpayee's visit, they maintain, compromised the situation for the Tibetans. While China recognized Sikkim as a part of India, India had to formally concede that TAR was an inalienable part of the Chinese territory. The Tibetans often describe this as 'a diplomatic bungle' on the part of India since Sikkim was never under Chinese authority and the clever move by the Chinese should not have been accepted by India as part of a 'barter' deal against the status of TAR.

Dharmasala also discerned a subtle message in New Delhi's reaction to the incident of protest by Tenzin Tsundue, General Secretary of 'Friends of Tibet' during former Premier Wen Jiabao's visit to New Delhi in 2005. While the TCiE had planned this to showcase their intent and demands, the Indian government responded in line with established diplomatic protocol and External Affairs Ministry expressed regret over the incident. This was read by the Dalai Lama setup as a major indicator of the shape of things to come in the future since increased political and economic engagement between the two neighbours would eventually persuade them to side-step certain contentious issues and move forward. Rather, Dharmasala would have liked New Delhi to 'treat Tibet as one of the core issues in Sino-Indian talks'. Interestingly, China itself considers Tibet issue as a 'sensitive' issue in its relations with India (former Premier Wen Jiabao, *Xinhua*, 18 March 2008); Beijing's official organ *People's Daily* (22 October 2009) was more explicit about this, by alleging that the 'Dalai Lama is colluding with India whenever Sino-Indian border talks are held'. In any case, it cannot be denied that the Tibet issue, though not in a formal sense, has come to stay as a bilateral matter of concern for New Delhi and Beijing.

However, the US for its part, reiterated its commitment to support the preservation of Tibet's unique religious, cultural and linguistic identity during the Dalai Lama's visit to the US in November 2005.[23] The international community also reprimanded China's response to the Tibetan uprising in 2008. The mounting external pressure must have surprised the Chinese authorities since it had fairly successfully created an impression that it was serious in its talks about settling the Tibet issue which was in turn acknowledged by the Tibetan representative, Lodi Gyari. The dialogue was perceived to be progressing well till the process plummeted significantly after the uprising in 2008. The Tibetans thus concluded that the geo-political interests and contemporary developments played a significant role in initially building and later on diffusing the momentum of the talks.

POLITICAL DEVOLUTION AND IMPLICATIONS FOR THE DIALOGUE

It is in this background that the announcement by the Dalai Lama to devolve political authority, though being contemplated for long, was as much of a surprise to the Chinese as to the Tibetans. It may be reiterated here that the main rationale behind this dialogue was to find a mid-way position between the Dalai Lama's demand for 'genuine autonomy' as per the Strasbourg proposal of 1988 and China's unwillingness to cede concessions related to the Tibetan Autonomous Region (TAR). Primarily, the Dalai Lama provided the pivot around which the deliberations were being carried out. Even though China continued to insist that it did not consider the TGiE as a legitimate government, it was willing to engage with it through 'representatives' of the Dalai Lama. The Dalai Lama was conscious of the fact that the Chinese strategy was to 'delay resolution of the Tibet issue till his death' and hence till that happened, they would like to preserve the legitimacy and the authority of the Central Tibetan Administration (CTA) as the only true government of Tibet.[24] Keeping this in mind the Dalai Lama, perhaps, decided on the devolution process to train a new leadership under the TGiE structure which could negotiate with the Chinese on a long-term basis on behalf of the Tibetan exiles.

The procedure of the devolution itself remained quite complex. It was based on the Dalai Lama's intention to devolve his powers as head of the *government*, which did not necessarily mean his resignation as a *head of the state*, which is purely symbolic or ceremonial in nature.[25] On 19 March 2011, the Dalai Lama stated 'what is happening is that *Ganden Phodrang* is relinquishing its political responsibilities' (*Ganden Phodrang* is the traditional form of government in Tibet established by the Dalai Lama in 1642 and continuing since then). This was to be followed by a redrafting of the Tibetan Charter.

The devolution has not only made the scenario more multifaceted but also unpredictable as there are several legal, political and practical complexities. First, the dialogue conducted between the Dalai Lama's special envoys and the Chinese leadership in the previous decade was never officially recognized by the Chinese government, which often dubbed them as 'private interactions' with the representatives of the Dalai Lama. It preferred to call them 'overseas countrymen' instead of special envoys.[26] So now with the devolution of authority, the first and foremost implication would be absence of the earlier established channel to continue the dialogue.

Second, since China does not recognize Central Tibetan Administration (CTA) as a legitimate entity, it would be unwilling to entertain any direct contacts with its functionaries. Accordingly, Lobsang Sangay the Kalon Tripa who used to earlier travel to China to participate in several workshops in Chinese territory as a research scholar from the US, will be denied any such opportunities as the head of a government-in-exile. Moreover, his position as an elected head is also not very clear. Though he has been bestowed with the political responsibilities which the Dalai Lama used to discharge earlier, the proposed Tibetan Charter (post-reform) addresses the Dalai Lama as the 'supreme leader.' This would suggest that he might still be able to override the Kalon Tripa's authority as he will continue to be the 'international spokesperson on behalf of the Tibetan people'.

Third, China's repeated attempts to defame Tibetan organizations like the Tibetan Youth Congress as a 'terrorist' organization has irked the TCiE. This tag of having been involved with a 'terrorist' organisation is now likely to be applied even to the new Kalon Tripa. In fact, he was described as such in an article published in the *People's Daily* for having served as an executive member in the pro-independence group, the Tibetan Youth Congress (TYC), which was earlier christened as a terrorist organization by China.[27] In this context it may be recalled that the first thing Sangay did after being sworn in, was to distance himself from his past connections with the pro-independence Tibetan Youth Congress by assuring that there would be no shift from the Dalai Lama's "Middle Path" guideline which seeks 'meaningful autonomy', but not 'independence', for Tibet.

Fourth, the dialogue process was designed by China more to act as a shield from the international community's pressure to engage with the Tibetans. The momentum was maintained even though no real and substantial progress was achieved through it over the years. Now with the increased dependency of the Western powers on China in the wake of the 2008 financial crisis, the international reactions to China's behaviour on the Tibetan issue's resolution is likely to be moderated, thereby reducing the imperatives for engagement or dialogue for China. In fact, the only pressing external factor on China to continue to opt for the dialogue is the presence of the Tibetan community in its bordering areas. Its policy on Tibet in future is likely to be driven by the need to maintain stable borders, both with Nepal and India. The recent developments in Nepal with the Maoist government in power in Kathmandu, has made the task so much easier as far as Nepal is concerned.

Fifth, the political changes occurring within China today have made it less conducive for the dialogue to continue. The United Front Work Department of the Communist Party of China, which was responsible for designing its Tibet policy and which was reinstated as the main policy formulation body again in 2003, does not have any pro-engagement policy-makers in it any longer. Thus, despite achieving stability and institutional and popular accountability for the TGiE, the devolution has not created any favourable stakes for the dialogue process.

The political shrewdness exhibited by the Dalai Lama through the devolution exercise, has generated a great deal of antagonism amongst the Chinese political leadership resulting in denial of fresh or renewed opportunities for exchanges of the type that used to take place earlier. It is argued that even the process of devolution has not been meticulously achieved in that, though it was to create genuine autonomy, with clear demarcation of powers and responsibilities between the two devolved entities, the two sides have not been able to create an administrative structure which will be able to implement it efficiently. In fact, the procedure has become even more complicated given a myriad of other emerging exigencies. The role of the youth is becoming more and more prominent in the decision-making process in both the new entities created through the devolution package. A schism is already visible amongst the Tibetan youth brought up in exile who find themselves at crossroads in opting to support either complete independence of Tibet from China or to abide by the Dalai Lama's 'Middle-way approach', while most maintain their utmost allegiances to the Dalai Lama.

The socio-economic conditions within Tibet are also changing. Through consistent efforts over the years China has fairly successfully created a class of 'citizens who would be loyal to the motherland' mostly bureaucratic elite. Much of the credit for this can be granted to the 'patriotic education' campaigns and the access given to the locals in regional administrative posts, howsoever restricted though. It is difficult to gauge how far these Tibetans will be able to identify with the new leaders of the TGiE as their association with the Dalai Lama was more as a spiritual guide rather than a political leader.

Meanwhile, the role of religion in Tibet has also been undergoing changes in recent times. The huge population of Tibetan Buddhists had traditionally observed non-violence and stayed aloof from political changeovers. However, with China's interference in nominating the key religious figures who are believed to be reincarnations of the previous ones, has piqued the Buddhist monks. The Buddhist monasteries are now being managed by Chinese appointed officials and the peaceful abodes are turning into grounds of protests and subterfuge. Chinese involvement in religious controversies within the TCiE have also not been ruled out. Many of these developments are driven by a sense of empathy for the exiled Tibetans and reflect the growing unrest within Tibetans in the TAR and Greater Tibet (as claimed by the TCiE) region.

LACK OF OFFICIAL CONDUITS AND THE SEARCH FOR ALTERNATIVES

The decision by two of the envoys of the Dalai Lama, Lodi Gyari and Kelsang Gyaltsen, in June 2012, to resign from the negotiations has yet again led to a roadblock in the process of negotiations. The representatives have apparently taken this decision in the wake of the deteriorating situation within Tibet since 2009 and the reluctance of the Chinese government to grant the demand of regional autonomy to Tibet. Thus, in their attempts to consolidate their demands and sense of identity, the Tibetans have been forced to look for different ways to showcase their demands to the Chinese state. One of these ways has been a resort to instances of self-immolations in the Tibetan Autonomous region and the surrounding provinces of China. There have been 90 cases of self-immolations reported so far, and it is speculated that many more might not be reported at all.

It is significant to note that the resort to these measures seems to be the primary responsive strategy of the Tibetans, undertaken as a strategic effort directed towards political goals; in this case, the return of the Dalai Lama to his birthplace and not simply as the product of irrational individuals or expression of fanatical hatred (towards the state). The aim is to compel the Chinese government to change its policy decisions on Tibet and acknowledge the desperation amongst Tibetans. However, considering the fact that the Tibetans are pitted against a hard-nosed authoritarian regime, the effectiveness of this strategy remains questionable.

Though the Dalai Lama has refrained from giving his opinions on the matter of self-immolations, it is quite clear that these instances are inherently antagonistic to the precepts of Buddhist ideology that most Tibetans adhere to. The Dalai Lama was recently quoted as saying "now, the reality is that if I say something positive, then the Chinese immediately blame me… If I say something negative, then the family members of those people feel very sad and thus the best thing is to remain neutral" (*The Hindu*). But the very fact that the Tibetans have been forced to resort to actions which are by nature antithetical to their religious beliefs shows the desperation amongst Tibetans currently. Yet, keeping in mind that these actions might not be able to garner sufficient attention from the government which prefers to negate their existence and even sidestep media queries regarding this matter along with the need for dialogue and direct channel of communications.[28]

THE ROAD AHEAD

With the 'delay tactic' sought to be made redundant by the Dalai Lama's astute political move through the devolution exercise, the future of the dialogue process portends much more scrambling and aggressive pursuit by either side. The historic opportunity to resolve the dialogue with the Dalai Lama while he is still alive and in a position to evolve a compromise deal would have been in China's long-term strategic interests. The chances of this to happen seem to be fading as the baton of political leadership passes on to the younger generation of exiles 'born in freedom'. Clearly, China is closely weighing its options; dubbing it as either a deception trick or, sometimes, still gesturing its willingness to communicate with the Dalai Lama. It is however cognisant that any adverse reaction to the Dalai Lama or the TCiE could entail serious consequences for the TAR, signs of which are evident in the rising number of cases of self-immolation amongst Tibetan Buddhist monks and frequent protest actions by the Tibetan community in different parts of China on local issues. A strong desire for the return of the Dalai Lama continues in the TAR where Tibetans identify with him as their leader par supreme.

The dialogue process will also continue to be hindered by the machinations involved in the nomination of key figures in the Tibetan setup, for instance, the Panchen Lama, the Karmapa and the Dalai Lama. While China would definitely want to nominate pro-Chinese individuals in these positions, the Dalai Lama would want to have his candidates nominated under the process of 'reincarnation'. China has already begun to woo the Buddhist monks by organizing two World Buddhist Forums within the last five years (China officially approved Buddhism as a religion in 2006). It is likely to further appropriate religion to achieve its strategic and domestic objectives in the future.

The Tibetans in exile have, by and large, depended on developments within China for their tactical posturing. The new Kalon Tripa, Lobsang Sangay, himself believes that much of Tibet's future will depend on circumstantial developments within Tibet and that the Tibetans in exile would have to adopt a wait-and-watch approach while continuing to prepare themselves for the future. Lobsang Sangay would personally prefer to follow a track II approach to reach out to Chinese academics, businessmen, dissidents and the common people to help them develop a better understanding of the issue of Tibet in the hope that this strategy would help in influencing the Chinese government.[29]

The stepping down of Lodi Gyari and Kelsang Gyaltsen, the Dalai Lama's official representatives from the dialogue process, could lead to several complexities. The continuous efforts made by these delegations to persuade China to implement the 17-point programme would fall by the wayside if they were to exit the negotiating team since they have been the most important negotiators in the talks held so far.[30]

A formal system of checks and balances needs to be established under a more 'constitutional TGiE'. This would be supported by the international community as part of a democratic endeavour. The reformulation and implementation of a new Tibetan Charter is an arduous task for the Tibetans-in-exile. The most challenging task will be to strike a balance between the charismatic authority of the Dalai Lama and the legal-constitutional authority of the new Kalon Tripa. The task of putting up a united face in their dealings with the Chinese authorities would be the real challenge, given the different streams of opinions amongst the older and younger generations of the TCiE.

The TCiE and the Chinese government need to exercise greater prudence to avoid derailing the process of engagement, failing which the future of the Sino-Tibetan dialogue seems bleak. Some of the recent utterances emanating from the leadership in Beijing are not really helpful in arriving at the conclusion that post-devolution, the dialogue process would still stay on course with the new political leadership. In this context, it may be mentioned that the Chinese Vice-Minister in the CCP United Front Work Department Zhu Weiqun, in charge of negotiations with the Dalai Lama, had said in an interview with *China's Tibet* journal, (14 May 2011) that the Tibetan government-in-exile, 'led by who so ever', was a "separatist political clique with no legitimacy, absolutely having no status to engage in dialogue with representatives of the Central government". The spokesperson of the Chinese foreign ministry, Hong Lei had earlier denounced Sangay's appointment (28 April, 2011) as a "political show by the Dalai Lama which no country in the world recognizes".

For the purpose of this paper, the main issue is whether China would be willing to continue the process of dialogue with the Dalai Lama's envoys after the devolution? According to an expert on Chinese affairs, Mr. D.S. Rajan, Director, Centre for China Studies, China, as a responsible global player now, needs to listen to international voices favouring its negotiations with the Dalai Lama side. On this basis, Mr. Rajan expects the CCP to open talks with Sangay's private representatives, on the same lines of nine rounds of unofficial negotiations held so far between the Dalai Lama's special envoys and the party's United Front Work Department officials. But some voices being heard from China are hinting that such expectations may not be accurate, For example, a People's Daily article (26 July 2011) said that the Dalai Lama during his recent overseas trips, has taken positions which are 'totally and diametrically opposite to those of the Central government showing that he has no interest in talks'. A question arises—Is Beijing by itself trying to scuttle the chances of holding talks taking the exiled spiritual leader's statements as a pretext?

Mr. Rajan goes on to argue in his article that the "period prior to the April 2011 election of Sangay, witnessed signs pointing to China's willingness to somewhat shed its rigidity on the Tibet issue, but without making any compromise on the country's basic stand on Tibet's sovereignty. The documents relating to the Fifth Tibet Work Forum (January 2010) held with former President Hu Jintao in the chair, for the first time since the 2008 riots, revealed a new trend—the rhetoric against the Dalai Lama was toned down and a fresh developmental approach centring round regional integration of all Tibetan areas of the PRC including the Tibetan Autonomous Region (TAR) was adopted. It looked like a Chinese acceptance of the Dalai Lama's 'Greater Tibet' concept but limited to economic terms. The Tibetan representatives participating in the ninth round of the Sino-Tibetan dialogue which closely followed the Forum took a positive note of such fresh nuances in China's Tibet policy.

However, the then Vice-President Xi Jinping, Mr. Rajan noted, "in a hard-hitting speech (Lhasa, 19 July 2011) said that his nation should "thoroughly fight against separatist activities by the Dalai clique and smash completely any plot to destroy stability in Tibet and jeopardize national unity". He especially praised the People's Liberation Army as 'loyal guardian' of stability in Tibet.

In view of the foregoing, it is unlikely that Beijing would try to find a way to re-engage with the Dalai Lama setup, now represented by Lobsang Sangay and even if it does, it would be at a time of its choice but with the clear understanding that it does not expect this process to eventually lead to a resolution of the conflict. China is likely to follow the same policy of endlessly dragging its feet to delay the whole process in the hope that the overseas Tibetan movement would eventually get weakened especially after the Dalai Lama is no longer on the scene. This fits in well with our assessment that the entire exercise of engagement during the nine rounds of talks between the two sides was not really designed to be a process of serious dialogue with the clear intent of seeking a resolution in the spirit of give-and-take by trying to find a middle ground acceptable to both sides. Beijing would not enter into negotiations with the new political structure in Dharamsala since any such move would amount to granting legitimacy to the move initiated by the Dalai Lama. Doing so now would bind Beijing to continuing with the dialogue process with the new political leadership for all times to come. This would go against Beijing's basic approach of engaging the Dalai Lama in the dialogue process only for tactical reasons and certainly not for finding a solution to the problem.

One should not, therefore, expect any quick or startling results and the state of agonising stalemate may continue in the years ahead. Beijing would, for strategic reasons, never agree even to an 'Autonomous', much less an 'Independent' Tibet. It would continue with the programme of Tibet's integration in every way with the mainland and also eventually weaken if not totally capture the important religious institutions post the 14th Dalai Lama. In doing so, it is unlikely to show any major sensitivity towards international pressures and persuasions unless the regime in Beijing itself collapses. That could be the only realistic hope for the Tibetans in exile.

In this near grim scenario, the road ahead for the Tibetan movement and the process of dialogue is bound to be long and arduous. The movement must prepare itself adequately for this long haul every which way and continue its international campaign in a more effective manner. It would be prudent to involve the community inside Tibet in a big way to continue to mount pressure on religious, political and economic issues affecting them. They could also consider building some synergy with the other disenchanted elements and groups within the PRC to co-ordinate their movement. And most importantly they must recognise the fact that their real strength lies in galvanising popular support amongst the Tibetans in exile both in India and in Nepal. It would also be important for both tactical and strategic reasons for New Delhi to reassess its Tibet policy in its own interest and in view of the fact that India is home to over a hundred thousand and growing number of Tibetan refugees who can pose serious internal problems if driven to desperation.

[The authors wish to thank Chok Tsering for providing inputs for this paper.]

ENDNOTES

1. Dawa Norbu, *China's Tibet Policy*, Richmond, Curzon Press (2001), p. 316.
2. Gyalo Thondup is Dalai Lama's elder brother and based in Hong Kong now. He was the main bridge between Beijing and Dharamsala during that time.
3. Claude Arpi, *Dharamsala and Beijing: The Negotiations that Never Were*, Lancer Publisher, New Delhi (2009), p. 57. See Tsering Shakya (1999), Dawa Norbu (2001), Melvyn Goldstein (1997) and Tashi Rabgey and Tsetan Wangchuk Sharlho (2004) for the detailed history of Deng Xiaoping's initial reform period in Tibet.
4. Though recent Chinese leaders have disputed this fact and assert that it was a made-up by the representative of the Dalai Lama.
5. Melvyn Goldstein, *The Snow Lion and the Dragon: China, Tibet and the Dalai Lama*, University of California Press, Berkeley, 1997, p. 61. Tshering Chonzom, "Chinese Preconditions and Tibetan Initiatives: Negotiating Narratives", *China Report*, Vol. 44(2), 2008, p. 186.
6. Central Tibetan Administration (CTA) is a de-facto government based in Dharamsala considered legitimate by the Tibetans. The other delegation members were Phuntsok Tashi Takla, Lobsang Samten, Tashi Topgyal and Lobsang Thargay.
7. Mentioned as reported by the Delegate to the Dalai Lama in *Freedom in Exile: The Autobiography of the Dalai Lama of Tibet*, Harper Collins Publisher, New York, 1990.
8. Jetsun Pema was the first woman minister of Kashag (the Cabinet) in Exile, though as a matter of fact the Tibetan government-in-Exile is not recognized by China, and she was at that time the President of Tibetan Children's Village (TCV) School.
9. Hu Yaobang became the Party General Secretary in 1980 and was considered a liberal leader and the major architect of China's Tibet

policy during the early initiatives. He was forced to resign as Party General Secretary in 1987 after a public demonstration.

10. Both the delegations were led by Juchen Thupten Namgyal, a cabinet minister, accompanied by Phuntsok Tashi Taklha and Lodi Gyari, who was then the chairman of the Tibetan Parliament-in-Exile.
11. Three provinces include all Cholka Sum, the traditional Tibetan inhabited areas which includes U-Tsang (present Tibet Autonomous Region), Kham and Amdo region which comprises of present Chinese provinces of Qinghai, Sichuan, Gansu and Yunnan.
12. Arpi, p. 78.
13. Rabgey and Sharlho, "Sino-Tibetan Dialogue in the Post-Mao Era: Lessons and Prospects", *Policy Studies* 12, East-West Center, Washington, 2004, pp. 8-10.
14. Dawa Norbu, "China's Dialogue with Dalai Lama 1978-90: Prenegotiation Stage of Dead End?", *Pacific Affairs*, Vol. 64(3), Autumn 1991, p. 354. Also see the detailed debate in Tsering Shakya (1999), Dawa Norbu (2001) and Tashi Rabgey and Tsetan Wangchuk Sharlho (2004).
15. Dalai Lama's genuine autonomy in Tibet implies foreign policy and defense matters to China while keeping internal matters like economy, culture, administration and education for the Tibetan people. This includes whole three traditional provinces of Tibet.
16. Rabgey and Sharlho, p. 11. The condition of one official to interact with the Dalai Lama was to emphasise the fact that Beijing still considered TGiE as illegal and unworthy of direct dialogue.
17. This change includes the collapse of Berlin Wall in 1989 and unification of the East and the West Germany. Along with this, Soviet leader, Gorbachev announced the liberal policy of democratization, glasnost and perestroika in mid 1980s.
18. Tiananmen Square incident triggered a reorganization of the PRC leadership, including the dismissal of Party's top leaders. It also threatened Beijing an isolation from the global table as its socialist partner, USSR also collapsed after a year.
19. www.tibet.net. http://tibet.net/important-issues/sino-tibetan-dialogue.
20. The four delegations members were led by Lodi Gyari, followed by Kelsang Gyaltsen, Sonam N. Dagpo and Bhuchung K. Tsering.

Since then Lodi Gyari was the head of the Tibetan delegation till the final dialogue in January 2010.

21. Rabgey and Sharlho, p. 21.
22. Arpi, 196.
23. Ibid., p. 198.
24. Jamyang Dorjee, "The Dalai Lama's Devolution of Power and What it Means to the Issue of Tibet", *The Tibetan Political Review*, 6 June 2011, Online URL: http://sites.google.com/site/tibetanpoliticalreview/articles/thedalailama%E2%80%99sdevolutionofpowerandwhatitmeanstotheissueoftibet.
25. Legal issues implicated by the Dalai Lama's Devolution of power, Tibet Justice Center, May 2011, Online URL: http://www.tibetjustice.org/dalailamadevolution/DevolutionMemo.pdf
26. Apri, p. 181.
27. Li Hongmei, "Terrorist Set to Rule Tibetan Government-in-Exile", 22 March 2011, *People's Daily Online*, Online URL: http://english.peopledaily.com.cn/90002/96417/7326988.html
28. Edward Wong, "Tibet: Negotiators Resign", 5 June 2012, Web URL: http://www.nytimes.com/2012/06/05/world/asia/tibet-negotiators-resign.html?_r=0
29. Interview with Dr. Lobsang Sangay, Nominee Candidate for Kalon Tripa, Mcleodganj, Dharamshala, 21 March 2011 cited in "A Paradigm Shift? Elections to the Tibetan Government-in-Exile" by Bhavna Singh, Special Report 105, IPCS, Web URL: http://www.ipcs.org/special-report/china/a-paradigm-shift-elections-to-the-tibetan-government-in-exile-105.html.
30. Circular from Special Envoy of His Holiness the Dalai Lama, Kasur Lodi G Gyari, 11 November 2011, Phayul.com, Online Url: http://www.phayul.com/news article.aspx?id=30357&article=Circular+from+Special+Envoy+of+His+Holiness+the+Dalai+Lama%2C+Kasur+Lodi+G.+ Gyari&t=1&c=2

REFERENCES

Abraham, Thomas, "Little can be Achieved through Negotiations in Tibet", *Economic and Political Weekly*, April 5 2008, pp. 8-11.

Arpi, Claude, *Dharamsala and Beijing: The Negotiations that Never Were*, Lancer Publisher, New Delhi, 2009.

Autonomy and the Tibetan Perspective, Tibetan Parliamentary and Policy Research Centre, New Delhi, 2005.

Boothalingam, Ravi, "For a 'Harmonious Resolution' of the Tibetan Question", *Economic and Political Weekly*, August 18 2007, pp. 3383-87.

Chonzom, Tshering, "Chinese Preconditions and Tibetan Initiatives: Negotiating Narratives", *China Report*, Vol. 44(2), 2008, pp. 185-93.

Dorjee, Jamyang, "The Dalai Lama's Devolution of Power and What it Means to the Issue of Tibet", *The Tibetan Political Review*, 6 June 2011.

Freedom in Exile: The Autobiography of the Dalai Lama of Tibet, Harper Collins Publisher, New York, 1990.

Goldstein, Melvyn, *The Snow Lion and the Dragon: China, Tibet and the Dalai Lama*, University of California Press, Berkeley, 1997.

Hongmei, Li, "Terrorist Set to Rule Tibetan Government-in-Exile", 22 March 2011, *People's Daily*.

Norbu, Dawa, "China's Dialogue with the Dalai Lama 1978-1990: Prenegotiation of Dead End?", *Pacific Affairs*, Vol. 64(3), Autumn 1991, pp. 351-72.

——, *China's Tibet Policy*, Curzon Press, Richmond, 2001.

Puri, Bharati, "Discourse and Method of the 'Earlier' Dalai Lama and the 'Later' Dalai Lama", *China Report*, Vol. 44(2), 2008, pp. 175-84.

——, "Deconstructing the Dalai Lama on Tibet", *Economic and Political Weekly*, August 24 2002, pp. 3500-03.

Rabgay, Tashi and Tsetan Wangchuk Sharlho, *Sino-Tibetan Dialogue in the Post-Mao Era: Lessons and Prospects*, East-West Center, Washington, 2004.

S. Verma, Virendra, "Post-Dalai Lama Situation and the Middle Path: Discussions with Chinese Scholars in Beijing", *China Report*, Vol. 45(1), 2009, pp. 75-87.

Sautman, Barry, "The Tibet Issue in Post-Summit Sino-American Relations", *Pacific Affairs*, Vol. 72(1), Spring 1999, pp. 7-21.

Shakya, Tsering, *The Dragon in the Land of Snows: A History of Modern Tibet since 1947*, Penguin Compass, 1999.

Singh, Bhavna, "A Paradigm Shift? Elections to the Tibetan Government-in-Exile", Special Report 105, IPCS, June 2011.

Chinese Build-up in Tibet and Implications for India

N.C. Vij and Rahul Bhonsle

> MOUNT EVEREST is singing for joy and the Brahmaputra River swirling with happiness.
>
> *An Official Chinese Newspaper [With Chinese Names for the features].*[1]

INTRODUCTION

China's build-up in Tibet follows a consistent policy of westward expansion over the decades. This includes extension of economic and social influence in the Autonomous regions of Tibet and Xinjiang. The Chinese use phrases as, "Western Development Campaign Policy", indicating a general trend or "Go West", which is the theme of the 12th Five Year Plan (2011–2015). Another oft repeated expression is the "South Asia Land Route." These typical phrases are policy catch words which are easy to remember and thus can permeate to the grass roots. Three southern land axes are of significance, of which Tibet is the central one. In the West is the Karakoram Highway through Pakistan

Occupied Kashmir (POK) extending to Gwadar in Balochistan while in the East Yunnan, the route connects to Kyaukpyu in Myanmar.

India is China's most populous neighbour. China has emerged as one of India's largest trading partners. Having fought one war (1962), a skirmish (1967) and a border standoff (1986) in the past 60 years plus, India's relations with its northern neighbour have been a mix of co-operation, contestation and coercion. The India-China boundary dispute and China's claims over Arunachal Pradesh continue to be a key challenge. India's special relationship with the people of Tibet and the presence of His Holiness the Dalai Lama in the country since 1959 and the deep Chinese resentment towards the same is another dimension of the relationship. Tibet is thus not just a physical but also a socio-cultural and ideological boundary between India and China. Given this legacy, internal dissonance or external machismo over perception of a weak India could act as drivers for China to trigger a conflict. China's build-up in Tibet, its likely impact on India-China relations and policy options for India thus need detailed examination.

CHINESE BUILD-UP—CONSIDERATIONS

Nations build-up infrastructure and expand their economy for a variety of reasons. The basic one is the welfare and development of the people which could be natural, demanded by the public or coerced due to an armed rebellion. Resource exploitation, be it oil and gas, minerals or timber is another reason for development of infrastructure. For such development to be carried out in border areas, defence and security would be the primary considerations. Build-up of infrastructure could also be undertaken to establish claims of sovereignty and integration where national boundaries are not well defined. Infrastructure is also a tool for extension of national power and strategic partnerships. In considering Chinese build-up in Tibet, some relevant questions do arise. Why is China developing infrastructure in Tibet? Is this development sustainable? What impact will this have on India and how should India respond? Briefly stated, the purpose of the Chinese build-up in Tibet in general and the Tibet Autonomous Region (TAR) in particular is envisaged to be for almost all the eclectic reasons stated herein which are subsequently elaborated in the Paper.

CHINA'S STRATEGIC PERCEPTION & IMPACT ON BUILD-UP IN TIBET

China's strategic perception has a major influence on build-up in Tibet. China feels it is a victim of history; many call it a "wounded power", a country which has been invaded rapaciously many times over by Japan and the West. The Communist Party sees itself as the saviour of Chinese nationalism and pride which has restored China to its rightful place in history. However over the years the Party has occupied a larger than life image and thus an impression is created that it is the Party which is the State and not a constituent of the state.

The Chinese think "long term". This is evident in various White Papers on Defence. China has already published a 100 year vision. The Chinese leadership is also flexible and adaptable in order to exploit opportunities as they come. Thus Mao's favoured dictum of, "Power flows through the barrel of the Gun", has now been converted to power flows through the Gun and Yuan by providing aid and loans to neighbours for building roads, bridges, oil and gas and power projects and extracting resources not just within the country but also across the world, extending to all of Asia and Africa. China's investments are however carefully calculated to expand its interests. The increasing proclivity for currency swap arrangements is a sign of this trend.

At the same time self-doubt and insecurity persist: thus China's approach can be seen as a mixture of confidence and diffidence. While the Party is extremely sensitive to political debates and contrarian views, there is extensive discussion on the economy and developmental issues. Thus all proposals on infrastructure expansion are discussed and debated by the Chinese hierarchy in the party, government, academia and think tanks. Academics have published papers critical of government's policies in this sphere. However, once the Party directive is issued, then there is no dissent and the instructions are implemented in letter and spirit. This perhaps explains the difference in approach to governance between China and noisy democracies such as India.

CHINESE APPROACH TO DEVELOPMENT

China's basic focus of development is on building infrastructure. China is said to spend about 50% of its GDP on building physical assets as roads, rail, bridges, ports, factories and office buildings. Compared to Japan and South Korea, who never topped 40 per cent of GDP during their phase of expansion in 1960s and 1970s, this seems to be a very large figure.[2] China's infrastructure development is also fuelled by savings rate at 53.2 per cent of GDP in 2008. Compared to China, India has a savings rate of 33.6 per cent, Japan 27 per cent and US 12.2 per cent of the GDP.[3] While the nominal GDP of the US is much higher and in absolute terms their savings may be large, comparatively, as China's economy grows, a high savings rate will provide the government substantial resources for investment. China's state companies have also acquired good expertise in project management and infrastructure development across the globe, thus execution is at a fast pace. How far this is sustainable in terms of human rights and ecology however remains to be seen.

CHINESE DEVELOPMENT IN TIBET

Contrary to the developments in Xinjiang, where the Chinese marched in their Construction Corps in the wake of the People's

Liberation Army (PLA), progress in Tibet has been relatively slower. This was undertaken in the 1950s with the main emphasis on rural development and primary infrastructure. There was also progress in the hydropower sector with Yamzho Yumco Hydropower Station, the Oiga One-Stage Hydropower Station, and the Mainla Water Control Project starting during these periods to increase installed capacity by 150,000 KW.[4] From the 1980s, gradual plans for extension of infrastructure in Tibet were undertaken to include 43 major projects including the Yanghu Hydroelectric Plant and the Gonggar Airport near Lhasa. Development progressed faster in the 1990s. 30 billion Yuan were invested by the Central Government towards the Three Rivers project and infrastructural development. In 2005 to mark the 40th anniversary of the founding of the Tibet Autonomous Region (TAR), 24 development projects were undertaken to include investments of over six billion Yuan in renovation and construction of infrastructure.[5]

The Eighth and Ninth Five Year Plans (1991–95 and 96–2000) saw allotment of 5 billion Yuan for development of the Three-river projects, these being the Yarlung Zangbo [Brahmaputra in India], Lhasa and Nyangqu Rivers which covered a total area of 65,700 sq kms. 40 construction projects and development of 100,000 hectares of cultivated land which is 45 per cent of Tibetan area was undertaken. 4.5 million hectares of grassland were also included in this plan.[6]

The Tenth and Eleventh Five Year plans (2001–2005 and 2006–2010) saw extensive development of road and rail infrastructure including the Qinghai Lhasa railway completed in 2006, apart from other projects which included telecommunications such as laying of fibre optic cables. For instance the central government earmarked 137.8 billion Yuan for 188 key infrastructure construction projects in Tibet in the 2006–2010 period. By the end of 2010, 109 of these projects had been completed and the other 79 were underway.[7] During this period Tibet had renovated 80 per cent of state highways and built blacktop roads to 54 counties, bringing the total length of roads to 58,000 kilometres.

Further impetus to development in Tibet has been given in the 12th Five Year Plan (2011-2015) under the "Go West" initiative for integration of Western provinces.[8] This Plan also includes the "South Asia Land Route", as indicated in the TAR People's Congress of January 2011.[9] The goals were approved by the 9th Tibet Autonomous Region (TAR) People's Congress in its session on 8–10 January. Most notably there were announcements relating to dual use infrastructure as well such as, "establishment of emergency relief and rescue bases, new railway projects, expressways and expansion of airports".[10] This approach indicates nominal involvement of the local government. At the same time, economic linkages and strategy are linked seamlessly by the government. Thus "Go West" and Western Development Campaign Policy provides not just an impetus to the economy but also expands connectivity to South, Central and even West Asia, though the latter linkages are presently being debated and discussed.[11]

For the 12th Plan an amount of US$ 1.98 billion has been allocated to extend the Qinghai-Tibet railway and an amount of US$ 7.5 billion has been earmarked for increasing the length of highways.[12] Announcements of investments to the tune of 138.4 billion Yuan ($21.4 billion) by 2016 in a series of infrastructure projects in Tibet have been made to include, as per Xinhua, 226 major construction projects. The total investment is likely to be 330.5 billion Yuan. A meeting of the State Council, China's cabinet, is reported to have approved these plans.[13]

The overall aim of these schemes ostensibly has been the development of Tibet. However, despite this, Tibet remains a region with the lowest per capita GDP as well as with lowest development indicators in China as would be highlighted in subsequent parts of the Paper.

INFRASTRUCTURE BUILD-UP IN TIBET

General

The key driver to any build-up in Tibet will be infrastructure development. Infrastructure can be mapped in terms of railways—single to double line, roads—highways and/or expressways, airfields and helipads, dams, power projects and power grids, fiber optical and telecommunication infrastructure, logistics nodes, oil and gas farms and staging camps and ballistic/cruise missile bases among other issues. Each of these is discussed below.

Railways

The Qinghai-Tibet Railway (QTR) which traverses a distance of 1142 kms from Golmud to Lhasa is a major achievement by Chinese engineers considering the challenges of terrain and permafrost in the region. The highest point over which the railway line passes is 5,072 metre (16,640 ft) at the Tanggula Pass in the Kunlun mountain range.[14] The QTR has been operational since July 2006. Ever since its launch the QTR has functioned continuously without a break, thereby indicating its operational stability.

The Chinese propose to extend the QTR to the border. Proposals in the 12th Plan 2011–2015 include completion of extension of the Qinghai-Lhasa railway line to Shigatse. Work on this section has already commenced and it is slated to be completed by 2015. The Lhasa-Nyingchi railway extension project is slated to commence in 2013 and is also expected to be completed within the 12th Plan period.[15] At the same time, feasibility studies on rail links between Lhasa - Chengdu and Kunming have been undertaken and there is renewed emphasis on linking Tibet with the Eastern regions. Previously Chinese authorities were not in favour of the same.

The project to extend the railway line from Hetian (Xinjiang) to Lhasa has reportedly been shelved, as it is perceived to be running along the border with India.[16] In the North, a project to link Lhasa with Urumqi through link between Golma (Qunghai) and Kurla (Xinjiang), reducing the travel distance by 1000 kms, is under consideration. The aim is apparently to integrate Tibet with the Chinese national rail network by 2020.[17]

The railway network is also planned to be extended to Dromo near Nathu La.[18] There are also plans to extend the Shigatse line to the Nepal border and to the Chumbi Valley, though so far these have not appeared in the official list and may be taken up based on the extensions during the 12th Plan in the subsequent plan periods and would have to be kept under close observation.

The QTR is a strategic game changer. In the 19th Century, Tibet was a buffer zone between British India, Chinese Qing Dynasty and Czarist Russia.[19] This perception was effectively shattered through the Chinese occupation of Tibet in 1950, and subsequent aggression against India in 1962. The QTR is an additional confirmation of the same trend. Extension of Chinese rail and road network to the border and to Kathmandu, as has been discussed from time to time, will result in overcoming the natural barrier that existed between China and India over the centuries. How feasible this is and what are the possibilities remains to be seen.

The QTR is thus a symbol of the 'Great Western Development Strategy' and is certainly a move to establish China's Great Power Status, in popular perception. QTR can also be seen as a very powerful tool to consolidate China's sovereignty over TAR.

Significantly about the same time that the railway became operational, the Chinese Ambassador in New Delhi announced that the whole of Arunachal Pradesh belonged to China. The linkage between the two is becoming very obvious.

China's plan to extend the line to Shigatse offers the dual advantage of boosting trade with Nepal as well as India and enhancing defence capability as the line is slated to be extended to Nyalam on the border with Nepal and to Dromo in the Chumbi Valley near Sikkim and Bhutan. The extension from Lhasa eastwards to Nyingchi will bring the network closer to the Indian state of Arunachal Pradesh claimed by China.[20] These plans are in the preliminary stages but their progress will have to be watched carefully.

Highways and Expressways

The total road network in Tibet was assessed to be 58,000 kms in 2010.[21] While the initial years did not see much development in linking major towns and cities, by the end of the 10th Plan, (2001–2005) about 42,700 kilometers of highway was opened to traffic.[22] This was partly a result of impetus given to Tibet as Hu Jintao took over leadership of the Communist Party.

The main highways in Tibet include Qinghai-Tibet road, a distance of 2122kms, which before QTR became operational carried over 80 per cent of goods to TAR. The Sichuan-Tibet highway links Chengdu to Lhasa over a distance of 2413 kms. This is lateral to South West China, an offshoot of the same is the Yunnan Tibet highway which links Xiaguan in Yunnan to Mangkam in Tibet with a distance of 315 km. The Xinjiang Tibet Highway is 1179 kms long and is considered to be the highest in the world as it connects Yecheng in Xining to Ngari. The Kodari road links China to Nepal and connects Lhasa to Kathmandu a distance of 736 kms.[23]

In the 12th Plan, it is proposed to increase the total road network from 58,000 to 70,000 kms and links between mainland and provinces are to be improved. There is a grand project named the "Four Hour Economic Zone" which will link five major cities—Lhasa, Xigaze (Shiagatse), NaQu(Nagchu), Shan Nan, Lin Zhi(Nying Chi) bringing these within four hour running time from Lhasa.[24] There is also a proposal for connecting all border defence posts by road. In relation to diversion of the water of the Brahmaputra, an important development is extension of the highway to Metok country which will enable transportation of heavy equipment and construction material for this project.[25] From the military point of view, while QTR provides strategic mobility, the highways and expressways as well as the border roads extend operational and tactical capabilities.

Oil and Gas

Simultaneous with the completion of the railway and road infrastructure, the Chinese are building and linking Qinghai oil and gas field with Lhasa with a gas/oil pipe line which is proposed in the 12th Plan.[26] A project known as the Lhasa Railway Oil Terminal Project with an investment of 180 million Yuan and 38,000 cubic meters of storage capacity is under way. This will have an annual oil turnover of 400,000 tons which can meet Tibet's demand for refined oil products, mainly gasoline, diesel and aviation kerosene. Loading and unloading oil depots have also been planned at the Lhasa railway terminals. Constructing the Lhasa-Shigatse–Shannan pipelines and launching work on the Naqu-Changdu refined oil products pipelines is also proposed.[27] These developments will obviate the necessity for transportation of oil and gas by road and rail considerably freeing the same for other commercial goods and/or military war-waging material.

Power Projects and Dams

The Chinese penchant for large power projects is evident in the construction of 90,000 KW Yamzhong Yumco Power Storage Station which started in 1997. This was built at a cost of 2 billion

Yuan. The power generating capacity has been expanded to 500,000 KW—an increase of 150,000 KW since 2000. In addition, construction of Chalong Power Station in Nagqu has been undertaken.[28] Chinese proposals to build dams in Tibet have received considerable attention in the recent past. There is some debate on whether these are run of the river dams and how these will impact the flow of the Brahmaputra into India and Bangladesh including the plan to dam the Great Bend.

Telecommunications

Given the criticality of telecommunications as a pathway for commercial, human as well as defence interaction, this facet has also received considerable attention by the Chinese. China's Advanced Info-Optical Network (CAINONET) project aims at connecting Tibet and has seen extensive spread over a period of time.[29] Three kinds of devices have been reportedly developed for this, "optical cross-connect (OXC), optical add-drop multiplexer (OADM) and core router (CR)". 3G mobile service is now available in TAR.[30] The Optical Fibre Communications (OFC) has been laid to military installations along the borders.[31] All military supply depots (MSDs) are connected to Lhasa by radio and OFC. There is also a grand plan by the National Committee on Border and Coastal Defence (NCBD) to build a "digital great wall" of fibre optical cables in Tibet and Xinjiang to improve PLA's command control structure and communication.[32] There are plans to considerably enhance military networking capacity to include border surveillance in the years ahead.[33]

Airfield Infrastructure

The Tibetan Plateau has five functional airfields, Gonggar, Linzhi, Bangda, Heping and Gar Gunsa. Gonggar Airport in Lhasa and Bamda Airport have been upgraded. In the 12th Plan it is proposed to connect Lhasa through Tibet Airlines to all domestic and international capitals.[34] Beijing, Shanghai and Chengdu were to be linked in 2011 and Nyingchi, Shigatse and Nagqu in 2012. Expansion of Gonggar, Linzhi, Bangda, Heping and Gar Gunsa Airports has also been proposed.[35] Gonggar and Bangda airfields are to be upgraded to cater to nearly 2.1 million transients per year. A new airport is to be constructed at Nagqu at an elevation of 14,639 ft.[36]. When completed this will be the highest airport in the world. There is a plan for the construction of Emergency Relief and Rescue Bases and Common use Air, Land and Take off bases as well as Tibet Aviation fuel distribution centres.[37] All this will provide the Chinese considerable dual capacity for civilian and military uses over a period.

CHALLENGES

The Tibetan plateau faces immense challenges for construction of roads and railways. Chinese road and rail construction capacity on the other hand is well established. The Chinese do not follow the Indian Border Roads Organisation model of outsourcing work to civilian contractors or hiring local labour. The PLA or its civilian construction counterpart march in to do the needful. Extensive mechanical equipment is used and they are now planning to keep the roads open throughout the year including the vital Karakoram Highway which is closed for six months during winter.[38] Yet one should not forget the vagaries of nature, which is supreme especially in high altitude perma-frost terrain. The area is oxygen-starved at an altitude of 3,550-4,000 metres. Construction work is also challenged by geothermal fields with hot springs. Kunlun Mountains are a permafrost area and Professor Wu Chenghu of the Chinese Academy of sciences has in a study indicated that, by 2050, the Tibetan Railway could collapse due to heat generated on the Plateau.[39] Whether China will be able to conquer Mother Nature, only time will tell.

IMPACT OF BUILD-UP

General

Tibet is a vast, sparsely populated table top. TAR has a population of 3,002,166 which is 0.2 per cent of China's total population. TAR on the other hand has the second largest area among the provinces of China at 1,228,400 sq kms, or 12.75 per cent of the Chinese land mass. The population density of TAR is 2.23 persons per sq km. Notably, together with the autonomous regions of Xinjiang and Inner Mongolia, it occupies an approximate area of 42 per cent of China. Low population density and vast area renders infrastructure development in Tibet expensive in economic terms, but the strategic importance of the region has rendered this imperative.

Economic Boost to Tibet-Chinese Claims

The Chinese claim that development of infrastructure has had a major impact in Tibet which has witnessed over 12 per cent economic growth annually in the 11th Plan. Tibet's local fiscal revenue is said to have reached 12.6 billion Yuan in the 2006 – 2010 period, up by 188 per cent from 2001–2005. Tibet received 21.25 million domestic and international tourists, a 30.6 per cent increase between 2005 and 2010. Local tourism administration estimates that tourist arrivals will reach 15 million in 2015.[40]

At the same time, the Chinese emphasise plans for alternate energy development in Tibet. Utilization of solar energy saves Tibet 127,000 tons of coal, annually priced at 100 million Yuan. Tibet has implemented the Sunlight Plan for employment of solar energy since 1980. The Ngari Photo electricity plan has a total investment of 100 million Yuan. Amdo Power Station is said to be the largest photovoltaic station in China. Total capacity of solar facilities in Tibet exceeds 2 MW.[41]

In the socio-economic field however Tibet is well below the national average and figures in the last few amongst all the provinces as is evident from the details given below:-

(a) Life expectancy - 33rd - 64.37 years
(b) Human Development Index - 31st - 0.630 in 2008.
(c) Per capita GDP – 28th – USD 2497.
(d) Literacy Rate 33rd – 62 per cent.

MINERAL WEALTH OF TIBET

Development of infrastructure facilitates the harvesting of Tibet's vast mineral wealth. Sources denote 3,000 proven mineral reserves containing 102 varieties in Tibet.[42] There are other claims of 1,800 mines of 17 minerals discovered in Tibet, of which 900 mines have an estimated value of USD 80 billion in the near future including 5,000 tonnes of silver, 10 million tonnes of lead and zinc and 400 million tonnes of iron ore.[43] Norbuse Chromite Mine in Shannan contains 2,500 sq kms of chromite deposits along Pangong Tso to Nujiang River. These could be China's biggest proven chromium and copper reserves, according to figures from the regional land and resources department in Tibet. Three large iron ore deposits between 50-100 million tons and oil reserves in the region, exceeding 10 billion tons have been reported.[44] Saline minerals and lithium is said to be located in the salt lake area in the northwest.[45]

For mining, Tibet has marked nine special zones for mineral industries. There is a special economic zone centred on the Yulong Copper Mine, one of China's biggest copper mines in the eastern Qamdo Prefecture.[46] It is claimed that by 2020, the mineral industry would contribute 30 to 50 per cent of Tibet's GDP. Chinese Officials claim that, "By then, Tibet will benefit more from its own advantages."[47] Thus infrastructure development will facilitate harvesting of this vast minerals potential.

INTEGRATION IN MAINLAND AND DEMOGRAPHIC SHIFT

China's emphasis on integration of Tibet and TAR to the main land is also evident with linkages established between the institutions at the local level. Municipalities and local governments in China have been contributing to Tibetan development which has been given significant publicity in the media. Over the past five years (2005–10), Tibet is said to have received 7.57 billion Yuan of aid from inland provinces and municipalities as well as government organizations, state firms and other institutions that are ready to nurture Tibet's development. 2,661 officials and professionals from inland areas worked in Tibet for periods of one to three years during the 11th Plan period as per Chinese sources.[48]

Increasingly, the development of Tibet is being managed through local bodies. For instance, the 9th Tibet Autonomous Region (TAR) People's Congress session from 8 to 10 January 2011 announced plans for the development of infrastructure in the 12th Plan. Some of the goals announced include, "establishment of emergency relief and rescue bases, new railway projects, expressways and expansion of airports," as per a Paper by Ashok Tiku of the Chennai Centre for Studies[49].

As per estimates indicated by Dr. P. Stobdan, a noted scholar, who has extensively mapped developments in the region, since 2006, over 4000 Han Chinese are entering the Tibet Autonomous region each day which could lead to substantial growth of Han population to 20 million by 2015.[50] Thus, road and rail infrastructure is also facilitating migration Westwards under the, "Go West" strategy which has raised fears of Hanisation of Tibet much as this has happened in Xinjiang over the past six decades.

SUSTAINABLE GROWTH

A related issue is the challenge of terrain in Tibet, with an average height of 4,900 metres. This is extremely inhospitable for survival in most seasons but particularly in the winters.[51] Thus there is reverse migration during this period. It is far from certain that mainland Chinese will be able to adjust to this hostile environment.

Can the Tibetan Plateau, with its fragile ecology sustain resource exploitation and population explosion? Tibet is facing an ecological crisis in terms of deforestation, effect on grasslands, soil erosion, logging, damming of rivers, mining, decrease in the amount of frozen soil and global warming leading to ozone layer depletion.[52] Water diversion schemes, Western Route Transfer Project, a South-North Water Diversion Project, and a West - East Power Transfer Project are other major areas of concern. Environmental challenges due to permafrost in the area of Kunlun by 2050 and beyond have their own impact. Can the Tibetan Plateau with a fragile ecology sustain large-scale infrastructure development and population explosion? It is one thing to carry out a demographic shift to regions as Xinjiang which has a far larger expanse in terms of area, is less ecologically sensitive and can sustain more numbers but Tibet has its own challenges.

IMPACT ON PLA MILITARY CAPACITY

Tibet is divided between the Chengdu and the Lanzhou Military Regions. The 13 and 14 Group Armies form a part of the Chengdu Military Region. As per noted Indian scholar on China's military, Professor Srikanth Kondapalli, PLA soldiers of Chengdu Military region are known as, "monkey" troops, implying good mountain warfare capability.[53] A US Department of Defence Report on the PLA 2011 indicates the role of the Two Group Armies of the Chengdu Military Region as offensive and defensive in nature in a complex terrain in high altitude. In addition, 13 Group Army is designated as the Rapid Reaction Force (RRF). The Lanzhou Military Region which is responsible for Western Tibet has 47 and 21 Group Armies with a similar role of offensive and defensive operations in high altitude terrain. In addition, 21 Group Army is designated as an offensive mobile force.

The Tibet military district as part of the Chengdu Military Region has nearly 40,000 troops.[54] QTR has reduced the travelling time for troops from Golmud to Lhasa from approximately 72 hours to 16 hours. 75 per cent of cargo also goes via the railway link. PLA has been stating that the railway would become "a main option" for transporting soldiers as well. A large number of military camps have reportedly come up in the region as observed through satellite imagery after development of infrastructure. Additional logistics nodes are also established for supply of ammunition. Road infrastructure has a combined capacity of 1,15,000 metric tonnes facilitating easy and swift movement of men, war-like material and equipment.[55]

Through development of infrastructure, 30 regiments of PLA stationed at Golmud can use the railway line and reach Lhasa while the Chengdu - Lhasa line can bring in five more PLA divisions to the border. Transfer of 12 divisions in 30 days is now possible with pre-positioned equipment as per some estimates.[56] PLA has also developed the capability to mobilise a Rapid Reaction Division into Lhasa within a period of 24-36 hours by a combination of rail and road movement.[57] Some estimates indicate that 30-plus divisions can be moved in one campaigning season to TAR. However, with a total of 54 divisions, will the Chinese risk putting over 50 per cent of their force in Tibet? This is open to debate, particularly when the high altitude and mountainous terrain is not suitable for employment of much of this force which is composed of mechanized forces.

Second Artillery

The Chinese have also inducted solid fuel medium range ballistic missile DF-21 (single warhead of 200-300 kilo-tons yield), which can engage targets at a distance of 2,150 kilometres in Tibet. This has also been confirmed in the 2011 Pentagon Report on China. A number of sites have reportedly been prepared at Delingha in Haixi Mongol and Tibetan Autonomous Prefecture in Qinghai, thus bringing Delhi within the 2,000 kms range of 812 Brigade of the Second Artillery Corps as per some estimates.[58] 58 launch pads and command and control facilities spread over a 2,000 sq kms deployed in the northern parts of Qinghai province on the Tibetan plateau were recently made public.[59] As per Dr P Stobdan, the missile launch brigades in Tibet include, "Da Tsaidam 412 Brigade; the Datung - Wulan 408 Brigade; the 9th Academy (Factory 211) in Amdo area; an Anti-frigate Missile Centre at Drotsang; a Missile launch site at Terlingka; a new site launch site in Amdo; bases at Risur in Nagchuka; and bases at Tago Mountain. There is also an underground site at Lhasa and Kangpo".[60] This will imply considerable enhancement of missile launch capability well forward in the Tibetan Plateau.

People's Liberation Army Air Force (PLAAF)

The most significant capability accretion through infrastructure development has been for the PLAAF. PLAAF has now a capability of airlifting a division, air drop a brigade and helicopter lifts of approximately two battalions. Su-27s are also being deployed in the Chengdu MR and in Tibet for short durations from other airbases. Frequent exercises including heli-drop have been reported. With 27 military airstrips in Tibet, the PLAAF ability to operate has been considerably enhanced. However, due to the effect of the high altitude terrain, the load carriage capacity will remain limited but this may be offset by operating from bases in Yunnan.[61]

Nagqu Logistics Centre

The Chinese are also developing a logistics centre at the Nagqu Township which can handle 2.23 million tonnes of cargo by 2015 and 3.1 million tonnes by 2020. This is located approximately

300 km northeast of Lhasa, at a cost of approximately Yuan 1.5 billion (US $ 220 million).[62] The oil and gas pipelines will also have a disbursal terminal at Nagqu with a new airfield and located on the main QTR as well as road highway. This logistics centre will facilitate placing of sufficient logistics in TAR for a campaigning season south of the Kunlun Mountains.

EFFECTS OF MILITARY CAPABILITY ENHANCEMENT

Development of infrastructure in TAR has enhanced mobilization capability of the PLA in three dimensions, time, space and forces that can be deployed. Combined with fast track modernisation with emphasis on Jointness and Informationisation, this has led to considerable capacity accretion which will also contribute to strategic surprise and deception. All this will provide the PLA ability to develop full spectrum operations employing land, air and Second Artillery forces despite the challenge of high altitude operations particularly for the PLAAF. Operations can now be undertaken at short notice, if need be, thereby definitely indicating the need for a higher level of preparedness on the Indian side. The PLA is *well poised* to conduct operations for sustained periods.

More importantly, the gap in military capabilities between India and China has expanded in absolute terms. This capability differential therefore needs to be critically evaluated and remedial actions taken. Under the circumstances, the PLA moving from a "self-defence counter-attack" perspective of 1962 to launching a major offensive extended over a prolonged period, to settle their border claims and humble India, is very much a live possibility and needs to be taken into reckoning by the national leadership and military hierarchy in India.

There is no doubt that the Chinese build-up will remain somewhat vulnerable as Tibet is an open flat table top without cover. Air and Missile forces will be able to play a major role in causing heavy casualties on the plateau. Some opine that troop ratios could be somewhat unfavorable for an offensive in the mountains but that is not likely to be the case and hence the Chinese capability for an offensive operation needs to be viewed seriously.

Thus, there is no gainsaying that infrastructure development in Tibet by the Chinese has considerably weakened India's dissuasive posture vis-à-vis China. This will have an impact on the larger strategic equation as well, and may tempt Beijing into exploiting this at a suitable opportunity in the near future unless India undertakes rapid capacity building to make up some of the operational deficiencies. As the strategic maxim goes, while military capability is finite, intent is determined by a variety of unpredictable strategic factors and is subject to change. Presuming that China does not have an offensive intent against India would be strategic imprudence on the part of the Indian leadership, particularly given the wide disparity in capability and a Two Front War scenario, involving Pakistan as well.

IMPLICATIONS AND OPTIONS FOR INDIA

Implications for India

Given the unsolved boundary dispute, there is likely to be an increase in mistrust due to expansion of capability for rapid deployment of military assets on the part of the Chinese. This will create a scenario which will place Indian forces at a relative disadvantage along the Northern borders especially in case of a Two Front War. Clearly after development of the QTR, the Chinese leadership has become more aggressive in articulating their claims to Arunachal Pradesh. The audacity of such an attitude is apparent from the manner in which they have decried the visit of the Indian Defence Minister to Arunachal Pradesh. The changing demographic pattern in Tibet could result in breaking the traditional cultural link between India and Tibet, which has to be preserved. The attendant challenges to India's water and ecological security due to the changes on the Tibetan Plateau also need to be flagged.

Indian Plans

Alarmed by the development of infrastructure in Tibet, India is now planning to build 558 roads at a cost of Rs 500 billion along the border. 27,986 kms of road infrastructure is likely to be completed by 2030 in a phased manner. In the first phase, 277 road projects have been earmarked to be completed at a cost of Rs 248.86 billion with a length of 13,100 kms. The Border Roads Organisation has already moved 46 units to Arunachal Pradesh, 21 units to Sikkim, 33 units to Uttarakhand, seven units to Himachal Pradesh and 61 units to Jammu and Kashmir for the purpose of developing border infrastructure.[63] ALGs like Pasighat, Mechuka, Walong, Tuting, Ziro and Vijaynagar are being upgraded. In the western sector, Daulat Beg Oldi, Fukche and Nyama in Eastern Ladakh have been developed. However, the Central Sector in Uttarakhand and Himachal Pradesh continues to remain neglected with lack of roads and airfields. However, speed is of the essence, since we have been planning to upgrade the roads and other infrastructure since the early 1950s.

While there is a debate on the possibility of water and ecological challenges due to Chinese activities of development including dam construction in TAR, moves to establish a co-operative framework with the Chinese have not been undertaken as Beijing has not been very encouraging in this sphere.

India's Options

Traditionally and geographically, Tibet has served the role of providing a buffer between India and China. It is in our interest that this status remains intact. Everyone in the entire region is very concerned with the Chinese policy and attitude of unilaterally trying to alter the status of even the regional commons like the use of water by way of making plans for dams and effort on changing the course of rivers. In our own case, we can ill-afford to overlook the reality of them having invaded us in 1962 and still being in possession of large chunks of our territory. We also need to take counsel of the age old dictum that "friendship is possible only amongst equals". Therefore, sound military preparedness, removing not only deficiencies in our dissuasive posture but developing a suitable deterrence along our Northern borders becomes a national imperative.

Thus there is a need for undertaking measures to develop infrastructure and military capability to ensure that as a starter the gap in India's dissuasive capabilities vis-à-vis China are reduced. This can be then raised to a level of deterrence in a phased manner in the medium term. For this, force accretion and military modernization is essential. Manoeuvre and fire power will be the main modes of successful war fighting on the India-China border and the Tibetan Plateau. Joint capability accretions will have to be directed in these dimensions in the armed forces.

The present model of infrastructure development and military modernisation has not produced results. Reviewing the same is therefore essential and the seminar held by the Vivekananda International Foundation (VIF) on Defense Vision has provided a large number of options, inputs from which could denote the way ahead. There is also a necessity for expanding road construction capability of the Border Roads in terms of technology as well as capability and also reviewing its model of contracting.

At the same time, India will have to employ the instruments of eco-politics, hydro-politics, human rights, and so on, to flag the hazards emanating from the shifting dynamics in Tibet.

Establishing strategic partnerships with countries impacted by Chinese expansion; be it in fields of water, ecology or military is important. India is already developing its relations with the United States, Japan and ASEAN countries to hedge against the threat from China. Realistically, though, we shall need to be ready to stand alone, for it is unlikely that any other country will come to our assistance through military action.

Finally, sustaining support to the Tibetan people's cause for freedom, equality and justice has to be the long-term vision for the bonds which have existed over centuries and need to be sustained for the future. This is not just in the interest of the people of Tibet and India but also for China, as this will provide Beijing long-term stability.

CONCLUSION

Rising powers tend to clash over issues of unsettled boundaries, sovereignty and disputed legacy. India and China have seen centuries of peace disturbed in the past few decades. The constraints of natural barriers of the Himalayas have now been removed through greater human capacity in developing infrastructure. This will increase the danger of conflict. It is now up to the leadership of these two great powers to act peacefully through mutual accommodation, or risk an unwanted contest over issues of territory, sovereignty and resources. The people of Tibet have been a singular example of peace and harmony in the modern world by drawing inspiration from their philosophy, and their sense of dignity and fairness. India and China could work to mutual advantage in the years ahead while meeting aspirations of the Tibetan people for freedom/ full autonomy in their own land.

Recent trends however denote a degree of bellicosity in China's posture in concert with growing strategic congruence with Pakistan. This could manifest itself in an open conflict in the short term, unless there is a radical change of perception in Beijing. India cannot afford to be ill-prepared for an unfavorable scenario developing along its northern borders and thus political resolve, diplomatic dexterity and sound military preparedness remain the way ahead

ENDNOTES

1. *The Economist.* Everyone else is worried. The Economist Report. Oct 7th 2010.
2. David Leonhardt. In China, Cultivating the Urge to Splurge. http://www.nytimes.com/2010/11/28/magazine/28China-t.html
3. China's savings rate to drop in coming decade: Research. http://articles.economictimes.indiatimes.com/2010-08-09/news/27577996_1_savings-rate-high-savings-chinese-researchers
4. China - SEMINAR REPORT. #190, 2 August 2006. IPCS New Delhi. http://www.ipcs.org/seminar/china/tibet-connectivity-capabilities-and-consequences-749.html
5. China - SEMINAR REPORT. #190, 2 August 2006. IPCS New Delhi. http://www.ipcs.org/seminar/china/tibet-connectivity-capabilities-and-consequences-749.html
6. Implications of Infrastructure Development in Tibet Centre for Land Warfare Studies Seminar Report. 29 July 2010. http://www.claws.in/index.php?action=master&task=612&u_id=36
7. Figures tell Tibet's development in five years. Jan. 16 2011. Xinhua. http://news.xinhuanet.com/english2010/china/2011-01/16/c_13693159.htm
8. Ashok Tiku, C3S Paper No 785 dated May 14, 2011. http://www.c3sindia.org/india/2320
9. Ashok Tiku, C3S Paper No 785 dated May 14, 2011. http://www.c3sindia.org/india/2320
10. Ashok Tiku, C3S Paper No 760 dated March 17, 2011. http://www.c3sindia.org/tibet/2212
11. Implications of Infrastructure Development in Tibet Centre for Land Warfare Studies Seminar Report. 29 July 2010. http://www.claws.in/index.php?action=master&task=612&u_id=36.

12. Ashok Tiku, C3S Paper No 785 dated May 14, 2011. http://www.c3sindia.org/india/2320
13. China to invest $21 bln in Tibet projects – Xinhua. Reuters Report 20 July 2011.
14. China - SEMINAR REPORT. #190, 2 August 2006. IPCS New Delhi. http://www.ipcs.org/seminar/china/tibet-connectivity-capabilities-and-consequences-749.html
15. Ashok Tiku, C3S Paper No 785 dated May 14, 2011. http://www.c3sindia.org/india/2320
16. Ashok Tiku, C3S Paper No 785 dated May 14, 2011. http://www.c3sindia.org/india/2320
17. Implications of Infrastructure Development in Tibet Centre for Land Warfare Studies Seminar Report. 29 July 2010. http://www.claws.in/index.php?action=master&task=612&u_id=36.
18. Implications of Infrastructure Development in Tibet Centre for Land Warfare Studies Seminar Report. 29 July 2010. http://www.claws.in/index.php?action=master&task=612&u_id=36.
19. China - SEMINAR REPORT. #190, 2 August 2006. IPCS New Delhi. http://www.ipcs.org/seminar/china/tibet-connectivity-capabilities-and-consequences-749.html
20. Everyone else is worried. The Economist Report. Oct 7th 2010.
21. Ashok Tiku, C3S Paper No 785 dated May 14, 2011. http://www.c3sindia.org/india/2320
22. Implications of Infrastructure Development in Tibet Centre for Land Warfare Studies Seminar Report. 29 July 2010. http://www.claws.in/index.php?action=master&task=612&u_id=36.
23. China - SEMINAR REPORT. #190, 2 August 2006. IPCS New Delhi. http://www.ipcs.org/seminar/china/tibet-connectivity-capabilities-and-consequences-749.html
24. Ashok Tiku, C3S Paper No 785 dated May 14, 2011. http://www.c3sindia.org/india/2320
25. Figures tell Tibet's development in five years. Jan. 16 2011. Xinhua. http://news.xinhuanet.com/english2010/china/2011-01/16/c_13693159.htm
26. Ashok Tiku, C3S Paper No 785 dated May 14, 2011. http://www.c3sindia.org/india/2320

27. Ashok Tiku, C3S Paper No 785 dated May 14, 2011. http://www.c3sindia.org/india/2320
28. Implications of Infrastructure Development in Tibet Centre for Land Warfare Studies Seminar Report. 29 July 2010. http://www.claws.in/index.php?action=master&task=612&u_id=36.
29. Implications of Infrastructure Development in Tibet Centre for Land Warfare Studies Seminar Report. 29 July 2010. http://www.claws.in/index.php?action=master&task=612&u_id=36.
30. Shailender Arya, "Infrastructure Development and Chinese War Waging Capabilities in Tibet". *Journal of Defence Studies*, Vol 5, No 3. July 2011. IDSA Publication. IDSA. New Delhi
31. Implications of Infrastructure Development in Tibet Centre for Land Warfare Studies Seminar Report. 29 July 2010. http://www.claws.in/index.php?action=master&task=612&u_id=36.
32. Shailender Arya, "Infrastructure Development and Chinese War Waging Capabilities in Tibet". *Journal of Defence Studies*, Vol 5. No 3. July 2011. IDSA Publication. IDSA. New Delhi
33. Shailender Arya, "Infrastructure Development and Chinese War Waging Capabilities in Tibet". *Journal of Defence Studies*. Vol 5. No 3. July 2011. IDSA Publication. IDSA. New Delhi
34. Ashok Tiku, C3S Paper No 785 dated May 14, 2011. http://www.c3sindia.org/india/2320
35. Ashok Tiku, C3S Paper No 785 dated May 14, 2011. http://www.c3sindia.org/india/2320
36. Implications of Infrastructure Development in Tibet Centre for Land Warfare Studies Seminar Report. 29 July 2010. http://www.claws.in/index.php?action=master&task=612&u_id=36.
37. Ashok Tiku, C3S Paper No 785 dated May 14, 2011. http://www.c3sindia.org/india/2320
38. China - SEMINAR REPORT. #190, 2 August 2006. IPCS New Delhi. http://www.ipcs.org/seminar/china/tibet-connectivity-capabilities-and-consequences-749.html
39. China - SEMINAR REPORT. #190, 2 August 2006. IPCS New Delhi. http://www.ipcs.org/seminar/china/tibet-connectivity-capabilities-and-consequences-749.html

40. Figures tell Tibet's development in five years. Jan. 16 2011. Xinhua. http://news.xinhuanet.com/english2010/china/2011-01/16/c_13693159.htm
41 China - SEMINAR REPORT. #190, 2 August 2006. IPCS New Delhi. http://www.ipcs.org/seminar/china/tibet-connectivity-capabilities-and-consequences-749.html
42. Tibet to step up exploitation of mineral resources. http://en.ce.cn/National/Local/201003/13/t20100313_21114321.shtml
43. China - SEMINAR REPORT. #190, 2 August 2006. IPCS New Delhi. http://www.ipcs.org/seminar/china/tibet-connectivity-capabilities-and-consequences-749.html
44. China - SEMINAR REPORT. #190, 2 August 2006. IPCS New Delhi. http://www.ipcs.org/seminar/china/tibet-connectivity-capabilities-and-consequences-749.html
45. Implications of Infrastructure Development in Tibet Centre for Land Warfare Studies Seminar Report. 29 July 2010. http://www.claws.in/index.php?action=master&task=612&u_id=36.
46. Tibet to step up exploitation of mineral resources. http://en.ce.cn/National/Local/201003/13/t20100313_21114321.shtml
47. Tibet to step up exploitation of mineral resources. http://en.ce.cn/National/Local/201003/13/t20100313_21114321.shtml
48. Figures tell Tibet's development in five years. Jan. 16 2011. Xinhua. http://news.xinhuanet.com/english2010/china/2011-01/16/c_13693159.htm
49. Ashok Tiku, C3S Paper No 785 dated May 14, 2011. http://www.c3sindia.org/india/2320
50. China - SEMINAR REPORT. #190, 2 August 2006. IPCS New Delhi. http://www.ipcs.org/seminar/china/tibet-connectivity-capabilities-and-consequences-749.html
51. Implications of Infrastructure Development in Tibet Centre for Land Warfare Studies Seminar Report.
52. China - SEMINAR REPORT. #190, 2 August 2006. IPCS New Delhi. http://www.ipcs.org/seminar/china/tibet-connectivity-capabilities-and-consequences-749.html
53. China - SEMINAR REPORT. #190, 2 August 2006. IPCS New Delhi. http://www.ipcs.org/seminar/china/tibet-connectivity-capabilities-and-consequences-749.html

54. Implications of Infrastructure Development in Tibet Centre for Land Warfare Studies Seminar Report. 29 July 2010. http://www.claws.in/index.php?action=master&task=612&u_id=36.
55. Implications of Infrastructure Development in Tibet Centre for Land Warfare Studies Seminar Report. 29 July 2010. http://www.claws.in/index.php?action=master&task=612&u_id=36.
56. China - SEMINAR REPORT. #190, 2 August 2006. IPCS New Delhi. http://www.ipcs.org/seminar/china/tibet-connectivity-capabilities-and-consequences-749.html
57. Implications of Infrastructure Development in Tibet Centre for Land Warfare Studies Seminar Report. 29 July 2010. http://www.claws.in/index.php?action=master&task=612&u_id=36.
58. Sakhuja quoted in Shailender Arya, "Infrastructure Development and Chinese War Waging Capabilities in Tibet". *Journal of Defence Studies*, Vol 5, No 3. July 2011. IDSA Publication. IDSA. New Delhi
59. Sakhuja quoted in Shailender Arya, "Infrastructure Development and Chinese War Waging Capabilities in Tibet". *Journal of Defence Studies*, Vol 5. No 3. July 2011. IDSA Publication. IDSA. New Delhi
60. China - SEMINAR REPORT. #190, 2 August 2006. IPCS New Delhi. http://www.ipcs.org/seminar/china/tibet-connectivity-capabilities-and-consequences-749.html
61. Shailender Arya, "Infrastructure Development and Chinese War Waging Capabilities in Tibet". *Journal of Defence Studies*, Vol 5, No 3. July 2011. IDSA Publication. IDSA. New Delhi
62. Shailender Arya, "Infrastructure Development and Chinese War Waging Capabilities in Tibet". *Journal of Defence Studies*, Vol 5, No 3. July 2011. IDSA Publication. IDSA. New Delhi
63. India plans major road projects on China, Pak borders. Rediff.com report. March 29, 2011. http://www.rediff.com/news/report/the-great-india-china-road-race/20110329.htm

8

India's Approach to the Tibetan Issue

Madhu Bhalla

As Tibet goes through another phase of domestic opposition to Beijing's control together with the Tibetan call for "genuine autonomy" at a significant post- Dalai Lama leadership shift, the issue of Tibet should be of wider concern within India. India's persistent problem on the India-China border, and its strategic fallouts in the China-Pakistan relationship, locates Tibet as the lynchpin in the strategic calculus of South Asia. Yet, because Tibet is now considered China's domestic concern—although it has external dimensions because of the political organization of the Tibetan Diaspora and the steady rise of the global human rights discourse—it has become increasingly difficult to bring any discussion of Tibet's strategic importance to South Asia and India, in particular, to centre stage in India, although not in China.[1] The time may, however, have come to deal with the centrality of Tibet in the India-China relationship. For India, in particular, there is need to define what, if anything, has changed in its perspective on Tibet and whether, in fact, the Chinese perspective of the centrality of Tibet in India-China relations needs to be addressed and policy options reassessed.

THE TIBET ISSUE IN THE GLOBAL CONTEXT

While Tibet is of central strategic significance to Indian security New Delhi has been influenced by a mix of pragmatic constraints and regional and global disincentives from which it is hard to extricate the issue of Tibet. The issue of Tibet is a perennial one that has seldom gained sustained global attention. China's rise explains partly why this is so, but it is not the only reason why governments and global governance institutions fight shy of taking the issue beyond cautiously worded admonitions and sporadic talk of human rights excesses.

Any effort to open a strategic dialogue over Tibet must contend with three factors that weigh against doing this. The first is the weakness of the global human rights regime which has been less than consistent in its attention to Tibet. Contesting definitions of human rights have allowed the regime to be effectively ignored and weakened. In addition, there has often been a selective use of pressure to ensure human rights, generally in keeping with strategic priorities. Thus, the case for human rights in Tibet was rarely made during the first two decades of the Cold War since Western strategic objectives were clearly focused on the erstwhile Soviet Union. Chinese isolationism and internal problems made China less threatening as a socialist state with, therefore, fewer incentives to focus on China's human rights record in Tibet. In the 1970s and 1980s, there was a convergence of Chinese and American strategic objectives against the Soviet Union when China's domestic political record was again ignored, with the western human rights agenda focused almost entirely on the Soviet Union. After the end of the Cold War, attention shifted to China's human rights record, especially after Tiananmen, but was short-lived. Economic sanctions against the PRC were effectively lifted within two years. However, the neoliberal argument for the emergence of democracy in China after its economic opening up ensured that China's democracy movement dissidents continued after Tiananmen to raise support on the basis of China's human rights repressions in relation to rights to free speech. Calls for democracy within China resonated with universal Western values. Tibetan dissidents were rarely that lucky when pressing for rights to self-determination or to autonomy. Hence major Western powers raised the issue of human rights in China more strongly when Beijing cracked down on democracy dissidents rather than on human rights abuses in Tibet. The Tibetan demand for autonomy was regarded as an internal matter which China was urged to resolve but without the threat of any serious sanctions or repercussions. Thus, Tibet was placed on the summit agenda between Bill Clinton and Jiang Zemin in 1998, yet four years later the US State Department acknowledged that little progress had been made on Tibet and that human rights excesses were an obstacle to fuller engagement with China.[2] After the People's Republic of China's (PRC) entry into the WTO, when its trade with the US could no longer be held hostage to the US Congress's annual review of its human rights record the last effective pressure to ensure some modicum of human rights within China ceased. In many ways China's Olympic Games triumph was a global recognition of the dangers inherent in pushing the human rights issue in Tibet to the foreground.

While strategic and economic interests overtook commitments to human rights in the West, within the non-Western world the human rights regime has been weakened by both its selective functioning and the argument for culturally specific notions of human rights. China was at the forefront of this argument with its White Papers on Human Rights arguing for community and economic rights over individual rights.[3] In the post 9/11 climate the US argument was irrevocably tarnished by Abu Ghraib and Guantanamo. In response to US reports of human rights excesses in China, the Chinese government has brought out successive rejoinders on human rights abuses in the US where the PRC's measure of human rights is to "protect the people's right to subsistence and improve their living conditions" as defined in successive Chinese White Papers on human rights.[4] China also translates rights in terms of power and, therefore, "human rights" as *renquan*, or "human power", which could become a domestic threat by contesting the political hold of the Chinese Communist Party and threaten the regime. As well it views the western human rights discourse as a neo-colonial threat to its stability, allowing it to dismiss human rights excesses at home.[5] In the wake of the 2008 global economic downturn, the argument for the right to subsistence and work has only gained greater currency. A significant corollary has been the celebration of the *China Model* of development and growth in which political stability is viewed as essential to the livelihood of the people.[6]

Secondly, since 9/11 and the "war on terror" China has had ample opportunity to indict movements for autonomy in its minority provinces as terrorist activities. This has been particularly true of Xinjiang where the Uighur separatist movement was quickly linked to Islamic movements elsewhere and China persuaded the US to place its chief organization, the East Turkestan Islamic Movement (ETIM), on its official list of international terrorist organizations.[7]

When the Tibetan protests gained support in the run up to the 2008 Beijing Olympics, the Tibetan movement began to be termed terrorist as well.[8]

Beijing's view that separatism is one of the "three evils", the other two of which are terrorism and religious fundamentalism, has often meant that all three are subject to the same policies of repressive and coercive police action, or hitting hard (*yan da*). When separatism is linked to religious groups it becomes an even more dangerous challenge to regime stability and requires extreme denunciations and repression. Thus, the barrage of abuse heaped on the Dalai Lama in official Chinese pronouncements and in the Chinese media as well as the excessive force used against protestors in 2008 in Tibet is justified within China as a response to acts of separatism which are interlinked with terrorism. China's acute sense of threats to regime security and hence to the state have made terrorism a part of internal security concerns. In what Fei-Ling Wang terms "Beijing's incentive structure", preservation of the political structure of the Chinese Communist Party (CCP) has motivated China to view the "war on terror" as a strategic opportunity to focus on a strategy for stability by 2020.[9] As a rising power in a period of US decline, Chinese nationalism makes China more assertive, not less, on issues of national integrity and security.[10] Hence, there is little, if any, debate within China on the definition of terrorism and what acts may be defined as terrorist ones, given the overwhelming focus on regime stability.[11]

As with acts of terror in Xinjiang, separatism is also seen as part of a colonial plan to dismember the state. While China is now well past its diatribe on righting the "century of humiliation" and viewing itself as a victim, its leaders still speak of the issues emerging from the "leftovers of history", the unequal colonial treaties, from that century. As such, China's recent experience of "terrorism" is cast within a historiography that privileges a narrative of challenges to the Chinese state from outside.[12] As Chien-peng Chung argues, ethnic autonomy movements and religious groups in the three restive provinces of Xinjiang, Tibet and Inner Mongolia are now routinely termed as terrorist challenges to regime security.[13]

This places constraints on the state and separatist groups while at the same time pushing them towards hard line policies. Neither the state nor separatist groups can afford to be seen as doing too much or too little. "For Beijing, playing up the issue would discourage foreign trade and investments in Xinjiang or Tibet, but playing it down would deprive the authorities of excuses to initiate actions against separatists and religious radicals. For the émigré activists, the problem is either discrediting their cause by associating it with terrorism, or demonstrating their hopeless lack of influence in rousing their fellow minorities in China."[14]

Thirdly, China's linking of "terrorism" to its sovereignty and territorial integrity also precludes foreign intervention in situations in Tibet or Xinjiang. The association of separatism with terrorism has meant that China's policies are taken as domestic issues. The reiteration by world leaders that Tibet is a part of China is intended to drive home the point that China will not tolerate any discussion of Tibet by outside powers. In an era where the doctrine of the "responsibility to protect" and "humanitarian intervention" has been used elsewhere, China remains immune to this threat. This has led to China's almost complete repression of the movement in Tibet—the recent immolations by Tibetan monks in neighbouring provinces being a desperate bid to break through the wall of silence—taking Tibet out of the focus of international concern.

The reluctance of foreign powers to separate movements for cultural autonomy from terrorism in China also shows up the strength and fragility of economic globalization. China's ability to use its economic clout to elicit positive behaviour from foreign governments was evident recently with Japan when it used its economic clout to shut down the export of rare earth materials for Japan's electronics industry over the arrest of the captain of a Chinese ship.[15] China's more globalised economy gives it the strength to fashion the debate on Tibet and the world's dependence on China in a global economy makes for a fragility and vulnerability that plays into the Chinese interpretation of the Tibetan issue.[16]

Yet, China's ability to manage situations like the one in Tibet are limited, especially if by labeling them as terrorist China absolves itself from dealing with the cultural, social and religious aspirations of the people. China's successive White Papers on Tibet have consistently refused to define the problem as anything but an effort by feudal forces to set back the revolutionary modernization of Tibet.[17] The doctrinaire Marxist analysis in the White Papers stands out in stark contrast to the market ethos of China's economy and the pragmatic, non-ideological rationale for the rest of China. However, it does echo the recent debates within the Chinese Communist Party on the *China Model* which view China's economic growth as dependent on its one party political system, the ideology of Marxism and the leadership of the Party. The resurgence of Marxism in inner Party debates is intended to shore up the Party's declining legitimacy after a difficult decade of criticisms of the social, economic and political fallout of rapid economic growth but also to provide a rationale for continuing a political system which is beset by a crisis of governance and by criticism of authoritarianism from within China and abroad as well. The outpouring of writing on the China Model within China can be read as an orchestrated effort to justify the present political system. Thus, Chen Jinhua's exposition of the China Model argues that China's success lies in following Marxism which provides the analytical framework for policy, the ability of the CCP leadership to mobilize and use resources effectively, the policy of freeing the "enterprising spirit of the people", and a democratic and legal system "suited to the conditions of the country" which maintains a balance between the Party, the people and the state. Other arguments for the Chinese Model have been made explicitly to rebut "the false call for democratizing 'authoritarian' states".[18] This at once positions the issue of minority rights, human rights and calls for autonomy within the ambit of domestic debate and action and a warning to critics from abroad.

Hence, since 2010 cautious suggestions by world leaders to revive the dialogue with the Dalai Lama have so far been ignored by Beijing. The series of talks between the Dalai Lama's representatives and Beijing have stalled ostensibly on Beijing's insistence that the aspirations of ethnic minorities must not go against the general direction of the country. The current direction of the Chinese state is set by an often shrill nationalism that conflates the unity of the Chinese state with China's rise to great power status. This brooks no obstacle such as the demand for ethnic political and cultural rights. The PRC's ability to manage dissent through coercive means, its view of Tibetan dissent as an issue of economic backwardness, the anticipation of the Dalai Lama's demise and the fragmentation of the Tibetan movement also add to the opposition to restarting the dialogue and fashion Beijing's response to demands for a resolution of the issue. [19] Clearly, "genuine autonomy" for Tibet is pitted against a view of the Chinese nation where federalist notions of the devolution of power are clearly unacceptable for provinces on China's unstable periphery. Ironically, this is a view that is beginning to be contested within China's heartland and is also at variance with the "two systems one country" approach which Beijing took with Hong Kong and espouses for Taiwan as well.[20]

INDIA, CHINA AND TIBET

On Tibet, India has found itself in an ambiguous position. Like the rest of the world, India has been no less susceptible to the context of the Tibet issue. As a post-colonial nation, the principle of territorial integrity, sovereignty and the issue of unequal treaties have resonated well within its broad foreign policy principles since 1947. These are all issues China has consistently linked to the Tibet issue. Yet, treaties as international law have also held some sanctity for India's policy-makers as the discussions before the 1962 India-China border war indicated.[21]

Since India's acceptance of the "One China" policy and the status of Tibet within China in 1954, the Tibet issue has been primarily viewed as a human rights issue by some groups in India, although the acceptance of Tibet as a domestic issue within China precludes any support for anti-sovereignty policies like "humanitarian intervention". India's own position in the UN Human Rights Commission has been opposed to allegations of human rights violations within India at the forum, especially when they have been linked to Kashmir. Here India and China have often found themselves on the same side in defending state policies in restive provinces. India has also viewed the uses and misuses of human rights positions by major Western states with misgiving, despite being a signatory to the Human Rights Convention. While India has active human rights institutions, in its current state of development the definition of human rights has been stretched to cover many of the developmental issues that underlie endemic poverty.[22] Hence, the opposition to China's "yan da" policies in Tibet has been limited and weak at best. At the level of the Indian state it translates into giving refuge to Tibetan émigrés.

China's linkage of separatism to terrorism creates difficulties of a peculiar kind for India since India's view on terrorism has changed in the last few years. From considering terrorism as a cross-border phenomenon, it is now confronted by a home-grown variety as well. Therefore, China's linkage between separatism and terrorism does not seem as unlikely as it would have even a decade ago. Yet, observers in India also make a distinction between the peaceful protests of Tibetan monks and Tibetan demonstrators and groups that use violent means and are linked to internationally recognized terrorist groups.[23] While India has dropped the reference to "Tibet as an *autonomous* part of the territory of China" from its statements with Chinese leaders, China's harsh opposition to the Dalai Lama's demand for "genuine autonomy" runs counter to its own principles where demands for cultural autonomy and demands for statehood on linguistic principles have been accommodated within the Indian state.

Finally, the economic rise of China has India in its thrall as it does the rest of the world. China is now India's foremost trading partner. While India is not as embedded in the Chinese economy in ways in which the US is, the India-China strategic economic dialogue which began in 2011 seeks to put economic relations on fast track for both countries.[24] For a trade averse nation, a targeted USD 100 billion trade with China has been a significant advance for India and domestic industry is seeking outward investments in the Chinese market. The contraction of investment in China as a result of the economic downturn and Europe's problems provides an opportunity to Indian entrepreneurs. Regionally and globally China's economic rise gives it increasing influence in financial and economic organizations and institutions. This prompts cautious responses by India which is concerned with its own development and growth objectives.

Yet, the global context of the Tibet issue has been overtaken in the recent past by changes within South Asia and the region, changes in the Tibetan movement, China's more assertive and nationalistic policy on the border and on Arunachal Pradesh and by India's redefinition of its security objectives in the new milieu. Paradoxically, in a more globalised security context, issues closer to home have gained greater salience speaking to more focused concerns with the implications of the Tibetan issue.

From the outset, Indian policy-makers saw the significance of Tibet to Indian security on its Himalayan borders. In the initial stages of the India-China conflict, Tibet was seen as central to the dispute by both the Chinese and the Indians. As most studies indicate, the Chinese invasion of Tibet in 1950-51 and the Tibetan uprising in 1959 became the catalyst for the dispute. [25] In fact, as Dawa Norbu noted, all legal documents on the India-China border talks were related to Tibet whether it was the Simla agreement on the McMahon Line or the 1954 Agreement on Trade between China and India. China's claims on the border rest on evidence from Tibetan records of the border and the principle on which India China relations were deemed to be based in the 1950s, the Panchsheel, were evolved in relation to Tibet.[26]

India's initial response to the Tibet issue was fashioned by British India's understanding of the importance of buffer states, and the definition of the McMahon Line, all pre-World War I strategies to keep Chinese irredentism at bay and safeguard British interests in India.[27]Nehru clearly felt the strategy was equally effective for the interests of independent India as well.[28]Although Nehru did not talk specifically of Tibet as a buffer state between India and China, he was conscious of the significance of the Chinese "invasion of Tibet", his words, for the security of the Himalayan region.[29]Thus, he wrote to the Indian ambassador in Beijing, K.M. Panikkar in 1950 that, "...this invasion of Tibet might well upset the present unstable equilibrium, and let loose dangerous forces." And again to V.K. Krishna Menon, "What happens in Tibet immediately affects some of our border states, like Nepal, Bhutan and Sikkim. As it is, there is tension in some of these States."[30] It was not surprising, therefore, that Nehru instructed his ambassador, after the Chinese army moved into Tibet, to persuade the Chinese to settle the issue in Tibet amicably with a solution that involved both Tibetan autonomy and Chinese suzerainty.[31] Tibetan autonomy would safeguard India against Chinese military threats and Chinese suzerainty would set the terms of Tibet-China relations.

It has often been argued that an idealist Nehru revealed little strategic sense over the Tibetan issue and India's policy of appeasement allowed the Chinese to strengthen their hold on Tibet without any strategic gains to India. It has also been alleged that Nehru gave away Tibet to China in the 1954 Agreement without an assurance on autonomy or the border, that he failed to heed the advice of the Secretary General of the External Affairs Ministry on getting a clarification on the McMahon Line in 1952, also that his sinophilia and bias towards Marxist states affected the choices he made, and that his agreement in 1954 with the Chinese government allowed China to gain recognition for its sovereign rights in Tibet.[32] As a consequence, Nehru's neutrality on Tibet amounted to an alignment with China against Tibet.[33] Nothing could be further from the truth. As Nehru told the Constituent Assembly on 4 December 1947, "Whatever policy you may lay down, the art of conducting the foreign affairs of a country lies in finding out what is most advantageous to the country. We may talk about international goodwill and mean what we may say but in the ultimate analysis...no government dares to do anything which ...is to the disadvantage of the country."[34] Nehru's pragmatic assessment of the choices before India in the early fifties—a weak military and little hope of intervention by either the British or the Americans—had him fall back on diplomacy and international treaty law. These elements remained strong aspects of Nehru's dealings with the Chinese throughout the 1950s until the 1959 uprising forced the issue. [35]

As some scholars have argued, Nehru worked within a strategic framework that was both realist and internationalist. Despite constraints, Nehru worked within a realist/pragmatic framework in trying to keep out the major Cold War powers from the conflict. Believing that the disadvantages would far outweigh the advantages, he sought to create buffering devices such as the proposal of Tibetan autonomy to enhance Indian security and fashioned policies for domestic administrative and military changes which would establish India's position on the border.[36] As Srinath

Raghavan points out, Indian policy-makers were considering the strategic implications of a Chinese takeover of Tibet even before the end of the Chinese civil war. K.M. Panikkar, then ambassador at the wartime capital of Nanjing, wrote to Nehru that once the Chinese took over Tibet, they would revive claims on the Himalayan states and undermine the McMahon Line.[37]

Together with his realistic perception of impending trouble in Tibet and the Himalayan region, Nehru also had a broader vision. His perception of what would today be called a 'new world order' in the post-war period expected cooperation among Asian powers, especially China, to prevent the conflicts of the major powers from pushing the world towards destruction.[38]

Somewhat ahead of his times, Nehru established an independent or non-aligned policy in what he essentially saw as an interdependent international context. From where we stand today his neo-realist assumptions do not seem amiss except that his perceptions of what drove Chinese foreign policy were misplaced. Thus, for example, he and other Indian policy-makers missed the fact that China's position on the unequal treaties forced on it during a "century of humiliation" were liable to have various definitions and objectives. In the Chinese discourse, unequal treaties have been differentiated as those which are unequal or those which have unequal clauses within them. The issue of unequal treaties has not been limited to the issue of inequity but has been used to reinforce the political authority and legitimacy of different political factions within Chinese politics. The debate over unequal treaties has also been instrumental in trying to persuade and confront in different ways through "moral persuasion of unfairness and legal invalidity addressed to elite constituencies" and consciousness raising through emotive slogans at the popular level.[39] As such, the unequal treaty discourse within China is liable to being interpreted differently at different times and therefore need not be taken as a definitive aspect of China's foreign policy conduct. The inability to contextualize the unequal treaties discourse within China has weakened the considerable legal argument for the Indian position when pitted against China's historical claims.[40]

As well, Indian negotiators were susceptible to Chinese historical claims of sovereign control over Tibet and, apart from Home Minister Sardar Patel, oblivious to the strength of Chinese historiography which has tended to construct a narrative of a strong territorial state despite evidence of China's absence of control for long periods of time over its periphery, or of the contradiction of terming once strong and threatening Central Asian empires as peripheral regions within China. China's claims to a political presence in Tibet are fairly recent and for the most part under the Manchu dynasty they took the form of a client-patron relationship.[41]

In addition, through the 1950s as China moved to secure its position in Tibet strategic concerns were voiced by Nehru, Girija Shankar Bajpai and Sardar Patel but the more pointed suggestions by Patel on opposing China in the UN and the urgent need for military preparedness were either ignored or not sufficiently well implemented. [42] Nehru's view, based on recognition of the asymmetry of power between the PRC and India, was that a two-pronged policy was likely to be more successful: one to ensure that the border was militarily defended against Chinese expansion and the second, to seek an understanding with the Chinese for the long-term resolution of the border problem.

Officially, the Indian government's stand separating Tibet from the border issue emerged around the signing of the 1954 Agreement on Trade and Intercourse between the Tibet region of China and India by which India recognized Tibet as a part of China. Nowhere in the document is there a reference to the autonomous status of Tibet that Nehru had asked his ambassador to place before Beijing.[43] This oversight, important as it was, may have arisen from the fact that if the Treaty did not address the issue of Tibetan autonomy it also did not touch on the Indian position of Chinese sovereignty or suzerainty in Tibet which India was to raise later. The Chinese assumed that its treaty-signing rights gave it sovereignty over Tibet, while the Indians assumed in turn, that the Treaty settled the issue of the border and that the Chinese had understood their position on Tibetan autonomy under Chinese suzerainty. There was little, if any, recognition of the fact that definitions of autonomy for ethnic minorities had changed from somewhat generous notion of autonomy in the early twentieth century to an extremely narrow or constrained one framed by an emphasis on nationalism and the definition of the nation within China's political discourse since 1911.[44]

In effect, therefore, Tibet had been divorced from the border issue by New Delhi in 1954. But, after the 1959 Tibetan uprising, the flight of the Dalai Lama to India and Beijing's suspicions of India's designs in Tibet, it became the centre piece of Chinese policy and rhetoric. Support for the Tibetan cause, both rhetorically and materially within the Tibetan community in India and at the UN, where India supported the UN Resolution on Tibet, surfaced up until the 1971 war with Pakistan.

Rajiv Gandhi's visit to Beijing in 1988 set the seal, as it were, on the public debate and official position on this separation.[45] Since the revival of the India-China relationship in 1988, the emphasis in India's China policy on confidence-building measures, managing border relations, and continuing border negotiations has maintained the myth of this separation. At each stage, Tibet was held hostage to the need to repair the relationship with China. This would give one reason to believe that the issue of Tibet in the relationship has been settled and that, in official reasoning, the issue of the border could be settled without reference to the fate of Tibet.

Contrary to the Indian position, Chinese analyses link the twin issues of the border and Tibet. For Beijing, an unsettled Tibet exposes China's southwestern flank to "expansionist" forces. The redrawing of the map of Tibet, divesting it of its two largest regions of Kham and Amdo and incorporating large tracts into China's western provinces of Yunnan, Sichuan, Gansu and Qinghai, was intended to secure this flank. The perception of the centrality of Tibet is still part of the Chinese understanding of the conflict and the current issues over the border. In China, the conflict with India is viewed almost entirely within the matrix of developments in Tibet, bringing home the fact that, "the root cause of the 1962 war was an Indian attempt to undermine Chinese rule and seize Tibet."[46] The Chinese reference to Tibet as the "lips and teeth" for China became, over time, even more true for India.[47]

However, changes in the Chinese stand, on what Neville Maxwell has called the Assam Himalayas, including Tawang, in the first decade of this century, political changes within the Tibetan émigré community, domestic unrest in Tibet and heightened Chinese suspicions of Indian support have brought Tibet into the centre of the dispute once again as far as India is concerned. When Tibetans inside Tibet confront the Chinese state in an almost decadal cycle of opposition the significance of the Dalai Lama and the Tibetan Youth Congress in exile is not lost on the Chinese regime. There is an active Tibetan government in exile which will fashion policies of some concern to both India and China. In fact, the anxiety over a cross-border threat to national integrity has encouraged the Chinese state and public opinion to expand their lexicon of opprobrium for the Tibetans in exile from separatists and splittists to terrorists.[48] Every time Indian and Chinese leaders meet, there is reference to Tibet which underscores Tibet as a core issue in India-China relations.

TIBET AND THE REGIONAL CALCULUS

While Nehru did not live to see it, the dispute over "Tibetan territories" has had far-reaching repercussions in the neighbourhood. Tibet became not just central to the border dispute but was also at the heart of the many strategic issues that have confronted the Indian state since the 1962 war. The Chinese occupation of and vulnerability in Tibet created a new strategic calculus in South Asia. It established a new frontier for incipient India-China rivalry in the cis-Himalayan states, between India and China.[49] Mao's anti-India policy had implications for China's involvement in insurgencies within India, especially in its northeastern states, during a period of heightened radicalism within China in the 1960s and 1970s. The treaty of friendship between China and Pakistan in 1963 established a special strategic relationship which aimed at holding back India in South Asia. The consequences of the militarization of the subcontinent and military conflicts were graver, given China's assistance for Pakistan's nuclear programme and military production facilities. China's alliance with Pakistan and vulnerability in its western provinces brought the Cold War into South Asia, something Nehru had most feared. The worst and by far the most far-reaching was China's support for the Pakistani jihadi state network on India's doorstep. This has had serious implications for India's internal security and for cross-border conflict with Pakistan. The centrality of Tibet to India's strategic calculus could not have been brought home with greater effect.

THE CHANGING CONTEXT OF INDIA'S TIBET POLICY

After a hiatus of slightly over two decades, Tibet is in the forefront of India-China relations again. The context of the Tibetan issue has changed dramatically in the last few decades alone. Economic growth agendas, terrorism, and internal security concerns increasingly fashion the foreign policy of both states. The economic rise of China and the relative rise of India have, with their focus on economic growth, precluded the possibility of open conflict on the border, although not differences over Tibet. India's policy still remains one of military and administrative preparedness in the border region while seeking a lasting understanding on the border. Yet, China's new assertiveness in foreign policy also draws attention to its rising power and a rethinking of India's strategies on ensuring stability on the border. In India in particular, Beijing's public positions on Arunachal Pradesh and Tawang have pre-empted any border resolution, raising the question of whether Beijing takes the border negotiations at all seriously. If public pronouncements on Arunachal Pradesh and Tawang are taken together with China's brutal reaction to the domestic opposition within Tibet and changes in the émigré Tibetan movement the contours of a new Chinese strategy for Tibet become obvious. In this context the South Asian turn in Chinese foreign policy is significant. From viewing South Asia as a region where its relations with Pakistan were aimed at keeping India at bay, China now looks at South Asia as a geopolitical and economic opportunity which will enable it to secure its western borders with the cis-Himalayan states through economic and political incentives. Humanitarian, security and political reasons, hence, combine to create arguments for looking at the Tibet issue afresh.

China's reluctance to settle the border issue with India, where it has done so with a host of other states on the basis of so-called "unequal treaties' and pre-1950 boundary demarcations, has been variously explained. According to one study, China tends to resolve border issues with states it views as status quo and stalls a resolution with those it views as expansionist. India falls into the expansionist category.[50] The Maoist construction of Nehru's motives in the 1962 war has become a part of Chinese mythology. Recent media stories and articles in China have tended to stoke the expansionist theory by slamming India as an over-reacher, out of its league with China.[51] In an examination of the various traditions upon which Chinese foreign policy draws Michael Hunt notes that China applies a power-oriented approach to states on its periphery. China's historical experience of threats from the periphery, and the fissiparous tendencies of border provinces during a time of internal instability lead the Chinese to deal with neighbours as the origin of threats to its self preservation.[52]

The Chinese perception of India as an expansionist state—and now as an ambitious one as well—will prevent the Chinese from moving ahead in the border negotiations. China's preference that the resolution of the border issue be left to the future should be viewed within the future that China envisages for itself. It is estimated that China will be the foremost economic power in 2040 and the world's dominant power by 2050.[53] This will allow China to press for its own terms on the border and primarily bring an end to any argument for Tibetan autonomy as well as the effective control of all disputed territories associated with its own authority and legitimacy in Tibet. This scenario does not preclude the ability of the PRC to create economic and political structures within Tibet in the interim which would effectively create a new post-Dalai Han-Tibetan elite which would shift the momentum of the Tibetan movement away from autonomy to assimilation with the political economy of the Chinese state and party. In this scenario, India would have lost its ability to negotiate a deal over the border in its own interests, it would have also "lost" the Tibetan issue to leverage its own position in the process. China's power-oriented approach to the border issue also puts into doubt the efficacy of the one-pronged policy on the border since 1988. The 1993 and 1996 agreements and the political guidelines (which China ignores) seem merely policies that hold India to the status quo until it can be revised in China's favour.

However, much of the perception of an unstable periphery is China's own doing. It is generally acknowledged that if a resolution to the dispute over autonomy is not reached in the Dalai Lama's lifetime it would unleash a less moderate trend within the younger émigré leadership. The Dalai Lama's middle path is related as much to his pragmatic approach to the problem of Tibet's existence within China as with the fact that he is the religious head of a faith that preaches non-violence. A more secular leadership may not have the same constraints. Paradoxically, as long as China puts off settling the boundary issue, it will be in India's interest to keep it alive. The Tibet issue will resurface in the India-China relationship keeping Beijing edgy about a perception of threat from its periphery.

But China does not just deal with the periphery in political and military ways. China's military and economic rise has provided a new impetus for social and economic cohesion and for addressing concerns over internal dissent, Han or ethnic. The policy direction for minority groups still comes from Mao's views on nationality policy in the 1930s. Mao argued that as minority nationalities are drawn into the economic mainstream, they will become a part of the larger Chinese nation.[54] As a consequence, Tibet is now in focus as part of China's geopolitical and geo-economic policy in South Asia.

The importance of economic and social engineering has led the PRC to focus on a development and class struggle approach to Tibet. China's White Papers on Tibet have routinely posited the solution for the Tibet issue in terms of the Tibetan people's freedom from the feudal hold of the monastic orders. Both the Chinese state and Chinese intellectuals like Wang Hui would prefer that the world direct its attention not on Tibet's nationalism but on the social conditions that triggered the historical and recent "Tibet crisis".[55] Tibet's social crisis needs to be addressed through a restructuring of its feudal social order and by applying to its economy the paradigm of economic growth and development. New transportation and communication infrastructure is intended to link Tibet to the cis-Himalayan states, border trade is viewed as having great potential and joint ventures in development and energy projects are slated to create opportunities for employment. Tibet increasingly serves as a showpiece for China's western development plan and is viewed as a bridge between China and South Asia.[56] While the policy is meant partly to leverage Tibet's potential as a bridge to South Asia, given its affinities with Buddhist states like Bhutan, it is also meant to address the issue of Tibet's backwardness which China sees as critical to Tibetan unrest and instability.

Hence the PRC's two-level policy deals with the Tibetan issue, internally as an economic issue, externally as a political one. Therefore, the geopolitical and geo-economic policies of the state converge in Tibet.

The geopolitical aspect of policy over Tibet calls for co-operation with its South Asian neighbours which might mean restraints on the movements of Tibetan exiles across their borders into Tibet, as with Nepal, or gaining neutrality, as with the resolution of outstanding border issues with Bhutan.[57] For India, China's focus on its smaller South Asian neighbours is not new but in the changed context, as for the example the one in Nepal, causes concern and has prompted India to engage in some holding operations. Thus, India has moved quickly to block China's generous contribution to the Lumbini complex, the birthplace of Gautam Buddha. China's control over the Lumbini complex would have been a significant symbolic gain in its strategy to gain legitimacy with Tibetan Buddhists. And it looks with some alarm at China's construction of road and rail heads up to the borders of the Himalayan states. The implications of the new transportation networks for transporting military reinforcements into South Asia are not lost on Indian policy-makers.

The effect of these policies on Tibetans within China will need to be assessed in the coming years. The Chinese state remains in denial over the real issue at the heart of the Tibetan problem: the demand for "genuine autonomy" for Tibet. The dichotomy between serfs and feudal lords does little to assuage the religious and cultural sources of Tibetan dissent since the development funds poured into Tibet seem directly to advantage the increasing number of Han residents in Tibet. The large-scale development of communications and transportation infrastructure in Tibet creates concerns over the implications for Tibet's fragile ecology and the pressure on land and resources. When the Chinese model of growth that has been so successful in China's coastal regions is applied to Tibet it not only aggravates ecological and environment problems but also transforms the economic structure of a largely nomadic population. The fact that until recently there was no ethnic Tibetan appointed to the top echelons of the provincial Party post, and that in general all higher positions in the TAR's administration are held by Han functionaries, also creates dissent and alienation. When internal dissent spills over in the immolation of monks it is viewed as being instigated by the "Dalai Lama Clique" and treated as splittist/terrorist act with *yan da* tactics, further outraging critics of the PRC's coercive policies within Tibet.

INDIA'S TIBET POLICY

India's approach to Tibet must take account of the fact that separating the issue of "genuine autonomy" for Tibet from the India-China border issue will not lead to lasting security on the border. The Chinese state is confronted with the challenge of balancing its rapid economic rise with widespread internal dissent on many counts providing India with a narrow window of opportunity to resolve the Tibet issue and the border issue with China. India must move on the understanding that while China's rise constrains the world from engaging China in a debate on the status of Tibet, China's internal challenges and India's own relative rise give it the negotiating advantages it can leverage. While China rises, so does India and a geopolitical and economic partnership between the two is essential for stability in China's western regions. India's diplomacy in the South Asian region, in support of democratic and representative political changes, has laid down a successful road map for new dialogues and created a critical mass of opinion in the subcontinent for negotiated solutions to political dissent. India must employ its influence and all the strategies at its command to deal with the Tibet issue. India has supported the dialogue between the Dalai Lama's representatives and the PRC since 2002 and must now take an active interest, along with other states, in convincing China that the path of dialogue is the one it should take. It must make the point that the Chinese government's refusal to take forward the dialogue with the Dalai Lama will keep the Tibetan issue in the forefront of India-China relations. If the issue takes a serious turn, Beijing's allegations against the Dalai Lama notwithstanding, the Chinese will only have themselves to blame. India is firmly convinced that a military response to Tibetan dissent is not the solution to the problem, as then External Affairs Minister, Pranab Mukherjee, told the Lok Sabha after the 2008 crackdown.

The Chinese proposal that the resolution of the border issue be left to the future is not, from China's internal and external behaviour, in India's favour. While India has little control over the domestic aspects of the Tibet issue, it must take a stand in supporting the Dalai Lama's position on "genuine autonomy" for Tibet. India should push for the Chinese to honour the 17-point agreement signed with Tibet in 1951 if China expects India and the rest of the world to reiterate the position that Tibet is China's territory.

A resolution of Tibet which satisfies Beijing's quest for legitimacy, albeit without full authority, will likely ease Beijing's suspicions about India's expansionist designs in Tibet. This will make it easier for China to move back from claims on symbolically important settled territories in Arunachal Pradesh and Tawang. Moreover, there is speculation that the next Dalai Lama may be appointed from outside Tibet, divesting the Chinese authorities of any hope of controlling Tibetan politics in the future. This may lead to more border tensions in an effort to control the most sanctified Buddhist shrines in India, the site of future Tibetan political authority and legitimacy. An early agreement on Tibet would make legitimacy issues irrelevant.

India should build on the Chinese policy of Tibet as a bridge between China and South Asia rather than obstructing regional economic integration. An example to keep in mind would be that of China and Vietnam where economic integration in the border regions has been an economic boon, despite their political differences. In fact, India's neighbourhood policy already has a large economic component and India could support aspects of cross-border trade and investment that complement its own initiatives. Finally, it is clear that China's plans for economic interaction with South Asia cannot ignore its largest economy, India. India could leverage this objective to pressure China to deal with the Tibetan issue. It must bring home the point that if Tibet is to become a bridge to South Asia, a negotiated settlement with the Dalai Lama and his government in exile for genuine autonomy would be required. It needs to point out to China the discrepancy between its position on Taiwan and Hong Kong with that in Tibet. This will ensure that at the least an autonomous Tibet will be at the forefront of the PRC's South Asia policy.

If India is to have any currency with China on the Tibetan issue it needs to move into the second phase of its neighbourhood policy. There are lessons to be learnt for its neighbourhood policy from its successful Look East policy. In the first phase of the Look East policy, India redefined its relations with the ASEAN states and established the basis for positive bilateral relations. In the second phase, India moved to make its presence felt in multilateral organizations and institutions, becoming a significant economic and strategic partner. While the situation in South Asia differs because of asymmetries of power and the burden of the past, India's recent flexible policy has established better relations with neighbours and enabled it to influence governments to support democratic forces in their own countries. A second phase of neighbourhood policy could likely focus on economic and strategic integration and greater influence in the SAARC. As an economic and strategic partner for China and other South Asian states, India would have the opportunity to suggest the conditions under which Tibet could become a political and economic bridge to South Asia.

India needs, in particular, to revive the interest in the humanitarian aspect of China's policy in Tibet. It is essential, in this context, to make a strong argument against branding the Dalai Lama, the Tibetan Youth Congress and Tibetan protestors within Tibet as terrorists. The case of the ETIM, where the PRC prevailed upon the US to place it on its list of terror organizations, should be a warning against tardiness on this issue. The ETIM's definition as a terrorist body has allowed the PRC to suppress the Uighur movement in Xinjiang violating all human rights norms. The Dalai Lama's demand for "genuine autonomy" within the laws and constitution of the PRC provide India a way of raising the issue of human rights in Tibet within the Chinese definition of human rights. In the process, the separation of terrorism from genuine demands for cultural and social autonomy must be addressed. Within China political discourses provide some encouragement towards this end. The recent 18th Party Congress has paid scant attention to the minority question indicating that the policy of economic development and *yan da* or "strike hard" is viewed as sufficient in dealing with the issue.[58] However, voices within and outside the Party have begun to argue first, for greater Party democracy and second, for a liberal rights-based regime. This creates a space for engagement between India and democracy advocates within China enabling a higher profile for democracy initiatives in India-China policy.[59]

Finally, New Delhi needs to treat the changing of goal posts by the Chinese in the border negotiations more transparently. Since China has no hesitation in making official announcements through its ambassadors, or taking official action on Indian travel documents, it is time for the government to make a clear statement on India's attitude towards China's position on Arunachal Pradesh, Tawang or Kashmir. It must be brought to Beijing's notice that if it continues to consider these areas as disputed then its own claims in Tibet may be considered to be disputed as well. It must also make clear to the Chinese side that the uprising in Tibet weakens its legitimacy to claim Buddhist places of worship on behalf of Tibet.[60] In particular, India's ad nauseum recognition of "One China" must be tied to a public reiteration of the political guidelines for the settlement of the border dispute from China. India has recently played the Tibet card to get China to revise its policy on Kashmir. It could continue to keep that option open.

India's ability to remove the constraints on dealing with Tibet—the weakness of a human rights discourse on the issue of Tibet, the Chinese conflation of separatism with terrorism and the further weakening of the humanitarian position on Tibet—would serve both the issue of Tibet as well as a more reasonable dialogue on the border dispute.

ENDNOTES

1. "Playing down irritants, India and China call for new, 'flexible' approach to ties". The report quoted External Affairs Minister S.M. Krishna as saying in Beijing that, "It is the Government of

India's position that the Tibet Autonomous Region is part of the People's Republic of China, and as a result of that we are dealing with the internal affairs of China…Hence we will have to be very cautious, and any help that we can render to ease the tension we are willing to do it but I don't think that situation will arise." 9th Feb. 2012 *The Hindu,* p. 11.

2. "State's Dobriansky Says U.S. Seeks Beijing-Dalai Lama Talks" USINFO East Asia iipgeap@PD.STATE.GOV US-CHINA@LISTS.STATE.GOV. Under Secretary Paula J. Dobriansky Remarks to House International Relations Committee March 7,Special Coordinator for Tibetan Issues, House International Relations Committee U.S. Policy Considerations in Tibet. Accessed 7 Mar 2002.
3. *Human Rights in China*, Information Office of the State Council of the People's Republic of China November 1991, Beijing. *Beijing Review* (November 4, 1991), 8-45. James C. Hsiung, ed., *Human Rights in East Asia: A Cultural Perspective* (New York, Praeger, 1985). Ann Kent, *Between Freedom and Subsistence: China and Human Rights* (Hong Kong: Oxford University Press, 1993).*The Human Rights Record of the United States in 2010*, April 8, 2011, Information Office of the State Council, Beijing. Release Date: 04/08/2011 [PDF] *UN COMMISSION ON HUMAN RIGHTS LOSES ALL CREDIBILITY*rsf.org/IMG/pdf/Report_ONU_gb.pdf.
4. *Human Rights in China*, Information Office of the State Council of the People's Republic of China November 1991, Beijing. *Beijing Review* (November 4, 1991), 8-45.
5. See Julia Ching for her discussion on the problem of translating "human rights" into Chinese. "Human Rights: A Valid Chinese Concept?" Panel convened by the Religious Consultation on Population, Reproductive Health and Ethics at the NGO Forum of the United Nation's World Summit on Social Development, March, 1995.
6. Chen Jinhua, "The China Model and the Chinese System", *Qiushi Journal(English edition),* Central Committee of the Communist Party of China, Vol. 3, No.4 October1,2011 | Updated:2011-12-29 15:11.Originally appeared in *People's Daily*, July 5, 2011.

7. Michael Clarke, *China's "War on Terror" in Xinjiang: Human Security and the Causes of Violent Uighur Separatism.*(London: Routledge,2008).'East Turkistan' Terrorist Forces Cannot Get Away with Impunity. Information Office State Council of the PRC, *People's Daily*, January 21, 2002.
8. Interview with Chinese academics in New Delhi. February 2008.
9. Fei-Ling Wang, "Beijing's Incentive Structure: The Pursuit of Preservation, Prosperity, and Power", in Yong Deng and Fei-Ling Wang (eds.), *China Rising: Power and Motivation in Chinese Foreign Policy.* (New York: Rowman and Littlefield Pub.: 2005), pp. 19-50.
10. Li Hongmei "India's Undue Worry about China Results from Inferiority Complex." Beijing, *Xinhua* 2011-11-24 http://news.xinhuanet.com/english2010/indepth/2011-11/24/c_131274625.htm
11. Andrew Scobell, "Terrorism and Chinese Foreign Policy," in Yong Deng and Fei-Ling Wang, op. cit., pp. 305-324.
12. Chien-peng Chung,"Confronting Terrorism and Other Evils in China: All Quiet on the Western Front?",*China and Eurasia Forum Quarterly*, Volume 4, No. 2 (2006), pp. 75-87.
13. Ibid., p. 82.
14. Ibid., p. 82.
15. "China Urges Japan to Resolve Fishing Boat Incident", *Reuters*, November 08, 2011. www.reuters.com.
16. Ely Ratner, "The Emergent Security Threats Reshaping China's Rise", *The Washington Quarterly*, 34:1, pp. 29-44.
17. China's White Paper on Tibet. *Fifty Years of Democratic Reform in Tibet.* Information Office of the State Council, PRC, Beijing, 2009. *Tibet: Its Ownership and Human Rights Situation*, 1992. www.china.org.cn
18. Chen Jinhua, "The China Model and the Chinese System", *Qiushi Journal (English edition),* Central Committee of the Communist Party of China. Vol. 3 No. 4 October 1, 2011. Updated: 2011-12-29 15:11. Originally appeared in *People's Daily*, July 5, 2011.
19. Pan Wei, "The Chinese Model of Development", Speech at the Foreign Policy Centre, London, Oct. 11, 2007.

20. Lodi Gyaltsen Gyari, "Tibetan Impasse", *South China Morning,* Post Op-ed. 10 September, 2010. http://www.scmp.com
21. Surya P. Sharma, "The India-China Border Dispute: An Indian Perspective," *The American Journal of International Law,* Vol. 59, No. 1 (Jan., 1965), pp. 16-47, www.jstor.org/stable/2197143 Accessed: 25/10/2010. 08:00)
22. Ted Piccone, "Do New Democracies Support Democracy? the multilateral dimension", http://www.brookings.edu/~/media/Files/rc/articles/2011/1026_democracy_piccone/1026_democracy_piccone.pdf. Elvira Dominguez Redondo, "Similar Positions, Different Perceptions: India and China's Approaches to Human Rights within the UN". www.chinalawsociety.com/admin/ewebeditor/.../200991116952784...
23. External Affairs Minister Pranab Mukherjee, March 17, 2008, speaking in the Lok Sabha, expressed distress over the "unsettled situation and violence" in Tibet and stated that the causes of trouble in this autonomous region of China should be resolved through dialogue and non-violent means. He also stressed that India's policy on China and Tibet was formed in 1959 and no government since then has changed it. "Tibetan Uprising and the 2008 Beijing Olympics: A Chronology", August 07, 2008, http://www.idsa.in/chronology/TibetanUprisingandthe2008BeijingOlympics
24. "India-China Strategic Economic Dialogue,", *TNN* Sep 24, 2011, 05.29am IST.http://articles.timesofindia.indiatimes.com/2011-09-24/india/
25. Steven Hoffman, "Rethinking the Linkage between Tibet and the China-India Border Conflict: A Realist Approach," *Journal of Cold War Studies,* Vol. 8, No. 3, Summer 2006, pp. 182-83.
26. Dawa Norbu, "Tibet in Sino-Indian Relations: The Centrality of Marginality," *Asian Survey,* Vol. 37 No. 11, 1997 p. 1095.
27. Premen Addy, "Imperial Prophet or Scaremonger? Curzon's Tibetan Policy Reconsidered', *Asian Affairs,* 14: 1, (1983), 54-67. http://dx.doi.org/10.1080/03068378308730098) Steven A. Hoffmann, p 169.
28. Yun-yuan Yang, "Controversies over Tibet: China versus India, 1947-49", *The China Quarterly,* No. 111 (Sep., 1987), pp. 407-20; Karunakar Gupta "The McMahon Line 1911-45: The British

Legacy," *The China Quarterly*, No. 47 (Jul. - Sep., 1971), pp. 521-45.
29. Dawa Norbu, "Tibet in Sino-Indian Relations: The Centrality of Marginality", *Asian Survey*, Vol. 37, No. 11, 1997, p. 1095.
30. Cable to K.M. Panikkar, New Delhi, 19 August 1950. *Selected Works of Jawaharlal Nehru*. 2nd Series, 15 part I (1 August-25 October 1950), Jawaharlal Nehru Memorial Trust, Teen Murti House. New Delhi: Oxford University Press: 1993, p. 431. To V.K. Krishna Menon, New Delhi August 18, 1950. *Selected Works*, p. 429.
31. *Selected Works*, p. 431.
32. Paul F. Power, "Indian Foreign Policy: The Age of Nehru", *The Review of Politics*, Vol. 26, No. 2 (Apr., 1964), pp. 257-286. Norbu, "Tibet in Sino-Indian Relations: The Centrality of Marginality," *Asian Survey*, Vol. 37, No. 11, 1997, p. 1095.
33. Claude Arpi, *Tibet: The Lost Frontier*, New Delhi: Lancer, 2008. pp. 1 and 138-39.
34. Quoted in Hiren Mukherjee, "The Debit Side" in Rafiq Zakaria (ed.), *A Study of Nehru*, New Delhi: Rupa, 1989, p. 266. V.K.R.V Rao, "Planning without Dogma', pp. 320-24, ibid. B. N. Mullik, *My Years with Nehru: The Chinese Betrayal* (New Delhi: Allied Publishers, 1971).
35. *Selected Works*, p. 431.
36. Steven A. Hoffmann, pp. 167 and 179. *Selected Works*, p. 431.
37. Srinath Raghavan, *War and Peace in Modern India: A Strategic History of the Nehru Years*. (Ranikhet: Permanent Black, 2010), pp. 230 and 233.
38. *Selected Works*, p. 431.
39. Dong Wang, *China's Unequal Treaties: Narrating National Histories*. (New York: Lexington Books, 2005), pp. 1-4, 135-40.
40. Surya P. Sharma, pp. 16-47.
41. Christopher I. Beckwith, *The Tibetan Empire in Central Asia* (Princeton: Princeton Univ. Press, 1987). Claude Arpi, pp. 36-37, Norbu, *China's Tibet Policy*. (London: Curzon, 2001), Ch. 8. "The Anatomy of Tibetan Autonomy: An Agenda for the 21st Century", pp. 15-100. Nie Hongyiy, "Explaining Chinese Solutions to Territorial Disputes with Neighbor States", *Chinese Journal of International Politics*, 2009, pp. 1-37. Wang Jiawei & Nyima

Gyaincain, "The Historical Status of China's Tibet", *Journal of the Washington Institute of China Studies*, Winter 2009, Vol. 4, No. 3, p. 24.

42. Patel's letter to Nehru, 7th November 1950 cited in Raghavan, p. 239.
43. "Agreement on Trade and Intercourse with Tibet Region, April 29, 1954", http://meaindia.nic.in/
44. Norbu, *China's Tibet Policy, 100-124.* Neville Maxwell, *India's China War* (New York: Pantheon Books, 1970). John Garver, *Protracted Contest: Sino-Indian Rivalry in the Twentieth Century* (Seattle: University of Washington Press, 2001), pp. 33-34.
45. "The Revolution in Tibet and Nehru's Philosophy", *People's Daily*, 6 May 1959.
46. John Garver, "China's Decision for War with India in 1962", in Alastair Iain Johnston and Robert S. Ross (eds.), *New Directions in the Study of China's Foreign Policy.* Stanford: Stanford Univ. Press, 2006, p. 89.
47. Norbu, *China's Tibet Policy*, p. 688. Xuecheng Liu, *The Sino-Indian Border Dispute and Sino-Indian Relations* (MD Lanham, University Press of America, 1994), pp. 23-26, 101.
48. Interview with Chinese scholars before the Beijing Olympics, March 2008.
49. Norbu, *China's Tibet Policy*, p. 694.
50. Ibid.
51. Li Hongmei.
52. Michael Hunt, *The Genesis of Chinese Foreign Policy* (New York: Col. Univ. Press, 1996), p. 24.
53. Arvind Virmani, *A Tripolar World: India, China and US*, ICRIER, May 18, 2005.
54. Hunt, p. 134.
55. Wang Hui, "The Tibetan Issue between East and West: The Case of Different Orientalisms", *Link Times*, Vol. 8, May 2011, pp. 10-15.
56. Thierry Mathou, "Tibet and Its Neighbors: Moving toward a New Chinese Strategy in the Himalayan Region", *Asian Survey*, Vol. 45, No. 4 (Jul.-Aug., 2005), pp. 503-21.
57. Mathou, p. 518.

58. Hu Jintao, Report to the 18th Party Congress, November 2012. news.xinhuanet.com/english/special/18cpcnc/2012-11.
59. Yu Keping, "Democracy is a Good Thing", www.chinesenewsnet.cn; Yang Jingjie, "Calls for Political Reforms Intensify," *Global Times*, 25 October 2012. Zhu Xueqin, "For a Chinese Liberalism," in Chaohua Wang (ed.), *One China, Many Paths* (London: Verso, 2005), pp. 87-107.
60. Brahma Chellany, "Why Tibet Matters", *The Hindustan Times*, March 19, 2008.

9

Tibet in India-China Relations: Civilisational Aspects

Madhuri Santanam Sondhi

Let me start by reflecting on three interwoven processes embedded in the agenda pursued by His Holiness the Dalai Lama vis-à-vis his homeland since his arrival in India in 1959:

First, right from the start he worked assiduously towards democratising Tibet's political system amongst the exiles as a dry run, so to speak, of what might be in Tibet. The Constitution for a democratic Tibet was drawn up and a Parliament-in-Exile established by 1961—no small feat for a traumatised group of exiles faced with the exigencies of life outside their sequestered home. Mr. Lobsang Sangay's position today as the directly-elected SiKyong (earlier Kalon Tripa) is the logical culmination of this process pursued in stages for over half a century.

Secondly, the changing positions in defining the status of Tibet vis-à-vis China, from complete independence to conditional autonomy, are responses to perceived external circumstances, shaped by Indian and Chinese attitudes towards Tibet, towards each other and by the attitudes of the world community. Although His Holiness has delinked himself from and thereby ended the dual Ganden Phodrang system of government, the fact that there is a SiKyong, an elected political leader, remains a challenge to the legitimacy and quality of the Chinese administration inside Tibet.

The third process stems from His Holiness's concern with the preservation of Tibet's unique civilization. As a living civilization under present circumstances it seems to have its best chances outside Tibet: Tibetan Buddhism fascinates scholars of religion and practitioners in the West; Europe, America, Australia are host to many monasteries and perhaps there are more practising Tibetan Buddhists amongst them than amongst Indians. But Tibetan Buddhism is undoubtedly part of the rainbow of Indian Dharmas, and in that sense, along with the Tibetan settlements and replicas of Tibet's major monasteries and traditions, with heads and incarnate Lamas of different sects residing in India, this country, in the immediate context, provides a natural ambiance for its development. But undoubtedly the goal is to see to its good health in Tibet, the habitat in which it flourished and achieved its distinct identity.

The whole world, including India, has accepted Chinese sovereignty over Tibet. His Holiness' Strasbourg statement itself was a unilateral acceptance of Chinese sovereignty, albeit conditional on China's granting of human and cultural rights within TAR and what we call Greater Tibet. Despite some nominal concessions, those rights can hardly be said to exist and so perforce the Dharamsala Administration continues in exile with its Parliament and Cabinet. There is a certain ambiguity in the Dharamsala position but its rationale, apart from administering to the needs of the exiles, is clearly both to leverage the situation inside and outside Tibet and establish a basis for negotiating with the Chinese, whenever opportunity presents itself.

This writing will concentrate mainly on the civilizational aspect especially within the context of what can be done now and is within the policy framework of His Holiness who stresses the preservation of Tibetan civilization both as an end in itself and for its universal values. I will also touch on some specific political matters that link with the civilizational imperatives especially since this goes to the press at a time when the wave of self-immolations in Tibet shows no sign of abatement.

CIVILIZATIONAL CONNECTIVITY BETWEEN INDIA, CHINA AND TIBET

There is a fundamental difference between Tibetan civilization with its unique form of Buddhism, often described rather narrowly as Lamaistic (deriving from the particular *form* of monastic organisation) and the Chinese Confucian-cum-Taoist-cum-Buddhist culture. It is important to stress this as the Chinese claim that Tibetans are racially, culturally and in every sense part of the Chinese family. It is a fact that for a long time, Buddhism has formed an important part of Chinese culture: Buddhism travelled from India up the 'Silk Route' to Central Asia from where it reached China: later the same route as well as the sea lanes were utilised by Indian and Chinese Buddhists for more direct interactions with each other, deepening Chinese understanding of the mother religion. Fa-Hsien and Hiuen Tsang were amongst the most famous scholar-pilgrims who visited India in the 4th and 7th centuries. China adopted Buddhism much before did Tibet, and it became, as is sometimes said, along with Confucianism and Taoism, the third leg of the 'Triple Religion'. However, as Hajime Nakamura has pointed out in his masterly *Ways of Thinking of Asian Peoples India-China-Tibet-Japan*[1], the ideographic structure of the Chinese language embodies a more particularistic rather than universal mode of thinking in contrast to Sanskrit's logic and categorical reasoning, embedded in its linear, grammatical structure. As a result, Indian scholar-translators and their Chinese counterparts experienced difficulties accurately conveying the true sense of Buddhist logical texts such as those of the Nagarjuna Madhyamika school in south India which became integral to the Nalanda curriculum. What developed in China as Dhyan Buddhism and went on to become Zen in Japan was a more intuitive a-logical grasping of the transcendent. Furthermore, although Buddhism was welcomed for providing a metaphysical and transcendent dimension to China's Confucian culture, it never replaced or absorbed the latter.

In Tibet on the other hand, Buddhism was a major all-encompassing civilizing influence: with the help of Indian masters, Tibetans not only established monasteries as centres of learning and practice, but they evolved a linear Indic-type script, in which the logic and metaphysics of the Indian Buddhist schools could be easily and adequately expressed. This is not to say that all Indian schools of thought are purely rational: there are also bhakti, ritualistic and tantric traditions which have also to a greater or lesser degree found their way into Tibetan Buddhist practice. However at the great Samye debate in Lhasa between Chinese and Indian Buddhist teachers lasting over two years, in which the former advocated their path of instant enlightenment, the Tibetans finally chose the Madhyamika or Middle Path of the Nagarjuna School, rejecting the former for all time to come. In time, Buddhism took over both state and culture in Tibet, not destroying but incorporating much of the pre-existing Bon religion which consisted of shamanistic and animistic practices. If in China Buddhism straddled a deeply entrenched Confucian high culture, in Tibet it absorbed popular Bon beliefs, and these, coupled with an excessively large monastic population, gave rise to a distinctive culture which flourished in relative isolation, differentiable from the Chinese and the Indian, but more closely linked with the latter. At its heyday, Tibet was non-violent, culturally expansive but not territorially aggressive. Tibetan Buddhism spread into Central Asia, into Mongolia, Manchuria and Eastern Russia; even in exile while labouring under the greatest of handicaps it continues in an inevitably minor way to find new converts. One may recall the civilizational studies of Amaury de Riencourt, who wrote three separate books on the cultures of China, India and Tibet, i.e. he regarded each of them as complete and distinctive. Nakamura himself recognised that although Tibet was not as politically important as the other three it had evolved a distinctive style of thinking which demanded separate attention.

To recapitulate, therefore, the adoption of a Sanskritic-derived script served the Tibetans as a conduit for the successful ingestion of Buddhism with essentially Indic features, and led to the evolution of the Tibetan into a vibrant and influential unique civilization which can by no means be described as an offshoot of the Chinese. If anything, there was some reverse influence when China was under the rule of the Manchus (Qings). Although they integrated into Chinese culture, as practitioners of Tibetan Buddhism, the Manchus encouraged the establishment of Tibetan Buddhist monasteries near Beijing, maintained the Guru-Patron relationship with Tibet and famously built a special palace to house the visiting 13th Dalai Lama. This served to accommodate the Fourteenth on his visit to Beijing in 1954 where he also received Mao Zedong. According to His Holiness, there are today at least 2 million followers of Tibetan Buddhism in mainland China.

Nakamura has been criticised for the reasons he proffers as to why the logical schools did not take root in China, especially in light of contemporary China's successful absorption of Western science, but the fact remains that fifteen hundred or so years ago they were uncomfortable with Sanskritic logic and reasoning. By contrast, the Tibetans absorbed not only Tantric Buddhism as personified in the person of the great Guru Padmasambhava but also the teachings of the Nalanda school from later Indian missionaries which involved highly skilled and sophisticated logical reasoning. Today Tibetans are adepts in the works of great masters like Nagarjuna—considered the equal of Aristotle of Greece—Dharmakirti, Chandrakirti and others, all carried along via the life-stream of the Sanskritic/Bengali-derived Tibetan script. What is remarkable is that not only did a significant number of these translations escape the ravages of the Chinese occupation and Cultural Revolution thanks to the refugees who carried out many manuscripts hidden in their capacious chubas, but also transliterations of Sanskrit works in the Tibetan script which are lost in India—a treasure waiting to be reclaimed.

As His Holiness is fond of pointing out, Tibet is a chela of India: this is not only a student-teacher relationship that carries its own duties and obligations but implies an overlapping worldview, a shared *parampara.*

ASIAN IMPERIALISM

It is very often the case that land or continental imperialism does not attract the same strictures as overseas colonialism. Russia's annexations of the bordering countries of Central Asia never received the same condemnation as Europe's colonisation of overseas Asia, Africa and Latin America. Had China laid claim to and occupied Singapore after a marine invasion, there could have been an international outcry despite the presence there of a Chinese majority with strong cultural links to the mainland: in the case of Tibet, racially and culturally distinct but a contiguous land neighbour, a hermit kingdom to boot barely known outside its borders, the PLA invasion in 1950 hardly caused an international ripple. Tibet, though a self-declared sovereign country with treaty-making powers, was not a member of the United Nations and lacked the means to put up an effective military resistance. When Chinese troops crossed her border not only did Tibet's appeals for help fall largely on deaf ears, but the aggression was never politically analysed in neo-imperialist terms. Two governments had inside knowledge of the real position, Great Britain and India, and both refused to lift even a little diplomatic finger.

However, although the Indian government did not much exercise itself about Tibet's political tragedy or its regional ramifications, which has in many respects proven costly for this country, when the refugees started pouring into India from the late 1950s onwards, it really bent over backwards to assist in their rehabilitation and preservation of their culture. To use His Holiness' metaphor, the guru welcomed the chela with open arms and saw to his material, cultural and spiritual needs. Tibet in India is one of the most successful international refugee rehabilitation stories. Tibetan language schools, Tibetan performing arts, Tibetan medicine, recreation of important monasteries—all these went towards helping the community-in-exile to remain connected to its cultural roots, while it got acquainted with the modern world through science, technology, politics, international relations, et al.

Preserving the Tibetan cultural identity has been important for several reasons: it contributes to the melange of world cultures necessary to maintain a healthy and interactive pluralism; apart from vibrant spiritual guidance it carries specific messages for individual compassion and global peace; for India it is an opportunity to reclaim her lost Buddhist traditions which virtually disappeared after the destruction of Nalanda and other Buddhist monasteries, a process aided by the competition between Sanatana and Buddhist dharmas. For the Tibetans, it maintains and projects a distinct Tibetan identity at a time when the Chinese government was out to deny and destroy it.

CULTURAL GENOCIDE

The Chinese policy in Tibet invites the name of cultural genocide. Outright racial genocide is against the stated principles of communism, but the demographic drowning of local people in a sea of Hans as happened in Inner Mongolia, once an ethnically distinctive country where today native Mongols are reduced to a minority (the 2000 census showing them about 17% of the population) accomplishes the same purpose. Added to which there has been the loss of a million odd Tibetans lives, i.e. one-sixth of their population, during the initial stages of China's occupation. Although bruited abroad in typical imperialist rhetoric as a mission of ideological, political and economic modernisation to save and uplift Tibet, it was more Chinese nationalism and strategic and economic interests that fuelled the so-called 'liberation'. If a non-communist culture is defamed as feudal and regressive, its destruction can be rationalised in the name of progress.

The Chinese at first resorted to a sustained policy of cultural destruction, razing about 3000 monasteries to the ground, killing and imprisoning thousands of monks, destroying precious manuscripts, etc., all repeated during the Cultural Revolution. After the passing of the Mao era, a brief lull brought some much-needed relief, but after Deng, and especially during Hu Jintao's tenure as Party leader in Tibet, the harsh repressive policies often under the banner of the Patriotic Education Campaign resumed and continue to this day. But the Tibetans proved surprisingly obstinate in clinging to their religious moorings and since religion and its pervasive influence could not be completely eradicated, the Chinese chose to co-opt it into their system under certain controlled conditions: it served as a fillip to the tourist industry and was useful for showing China's so-called forbearing minorities policy to the rest of the world. Perhaps half the destroyed monasteries have been restored and surviving cultural artefacts are now preserved in museums. However, religion is kept under the strict political control and surveillance of a self-declared atheistic government, which can only serve to stultify its vitality and growth.

Furthermore, China for both political strategic reasons and demographic compulsions looks upon Tibet as a legitimate lebensraum for her huge population and for several decades has been flooding the Tibetan Plateau with her citizens, slowly but surely marginalising and downgrading the Tibetan people and their culture. Clearly, the Chinese long-term goals, which they are known to pursue with unflinching ruthlessness, are to dilute the hold of Tibet's culture by state management of religion, if not to Sinicise the Tibetans by prioritising Chinese as the language of advancement. The state reserves the right to identify and legitimise incarnations, interfere in monastic curricula, etc., i.e. it seeks to fit Tibetan religious culture into an acceptable-to-the Chinese-state Procrustean framework. Ultimately, they would no doubt be happy to be left with just the grin of the Tibetan-Buddhist Cheshire cat.

The Patriotic Education Campaign (PEC) is an effort to achieve these goals by indoctrinating the Tibetan people, especially monks who, against all canons of self-preservation, prove the most recalcitrant in their persistent loyalty to the Dalai Lama and attachment to Rangzen or independence. This somewhat echoes the role of the Catholic Church in Poland during the Cold War when it acted as a centre of cultural resistance to Soviet domination. The PEC's agenda is holistic: it writes revisionist history, claiming that since ancient times Tibet has been part of China; it condemns the idea of Tibetan independence as a foreign invention and the current Dalai Lama's non-violent demands for autonomy and human rights as 'splittism' of the motherland; politically it castigates old Tibet's theocratic-political system as a feudal structure which denied human rights to all citizens except feudal lords, and projects Chinese communism as modern and, against all objective assessments even in mainland China, as a true guarantor of human rights. The PEC agenda also condemns Tibet's otherworldly religion for miring the country in social backwardness which has only now improved thanks to China's replacement of the archaic politico-religious structure by this-worldly socialist and legal systems.

Thus the Chinese agenda is even stronger than that of the erstwhile European colonial powers: they were not assimilationist and did not completely distort and deny local history and culture. The pragmatic Chinese learn from others' 'historical mistakes': from Russia they digested the perils of and avoided glasnost while adopting perestroika, from imperialist history, they learnt that to tolerate the identity of the colonised is to leave the door open for future demands for independence. Hence the compulsion to totally negate Tibet's separate historical, political, and cultural existence to obviate any potential grounds for national self-determination. The intensity of this felt need and the magnitude of the distortions of reality it engenders can only be explained by its total lack of basis in objective reality. Although their revisionist propaganda is resented by the populace at large, there are always opportunists and pragmatists willing to compromise for a few perks and privileges. Pursued over a sufficiently long period of time, i.e. significantly longer than the 50 years of their rule so far, this pervasive method of brain-washing combined with demographic aggression might prove successful especially if simultaneously the Chinese language remains the medium of (and thereby controls) higher education and research and the route to economic and social advancement.

DISCONTENT ON THE PLATEAU

It is suggested that the Chinese in a perverse manner base or justify their policies in Tibet on the Native American model. There are indeed some disturbing parallels to what happened to the indigenous people of America: they were defeated in battle, humiliated, pressured to sign treaties which divested them of their rights and lands (as were the Tibetans by the 1951 17-point Agreement); incentivised to embrace the religion and culture of the conquerors (in this case the victor's ideology), decimated and pauperised through war, exposure to infectious diseases, deprived of their traditional means of livelihood et al. Surviving tribes were finally ghettoised into a few reservations which have serviced the tourist industry as do monasteries on the Tibetan Plateau. While this is a matter of embarrassment and regret to some section of Americans today, several of whom are engaged in rectifying history and attempting some restitution where possible, as where original contracts and records are still available, the Chinese have seized upon this unfortunate history as an example of how things ought to be done.

Thus, when we come to the present day, it appears that the predicament has reversed from when Tibetan refugees first entered India—at that time the need of the hour was to help preserve the identity of the refugees through their language and culture, which also though not solely served a political purpose. Now the urgency is in the opposite direction, to save Tibetan identity, language and culture inside Tibet on humanitarian, cultural and political grounds.

This has become more urgent in the light of the series of self-immolations that have taken place, largely but not solely in Greater Tibet over the last several months, reaching as at the date of this writing to over 95 instances. The immolators are mostly young people who have grown up in modern Tibet with no personal memories of the Dalai Lama and his government. Yet the slogans they chant as they burn to death are of political freedom and the return of the Dalai Lama to Tibet. What they are asking for may just be a dream, but what they are protesting against is very real—the suffocating lack of freedom and political-cum-cultural suppression under Chinese rule.

WHAT CAN BE DONE?

There is much speculation about China's future prospects, as to whether she will be able to maintain and manage current economic growth, indefinitely suppress democratic aspirations within the mainland, whether her tightly controlled one-party system will implode, opening spaces for minorities like the Tibetans, all of which entail a wait and watch policy. But, as of today the CCP is firmly in control of the country and China's growing economic and military clout is intimidating.

Still, there is much that we in India can do alongside our Tibetan friends. There is an overriding need to speak out on the horrific self-immolations in Tibet, and reports emanating from the Dharamsala Administration indicate some success in mobilising international concern, which needs to be sustained and expanded to bring pressure to bear on the Chinese government.

Working on ways of keeping Tibetans inside Tibet connected to their own language, history and culture is a doable option in the present especially with the means afforded by modern electronic communications. Refuting China-centric history, righting its distortion of religion, spirituality, political history (including its too slick dismissal of the Ganden Phodrang dual system as feudal which though outdated merits further study as a pre-modern attempt to institutionalise power checks and responsibility); its meretricious sociological and anthropological theories to support its theory of one Han family; in sum, a review of the whole gamut of the revisionist campaign to Sinicise Tibet's history and culture is a political and a scientifically objective necessity. Creating language CDs, popular film and documentary material for circulation on Tibetan themes inside Tibet is a possibility, they could be distributed also amongst the large numbers of Tibetans who live outside the TAR and have less guarantees, such as they are, about their language and culture. And if Tibetans are ready to expand their cultural horizons beyond pure tradition, why not a dose of Indian soft power both popular and classic? No doubt, some of this is already happening but much more could be done at relatively low cost; for sure China makes interaction between the home and exile communities more difficult by the day, but as yet there is no foolproof way to curb electronic communication.

There are also two matters in the state domain where perhaps the Indian government and the Indian political system could take some concrete steps.

India's first Prime Minister followed an ambiguous policy towards Tibet—he privately described China's occupation as an act of imperialism but refused to raise his voice against it. Rather, he equivocated by adopting the British notion of Chinese suzerainty over Tibet, which the British themselves implicitly abandoned when they signed the Simla Agreement with the sovereign government, of the 13th Dalai Lama. When Nehru declared that the Tibetan people had the right to choose their own form of government he did not clarify whether this was on grounds of sovereignty or autonomy, he did not use the term 'self-determination' but recognised that the PLA was in occupation and advised the occupiers or their masters to be gentle with the Tibetans. In India, he permitted the Tibetans to set up their Government-in-Exile but did not recognise it (if it was never a GIE he never demanded clarification and let the matter rest with studied ambiguity), and forbade them to indulge in any political activity from Indian soil. He initiated a policy of friendship with China, lobbied for her membership in the UNSC, embarked on intelligence operations in the Himalayas and was intransigent over the Indo-Tibetan border. All of the above has been described by apologists as sophisticated diplomacy but when Nehru declared himself betrayed in 1962 it rather suggested failure. Subsequent administrations, i.e. those of Indira Gandhi, Rajiv Gandhi, Atal

Bihari Vajpayee, step by step renounced several of Nehru's stronger and more obdurate positions: by degrees they forfeited the concept of Tibetan sovereignty, began to negotiate the Himalayan border, and became for a while more stringent in denial of public activity to the Tibetans and their supporters. More recently, however, the government has been tentatively and selectively using the Tibet card in the course of playing an increasingly aggressive China, as for example, when it allowed or encouraged the Dalai Lama to visit Arunachal at a time when the Chinese were asserting their claims to what they call Southern Tibet.

Given the fact that card-playing is essentially a tactical and not a strategic exercise, it is not the most reliable. Given regional tensions accompanying China's rising might and assertiveness, it may last for yet a while, especially as long as His Holiness is with us. But even otherwise it is as much in India's interest as in Tibet's that the exiles maintain their identity and help towards maintaining that of their confreres in Tibet. The rationale is both civilizational and strategic. One worst case scenario is that after the passing of the present Dalai Lama when the next outbreak of riots takes place in Tibet, China will again put the blame on the 'Dalai-clique' in Dharamsala as it does today over the immolations, and demand the dissolution of the Dharamsala administration. It is fervently to be hoped that India will draw the line at this point, and not succumb to Chinese pressure. Clearly, it would be best to draw a red line well in advance. The pro-Tibet lobby in India's Parliament which cuts across political parties, her civil society and the media could be primed to impact more long-term policy-making.

A second course of action for the Government of India is to work for restoration of Tibetan people-to-people links, an item to take up with the Chinese government. Although the Indian government has been publicly unequivocal in its acceptance of Chinese sovereignty over Tibet, reiterated at almost every Sino-

Indian summit, the Chinese remain distrustful. Nevertheless, it will at the very least put moral pressure on China and perhaps open some space for Indo-Tibetan soft power to compete with the enticements of Chinese consumerism.

POSTSCRIPT

Since the last two years, there has been a spate of fiery protests by Tibetans to capture international attention which indicates the extent of discontent and the absence of normal democratic avenues to register protest. Apparently adding to the policies of cultural attenuation, recent provocations include forcible settlement of nomads, increased imposition of the Chinese language over Tibetan as the medium of instruction, and tighter political control over monasteries.

In response, several resolutions on Tibet have been passed in parliaments and congresses in EU, France, Italy and the United States, and supportive statements by parliamentarians in Australia, Brazil, Canada, European Union, France, Germany, Italy, India, Japan, South Africa, the United States. Individuals like Ms. Navi Pillay, the UN High Commissioner on Human Rights, Mr. Gary Locke, the former US Ambassador to China[2] and Shinzo Abe, Prime Minister of Japan have also voiced their concerns.[3]

However, China's response had been couched in typically Orwellian newspeak: "A joint legal opinion issued by China's Supreme Court, top prosecution body and police says that the charge of 'intentional murder' should apply to anyone urging Tibetans to set themselves alight."[4] The immolators are treated as criminals and their families severely punished.

Several suggestions have been proffered in the course of recent deliberations for responding to these desperate appeals for help.[5] Apart from the need to continue activating interest amongst Indian religious and political leaders as well as of the international community, the issue of human rights violations could be vigorously pursued at the UN and if possible, at the International Court of Justice. If Tibetan women are still being subjected to forcible sterilization, it is a proper case for invoking the UN Convention on Genocide of 1948.

Since the Tibetans have obviously been denied their promised cultural autonomy, the international community should insist on China's adherence to the clauses of the 17-pt Agreement signed by her and representatives of the Tibetan Government in 1951. Her legal claim to Tibet rests basically on this document. The *spirit* of this Agreement would allow for reduction of Han immigration into TAR if not for trimming their already overwhelming presence, apart from the cultural and religious rights of Tibetans.

In particular India, in line with the civilizational theme of this paper and given her natural historical advantages, should make strenuous efforts to reclaim a leadership role in the Buddhist world, countering non-religious China's opportunistic attempts to do the same. In a non-formal way, this has already started: "In the middle of the expanses of Siberia, it is most interesting to come across monks, all of whom speak Hindi as they have received their Buddhist education in India."[6]

At the same time the government could increase promotion of research into Tibetan affairs, both by Indians and Tibetans, and also try to recover some of its old presence in Tibet by asking for the re-opening of the Lhasa consulate. Concomitantly, there is need to spread awareness amongst the Chinese people about Tibetan political rights and culture, especially among their liberal intellectuals at home and abroad.[7]

It is also fervently to be hoped that, although it is realistic to follow a flexible, tactical policy, given projected trends India may also think in the longer term of a stable regional architecture along the lines of the Zone of Peace proposal (with possible demilitarisation and denuclearisation of Tibet) spelt out by the Dalai Lama at Strasbourg, which will link the genuine autonomy of the Tibetan people with the strategic and environmental security of the region.

ENDNOTES

1. East West Centre Press, 1964.
2. CTA (Central Tibetan Administration), 5 December 2012 report on Sikyong Dr. Lobsang Sangay's March 10, 2012 statement.
3. Shinzo Abe (*Ft.com Nov. 13*th *2012*): "I swear I will do everything in my power to change the situation in Tibet where human rights are being suppressed ...Tibet seeks freedom and democracy and we agree on those values."
4. Olga Khazan, China; Self-immolators and their abettors will be charged with murder (*The Washington Post*, Dec 6 2012), quoting *Gannan Daily*
5. These suggestions are amongst a few thrown up at a Roundtable held under the auspices of the M.L. Sondhi Institute for Asia Pacific Affairs in collaboration with the TPPRC. Contributors included George Verghese, K.P.S. Gill, Thubten Samphel, N.N. Jha, Yeshi Choeden, Rajiv Vohra, Dagmar Bernstorff and J.M. Mukhi.
6. Benoy K. Behl, Signs of a Revival (*Frontline* Vol. 29, Issue 24 Dec. 01-14, 2012)
7. Andrew Jacobs (with research contributed by Shi Da, Amy Qin and Chang Lu), Many Chinese Intellectuals are silent amid a wave of self-immolations (NYT Nov 12 2012). Hu Yong, a professor at Peking University's School of Journalism and Communication. said: "the authorities have deliberately created a barrier between the two cultures," and . ..."such attitudes were reinforced by China's army of Tibet specialists, nearly all of whom are employed by government-affiliated institutions and who faithfully parrot the party's official narrative on Tibetan history and politics." ... Tsering Woeser, a blogger of mixed Tibetan and Han ancestry, commented that many Chinese see Tibetans as the "other"; ... "even her most open-minded friends are confounded by Tibetans, with their fierce

religious devotion, their demands for greater autonomy and their aching for the return of the Dalai Lama, whom Beijing regularly dismisses as a 'wolf in sheep's clothing'."

The Art of Non-violence: Winning China Over to Tibet's Story

Thubten Samphel

With the possible exception of the island nation of Taiwan, never in its more than 5,000 years of history has China's imperial throne met a match like that of Tibet. The Mongols, on whose mighty imperial enterprise communist China lays its claim of legitimacy to rule the minorities, are now a people divided in two. Chinese settlers' demographic assault on the traditional grazing grounds of the Mongols goes on at a ferocious pace. The Manchus, another nomadic people, who whipped China into its present imperial shape and size, are so totally assimilated into the mainstream that they are indistinguishable from the Chinese whom they ruled from 1644 to 1911. Today at the last count, only about twelve ageing Manchus can speak the language. The Uighurs of Eastern Turkestan or what the Chinese call Xinjiang, are politically and militarily suppressed and like other minorities, demographically flooded by Chinese settlers.

Tibet grapples with all these problems faced by China's other minorities. The Tibetans, like the Mongols and Uighurs, bristle under Beijing's subjugation and have been doing so for these last sixty years. However, in all three regions, China has not succeeded in either snuffing out their separate identities or winning their loyalty. On the contrary, resistance, violently in Eastern Turkestan and non-violently in Inner Mongolia and Tibet, is growing. The recent prolonged and peaceful protests in Inner Mongolia, the outburst of violence in Eastern Turkestan and the fiery death of two monks in Eastern Tibet are clear indication that the minorities in these regions are deeply unhappy with the nature of Beijing's brutal rule over them.

The Mongols of Inner Mongolia, the Uighurs of Eastern Turkestan and Tibetans in Tibet are served by active exile communities in the free world. In the case of the Tibetans, they are served by an organized and productive community, mainly based in India, that has preserved the values of the Tibetan Buddhist civilization and successfully promote these in the larger world. The Dalai Lama has empowered and truly liberated his people by persuading them to elect their political leader. This event will resonate far beyond the Tibetan people and into the hearts and minds of the Chinese who will one day want the same gift of democracy to decide who they want their leaders to be. At the same time, the Tibetan exiles maintain and run an education system that produces successive generations of teachers, doctors, writers and social activists and professionals in other vital fields. They are all committed soldiers in Tibet's non-violent struggle for freedom. In this freedom struggle, the Tibetans are supported by the selfless efforts of thousands of non-Tibetans, Indians and others across continents, who form the worldwide Tibet support group movement. For these reasons, the Tibet movement constitutes one of the most dynamic, sustained and yet non-violent struggles of our times.

But all these efforts by the Tibetans on both sides of the Himalayas pale in significance and import when seen against their decision to reach out to the Chinese people. The success of this new effort will decide the political fate of Tibet.

However, the decision to reach out to the Chinese people on the issue of Tibet threw up several serious challenges. One is the sheer scale of China's teeming masses. As one seasoned Western diplomat observed in disbelief at this Tibetan audacity to do what he perceived as the impossible, "There's 1.3 billion Chinese! Best of luck!" The other is the nature of the Chinese state. Ever since its founding in 1949, the People's Republic of China underwent tumultuous changes, from party-induced political upheaval to state-guided economic transformation. Overseeing all this is China's communist party, determined at all cost to keep the country under its vigilant rule. In such a circumstance, even if the six million Tibetans were able to convince all the 1.3 billion Chinese about the true nature of their non-violent struggle and win their support, would the opinion of the 1.3 billion Chinese in a one-party state matter in shaping Beijing's Tibet policy?

Then there is an even bigger challenge. These days, in the age of the Internet, the greatest obstacle to the Tibetan exiles' effort to reach out to the Chinese people is the Great Firewall. Like the Great Wall of China, this wall erected by Beijing in cyberspace is meant to prevent barbarian thoughts from infecting the health and harmony of the Middle Kingdom. Like all rulers of one-party states, China's communist leaders know that knowledge will set the Chinese people free.

These challenges either individually or collectively make the Tibetan effort to reach out to the Chinese a horrendous task.

Accomplishing this task is made well-nigh impossible by the fact that the resources, both in manpower and otherwise, available to the exile Tibetan community are limited. At the same time the political, economic, commercial and media reach of China both domestically and internationally is enormous and growing at a ferocious pace.

Though these challenges are compelling enough, for some Chinese there is a bigger problem. They consider the Tibetan exiles' incorporation of the pacifist doctrine of non-violence into their struggle against a highly militarized Chinese state as "mosquitoes stinging a bull's horn." Others, no less caustically, liken the Tibetan effort to "beating a dead yak to life" or as Beijing is condescendingly fond of pointing out, "a fly flapping its wings against the king of mountains." The latest Chinese government description of the Tibetan exile community is "Dalai and his scattered monkeys."

Whether as mosquitoes, or a dead yak or a lone fly or scattered monkeys, the Tibetan effort to reach out to the Chinese is producing results. These results are slow but they are inexorable. This is as much a credit to the Dalai Lama's unshakable conviction in the power of human persuasion as to the keen sense of justice of millions of Chinese, who themselves suffer the same boot-heel treatment from their rulers.

Chinese expression of sympathy and support for the Tibetan people came when it was most needed. The spring of 2008 saw Tibet swept away by a wave of prolonged protests that called for freedom in Tibet and the return of the Dalai Lama. China responded by massive force. On 15 May that year about 368 Chinese intellectuals signed an open letter to the Chinese government[1]. This letter, signed by Liu Xiaobo, the 2010 Nobel laureate, among many other Chinese luminaries, urged the official Chinese media to stop "stirring up inter-ethnic animosity and aggravating an already tense situation. This is extremely detrimental to the long-term goal of safeguarding national unity. We call for such propaganda to be stopped."

The letter added, "We support the Dalai Lama's appeal for peace, and hope that the ethnic conflict can be dealt with according to the principles of goodwill, peace, and nonviolence. We condemn any violent act against innocent people, strongly urge the Chinese government to stop the violent suppression, and appeal to the Tibetan people likewise not to engage in violent activities."

To explain both the violence meted out to the largely peaceful Tibetan protesters and to shirk responsibility for China's appalling misrule in Tibet, Wen Jiabao, the former premier, went on air with these words, "There is sufficient evidence to prove this incident was organized, premeditated, and meticulously orchestrated by the Dalai clique."

The challenge to ascertain the accuracy of the Chinese premier's accusation was taken up by Gongmeng, which translates into English as the Open Constitution Initiative, also known as the Gongmeng Law Research Centre, an organization based in Beijing. It consists of lawyers and academics who advocate the rule of law and greater constitutional protections in the People's Republic of China. It was established in 2003 by Xu Zhiyong and other lawyers.

Gongmeng sent four researchers throughout Tibet to find out the causes of the Tibetan people's discontent. In May 2009 it issued its findings[2]. The report said that the causes of the Tibetan people's unhappiness lay within Tibet and not outside. It said that the Chinese government's hard line policy on Tibet threw up a new aristocracy of corrupt officials whose chief concern was the protection of their personal interests and not the formulation and the implementation of just governance. The report presented to the Chinese government a nine-point recommendation. The first of these recommendations urged the Chinese government to "Earnestly listen to the voices of ordinary Tibetans and on the basis of respecting and protecting each of the Tibetan people's rights and interests, adjust policy and thinking in Tibetan areas to formulate development policies which are suited to the characteristics of Tibetan areas, and which accord with the wishes of the Tibetan people."

On 17 July 2009, Beijing declared Gongmeng "illegal" and shut down the law firm. The same month one of its founding members, Xu Zhiyong, was arrested for "tax evasion" and released on bail a month later.

To further intensify the Tibetan efforts to reach out to the Chinese, the Dalai Lama himself started a conversation on the Internet with the Chinese people. Moderated by Wang Lixiong, a well-known Chinese writer on Tibet, the Dalai Lama tweeted with Chinese netizens in May and July 2010, answering questions on his successor, his approach to resolve the issue of Tibet with Beijing, the nature of autonomy for Tibet, whether Tibetans would stick to non-violence after his demise and relations between Tibetans and Chinese. According to the Radio Free Asia's broadcast of this event on 21 July 2010, "A total of 1,543 netizens submitted 326 questions with a further 12,771 votes submitted online to select a final 10 questions."

The same broadcast, quoting Yu Jie, the author of *Wen Jiabao: China's Best Actor*, a book, banned in China but published in Hong Kong and critical of the Chinese prime minister, assesses the impact of this interaction between the Tibetan leader and the Chinese. "Beijing-based writer Yu Jie said Tuesday that the Dalai Lama's online dialogue will be very helpful in addressing false propaganda created to attack his image.

"The scale of the dialogue is not that big, just several thousand [participants]. However, I believe its influence and impact are getting bigger and bigger," Yu said. "One day it will defeat all distorted propaganda on the Dalai Lama and truth in Tibet, which has been overwhelmingly portrayed in the newspaper, on the radio, on television, and via the Internet controlled by the Chinese Communist Party will prevail."

Regardless of Beijing's determined efforts to control and supervise the Internet traffic, the Internet has empowered the Tibetan people. Lui Xiaobo, the imprisoned Nobel laureate, considers the Internet God's gift to the Chinese people. Likewise for Tibetans the Internet has exponentially increased their capacity to reach out to the Chinese people in order to tell their side of the story.

And the Chinese people are listening to the Tibetan story with increasing sympathy and understanding because the Tibetan effort to seek greater freedom for Tibet embodies all the values which the Chinese people cherish but are denied to them: democracy, freedom, human dignity, tolerance, compromise and cultural diversity. These are the political attractions of the Tibetan diaspora for an increasing number of Chinese.

For a different group of Chinese, there is another Tibetan attraction, and that is, Tibetan Buddhism. China today is roiled by sweeping economic and social changes. Communism, the ideological foundation of socialist and egalitarian China, lies in ruins except for the determined assertion of the Chinese communist party to its right to rule a hugely successful capitalist China. Communism as a discredited ideological force has created a spiritual vacuum and young Chinese are flocking to traditional beliefs like Taoism, Confucianism, Christianity and Buddhism or extreme nationalism to make sense of their lives and their rapidly changing society. Young and well-to-do Chinese are turning to Tibetan Buddhism, inviting Tibetan Lamas to their homes, joining monasteries in Tibet and even coming to India to attend the teachings of the Dalai Lama.

The story of Chinese fascination with Tibetan Buddhism is told in a new book, *Tragedy in Crimson: How the Dalai Lama Conquered the World but Lost the Battle with China*, by Tim Johnson, a veteran reporter who had covered China for Knight-Ridder and McClatchy for six years from Beijing. One of the stories the book tells is about the Serthar Buddhist Academy, founded in Eastern Tibet more than thirty years ago by the late Khenpo Jigme Phuntsok, a charismatic and deeply venerated master both in Tibet and the outside world. In Tibetan the Serthar Buddhist Academy is known as Larung Gar, which invokes a vast nomadic encampment that downplays its monastic character to circumvent China's restrictions on the construction of new monasteries. At its height the academy attracted over 10,000 students from all over Tibet, China and Southeast Asia and at least about 1000 students were Chinese, mostly from mainland China.

Unfortunately, China in the late 1990s and early 2000s suffered from the Falun Gong fear which led to the organisation's uprooting from the country. Just as the Chinese Communist Party feared Falun Gong which at one point is said to have more than 70 million members, more than that of the Chinese Communist Party, the provincial authorities in Sichuan grew nervous about the potential for trouble from such a large body of people outside Party control.

In July 2001, the authorities declared the academy "illegal." Soon after, demolition squads descended upon the academy and by their own admission the authorities said 1,875 dwellings were razed to the ground. All students not native to the region were expelled.

Tim Johnson visited Larung Valley in which the academy is located after the sustained protests that swept Tibet in the spring and summer of 2008. Despite the mauling that the Serthar Buddhist Academy received from the provincial authorities nearly a decade ago, what the author saw in Larung Valley astonished him.

> While thousands of monks and nuns were forced to leave Serthar in 2001, many climbed over the mountains and returned to the academy later. The population has swollen now to an even higher number … Thousands of simple rustic cabins climbed the slopes as far as the eye could see … A few minutes later, lower in the valley, several thousand nuns flooded out of wooden buildings at the end of classes … I'd never been to a Tibetan Buddhist center with so many ethnic Han Chinese. I wondered what was different here. While clearly some of the Chinese were from Taiwan, Singapore and Malaysia, many were from the Chinese mainland.

The presence of a large body of Chinese students at the academy certainly indicates that Tibet's political struggle with Beijing does not deter ordinary Chinese men and women from embracing and benefiting from the universal values embedded in the Tibetan Buddhist culture.

The Tibetan ability to tell their story effectively to the Chinese might determine the outcome of the story itself. Joseph S. Nye, the coiner of the "soft power" concept, explains this in his new book, *The Future of Power*, "On an increasing number of issues in the 21st century, war is not the ultimate arbiter... Outcomes are shaped not merely by whose army wins but also by whose story wins." In articulating this view, Joseph Nye echoes the military precepts of Sun Tzu, who lived around the same time as Confucius. In his classic text on military strategy, *The Art of War*, ancient China's master military strategist reveals this gem, "Ultimate excellence lies not winning every battle but defeating the enemy without ever fighting."

The best example of the changing attitude of the Chinese to the issue of Tibet is the self-immolations that are going on in

Tibet. So far, since 2009, over a hundred Tibetans in Tibet have set themselves ablaze. All of them have called for the return of the Dalai Lama to his homeland and freedom for the Tibetan people. This is the burning topic of discussion between Tibetan exiles and the Chinese on the Mainland. When informed of these self-immolations, the reaction from the Chinese netizens is one of shock and disbelief. Even when images of self-immolations were sent to them, the sentiment of the majority Chinese netizens is, this can't be happening in China.

Buried in the widespread sentiment of disbelief are also expressions of support and understanding, says Tsering Wangmo, who heads Drelwa, a Tibetan NGO based in Dharamsala, the seat of the Dalai Lama in north India. Drelwa consists of six young Chinese-speaking Tibetans who daily surmount the Great Firewall of China to carry on a conversation with netizens in China. One netizen writes, "You Tibetans are not alone. We are also frustrated by rising food and rent prices. Though we haven't heard about the self-immolations, we understand the reasons for the frustration arising out of a loss of hope."

Another blames the Chinese Communist Party for the increasing cases of Tibetans resorting to self-immolation. He says, "The CCP hides the truth and spreads distorted information. The CCP suppresses not only Tibetans, Mongols, Uighurs but the Chinese people. The Chinese people don't know the truth because all channels of free information are blocked. To solve all these problems, China must tread on the path of democracy."

These are some of the sentiments of support and sympathy whispered beyond the radar of China's censor and below the din of China's Internet chatter.

Others openly express what they feel about the self-immolations going on in Tibet. For example, in an interview for the *Foreign Policy* magazine in its September-October 2012 issue, Ai Weiwei, the world famous Chinese artist, made these comments,

"The one exception is Tibet, because of its natural resources, but the Tibetan people are burning themselves to death. Already over 40 of them in the past two years, and nobody's talking about it."

When asked whether he had been to been to Lhasa before, Ai Weiwei said, "No. I would feel ashamed to go. I think to respect [the Tibetans] is not to touch them, to leave them alone."

Ran Yunfei, one of China's most outspoken public intellectuals, in an interview to Ian Johnson for the *New York Review of Books,* said, "The communists really destroyed religion. They don't understand it at all. Look at Tibet. I told the guobao (state security agents) that, "you guys have gone too far. You don't allow them to hang pictures of the Dalai Lama. You don't have faith so you don't understand. So the Tibetans get very angry and depressed. And then you go into temples and instead hang pictures of Mao and Jiang (Zemin) or Hu (Jintao). You've gone overboard! This isn't right. Think about it. No wonder they set themselves on fire."

On 21 November 2012, Human Rights in China, an advocacy group of Chinese who promote human rights in China, based in New York, posted a news item on its website which said, *Chinese Netizens Speak Out on Tibetan Self-Immolations Despite Censorship.* Perhaps, this is in response to a *New York Times* article which commented on the deafening silence of Chinese scholars to the self-immolations in Tibet. The news item says, "In recent weeks, Chinese netizens have helped spread reports of Tibetan self-immolations online and expressed their concerns by posting comments on Twitter. They have done so despite intensified government crackdowns and Internet censorship in the lead up to and during the 18th Party Congress."

Human Rights in China posted eight comments made by Chinese netizens. The human rights organization posted these comments in their original Chinese and English translation. One post says, "Some say the world is numb towards Tibetans' self-immolation. I deeply agree. Especially Han Chinese, it seems as if it is not relevant to them, or they are intentionally avoiding the problem."

Another post says, "Support! Treasure life! Peaceful and rational resistance. We request, from now on, do not self-immolate. We believe that the future of the Tibetan people can rely only on the Tibetans themselves."

Another post says, "I hope more people will pay attention to the Tibetans' situation and their wishes. Put an end to the authoritarian and decrepit one-party system and the oppression of ethnic minorities."

One post says, "Communist Party of China must understand that the way to prevent Tibetans from self-immolation is to stop the colonial oppressive rule in Tibet. In another words, self-immolation will not end as long as (Tibet) is not liberated."

These comments made by Chinese netizens on the situation in Tibet constitute a drop in China's 1.3 billion ocean. However, if they are allowed to grow to their full potential within an evolving China, these comments will help positively shape how China treats its minorities.

ENDNOTES

1. Google search by typing 'Twelve suggestions for dealing with the Tibetan situation.'
2. The report can be google searched by typing 'Gongmeng Tibet report.'

11

China's Approach to Tibetan Issue

Sujit Dutta

The principal actor here is China and how it thinks about Tibet and what it has done in terms of shaping its policies towards Tibet, have deep implications for India, not to speak about the fate of Tibet itself. So keeping those factors in mind, a few broad comments are offered, as to how Chinese policies have evolved over time and what has been their overall impact on Tibet and what it means in terms of the next phase of the Tibetan struggle for autonomy/independence and how it will shape up.

Chinese claims on Tibet are deeply nationalist and are intertwined with the entire nationalist historiography that have been internalized by the Chinese students, scholars, elites both of the Kuomintang and the Communist Party over the past century. Since it began and since it had the backing of people like Sun Yat-Sen and Mao Zedong and others, it has gained a huge amount of political weight in Chinese thought, and so it is taken for granted that Tibet has been part of China and that it was somehow conspired and sought to be weakened by the foreigners. Now that China is stronger and China has come back as a powerful actor in the international system, this is the way that the Chinese must create their own justice, history must be recovered and attenuation must be done. That is basically the first point.

The internalization of this idea through books, literature, other writings and propaganda has taken it to a very extensive level so that the basic question of sovereignty is not an issue for the Chinese and does not raise any question in the Chinese mind.

Secondly, the Chinese attempted to go about settling the issue by seizing it by force. Power was seized in Beijing from the Kuomintang through the gun. So power had to be seized in Lhasa similarly and the PLA was an instrument of China's control and occupation of Tibet in 1950-51, which they called liberation. So their actions fitted well within the concept of what the Chinese Communist Party was doing, liberating both China and Tibet from the old system and creating a new society and bringing a new type of freedom to the Tibetans. So the Chinese have always conceptualized in their writings and in their talks: Tibet is a question of feudalism being liberated into modernity and socialism. Therefore, removing backwardness and medievalism from Tibet has been a principal mission as far as the articulation of China is concerned. So economic development as well as questions relating to new social foundations of Tibet have been a deep driving force behind Chinese policy/Chinese thought as far as Tibet is concerned. In addition, the use of force has not been seen in China in any manner as something illegitimate. So it does not create moral questions as far as China is concerned. Since it has been called liberation, it is seen as liberation.

Thirdly, the Chinese have tried to overcome the fact that for very vast periods of Tibet history, Tibet was independent. It had its own culture, its own territorial make-up, state systems, currency and its relationship with China, parts of China were occupied by the Tibetan state. In addition, the fact is that in the 1914 Simla

Conference, China was quite willing to sit with Tibet and British India as independent actors. If they did not accept Tibet as an entity how were they sitting in that conference? So these questions raise very important dilemmas which current Chinese historiography tries to wipe out by calling the entire Simla Agreement and therefore the McMahon line a charade, basically a British-crafted manoeuvre which the Chinese were tricked into. But the issue is that the question essentially boiled down to the inner Tibet- outer Tibet division for which reason the Chinese did not sign and ratify the Agreement. If that had been settled, the Chinese would have signed it. The British kept on asking for that signature for a very long time. Only by 1938, Olaf Caroe insisted that the Treaty be published since the Tibetans and the Chinese were not reaching an agreement.

So that sets the backdrop: there is a legitimacy question as far as Tibet is concerned. There is a question relating to 1914, the fact that China participated in that conference as equal to Tibetans and that it was essentially a territorial question that kept them from signing it [though they initialed it] and not a fundamental disagreement with the arrangement. All these historical facts cannot be denied but Chinese historiography has sought essentially to cloud it and just bury it, so that there is no complication in the mind of the Chinese elites and intellectuals about where Tibet belongs in terms of the long history of Chinese sovereignty over Tibet in terms of their interpretation.

Now in all this of course the Chinese have crafted a national strategy like the rest of China but more importantly because of the specific conditions of Tibet and its history and culture. They have established a formal structure of autonomy, Tibet Autonomous Region (TAR), while other ethnic Tibetans have been merged into some of the other provinces around Qinghai, Gansu, Yunan and Sichuan. But Tibet Autonomous Region (TAR) remains on the front burner as the symbol of the so-called autonomy. And yet the Chinese have not been able to implement that autonomy in practice.

Self-determination of nations was very much part of the communist theology, both within Leninism and which Stalin and Mao inherited as well. And from time to time, there is talk about self-determination of nationalities and the suggestion that the Tibetans could choose their way. But when it came down to actual practice, the Chinese Communist party was competing with the Kuomintang and becoming more and more nationalist. In such a competition, no compromises on such territorial issues and sovereignty questions could be made because otherwise it would be seen as the weaker party making the weaker argument. So nationalist competition determined that there would not be any quarter given to such ideas which Mao from time to time and others reflected, essentially flowing from the Leninist understanding of nationalities. So autonomy formally in practice would be the way forward and between 1954 when India recognized Tibet as part of China and the 1980s, there would be a series of continuous aggravation to deny the essential issues of autonomy that the Tibetans were asking for, based on the 1951 Agreement.

Even that Agreement was imposed; nonetheless, even on the basis of the Agreement that promised to grant autonomy and the constitution that promised it again, the Chinese were not quite willing to adhere to the letter as well as the spirit. By 1965, the Tibetan Autonomous Region had been created, just about the time the Cultural Revolution was beginning and by this point in time the cultural destruction of Tibet along with much of China began. All that was old had to be destroyed and the Tibetan monasteries were among the heaviest losers in the Cultural Revolution. Many monasteries and cultural artefacts were destroyed just as Confucian artefacts were destroyed in the rest of China. So the restructuring of Tibet, Tibetan history, reconstruction of its identity, began. And till about the middle of the 1980s, very little economic development or political development beyond this took place. There was some attention given to it during the Maoist period but major economic development did not happen. It is therefore in the post-Mao phase and its reform and modernization that we must locate current Tibetan autonomy/devolution of power and questions relating to the negotiations.

One of this of course is the Deng Xiaoping strategy of opening up Tibet that began with an initial genuine humanistic face articulated by Hu Yaobang, the General Secretary of the Party. In his 1980 visit, Hu Yaobang accepted frontally the Red Guard destruction that the Communist Party's movement had inflicted during the Maoist period in Tibet, the great loss of life and many other weaknesses of the party policies that had created havoc. Therefore, he sought out a way to reconcile the two and move forward. Unfortunately, Hu Yaobang represented a very liberal reformist phase that the larger Chinese political elite were unwilling to accept. They were willing to accept a reformist economic state but not the political reforms represented by Hu Yaobang and his supporters, who even articulated a very different kind of approach on the question of autonomy vis-à-vis Tibet. Some important writings of that period talked about a far greater attempt to create autonomy in Tibet and a new cultural and political policy. Unfortunately, the phase ended with Hu Yaobang himself being overthrown and sacked from the Party.

Thereafter, Deng Xiaoping's hard approach regarding politics was followed. Hu Jintao, the current president, was a principal instrument as the Party Secretary of the Tibet Autonomous Region to enforce that policy of holding it together. Stability and security being the foremost goals of the party in Tibet while economic and infrastructural questions would be looked at in a very different manner. China has pursued these two goals since then. One, the principal focus is on stability and security, with no questions regarding sovereignty; secondly, opening up Tibet to infrastructure, railway development, road construction and urbanization, which in turn would draw in tourists, etc. that would open Tibet to the rest of the world. Now these twin policies are therefore the feature of the reform period as far as China and Tibet are concerned.

In terms of economic growth, just the sheer size of Chinese GDP growth statistics will indicate the scale of rapid economic growth over the past 10 years at least. GDP grew at a CAGR of 10+ % and the rise in per capita income is equally impressive. The reality, of course, is much more difficult, much more crass and, in terms of the Tibetan experience, not a happy one either. Firstly, the bulk of the Tibetans live in the rural areas and the Chinese strategy is essentially urban centric, and infrastructure centric and the focus is on essentially development of this kind plus stability and security. The military and the Party play a very important role in creating this kind of stability and security.

Secondly, on the economic side, China has promoted urbanization and the re-casting of Lhasa and several cities and towns. In order to pursue this, entrepreneurs and semi-skilled workers from the rest of China have been brought in on the grounds so that they can provide economic development. However, since the bulk of the Tibetans are in the rural areas, urbanization and administrative growth of this type has no real effect on their lives or their needs. Therefore the Chinese model of the post-reform period has a major disjunct, on the one hand data show high rates of economic growth, and urbanization which changed Lhasa, Shigatse and other cities. There has also been huge growth in tourism and other connectivity with the rest of the world, and entrepreneurship is also growing. However the bulk of the Tibetans, around 80-85%, that stay in rural areas have little connection with this world and this economic growth model. Here lies the great dichotomy of the past two decades of high growth, yet coupled with missed opportunities and arrested growth for the Tibetans.

The Chinese strategy therefore has a major weakness since it is crafted from Beijing or the nearby cities of Xian and Chengdu and hence does not have the integrated view that the Tibetans need, both within TAR and also the Tibetan communities across the other four provinces mentioned earlier. As a result, the Tibetans are unhappy over the loss of identity, culture and their political autonomy. This feeds into the Tibetans yearning for independence.

However, the Tibetans have not allowed the Chinese to forget the Tibetan question. Earlier in 1950s, then in 1987, 1990 and 2008, especially during the Olympics, tens of thousands of Tibetans protested on the streets, despite the huge presence of military and security forces, resulting in the arrest of thousands of them. They are political prisoners, including monks and nuns from the monasteries and they languish in prisons. Every time some relaxation takes place, a new crisis follows, and the state clamps down with brutal suppression of these movements. Therefore it is a recurring cycle.

However, in between this, these movements have been kept alive and have forced China to initiate talks from time to time. The Chinese have insisted on several conditions as far as negotiations are concerned, demanding pledges of no splittism, acceptance of one China policy, Tibet as part of China, Taiwan as part of China, etc. The talks have not really moved forward to settle anything; nonetheless the fact that these talks have taken place from time to time indicates that Tibetans have kept alive their movement. Therefore, much will depend in the coming years on how Tibet and the Tibetans in exile develop that movement, use international opportunities of today, the internet and other means to create a greater awareness of Tibet's culture, identity, political history and its demand for the exiles to return to their homelands.

These are all major factors around which movements can be constructed. China will not always be the monolith that it is today. It is undergoing great changes and the coming years will see huge social upheavals in China in which the middle class of China would be demanding their own rights. As Hu Yaobang recognised at one point of time during the political reformist phase, the Tibetans are going to be part of the larger movement for changing China and Tibetans in exile as well as within must prepare for that day.

Tibetan Autonomy—Myth or Reality ?

Vijay Kranti

On 23rd of May 2011 the People's Republic of China (PRC) celebrated the 60th anniversary of what its leaders termed the 'peaceful liberation' of Tibet. It was on this day in 1951 that a 17-point agreement was claimed to have been signed in Beijing between the representatives of the Chinese government and a delegation of the government of Tibet in Lhasa. This delegation was forcibly sent to Beijing by the Chinese communist establishment for 'discussions' following the invasion and occupation of a large part of Eastern Tibet by the People Liberation Army (PLA) a year earlier.

In the light of the threatening postures of the communist neighbour, the 16-year-old monk ruler of Tibet, the Dalai Lama, had been shifted by his government functionaries from the capital Lhasa to Dromo, a safe place near the Indian border in the South.

The Chinese delegation was led by the Chairman of the Commission of Nationalities Affairs, traditionally a Han dominated organ of the Chinese government whose main responsibility was to keep the 55 non-Han 'nationalities' under Chinese control. The Tibetan side was led by Ngapo Ngawang Jigme, a junior minister in the Dalai Lama's Kashag (Cabinet of Ministers) and apparently a preferred choice of Beijing. In principle, the 17-Point Agreement assured Tibet complete autonomy within the Chinese framework.

17-POINT AGREEMENT

The language of the 17-Point 'agreement', though claimed by China to be the outcome of a 'dialogue' between the two sides, leaves little doubt that it was outright a Chinese draft which was simply pushed down the throat of a meek, defeated Tibetan government. Although the title *"The Agreement of the Central People's Government and the Local Government of Tibet on Measures for the Peaceful Liberation of Tibet"* presumes Beijing's unquestionable authority as the 'Central' government over just a 'local government' of Tibet, yet the very opening paragraph of the main statement admits Tibet's status as a separate entity where, for whatever reasons, China did not enjoy any direct, effective control for *"over the last hundred years and more"*.

Most of its clauses simply testify to the status of the Tibetan government, led by the Dalai Lama, as an independent entity until the day China decided to walk in. Seeking support of Tibetans on so many counts, the 'agreement' also exposed the status of the invading Chinese army as 'outsiders'. For example, the very first point of the 'agreement' starts with calling upon the Tibetan people to '*drive out*' some imaginary '*imperialist aggressive forces*' from Tibet and expects that the Tibetan people "*shall return to the big family of the motherland—the People's Republic of China.*"

The second point, which reads: "*The Local Government of Tibet shall actively assist the People's Liberation Army to enter Tibet and consolidate the national defences,*" too exposes what level of control the 'Central Government' or its army enjoyed in Tibet prior to this 'peaceful liberation of Tibet'. This simply exposes the falsity of the PRC leadership's claims that *'historically Tibet has been an inalienable part of China'.*

While assuring the people of Tibet that they "*have the right of exercising national regional autonomy*" (Point-3), the same clause takes it back simultaneously through the rider which clarifies that this autonomy would operate "*under the unified leadership of the Central People's Government.*"

The 'agreement' made many other promises to the Tibetans which included "*not* (to) *alter the existing political system*", especially the "*established status, functions and powers of the Dalai Lama*" (Pt-4); freedom of religious belief (Pt-7); development of the Tibetan language (Pt-9); and "*no compulsions*" on reforms on the part of the '*Central Authorities*' (Pt-11). The 'agreement' even went to the extent of assuring the Tibetans that the funds for the Chinese Army and administration would be provided by the '*Central People's Government*' (Pt-16) and that "*the PLA entering Tibet ... will also be fair in all buying and selling and will not arbitrarily take even a needle or a thread from the people.*" (Pt-13).

In lieu of all these 'concessions', the 'agreement' also announced the privileges which China was going to enjoy in Tibet. These included the predominance of PLA through dissolution of Tibetan troops as "*Tibetan troops will be reorganised step by step into the People's Liberation Army*" (Pt-8); and an end to all ties of the Tibetan government with the outer world as PRC decided to take charge of '*all external affairs of the area of Tibet*" (Pt-14).

The signing of this '17-Pt Agreement' in Beijing came as a bomb shell to the young Dalai Lama and his government colleagues in Dromo when Radio Beijing broke the news of the 'peaceful liberation' of Tibet through this agreement. They did not expect that a junior ranking 'discussion' team could sign an 'agreement' which had the potential of changing their nation's history.

Recalling those moments in his autobiography *Freedom in Exile*, the Dalai Lama writes,

> ....Every evening I would listen to the Tibetan language broadcasts of Radio Peking...... However, one evening, as I sat alone, there was a very different sort of program. A harsh, crackling voice announced that a 'Seventeen-Point Agreement' for the Peaceful Liberation of Tibet had that day been signed by representatives of the Government of the People's Republic of China and what they called the 'Local Government' of Tibet. I could not believe my ears. I wanted to rush out and call everybody in, but I sat transfixed....... What was most alarming, however, was that Ngabo[1] had not been empowered to sign anything on my behalf, only to negotiate. I had kept the seals of state with me at Dromo to ensure that he could not. So he must have been coerced....

Later, it became clear that Beijing forced the Tibetan group leader to sign an already prepared 'agreement' under a Tibetan government seal which was hurriedly forged by Beijing especially for this purpose.

In the recorded history of China and Tibet, it was the second time that an 'agreement' based on a 'dialogue' was being claimed to have been 'signed'. The first recorded treaty dates back to 821-822 AD which was signed between a powerful Tibetan king Trisong Dretsen and the Chinese king Hwangti (Wen We Hsiao-te Hwang-ti). This treaty remains engraved in Tibetan and Chinese languages on two identical stone pillars, one installed in the Tibetan capital Lhasa and other in China. Opening with the declaration of an 'alliance' between the two kingdoms, this treaty clearly defines the independent character of the two countries and calls for conditions that ensure that 'Tibetans shall be happy in the land of Tibet, and the Chinese in the land of China' in future. The operative sections of the 821-822 AD Treaty[2] read:

> The Great King of Tibet, the Miraculous Divine Lord, and the Great King of China, the Chinese Ruler Hwang-ti being in the relationship of nephew and uncle, have confirmed together for the alliance of their kingdoms.....Tibet and China shall abide by the frontiers of which they are now in occupation. All to the east is the country of Great China; and all to the west is, without question, the country of Great Tibet. Henceforth on neither side shall there be waging of war nor seizing of territory..... According to the old custom, horses shall be changed at the foot of the Chiang Chun pass, the frontier between Tibet and China. At the Suiyung barrier the Chinese shall meet Tibetan envoys and provide them with all facilities from there onwards...... Between the two countries no smoke nor dust shall be seen. There shall be no sudden alarms and the very word 'enemy' shall not be spoken...... This solemn agreement has established a great epoch when Tibetans shall be happy in the land of Tibet, and the Chinese in the land of China.... If the parties do not act in accordance with this agreement or if they violate it, whichever it be, Tibet or China, nothing that the other party may do by way of retaliation shall be considered a breach of the treaty on their part......

AN INDIFFERENT WORLD

In 1951, the civilised world took note of the forcible takeover of Tibet by PRC as yet another case of colonising a powerless country. But no government or international organisation like the UN, demonstrated the guts to challenge the government of China on this issue. Even a country like India, the most affected by this sudden change in the Asian map, chose to discourage the UN from taking any steps against China. The government of India decided to give more importance to the personal assurances that Chinese Premier Chou En-Lai gave to Indian Prime Minister Pandit Jawahar Lal Nehru, that the PRC would honour the unique cultural identity of Tibet and Tibetan people. No wonder, this meek and indifferent international response only encouraged the PRC leaders to take their own course in occupied Tibet.

In the next few years, the much hyped 17-Point 'agreement' was observed more in the breach of most of the clauses than following it in letter and spirit. The promises of autonomy were overturned as the control of the political and administrative system shifted to the hands of communist cadres and PLA's machinery, thus leaving no scope for the Dalai Lama to play any meaningful role. The sudden arrival of hundreds of thousands of PLA soldiers and cadres in a thinly populated Tibet pushed up food prices to unheard-of levels. Forced cultivation of wheat in place of traditional barley too led to unprecedented food shortages and anti-China food riots all over Tibet. The cadres' intolerance for Buddhist practices led to the closures of monasteries and of monastic schools in favour of Chinese language schools. PLA's armed attacks on monasteries forced a sizeable section among the monks and nuns to join the resistance movement which was already spreading across Tibet, especially in the eastern regions of Kham, Golok and Amdo.

Things came to a head in March 1959 when a 100,000-strong crowd of local citizens and pilgrims in Lhasa clashed with the PLA. Soon this clash morphed into a Tibetan uprising against the occupying Chinese army. What followed was the escape of the Dalai Lama to exile in India and PLA killing tens of thousands of Tibetans across Tibet in order to put a decisive end to the uprising. In its report on Tibet *"The Question of Tibet and the Rule of Law"* (July 24, 1959) the International Commission of Jurists, Geneva referred to its own earlier press statement of June 5th, 1959 which said, ".... the number of the Tibetans killed by the Chinese was given as 65,000....". But in its report it quoted the Dalai Lama's reply to a media person's question as saying that, "The number of Tibetans killed in fighting the Chinese occupation forces since 1956 is actually more than the Indian report." (p. 60)[3]

TIBET AUTONOMOUS REGION: THE SECOND COMING OF 'AUTONOMY'

Following the escape of the Dalai Lama to exile which led to the formal end of the Dalai Lama-led social, political and cultural system, the Chinese leadership gave final shape to their Tibetan agenda by reorganizing the geographic and administrative map of Tibet in 1965. A new region, designated as the 'Tibet Autonomous Region' (TAR) ('Xizang' in Chinese) was carved out of the newly acquired Tibet which was only about a third of the original Tibet. Its boundaries were largely limited only to U-Tsang, one of the three traditional provinces of Tibet. Large chunks of the other two provinces, namely Kham and Amdo, were chopped off the original Tibet and these chunks were absorbed into adjoining Chinese provinces of Sichuan, Yunnan, Quinghai and Gansu. Interestingly, this exercise was undertaken in the name of further advancing the 'autonomous' status of Tibet.

One major goal of Beijing behind this exercise was to restrict any future claims of Tibetans and their prospective international supporters to TAR only. Obviously, this idea of the PRC leadership to insulate the original Tibetan regions of Kham and Amdo from any international dispute or Tibetan claims has become a serious stumbling block in the progress of Beijing-Dharamsala dialogue in recent decades.

THE IRON CURTAIN

The following two decades saw a completely closed and non-communicative PRC as far as Tibet was concerned. This was the period when Tibet witnessed an intense spell—its longest so far—of political suppression and cultural destruction. Believing that the religious faith and unique culture of Tibet were the only barriers holding the Tibetan masses back from assimilating emotionally into the socio-political system of 'Motherland China', the regional administrators of Tibet and communist party cadres did everything that they could do to destroy each visible symbol of Tibet's religious, cultural, social and national personality. Far from the eyes and physical control of the central leadership in Beijing, a remotely located Tibet went through the worst excesses of the 'Cultural Revolution' [and the 'Great Leap Forward' before it], at the hands of overenthusiastic Red Guards for a much longer time and with a far more devastating impact than what happened in mainland China. Exiled Tibetans claim that over 1.2 million Tibetans have died unnatural deaths out of a total population of about six million since the Tibetan occupation in 1951. A majority of these deaths are attributed to the happenings during the Cultural Revolution days and the 'Great Leap Forward'. The reasons for these deaths include direct execution of citizens by the Public Security Bureau (PSB) for various 'crimes'; torture in jails; public death sentences in humiliating 'Thamzing' (public street trial sessions which were an integral part of indoctrination and cleansing of "peoples' enemies" in towns and villages across PRC); PLA's killing of rebellious Tibetans who took to armed resistance against the Chinese occupation; and starvation due to perpetual food shortages caused by the state's colonial policies in Tibet. According to the Central Tibetan Administration (CTA), informally also known as the 'Tibetan Government in Exile' (TGIE), barring very few (less than 10) among the 6259 monasteries and other religious centres, almost all were either closed, destroyed or taken over by the PLA and the Party cadres to accommodate their soldiers, cadres and their animals (horses, mules and pigs). In the fateful days of the Cultural Revolution, even a 'crime' like making '*Bod-Chha*' (traditional Tibetan tea with yak butter and salt) was labelled a 'reactionary' act or even 'treason', which could end up in public execution in a 'Thamzing' trial. In later years, Communist Party leaders did admit and express regret over these atrocities in Tibet, but also tried to brush them off as of 'little consequence' as compared to what happened in mainland China during the Cultural

Revolution. It is now acknowledged in China that over 30 million people died during Mao's fanciful but disastrous 'Great Leap Forward'.

THE DALAI LAMA RETURNS TO CHINESE FOCUS

However, things started changing when Deng Xiaoping re-emerged after Mao's death on the scene with a new economic and political outlook. The Tibetan situation made him realise that attempts to win Tibetan hearts through attack on faith and coercion had proved counter-productive. He could see that the Tibetan people's faith in their exiled ruler and religious leader, the Dalai Lama, had only increased during two decades of Tibetan occupation. His own pragmatic approach and the PRC's new interface with the civilised world made him realize that if handled properly, the Dalai Lama could be made a part of the solution. It was at this stage that the Chinese leadership started realising that the Dalai Lama was the key that could unlock the Tibetan problem and, hence, deserved the PRC's special attention.

An extreme view that emerged from this thinking, and still dominates the minds of a section of the Chinese leadership, is that the real problem is the Dalai Lama, not the Tibetan people. Most of their policies emerge from the assumption that the return of the Dalai Lama to China on China's terms will end the Tibetan problem or, in the absence of such an eventuality, the death of the ageing Dalai Lama will automatically see the end of the Tibetan headache of PRC.

This encouraged Deng to establish a dialogue with the exiled Dalai Lama. In early 1979 he sent a message to the Dalai Lama in India through the latter's elder brother Gyalo Thondup. A senior political functionary of the government-controlled news agency Xinhua, who personally knew Gyalo Thondup from their Hong Kong days, played a pivotal role in fixing his meeting with Deng in March 1979. To many Tibet observers, Beijing's choice of using Gyalo Thondup as its link to Dharamsala, the seat of the Dalai Lama and his Tibetan Government-in-Exile (TGiE) in northern India, came as a surprise. For it was Gyalo Thondup who had worked as the main link between the American intelligence agency CIA and *"Chu Shi Nga Druk"* (meaning 'Four Rivers, Six Ranges'), the fiery Tibetan guerrilla force that spearheaded the armed resistance against occupying Chinese forces inside Tibet until the CIA withdrew its support in the mid-1970s and paved way for the PLA and Royal Nepal Army to hunt down the Tibetan guerrilla fighters. Those who were gunned down by the RNA and PLA included Wangdu, a much revered guerrilla general inside and outside Tibet.

But for some other observers, who were aware of Gyalo Thondup's close personal links and relations with some key Chinese functionaries, he was an obvious choice as Beijing's main link to Dharamsala. According to Tsering Shakya, an acclaimed authority on the history of modern Tibet and the author of history book *The Dragon In The Land Of Snows*, Gyalo Thondup is the son-in-law of Zhi Shiguai, the first director of the 'Mongolian and Tibetan Affairs Commission' (p. 35)[4]. Originally established by the Chiang Kai-Shek regime and later taken over in toto by the Communist government, the sole mandate of this Commission has been to expand China's control over Tibet and Inner Mongolia.

It has been repeatedly claimed by Dharamsala, that Deng asked Thondup in 1979 to communicate to the Dalai Lama that *"except independence, all other issues can be resolved through negotiations"*. This marked the opening of a new door between Beijing and Dharamsala. TGiE functions through a democratically elected Parliament and an impressive paraphernalia of 'ministries' and representative offices in over a dozen important countries. However, it was much later following the death of Deng that Beijing leaders publicly denied that Deng ever made the above-mentioned statement. The reality on this issue has yet to unfold itself either in Beijing or Dharamsala.

HISTORIC APOLOGY

Even though these talks broke down in 1993 and Beijing-Dharamsala contacts remained almost frozen until 2002, the period between1979–1993 saw some significant developments in these ties. The hope of bringing back the Dalai Lama to the fold of the 'great motherland' encouraged Beijing leaders to usher in some liberal policies which brought some relief in the life of the Tibetan masses inside Tibet who have been used to seeing oppression and difficult days.

This welcome change provided some fresh breathing space to the Tibetan masses in matters like religious practice, social interaction and travel to other parts of Tibet and China. It was in this atmosphere that something happened which was considered unimaginable in PRC's political culture. Communist Party Secretary Hu Yaobang offered a public apology[5] to the Tibetan people in his public speech at Lhasa on 23 May 1980. Admitting that the Tibetan people were 'let down' by the Chinese rulers, Hu said,

> Our present situation is less than wonderful because the Tibetan people's lives have not been much improved. .... in general, Tibetans still live in relative poverty. In some areas the living standards have even gone down. We comrades in the Central Committee, Chairman Hua as well as several vice-chairmen, were very upset when we heard about this situation. We feel that our party has let the Tibetan people down. We feel very bad!..... We have worked nearly thirty years, but the life of the Tibetan people has not been notably improved. Are we not to blame? If we don't make this clear, people won't let us off the hook; party members won't let us get away with it!

FROM 'RANGZEN' (INDEPENDENCE) TO 'GENUINE' AUTONOMY

It was much later that these liberal policies were condemned and reversed in China following the unceremonious fall of Hu Yaobang. It was believed among the dominant section of the Communist Party that Hu Yaobang's relaxations gave Tibetan 'reactionaries' fresh opportunities to reorganise themselves and to rise against the 'central' government.

However, openness on the part of PRC in Deng's days had its demonstrable impact on the Dalai Lama's side too. It encouraged the Dalai Lama to publicly climb down from his people's popular demand for *'Rangzen'* (total independence) to a more 'liberal' concept of 'Middle Path' that calls for just 'genuine autonomy' for Tibet within the political framework of PRC. But subsequent developments proved that Chinese leaders' expectations were far beyond what Dalai Lama could offer, and vice versa.

What followed the opening of doors in 1979 between the two sides reads more like a war of wits. The PRC leaders remained focused on enhancing their physical grip on Tibet during this period and prolonged the dialogue process to buy more time to achieve their goals of population transfer to Tibet to such levels that Han migrants could overwhelm the local Tibetans by sheer weight of numbers. The Dalai Lama too made a few smart moves to make the most of this Chinese enthusiasm about bringing him back to their fold. Following the open invitation from Deng's government for a dialogue, the Dalai Lama went public to express his eagerness to visit Tibet provided he was convinced that conditions inside Tibet were normal and as good as the Chinese claimed. Biting the monk statesman's bait, an overenthusiastic Beijing offered him an invitation to come, even if on a short visit 'to see things with his own eyes' and to 'seek truth from facts'.

FIRST CONTACT WITH TIBET

In his response, the Dalai Lama accepted the offer 'in principle' but proposed to start the process by sending his 'fact-finding' delegations from among the exile community to verify the Chinese claims of 'progress, prosperity and happiness' of the Tibetan community under the Chinese rule. Between August 1979 and 1985, Dharamsala sent four such 'fact-finding' delegations. The first three delegations, namely the High Power Delegation of senior Tibetan leaders, the Delegation of Youth Leaders and the Educationist Delegation, were sent in quick succession between August 1979 and September 1980. The nature of study of each delegation was designed in such a manner that each got the privilege of travelling to all the three Tibetan provinces of Kham, Amdo and U-Tsang. Citing reasons like the huge geographic area and lack of good transport system, the travel plans of these delegations were spread over 2-3 months each to ensure that the delegates had enough time to see things and meet the maximum number of Tibetan people.

The delegations were comprised of senior serving and former cabinet ministers of the exile government, senior religious leaders, members of the parliament-in-exile, and other well-informed community leaders. Almost all of them were individuals who were familiar with pre-1959 Tibet and, hence, could make sense of the changed situation. An interesting aspect of this delegation diplomacy was that even though Beijing has been highly sensitive about presenting only 'Tibet Autonomous Region' (TAR) as the 'real Tibet', yet it permitted the delegates to visit those areas of Kham and Amdo provinces of Tibet which now belonged to the adjoining Chinese provinces of Yunnan, Sichuan, Qinghai and Gansu.

These delegation visits proved a bit too shocking for the Beijing leaders as far as the response of the Tibetan masses was concerned. Relying heavily on the feedback of self-serving party leaders and government functionaries in TAR, the Beijing leadership had come to believe genuinely that the Tibetan masses were 'extremely happy' under the Chinese rule and that the country of 'former serfs' was too strongly opposed to the Dalai Lama to see him back in Tibet. In their enthusiasm to make the guests comfortable in their former homeland and to save Beijing from any possible 'embarrassment' caused by public hostility, the government propaganda machinery went into overdrive to educate the Tibetan masses on how, and how not to, treat the visiting guests. In addition to regular radio broadcasts, loudspeaker-fitted propaganda vans were specially sent to villages and towns to warn the Tibetan masses against 'stoning', 'spitting' or any other kind of 'misbehaviour' against the visiting representatives of the exiled Dalai Lama.

However, the actual public response turned out to be just the opposite of what the Chinese leadership was expecting. The delegations were mobbed by massive cheering crowds who listened respectfully to them, cried and competed with each other to shake hands or touch them to seek their blessings. At places the crowds swelled into such huge gatherings that the Chinese Public Security Bureau personnel were finally left with no choice but to stand aside and watch this unimaginable surge with surprise. This experience had its own message for all three parties, viz. the Beijing rulers of Tibet, the exile government as well as the Tibetan masses. For the Tibetans representing the Dharamsala CTA, the main message was that despite all the Chinese claims, the 'autonomy' promised to Tibet in the 17-Point Agreement was either missing or just not enough. And for the Beijing leaders one of the most important messages was that the policy of winning control over the Tibetan hearts through coercion had simply not worked and that the exiled Dalai Lama still dominated their mindscape. And a common point for both sides was that they needed to discuss how to find a meeting ground.

TALKS ABOUT TALKS

Following this unexpected experience, the fourth and last fact-finding delegation was kept on hold till 1985 when some senior religious leaders from exile were allowed to have a look at the religious situation in Tibet. The intervening period between the first three delegations and the fourth witnessed the beginning of a new process of negotiations between Beijing and Dharamsala. In 1981, Beijing invited Gyalo Thondup again. His meeting with the Chinese leader Hu Yaobang on July 28 paved the way for opening a discussion process that was aimed at 'probing the possibilities of detailed talks on the future of Tibet'. This was the real beginning of what many call the phenomenon of 'Talks about Talks' between Beijing and Dharamsala.

Two teams of high-level Tibetan representatives under the leadership of Kalon Tripa (Prime Minister) Juchen Thupten Namgyal of the CTA visited Beijing in 1982 and 1984. Interestingly, the Chinese perceptions of the Tibetan problem could never move beyond the persona of the Dalai Lama. From the very outset, Beijing appointed the Central United Front Work Department, as the exclusive interface between PRC and Dharamsala to underline the 'local' and 'internal' nature of the Tibetan issue. This Front, an internal organ of the Communist Party of China, was created by Chairman Mao during his Long March days to win the 'co-operation' of all those non-Chinese nationalities that Mao intended to absorb in his 'People's Republic of China'. Though the Front appears to be headed by a 'Minister', the overall status of the Front is nothing more than a 'department' of the Communist Party of China. Its focus remains till this day on how the Dalai Lama and/or his fellow exiles are to be won back to the fold of PRC as just any other 'Chinese' citizens. The Beijing government's official communiqués too have been consistently presenting these delegations from Dharamsala as 'overseas Chinese' who were on 'private' visit 'to meet their relatives'. At no stage did Beijing recognise the Tibetan delegates as the 'representatives of Tibetan people' or that of a 'Tibetan Government-in-Exile'.

GENUINE AUTONOMY?

In addition, almost on each occasion China has been demanding that the Dalai Lama must give certain undertakings. One such undertaking demands that he should accept and declare that "Tibet has been an integral part of China through history". To this, the Dalai Lama's consistent response has been that although this is untrue and though he cannot go back in history to rewrite it, yet he will not raise the question of Tibetan independence and is ready to accept Tibet as a part of PRC provided 'genuine autonomy' for Tibet and Tibetans is ensured. Another Chinese condition which the Dalai Lama has consistently resisted meeting is to declare that "Taiwan is an integral part of China". To this his response is that since he has no authority to speak on behalf of the people of Taiwan, Chinese leaders should better contact the Taiwan government directly on this issue.

On the other hand, the Tibetan side has been showing keen interest in evolving a special, long-term and mutually acceptable arrangement for Tibet and Tibetans within the framework of PRC. They have been keen to have a special arrangement which ensures some special status for Tibet on lines similar to what was granted to Hong Kong or was being discussed by Beijing for Taiwan under a 'one country, two systems' idea at that time. But Beijing's approach was limited to reaching only an arrangement which ensured that the Dalai Lama could return and settle in Beijing. In response to this, the Dalai Lama's consistent stand has been that *the Dalai Lama is not the real issue. The real issue is the happiness of six million Tibetans living inside Tibet.* In his annual address to Tibetans on March 10, 1980, the Dalai Lama said,

> .... I would like to remind everybody that the core of the Tibetan issue is the welfare and ultimate happiness of six million Tibetans in Tibet. The limited leniency that the Chinese have introduced is a welcome first step. But we are still nowhere near being satisfied that the Tibetans in Tibet are content... [6]

However, he also took care that Beijing's interest in the dialogue was not lost. In February 1983, he pleased Beijing by repeating that he was very keen to visit Tibet.

BEIJING'S CHANGING PRIORITIES

However, following the visit of the fourth fact-finding delegation of religious leaders in 1985, Beijing cooled down the dialogue process with Dharamsala. In the wake of a major Tibetan public uprising in Lhasa in 1987 against the Chinese regime, the talks suffered a serious setback. Later in December 1988, Hu Jintao took over as the the Party Secretary of Tibet Autonomous Region (TAR). Very soon, Hu Jintao had to face an unprecedented uprising of Tibetans in Lhasa in March 1989. It was a great challenge for Hu to save his position in the Party. Using armoured vehicles and army tanks, he ruthlessly crushed the uprising and imposed Martial Law in TAR. It was Hu's 'Lhasa Model' which Jiang Zemin and Deng used successfully to crush the democratic uprising at Tiananmen Square in Beijing three months later.

This upheaval inside China and later the collapse of world's most prominent communist heaven, i.e. the Soviet Union, nearly wiped out whatever enthusiasm remained in the hearts of the Beijing rulers for a dialogue with the exiled Dalai Lama. The Chinese embassy in New Delhi functioned as the only contact point between Dharamsala and Beijing till 1993 when relations broke down completely.

1989 also saw the death of the Panchen Lama who lived in China and was used by Beijing leaders extensively as a counterbalance against the Dalai Lama. On a rare visit to Shigatse, the town of his main religious seat at Tashi Lhumpo monastery, the Panchen Lama died under suspicious circumstances in February 1989 only a day after his public argument with Hu Jintao who claimed in the same public meeting that Tibet had gained in a big way after joining the 'motherland'. In his response to Hu's claims, the Panchen Lama's speech was highly critical of the Chinese regime for its mistakes in Tibet and failure to deliver the promises which were made to the Tibetan people under the 17-Point Agreement. Interestingly, it was not the first time that the Panchen Lama had openly criticized Beijing leaders for their mistakes in Tibet. Despite siding with Beijing during the fateful period of the 1950s vis-à-vis the Dalai Lama, the Panchen Lama showed courage in pointing out the Chinese failures and misdeeds in Tibet in his historic 70 thousand character long memo to Chairman Mao. For this 'crime', he had to undergo public humiliation and a 12-year long confinement in a labour camp during the Cultural Revolution.

Beijing-Dharamsala relations nosedived to their lowest ever levels in 1995 when the Chinese government arrested the 5-year-old boy Gedhun Choeky Nyima, authenticated by the Dalai Lama from exile as the next reincarnation of the deceased Panchen Lama. This boy was quickly replaced by Beijing with another boy of its choice. Despite all efforts by the Dalai Lama and his supporters across the world, Beijing has refused to give any information on Gedhun during the past 18 years.

A MONK'S PEACE OFFENSIVE?

While maintaining his contacts with Beijing, the Dalai Lama has been busy in evolving a long-term strategy and winning support from the world community to find a lasting, acceptable solution to the Tibetan problem. The sad and tragic experience of Chu-Shi-Nga-Druk and other unorganised and sporadic violent resistance to the Chinese occupation over the years inside Tibet had already proved beyond doubt that any violent approach was bound to be suicidal for the Tibetans. More so because of the mammoth difference in the size and capacities of the two sides. With ever increasing Chinese might and the proportional waning of the world governments' capacities, their desire to confront China on the Tibetan issue too has been diminishing and, with it, the Dalai Lama's chances of winning much political support for the demand for complete independence. Then news emanating from inside Tibet through friendly visitors and second line mediators too was presenting a very hopeless scenario. The Dalai Lama had been frequently heard expressing fears of Tibet losing its culture and Tibetan identity in the wake of an ever increasing pace of systematic transfer of Han Chinese into Tibet. That explains why the Dalai Lama decided to probe the efficacy of a renewed peace offensive.

His address to the US Congressional Human Rights Caucus on September 21, 1987 was the first milestone in this direction. It was here that he launched his peace offensive against the Beijing regime. Addressing the Chinese sentiments about maintaining Tibet as an 'integral part of China', he presented a five-point peace plan which underlined the basic problems of Tibet under Chinese occupation. These five points were:

1. Transformation of the whole of Tibet into a zone of peace;
2. Abandonment of China's population transfer policy which threatens the very existence of the Tibetans as a people;
3. Respect for the Tibetan people's fundamental human rights and democratic freedoms;
4. Restoration and protection of Tibet's natural environment and the abandonment of China's use of Tibet for the production of nuclear weapons and dumping of nuclear waste; and

5. Commencement of earnest negotiations on the future status of Tibet and of relations between the Tibetan and Chinese people.[7]

AUTONOMY AND STRASBOURG PROPOSAL

But Beijing rejected his demands outright, saying that it smacked of asking for independence for Tibet from China. Next year at Strasbourg (France) the Dalai Lama presented a refined and detailed version of this proposal before the European Parliament on June 15, 1988. In this version, the Dalai Lama clearly offered to let Tibet remain within the framework of PRC and accepted Beijing's right to conduct the foreign relations of Tibet. In return, he demanded a 'self-governing' democratic system for entire Tibet which, as against the Chinese concept of Tibet as a much truncated 'Tibet Autonomous Region', comprises of 'Cholka-Sum' the traditional Tibet comprising of U-Tsang, Kham and Amdo provinces.

In his address, the Dalai Lama elaborated each point in detail:

> The whole of Tibet known as Cholka-Sum (U-Tsang, Kham and Amdo) should become a self-governing democratic political entity founded on law by agreement of the people for the common good and the protection of themselves and their environment, in association with the People's Republic of China.
>
> The Government of the People's Republic of China could remain responsible for Tibet's foreign policy. The Government of Tibet should, however, develop and maintain relations, through its own foreign affairs bureau, in the field of commerce, education, culture, religion, tourism, science, sports and other non-political activities. Tibet should join international organisations concerned with such activities.
>
> The Government of Tibet should be founded on a constitution or basic law. The basic law should provide for

a democratic system of government entrusted with the task of ensuring economic equality, social justice, and protection of the environment. This means that the Government of Tibet will have the right to decide on all affairs relating to Tibet and the Tibetans.

As individual freedom is the real source and potential of any society's development, the Government of Tibet would seek to ensure this freedom by full adherence to the Universal Declaration of Human Rights, including the rights to speech, assembly and religion. Because religion constitutes the source of Tibet's national identity and spiritual values lie at the very heart of Tibet's rich culture, it would be the special duty of the Government of Tibet to safeguard and develop its practice.

The Government should be comprised of a popularly elected Chief Executive, a bi-cameral legislative branch, and an independent judicial system. Its seat should be in Lhasa.

The social and economic system of Tibet should be determined in accordance with the wishes of the Tibetan people, bearing in mind especially the need to raise the standard of living of the entire population.

The Government of Tibet would pass strict laws to protect wildlife and plant life. The exploitation of natural resources would be carefully regulated. The manufacture, testing, stockpiling of nuclear weapons and other armaments must be prohibited, as well as use of nuclear power and other technologies which produce hazardous waste. It would be the Government of Tibet's goal to transform Tibet into our planet's largest natural preserve.

A regional peace conference should be called to ensure that Tibet becomes a genuine sanctuary of peace through demilitarisation. Until such a peace conference can be convened and demilitarisation and neutralisation achieved, China could have the right to maintain a restricted number

> of military installations in Tibet. These must be solely for defence purposes.
>
> In order to create an atmosphere of trust conducive to fruitful negotiations, the Chinese Government should cease its human rights violations in Tibet and abandon its policy of transferring Chinese to Tibet.....[8]

As expected, this too was rejected, rather more strongly, by Beijing. Besides strong objections to almost all other points, it specifically refused to accept the concept of 'Cholka-Sum' for defining Tibetan boundaries.

DEMOGRAPHIC COLONIALISM AT PLAY

This Chinese reaction to the Dalai Lama's Five-Point Peace Plan was natural because, since absorption of most parts of Kham and Amdo provinces into adjoining Chinese provinces, China had already settled millions of Han Chinese in these areas to reduce the Tibetans into an insignificant minority in their own home regions. Today, only a few Tibetan pockets remain in Yunnan, Sichuan, Gansu and Qinghai with some Tibetan character amidst a sea of Han towns and villages. During a recent visit to Xiling, the captal of Qinghai, the home province of the present Dalai Lama, this author was surprised to note that one would have to watch over 500 Chinese pass a road junction before one could see the first Tibetan face. Things were no different in towns and villages of Kham in Yunnan and Sichuan either.

According to the TGiE's data, the population of entire Tibet (Cholka-Sum) was 6 million before occupation by China. Today, the Tibetan population accounts for 0.5 per cent of the Chinese population while Tibet accounts for over 25 per cent of the land area in PRC's present geography. Figures from China's official Statistical Year Book-2002, (China Statistics Press, p. 100) show that only 3.5 million Tibetans live among a total population of

154.7 million in these four Chinese provinces of Sichuan (82,348,296), Yunnan (42,360,089), Qinghai (4,822,963) and Gansu (25,124,282). The population of TAR is 2,616,329. According to the Dalai Lama-led Tibetan Government-in-Exile (TGiE) the total populaiton of Tibet was 6 million before China occupied Tibet in 1951.

THE EUROPEAN ULTIMATUM

On July 6, 2000, which happened to be the 65th birthday of the Dalai Lama, the European Parliament passed a resolution (nr. B5-0608, 0610, 0617, 0621, 0641/2000) which called upon the Beijing authorities to restart their negotiations with Dharamsala. In stern language it underlined that "*Tibet was invaded and occupied in 1949 and 1950 by the Chinese armed forces*" and called upon the PRC government to "*....reach a new status for Tibet which guarantees full Tibetan autonomy in all areas of political, economic, social and cultural life, the only exceptions being defence and foreign policy.*" [9]

Since the fateful events of 1959, it was the first time when an international forum of this stature threatened Beijing with as serious consequences such as recognising the 'Tibetan government-in-exile as the 'legitimate representative of the Tibetan people'. The operative part of this resolution "*Calls on the governments of the Member-States to give serious consideration to the possibility of recognising the Tibetan Government-in-exile as the legitimate representative of the Tibetan people if, within three years, the Beijing authorities and the Tibetan government in exile have not, through negotiations organised under the aegis of the Secretary-General of the United Nations, signed an agreement on a new Statute for Tibet.*"

Though Beijing demonstrated all its contempt to this resolution, yet it finally announced in 2002 that it was keen on restarting the talks with Dharamsala on how to find a solution to the Tibetan issue. Beijing had its own compelling reasons and designs behind eating this humble pie. It had already moved ahead on its ambitious plans of hosting the Olympics in 2008. The PRC leaders were in no mood to invite direct confrontation with the European community and the rest of the Western bloc and thereby run the risk of seeing the Beijing Olympics going the Moscow Olympics way. The projects of connecting Tibet by rail and other means to the rest of China and developing new townships for future Chinese settlers too were in full swing at that time. Any major confrontation with Dharamsala would have rocked the boat inside Tibet to create problems for these projects which were essential requisites for Beijing's plans of implementing the 'final solution' to the Tibetan problem through population transfer.

Moreover, the Beijing leaders who have high hopes of seeing the Tibetan issue end with the death of the current Dalai Lama, know well that each passing year in the life of an ageing Dalai Lama is 'precious'. No surprise that Beijing decided to buy this precious time by agreeing to 'talk about talks'. This, surely, did not surprise those Tibetans and international friends of Tibet who had reservations about the Chinese approach towards dialogue despite the Dalai Lama's climbdown from 'Rangzen' to 'Genuine Autonomy' and who believed that talks were just a ploy of Beijing leaders to buy time.

BEIJING'S U-TURN

The fears and warnings of these groups came true in November 2008 when the Beijing leaders slammed the door shut on the face of the visiting Tibetan delegation by rejecting the Tibetan memorandum on autonomy with all the contempt at their command. Anybody could see now how Beijing had been dragging its feet on talks for six years and that it had not allowed the talks to move an inch further from where they stood in 1993. Only a month before the Beijing Olympics, Beijing had asked Dharamsala to present its concept of 'Genuine Autonomy for Tibet', a step which both sides should have taken on day-one when the dialogue restarted in 2002. It is surely not a coincidence that Beijing outrightly rejected Dharamsala's memorandum at the first available opportunity after the successful conclusion of the Olympics, and called off the talks on the grounds that the memorandum was a hidden way of asking for full independence from China.

Strangely, the Tibetan memorandum refers to the Chinese side as 'the Central Government' and (late) Deng Xiaoping as the 'paramount leader'. It also makes it amply clear that Dharamsala expected the final solution "within the PRC". Adopting an assuring tone the memorandum says, "His Holiness the Dalai Lama's commitment to seek a solution for the Tibetan people within the PRC is clear and unambiguous. This position is in full compliance and agreement with paramount leader Deng Xiaoping's statement in which he emphasised that except for independence all other issues could be resolved through dialogue. Whereas, we are committed, therefore, to fully respect the territorial integrity of the PRC, we expect the Central Government to recognise and fully respect the integrity of the Tibetan nationality and its right to exercise genuine autonomy within the PRC. We believe that this is the basis for resolving the differences between us and promoting unity, stability and harmony among nationalities."[10]

The scope of autonomy in this memorandum is also clearly defined as limited to specific subjects, namely Language, Culture, Religion, Education, Environmental Protection, Utilisation of Natural Resources, Economic Development and Trade, Public Health, Public Security, Regulation on population migration, Cultural and educational and religious exchanges with other countries.

Defining the nature of powers to be enjoyed by the local autonomous government of Tibet, the memorandum mentioned specifically that, "The exercise of genuine autonomy would include the right of Tibetans to create their own regional government and government institutions and processes that are best suited to their needs and characteristics. It would require that the People's Congress of the autonomous region have the power to legislate on all matters within the competencies of the region and that other organs of the autonomous government have the power to execute and administer decisions autonomously. Autonomy also entails representation and meaningful participation in national decision-making in the Central Government. Processes for effective consultation and close co-operation or joint decision-making between the Central Government and the regional government on areas of common interest also need to be in place for the autonomy to be effective."[11] Adding insult to injury, Zhu Weiqun, executive vice minister of the United Front Work Department (UFWD) issued a press statement after the meeting in which he advised the Dalai Lama "to do something beneficial for the people of Tibet....... before he dies". He categorically rejected the memorandum saying that the ideas were just unacceptable. He termed the concept of 'Cholka Sum' as that of a 'Greater Tibet' which 'never existed' before 1951. "The unification of the motherland, territorial integrity and the national dignity are the greatest interests of the Chinese people. We will never make a concession,"[12] Zhu Weiqun, told reporters in Beijing on November 10, 2008

He ruled out any kind of special status for Tibetan areas. "China is a country in which various ethnic groups live together. If all ethnic groups in China ask for an autonomous region in which only people of their own groups could live, the whole country would be cast into chaos", Zhu said.

As expected, China also refused to take the Dalai Lama's call on 'demilitarising' Tibet. "Everybody knows that the army is a basic guarantee of territorial integrity, national security and social stability... I believe not a single nation would agree to withdraw its own army from its own territory", Zhu declared.

Zhu also reiterated that the door for the Dalai Lama's return to a patriotic stance had always been open and would remain open, "But the door for 'Tibet's independence', 'half independence' and 'independence in a disguised form' had never been open, nor would it be open in the future", he clarified.

On the issue of settlement of the Chinese population in Tibet, Zhu made it clear that Beijing has no intention of stopping or undoing what the Dalai Lama side terms 'demographic aggression'. He even went to the extent of accusing the Dalai Lama of having intentions to "... carry out ethnic discrimination, apartheid and ethnic cleansing..." in the name of restoring Cholka-Sum to the Tibetan population.

THREE-DECADE LONG WAR OF WITS

The net result of this three-decade long contact is a mix of gains and setbacks for both sides. Although the two sides have been engaged in talks since 1979 with the aim of finding a mutually agreeable solution, they have been simultaneously busy in their own ways to prepare for the future. Beijing has been frantically focused on ensuring a permanent and 'final solution' to the Tibetan problem by fortifying its position inside Tibet. Its major focus has been on cementing its military position inside occupied Tibet through a widespread network of roads, other transport and communication facilities and defence installations inside Tibet as well as along its borders with other countries in South Asia.

Of late, Beijing has been busy ushering in a new economic environment in Tibet to accommodate millions of new Han settlers. By extending the Chinese railway network up to Lhasa in 2006, China has successfully removed the last hurdle that discouraged mainland Chinese from settling permanently in Tibet. Beijing has already seen the fruits of this strategy in taming most of its other 55 national minorities like the Manchurians and Mongols. Thanks to the abundance of invaluable minerals and timber across the Tibetan Plateau, establishment of this rail link has converted Tibet from a net financial liability to a 'national profit centre' for China. Beijing is already working on at least three more similar rail links to Tibet in addition to its plans to extend the present Gormo-Lhasa rail to the Nepalese border.

PREPARING FOR THE NEXT LIFE?

The Dalai Lama too, like a typical Buddhist monk who would use his current lifetime to prepare for his next life, has been busy preparing for a Tibetan system that can last beyond his own life time. Internally, he has already succeeded in replacing an outdated theocratic political system of old Tibet into a highly modern democratic system which functions through an elected Parliament and is presided over by a Prime Minister who is elected through a direct secret vote by the Tibetan community. The Dalai Lama brought this process of democratization to its logical conclusion in 2011 when he handed over his political powers into the hands of an elected 'Kalon Tripa' (Prime Minister), an elected Parliament and other statutory democratic organs of the TGiE. This historic decision has, on the one hand, given an endless shelf life to the Tibetan national identity in exile as well as effectively pre-empted Beijing leaders from installing a puppet Dalai Lama in the event of the death of the current Dalai Lama.

WHAT NEXT?

This sudden breaking off of the dialogue process has its own implications for both sides. Having already put all his bargaining chips on the table, the Dalai Lama is left with no further climb down options in the event of a renewed dialogue. After declaring his stand for 'Choka-Sum' as the real Tibet and PRC's outright refusal to include those areas of Tibet which it has already dissolved in other Chinese provinces the Dalai Lama's side no longer has the choice of making any major change because he cannot afford to lose the support of either Khampa Tibetans of Kham province or of Amdo Tibetans.

He also cannot afford to abandon his concept of 'genuine autonomy' for Tibetans in lieu of the PRC's offer of the existing 'autonomy for nationalities' which has already seen nationalities like the Manchurians and Mongolians of 'Inner Mongolia' and a few dozen other nationalities vanish slowly into almost nothingness. Even PRC will not propose this idea fearing an admission that all its past claims of implementing its constitutional autonomy in Tibet were bogus. With less than 8% of their total share amidst a sea of over 92 per cent Hans, most of these 'Autonomous' nationalities have been already reduced to 'museum' pieces along with their cultural and lingual identities. After having seen the fate of most other nationalities, the Tibetan are aware that further Hanization of Tibet will bring a similar fate to their identity in not very far future.

THE PRICE OF MIDDLE PATH

No doubt, the Dalai Lama's stature as a statesman and the international acceptance of his struggle for Tibet has considerably increased among the community of nations who found it relatively convenient to support a 'reasonable' Dalai Lama in his fight with China. His 'Middle Path' based on 'genuine autonomy for Tibet within the structure of PRC' provided enough elbow room to those governments and heads of state who wanted to take up the Tibetan leader's cause with the leaders of China. It is a different matter that the Communist leaders of China have yet to come up with their first meaningful response to any such request in past over 20 years. Moreover, as a matter of fact, with the ever increasing economic and political power of PRC during past many years, the efficacy of such governments vis-à-vis PRC has only reduced.

It could be a coincidence that within a couple of years of publicly abandoning Tibetans' original demand for complete independence from China, the Dalai Lama was honoured with a Nobel Peace prize for his campaign for Non-violence and Universal Responsibility. Since being decorated with this honour, the Dalai Lama's international appeal and struggle for Tibet has received ever increasing support among the international audience. The European Parliament too passed a strong resolution on Tibet with an ultimatum to China. The American nation bestowed its highest honour—the US Congressional Medal (an equivalent of Bharat Ratna in India). To put it in simple words, the Dalai Lama's personal image has attained new heights of universal acceptance and respect since he adopted the 'Middle Path'. Rather, his outstanding international stature has emerged as the greatest strength of Tibetan people along these years.

But the accompanying internal costs of 'looking good' by adopting a very accommodating approach towards PRC too have not been small — either for the Dalai Lama or his Tibetan 'Government-in-Exile' or for the Tibetan community — especially since the last phase of Dharamsala-Beijing dialogue started in 2002.

One major fallout of the six-year long dialogue has been the loss of sense of direction and of confusion among the Tibet support movement — both at the refugee community level as well as among the community of international Tibet Support Groups (TSG). It has had its fallout on the morale and enthusiasm of the freedom movement inside Tibet where Tibetan masses have already had enough taste of 'autonomy' at the hands of their colonial masters. Significantly, there has never been any public expression of support for 'Autonomy' vis-à-vis 'Rangzen' from inside occupied Tibet in all these years. In all reports of anti-China demonstrations from inside Tibet reaching the free world during the past over 50 years, the only two expressions used by the Tibetans to express their collective national aspirations were 'Rangzen' (independence) or 'Rangwang' (freedom). For ordinary Tibetan, living under occupation, both words have been always synonyms of the same sentiment — getting rid of Chinese rule.

In their enthusiasm to keep the Chinese happy during the dialogue process, the Tibetan exile leadership sought two major changes in the approach of Tibet support movements. One, they asked the Tibetan community and the TSGs to drop the demand of 'Rangzen' from their philosophy and replace it with 'Autonomy'. Second, they wanted the TSGs in different countries to stop holding demonstrations against the visiting Chinese leaders lest they get offended and embarrassed.

For most TSGs who stand by Tibet mainly because of their commitment to values like democracy, anti-colonialism and anti-communist dictatorship, this embargo was too demoralising. To most of them, opposing a visiting Chinese leader was the basic demand and expression of their commitment to human rights of suffering Tibetan people under the Chinese colonial rule. As the dialogue dragged on for years without any visible or specific results, a substantial section among these Tibet supporters either dropped out or stood by their Tibetan friends with a confused mind.

Luckily, Beijing Olympics-2008 came as a great blessing which enabled most of the TSGs to maintain some spirit and enthusiasm because they could oppose China on this issue even without raising the issue of Tibetan freedom. In their opinion the allotment of Olympics to Beijing was an open insult to those millions of Chinese citizens who were living under communist oppression as well as to colonized countries like Tibet, East Turkistan or Inner Mongolia. That explains why Tibetan flags dominated the visuals of anti-Beijing Olympics campaign.

However, many TSGs who strongly believed in Rangzen for Tibet adopted the strategy of staying out of the mainstream TSG movement and pressed their own agenda through their own pro-independence campaigns. The Dalai Lama's elder brother (now late) Taktser Rinpoche, who was a professor in California and an unbending vocal Rangzen enthusiast, became the rallying point of such TSGs in the USA. He and his supporter TSGs kept the Rangzen flame burning till his last day. After his death, his son has taken over the Rangzen flame.

Germany, where Tibet Initiative Deutschland (TID) has emerged as one of the most effective TSGs, presents a unique example of how Tibet supporters have been able to maintain their enthusiasm and tempo from cooling down due to the prevailing confusion at some other places. For many years TID is running a unique 'Tibetan Flag on The Town Hall' campaign in various German cities. In a recent count, TID has been successful in persuading over 1200 municipalities across Germany to adopt resolutions to the effect that all of them hoist the Tibetan flag on the city Mayor office every 10th March, the uprising day of Tibet against Chinese occupation.

But the impact of down-grading the Tibetan public movement from 'Rangzen' to 'autonomy' has been far more pronounced among the Tibetan exile community, the majority of whose ordinary members have yet to accept the change at their conscience levels. An atmosphere has consistently been created by a dominant section among senior political and bureaucratic functionaries which has made people believe that opposing 'autonomy' or standing by 'Rangzen' as the final goal of Tibetan struggle means directly opposing the Dalai Lama. That explains why, despite their deep faith in 'Rangzen', no ordinary Tibetan would publicly denounce 'autonomy' or shout slogans in favour of 'Rangzen' in public demonstrations. This drop in public enthusiasm and prevailing demoralisation has started showing in annual 10 March processions and during most other public demonstrations. Having seen most of the 40 uprising days from a close distance during many years, this author was shocked to notice on 10 March 2009, the 50th anniversary of Tibetan uprising, that a substantial section of the Tibetan demonstrators had left the public meeting midway at the Parliament Street in New Delhi to eat Chhole-Bhatoore at food stalls in the adjoining lane.

This missing enthusiasm towards 'autonomy' among ordinary masses, is reflected in the fact that in the past 10 years, since TGiE abandoned 'Rangzen' for 'Autonomy', not a single slogan has been coined by the Tibetan demonstrators that calls for 'autonomy' for Tibet from China. While the key slogan "We want — Rangzen!" is now heard only in TYC or FOT sponsored demonstrations, old traditional slogans like "Dusht Cheenio! Tibbat Chhoro!" (Evil Chinese! Quit Tibet!) or "Hamein Kya Chahiye? Azaadi!" (What do we want? Freedom!) still rend the air in all Tibetan demonstrations across India.

On the other hand, almost all vocal and major Tibetan organizations like the Tibetan Youth Congress (TYC), Students For A Free Tibet (SFT), Gu Chu Sum (association of former political prisoners in occupied Tibet) and the National Democratic Party of Tibet (NDPT) have openly expressed allegiance to 'Rangzen'. Interestingly, none of these groups advocates violence to achieve independence for Tibet.

Since coming to India in exile, the Dalai Lama has been consistently promoting democracy among the exile community. After adopting a democratic charter for the future Tibet in 1963 and introducing an elected 'Chitue' (Parliament), the Dalai Lama first gave autonomy to the TGiE through nominated ministers. Then he slowly but consistently democratised the system by introducing an elected Prime Minister and finally introduced a constitution in 2011 through which he handed over all his traditional political powers as the 'head of state' to a 'Sikyong'

(Prime Minister) who is elected directly by people through a secret universal vote.

While the Dalai Lama has been advocating democracy and freedom of expression among the exile community, there have been many instances indicating that a substantial section among the influential and vocal members of the ruling elite among the refugee community have not been able to keep pace with their supreme leader in practicing democracy in the intra-community political dialogue, especially on the Rangzen-vs-Autonomy debate.

In sharp contrast to the prevailing confusion in the Tibetan exile community over the future status of Tibet, the colonial masters of Tibet in Beijing look clear and confident about their plans over Tibet. On the occasion of the 60th anniversary of 'Tibetan Liberation' in 2011, Xi Jinping, the then Vice President of the PRC, announced in a commemorative Lhasa rally on 20 July 2011 that, "Without the Chinese Communist Party, there would be no new Tibet. ....We should thoroughly fight against separatist activities of the Dalai clique by firmly relying on ethnic groups, and completely smash any plot to destroy stability in Tibet and jeopardize national unity."

These words of Xi Jinping expose the helplessness of a superpower that has failed miserably in taming a microscopic minority under its own iron control. In reality he is testifying to the power of ordinary Tibetans, living under China's colonial control for the past over sixty years, who have refused to give in. Denied any third party support over the past sixty years, these Tibetans have made the best use of whatever elbow room their Chinese masters leave for them. These Tibetan masses inside Tibet have been consistently expressing their resentment and resolve against their Chinese colonial masters in unambiguous terms since Mao's first PLA columns marched into Tibet in 1950.

THE FOURTH STAKEHOLDER

And finally the fourth group of stakeholders whose fate will be directly impacted by the direction that any Tibetan solution takes — the Himalayan Asian countries which are immediate neighbours of Tibet. Before China occupied East Turkistan ('Xinjiang' in modern Chinese vocabulary) in 1949 and Tibet in 1950-51, neither India, nor Nepal, nor Bhutan shared borders with China. Over 95 per cent length of this 4000 kms border was shared between these countries and Tibet. The remaining about 5 pc was with East Turkistan. With the fall of Tibet and arrival of PRC along their Northern borders, all these countries today live in a vulnerable situation. Pakistan, for obvious reasons (inter alia, it is in illegal occupation of part of Jammu & Kashmir), felt a sense of relief in watching India under pressure from its new neighbour China in earlier decades, and continues to do so. While some Western governments might find it convenient to see the Tibetans and Chinese agreeing over a certain degree of autonomy for Tibet within the PRC framework, most Asian neighbours of Tibet shudder over such a prospect. A solution of this kind is going to make the PRC a permanent neighbour on their borders. An uncomfortable China with an unsettled Tibetan issue looks more comfortable for these Asian neighbours of Tibet because it leaves some hopes for these countries. They can hope for a favourable day in future when Tibet's luck smiles like that of over a dozen occupied members of erstwhile USSR. Unfortunately, the Tibetan Diaspora and the Tibet support movement has utterly failed in cashing in on this sentiment among the South Asian countries.

ENDNOTES

1. Ngabo Ngawang Jigme: a junior minister and leader of Tibetan delegation. He was the Governor of Kham provice when China's PLA attacked and defeated Tibetan army to occupy Kham in 1950.

2. TREATY BETWEEN TIBET AND CHINA A.D. 821-822 (Translation from the Tibetan text) http://www.tpprc.org/documents/agreements/821-822.pdf. Two translations of the Chinese text of the treaty can be seen in G. Timkowsky's *Travels of the Russian Mission through China*, etc. London 1827 and one by S.W. Bushell in JRAS 1880
3. "The Question of Tibet and the Rule of Law" (July 24, 1959) the International Commission of Jurists, Geneva (p. 60)
4. Shakya Tsering, *The Dragon in the Land of Snows* (p. 35)
5. Hu Yao Bang in Tibet: Report of his visit written by one of his close collaborator, Wang Yao. Reproduced by EPOCH TIME (affiliated to FALUN GONG), on death of Hu Yaobang in 1989. http://claudearpi.blogspot.in/2012/04/return-of-hu-yaobang.html
6. Text of Dalai Lama's Annual message on 10th March, 1980 http://www.dalailama.com/messages/tibet/10th-march-archive/1980
7. Address to the U.S. Congressional Human Right's Caucus, 21 Sep 1987 http://www.dalailama.com/messages/tibet/five-point-peace-plan
8. Dalai Lama's Address to the Members of the European Parliament, Strasbourg, France, June 15, 1988 http://www.dalailama.com/messages/tibet/strasbourg-proposal-1988
9. Resolution Nr. B5-0608, 0610, 0617, 0621 and 0641/2000. European Parliament resolution on the Western China Poverty Reduction Project and the future of Tibet, 6 July 2000 http://www.tpprc.org/documents/resolutions/european_parliament/6_july_2000.pdf
10. Memorandum on Genuine Autonomy for the Tibetan People (Translated from the original Tibetan) http://tibet.net/important-issues/sino-tibetan-dialogue/memorandum-on-geniune-autonomy-for-the-tibetan-people/
11. Same as above.
12. Press release by the Chinese Consulate Chicago on the Statement of Zhu Weiqun on Nov 10,2008 http://www.chinaconsulatechicago.org/eng/zt/tibetissue/t521736.htm

SECTION III

Humanitarian and Socio-Economic Aspects

13

China's Water Diversion Plans: Will the Brahmaputra Be Diverted?

Claude Arpi

Sometimes news found in the main Indian press can be misleading. Take the case of the purported 'diversion' of the Yarlung Tsangpo.

A serious national newspaper spoke of the "Yarlang Tsangpo, the name of Brahmaputra River in Mandarin". The Yarlung (and not Yarlang) Tsangpo is the Tibetan name for the river originating near Mt Kailash on the Tibetan Plateau; it has nothing to do with Mandarin.

A minor, but telling, detail about the confusion about the Chinese projects on the mighty river!

The same article further says that the Ministry of Water Resources has asked the Hyderabad-based National Remote Sensing Centre (NRSC) for a report on the Chinese building activities near the Great Bend of the Yarlung Tsangpo, as it enters into Indian territory: "Sources do not rule out the possibility that the 'new' images could be of existing structures, since the resolution of India's satellite images has increased substantially in recent months. The resolution has gone up from 181m to 10cm. This means structures, which have been there, are now visible in much greater detail."

Great news, but the NRSC scientists are wasting their time looking for the 'diversion' near the Grand Bend of the Brahmaputra: the project is planned a few hundred kilometres upstream, near the city of Tsetang.

Had the Ministry done its homework before sending a request to NRSC?

In Parliament also, the 'diversion scheme' is mixed up with the dams being built on the Brahmaputra, the Minister nevertheless affirmed that the Zangmu Dam, the first dam being built on the Brahmaputra "is no cause of concern to India as it is a 'run of the river' dam" (Beijing is planning a string of 6 dams in this area in Lengda, Zhongda, Langzhen, Jiexu, Jiacha and Zangmu).

What about the utopian Chinese dream of a 38 GWs power station (nearly twice the size of the Three Gorges Dam) at the Great Bend, near the Indian border?

One needs to understand the rationale of the Chinese government to grasp the importance of these mega hydro projects on Tibetan rivers for the Middle Kingdom's leadership.

CHINA'S GRAND PROJECTS

Traditionally, the Chinese people's respect for their Emperor increases when the ruler is able to undertake projects that no human mind can conceive. After all, the Emperor is the Son of Heaven, and only in Heaven can projects such as the Grand Canal or the Great Wall be envisioned. It is also the role of the Emperor to bring Heaven's vision down on earth. If he fails, his Mandate is terminated by Heaven and a Revolution or a Rebellion occurs.

In an article in *The Independent* in 2001, four mega projects were described by Zhao Qinghua, the Chinese Ambassador to

Bangladesh[1]. To quote him: "Four gigantic projects to be built in the next five years in China are expected to balance the supply of the nation's water, energy, mineral and human resources, which are vital to a coordinated development of the national economy but unevenly distributed in the vast land.... The four projects are designed to solve these problems. They are the diversion of southern water to the north, a west east natural gas pipeline, transmission of electricity from west to east and a railway linking Tibet with the rest of the country[2]."

But what is the rationale of the water projects?

Two of the most acute problems facing China today are the questions of food and water. These two issues are closely interlinked and, if not solved, are bound to have grave social and political consequences for the country.

The leadership in Beijing has proclaimed: "China can feed itself in the next century"[3], but the mere fact that the problem is often discussed at the highest level of the Chinese hierarchy shows that the problem is not solved, that the leadership is not sure where the solution lies or even if there is a solution.

This has been pointed out in a remarkable book written by one of the foremost world experts in agriculture, the American Lester Brown. His book, *Who Will Feed China*[4] published in the mid-eighties in the World Watch Environment Alert Series, forced the Chinese leadership to rethink their agricultural strategies a few years ago.

According to global statistics, the conversion of agricultural land into other uses (factories, residential areas, airports, roads, fly-overs, etc...) has provoked the loss of 52% of Japan's grain harvest areas, 46 of Korea's and 42% of Taiwan's in the early 1960's. China's development is not different from these three countries though it started later.

Lester Brown concludes his study by citing again the examples of the industrialised Asian countries Japan, Korea and Thailand which in spite of the best conditions have become grain importers. He prophesies: "In an integrated world economy, China's rising food prices will become the world's rising food prices. China's land scarcity will become everyone's land scarcity. And water scarcity in China will affect the entire world... It could well lead us to redefine national security away from military preparedness and toward maintaining adequate food supplies."

A small mercy for India, a large percentage of the population is still vegetarian.

THE PROBLEM OF WATER: SOUTH-NORTH WATER DIVERSION

This leads us to the problem of water. According to a study of the *World Watch Institute*[5], "In 1999, the water table under Beijing fell by 2.5 meters (8 feet). Since 1965, the water table under the city has fallen by some 59 meters or nearly 200 feet, warning China's leaders of the shortages that lie ahead as the country's aquifers are depleted."

The problem can be analyzed but not wished away.

The Draft Outline of the Tenth Five-year Plan for National Economic and Social Development already mentioned the 'gigantic' project to divert the waters of three major Tibetan rivers (Yangtse, Yellow River and Brahmaputra) to China's drought-stricken north involves the construction of massive canals, aqueducts and tunnels.[6]

The Chinese engineers are aware that Tibet is the water tank of Asia with 11 major rivers having their sources on the high plateau.

THE CASE OF THE YARLUNG TSANGPO

The Yarlung Tsangpo, or Brahmaputra as it is known in India, has an immense bearing on the lives of hundreds of millions in the sub-continent.

It is the largest river on the Tibetan Plateau, originating from a glacier near Mt Kailash. It is considered to be the highest river on earth with an average altitude of 4,000 metres. It runs 2,057 kilometers in Tibet before flowing into India, where it becomes the Brahmaputra. One of its interesting characteristics is the sharp U-turn it takes at the proximity of Mt. Namcha Barwa (7,782 meters) near the Indian border.

Like the Nile in Egypt, the Yarlung Tsangpo has fed the Tibetan civilization which flourished along its valleys, particularly in Central Tibet. The two larger tributaries of the Tsangpo are the Kyichu (or Lhasa River) and the Nyangchu.

Near Shigatse region, the Yarlung valley is 20-30 km wide. This area with its sand dunes and lakes is the cradle of a two thousand year-old civilization. *China's Tibet*, a Chinese magazine describes the scenery: "The complex and unique geographic and climatic conditions created by this great river provide Tibet with a wide array of wildlife. Black-necked cranes, Tibetan antelopes, wild Tibetan donkeys, sheep and Tibetan gazelles are among the larger animals found in the river valley[7]." In Tibet, the river is often navigable, local people use coracles (made of yak hide and bamboo) to cross it.

The Yarlung Tsangpo enters India in Siang district of Arunachal Pradesh. When it penetrates Assam, it is joined by two other rivers (the Dihang and Lohit).

In Assam, the Brahmaputra has always been considered as the very soul of the State by poets and ordinary people alike. The valley has fertile farmland, with large areas covered with Sal forests, a valuable tree that yields resins. Crops of tea, rice and jute bring wealth to the region. The River floods over much of the valley in the rainy season providing natural irrigation to rice growers. The rare one-horned rhinoceros, extinct in other parts of the world, is still found in Assam, along with tigers, elephants and a large variety of fish. Around the settlements in the Brahmaputra Valley many fruit-bearing trees like mango, jackfruit and papaya are easily grown.

Entering Bangladesh, the river unites with the Ganga and is known as the Padma, before becoming the Meghna-Brahmaputra after merging with the river Meghna. Finally it divides into hundreds of channels to form a vast delta which flows into the Bay of Bengal.

THE GRAND CANYON

When the Tsangpo reaches its easternmost point in Tibet, it takes a sharp U-turn known as the Great Bend. In recent decades, it has been established that the Yarlung Tsangpo gorge forms the longest and deepest canyon in the world.

For the first time in May 1994, *Xinhua News Agency* mentioned the length and depth of the canyon: "Chinese geologists claim that a remote Tibetan canyon is the world's largest, bigger and deeper than the Grand Canyon. The Yarlung Tsangpo Canyon, in the vast Himalayan range that encircles China, averages 3.1 miles in depth and extends 198 miles in length. The Grand Canyon in the southwestern U.S. state of Arizona is, by comparison, a mere 1 mile deep but 217 miles long, with a width of between 4 and 12 miles. The dispatch did not reveal the width of the Yarlung Tsangpo[8] Canyon. The canyon was cut during the Pliocene Epoch two million years ago by the Brahmaputra River, which flows from the Tibetan capital of Lhasa (sic) before swooping down to the Indian subcontinent. Scientists found that the canyon, located in the Himalayan range, averages 5,000 meters in depth (sic), with the deepest section reaching 5,382 meters.[9]"

A few years later, it was realized that near Mt. Namchakbarwa (7,756 metres), the Tsangpo Gorge is eight times as steep and three times as large as the Grand Canyon.

In the early 1980s, it was assumed that China planned one of the most important components of the 'western route' diversion scheme at the Great Bend. This pharaonic project was the most mind-blowing part "of the national strategy to divert water from rivers in the south and west to drought-stricken northern areas."

THE HISTORY OF THE PROJECT(S)

Through articles in the Chinese and world press, one can reconstruct the history of the project(s); because in fact there are two projects: a mega dam to produce electricity and a diversion scheme.

Let us first have a look at the mega hydropower project.

The Three Gorges Dam on the Yangtze River, which has an 18,200 megawatts capacity, could be dwarfed by a hydroelectric plant at the Great Bend of Yarlung Tsangpo with a planned capacity of 38,000 megawatts.

For the Chinese leaders, it is enough to know that the Tsangpo river tumbles down over 3,000 metres in less than 200 kms. This gives the Gorge one of the greatest hydropower potentials available in the world. It makes emperors dream.

For the Tibetans, it is one of the most pristine regions of their country. They consider the area around the Bend as the home of the Goddess Dorjee Pagmo[10], Tibet's Protecting Deity. Many believe that this place, locally known as Pemakö is the sacred realm often referred to in their scriptures: the last hidden Shangrila.

For South Asia and more particularly for India, the enormity of the scheme and its closeness to the Indian border cannot be ignored. It is not only the sheer enormity of the project which has to be considered, but the fact that if it is accomplished, the project will have ominous consequences for millions of people living downstream. Their basic need for water and thus their survival would be endangered.

Ismail Serageldin, a former Senior Vice President of the World Bank, once said: "The next World War will be over water[11]." China's green light for the project could be considered by South Asia as a declaration of war.

In the initial years, the mega dam at the Great Bend and the diversion project were often mixed up. A gigantic project was first mentioned at a conference in Alaska in July 1986. Projects under the Global Infrastructure Fund[12] (GIF) were discussed and the 'Himalayan Hydropower project' was shortlisted. At that time, it was envisaged to have a series of 11 dams around the 'Brahmaputra loop'[13]. It included a tunnel through the mountains bringing water to a powerhouse projected to have a capacity of 48,000 megawatts. The overall capacity of the 'loop' was speculated to be 70,000 megawatts.

Later, the GIF stopped mentioning the project, but engineers in Beijing had not shelved it. On the contrary, its new avatar appeared a few years later, as a single mega power station with an installed capacity of around 38,000 megawatts.

But suddenly, a diversion scheme was added on to it.

The project was reported in the *Scientific American* in June 1996. This article gave credence to the Chinese plans. The journal wrote: "Recently some Chinese engineers proposed diverting water into this arid area [Gobi Desert] from the mighty Brahmaputra River, which skirts China's southern border before dipping into India and Bangladesh. Such a feat would be 'impossible' with conventional methods, engineers stated at a meeting held in December 2011 at the Chinese Academy of Engineering Physics in Beijing. But they added that "we can certainly accomplish this project" with nuclear explosives."

The journal continued: "This statement is just one of the many lately in which Chinese technologists and officials have touted the potential of nuclear blasts for carrying out non-military goals."

At that time, it was said that one of the reasons for China's refusal to sign the Comprehensive Test Ban Treaty (CTBT) was because their desire to keep the possibility of experimenting with what is called PNE (Peaceful Nuclear Explosion). The Chinese argument was "why should promising and potentially useful technology be abandoned?"[14]

The first (and almost the only time[15]) that the matter was reported in the Indian Press was in June 1997 when *Outlook* magazine wrote a piece entitled: "A river runs through it—China proposes to divert the Brahmaputra at source to green the arid Gobi desert."

The Delhi magazine said: "The initial report—that the Chinese were planning to raise their food output in the decades ahead—was hardly stop-press material. But as details leaked out, policymakers in India and Bangladesh felt a shiver of apprehension: the Chinese proposed to divert the Brahmaputra river at source, in Tibet, even set off a peaceful nuclear explosion, to serve their purpose[16]."

At that time, the only thing that a former director, Asian Development Bank said was that under international law, no one could stop China and that "The Chinese government has equal rights to the use of the river."

However, *Outlook* revealed that "the concern in Assam and Bangladesh is understandable. The Luit—as the river [Brahmaputra] is locally called—figures prominently in the folklore and culture of Assam and the Northeast; has been the theme of countless Bhupen Hazarika songs. The river is crucial to the economy of the entire region, where the concept of irrigation through groundwater sources has not really taken off."

In the coming months, more publicity was given to the dam as well as the diversion proposals. In September 1997, *Agence France Press* in Beijing[17] reported: "Three experts propose construction of giant dam in Tibet". It stated: "After a long experience of exploration on the site, we believe that the project could begin to be included in the agenda of the concerned department". Electricity produced was claimed to be: "available for export to Bangladesh, Burma and

India, [a feature of the GIF plans] and the diverted water could irrigate the northwestern deserts of the country".

The project was also mentioned in news briefs in the *China Daily Business Weekly* (21 September 1997) and the *International Water Power & Dam Construction Monthly* (November 1997).

In January 1998, the German TV channel ZDF presented a feature on the Yarlung Tsangpo project, in a programme entitled "Die Welt" [The World]. The Chief Planner, Professor Chen Chuanyu was interviewed. He described the plan to drill a 15 kms (9.3 miles) tunnel through the Himalayas to divert the water before the U-turn and direct it to the other end of the bend. This would shorten the distance of the approximately 3,000 metres altitude drop from 200 kms to just 15 kms. He explained that the hydropower potential of 40,000 megawatts could be used to pump water to Northwest China over 800 kms away.

An interesting aspect that we have briefly mentioned is that this area known to the Tibetans as Pemakö was considered to be a sacred area, rarely visited by outsiders. The difficulty of access to this unexplored region must have created one of the greatest obstacles for the engineers in Beijing. At the end of the 1990s, the Chinese government decided to permit foreigners to explore the canyon. The well-known National Geographic expedition, with ultra sophisticated materials and highly professional rafters made the first discoveries. Though it resulted in the death of an American kayaker, Doug Gordou in October 1998, it permitted a far greater knowledge in several previously unexplored parts of the gorges. Books and video footage of this expedition (as well as subsequent ones) certainly helped the Chinese planners to get a more accurate picture of the difficulty of the terrain (as well as the potentialities).

The opening of the area to adventure tourism was also a first step to find an approach way for dam site.[18]

In recent years, the Chinese have been more discreet on the project, although a few reports have continued to come in. The correspondent of *The Telegraph* in Beijing wrote in October 2000: "Chinese leaders are drawing up plans to use nuclear explosions, in breach of the international test-ban treaty, to blast a tunnel through the Himalayas for the world's biggest hydroelectric plant."

The Telegraph rightly warned: "China will have to overcome fierce opposition from neighbouring countries who fear that the scheme could endanger the lives and livelihoods of millions of their people. Critics say that those living downstream would be at the mercy of Chinese dam officials who would be able to flood them or withhold their water supply."

According to the London paper, the cost of drilling the tunnel through Mt Namcha Barwa appears likely to surpass £10 billion. The article gives further details: "At the bottom of the tunnel, the water will flow into a new reservoir and then be diverted along more than 500 miles of the Tibetan plateau to the vast, arid areas of Xinjiang region and Gansu province. Beijing wants to use large quantities of the plentiful waters of the south-west to top up the Yellow River basin and assuage mounting discontent over water shortages in 600 cities in northern China."[19]

However, it seems that the proposal has drawn flak from several Chinese scientists. Yang Yong, a geologist who had explored the river, stated that the dam could become an embarrassing white elephant amid growing signs that the volume of water flowing in the Yarlung Tsangpo could shrink over the years.

But in 2000, before becoming Premier, Wen Jiabao had declared: "In the 21st century, the construction of large dams will play a key role in exploiting China's water resources, controlling floods and droughts, and pushing the national economy and the country's modernization forward."[20]

Wen seemed to have had a more moderate approach later.

In the first years of the new millennium, one pertinent question in China was: does a Chinese emperor have a choice other than to take up pharaonic works, if he wants to remain emperor?

A MOST SEISMIC AREA

To understand the difficulty of the project, it is necessary to go back to an event in 1950. In the evening of August 15, a terrible earthquake shook Eastern Tibet[21]. "This was no ordinary earthquake; it felt like the end of the world," wrote Robert Ford, the British Radio operator working in Eastern Tibet. "Mountains and valleys exchanged places in an instant, hundreds of villages were swallowed up, the Brahmaputra River was completely rerouted and for hours afterwards, the sky over south-eastern Tibet glowed with an infernal red light, diffused with the pungent scent of sulphur.[22]" It is a fact that the course of the Brahmaputra changed during those few hours. One may argue that only nature can produce such an upheaval, but nothing is less certain.

Nehru visited the Indian side of the border in September and made a long vivid description of the damage and sufferings of the people. On his return from Assam, he made a broadcast to the nation on All Indian Radio[23]: "It is said that the epicentre of the earthquake was somewhere in Tibet, near a place called Rima, some miles from the Assam frontier. We know nothing of what has happened in Tibet or on the mountainous regions of the border. As a result of the landslides, rivers were blocked up for a while, and when they broke through, they came down with a rush and a roar, a high wall of water sweeping down and flooding large areas and washing away villages and fields and gardens. These rivers have changed their colour and carried some sulphurous and other material which spread a horrible smell for some distance around them. The fish in them died. The remains of villages, animals (including cattle and elephants), and large quantities of timber floated down these raging waters. Paddy fields were destroyed, stocks of grains were washed away and some tea gardens also suffered great damage."

This was a month after the earthquake and a few hundred kilometres south of the epicentre. One can imagine what happened in Tibet; this broadcast also gives an idea of what could happen on a much larger scale, if the hydro power projects are carried out.

THE DIVERSION SCHEME: THE LI LING-GAO KAI PLANS

But let us look at the 'diversion' story.

Some ten years ago, one Chinese engineer Li Ling and a retired PLA General, Gao Kai, seriously worked on the diversion scheme. Li Ling then published a book called *Tibet's Waters will Save China* in which the Chinese engineer details the diversion scheme, also known as Shuomatan Canal (from Suma Tan in Central Tibet to Tanjing in China).

Many 'experts' denounced the plans of Li Ling and Gao Kai; Qin Hui, a professor in the School of Humanities and Social Sciences of Tsinghua University declared: "We have to take the international response into consideration. It is undoubted that the lower reaches of Yarlung Tsangpo River are within India's Assam Province, where it is a lifeline for local agriculture and backbone of the economy, just as it is further downstream in Bangladesh."

Qin added: "It is so obvious that the proposed damming project will have a cascading effect leading to a natural disaster in the lower foreign reaches of the Brahmaputra, Salween and Mekong rivers."

Liu Changming, a hydrologist at the Chinese Academy of Sciences who had advised the government on these proposals, confirmed that a team of water experts from the Chinese Academy of Engineers, an advisory group of prominent scientists "had concluded that the proposal to tap the Brahmaputra River would be far too expensive, technologically unfeasible and ...too controversial". He nevertheless admitted: "There may be some retired officials that support the plan, but they're not the experts advising the government."

We heard again about the diversion of the Brahmaputra in November 2006 when President Hu Jintao visited India. China had decided to assuage the legitimate worries of the Indian government.

Water Resources Minister Wang Shucheng, a hydraulic engineer himself, affirmed that the proposal was "unnecessary, unfeasible and unscientific. There is no need for such dramatic and unscientific projects."

He, however, admitted that there was a plan in the drawers, but "the project involves major financial and technical difficulties". Further, "the cost of diverting water from the Yarlung Tsangpo would be much more expensive than any of the current water projects."

Chinese Foreign Ministry spokesman Liu Jianchao also confirmed: "The Chinese government has no plans to build a dam on the Yarlung Tsangpo River (the China part of the Brahmaputra) to divert water to the Yellow River."

This reminds me an interview with the Dalai Lama in 2003. He said: "I remember that one day in the early sixties; one man from Xinjiang[24] came to see me. He was an ex-minister of the local government belonging to the Ugyur nationality. While we were having some food, (it was not here, it was in my previous residence in Dharamsala), he told me that there is a real danger in the future of China changing the course of the major Tibetan rivers towards the deserts of Xinjiang or Gobi areas. The Chinese can do it! If that happens, what will happen to India? At that time, I thought that it was very difficult, but now I think that it is possible. For example, look at the Three Gorges project, the Chinese can undertake such big projects. In fact, in Tibet, it is easier, arrangements can be made to divert rivers because [the Tibetan plateau] geographically slopes from higher areas to lower areas. [To make such a diversion] on a few hundred kilometers, from Kongpo in Southern Tibet to Northern Tibet, is not that difficult."

The Dalai Lama knows how the minds of the Chinese leaders function: he met Mao for the first time 50 years ago. His interview tends to confirm the apprehensions of many experts.

THE MEGA HYDROPOWER PLANT

During the following years, we did not hear anymore about the 'diversion' project, though the mega hydropower plant was definitely on the cards.

On July 17, 2003 *The People's Daily* published a small item "China to Conduct Feasibility Study on Hydropower Project in Tibet." It ran thus: "China plans to conduct a feasibility study in October on the construction of a major hydropower project on the Yarlung Tsangpo River, in the Tibet Autonomous Region... an expert team [was sent] to the area for preliminary work between late June and early July. The Chinese section of the river, 2,057 kilometers long, boasts a water energy reserve of about 100 million kilowatts, or one sixth of the country's total, ranking second behind the Yangtze River. The location for the possible hydropower plant is the U-shaped turn of the river in the southeastern part of Tibet. The river drops by 2,755 meters in the 500 kilometer-long "U" section."

Though very few people noted it, the cat is out of the bag.

CHANGING SCENE?

In May 2011, the hydrological scene seemed to change in China. For the first time, the State Council (the Chinese Cabinet) acknowledged various serious problems faced by the mega Three Gorges Dam. A statement on the government's website affirmed:

"At the same time that the Three Gorges project provides huge comprehensive benefits, urgent problems must be resolved regarding the smooth relocation of residents, ecological protection, and geological disaster prevention."

The statement was dictated at the end of a meeting chaired by the then Premier Wen Jiabao: "Problems emerged at various stages of project planning and construction but could not be solved immediately, and some arose because of increased demands brought on by economic and social development", it explained.

An article from *Reuters* quoted Dai Qing, an environmental activist who said the damage caused by the dam in some cases is irreversible: "The most serious threat is that of geological disasters. Now that the dam is in place, no amount of money can fix the problem. It fundamentally cannot be resolved."

Dai affirmed that the then Premier Wen and then President Hu, respectively trained as geological and hydraulic engineers did not turn up at the opening function of the dam because they knew 'the risks of the project'.

In the post-Fukushima era, it is logical to expect any government to honestly study the geology and other environmental issues linked to these mega projects.

These 'irreversible' hitches should trigger fresh researches into the most seismic region on the planet: the Tibetan Plateau. This is the least that one would expect.

Officials are planning the construction of myriads of dams on the Tibetan rivers without taking into account the local seismic conditions, although the State Council has now admitted that this issue cannot be sorted out once the dams are built.

THE IMPLICATIONS OF A MEGA HYDROPOWER PROJECT

Based on mean annual flow, the Yarlung Tsangpo constitutes about 33 per cent of the total flow of the Brahmaputra when it enters

India. In other words for the sub-continent, it is the largest proportion of stable flow from glacial sources. The implications of the diversion of the waters of the Yarlung Tsangpo (even if it is a percentage only) to northwestern China will have far-reaching consequences for Tibet. Most importantly, this project also represents a direct threat to the people living downstream in India and Bangladesh.

For Tibet and the Surrounding Areas

A 38,000-megawatt capacity hydropower plant would destroy vast areas of virgin forest within the canyon and beyond. Rare species of flora and fauna[25] will be lost for scientific study. The Chinese authorities themselves admit that the Canyon is the home for more than 60 per cent of the biological resources on the Tibetan Plateau.

Although the population in the canyon is rather small, the indigenous people would suffer great hardship and be forced to leave their ancestral lands. It may not be a problem for Beijing which has 'resettled' more than one million Chinese Hans since the beginning of the construction of the Three Gorges Dam, but for the Tibetans, it would mean the loss of a last sacred place and the home of their Protecting Deity. Furthermore, Tibetans would not benefit in any way from the power produced by the hydroelectric plant, as it would be sold to China's southern neighbours or used to send the water upstream to northwestern China.

If the project comes to fruition, Tibet and the world would have lost this virgin region and its canyon, a great treasure heritage. The Central Tibetan Administration of the Dalai Lama even suggested recently that the "Yarlung Tsangpo canyon is a unique and magnificent natural phenomenon with diverse plant and animal life which should be considered as a UNESCO World Heritage Site or similar preserved site of international significance[26]." But, when the stakes are so high and the ego of the emperors so big, one can have no doubt that such scheme could be implemented.

For South Asia

India and Bangladesh would be at the mercy of China for adequate release of water during the dry season, and for protection from floods during the rainy season. India knows from its own internal problems how difficult it is to solve a water dispute. When it comes to a trans-boundary question (when the boundary is not even agreed upon), it seems practically impossible to find a workable understanding. The Cauvery dispute in the South or the Ravi-Beas disagreement between Haryana and Punjab are nothing compared to a possible confrontation between India and China over the use of the Himalayan waters.

Precipitation in North India (particularly Assam) and Bangladesh is very high (80%) during the four monsoon months (between June and September), and low (20%) during the remaining eight months. China, seeing her own interests, could withhold water for power generation and irrigation during the dry season and release water during the flood season with catastrophic consequences for eastern South Asia.

But there is worse, the 'diversion' project is back on the scene.

THE NEW PLANS OF WANG GUANGQIAN

It is very unfortunate that for the first time in 5 years, a Chinese official spoke again of the possibility of diverting the Yarlung Tsangpo/Brahmaputra towards northern China.

The website *2point6billion.com* quoted Wang Guangqian, a scholar of the Chinese Academy of Sciences as saying: "Chinese experts have raised a new proposal to divert water from the upper reaches of the Brahmaputra River to the country's northwestern province of Xinjiang. The water diversion route in the proposal, named the 'Grand Western Canal', is slightly different from the 'Western Canal' mentioned in China's well-known South-North Water Diversion Project[27]."

Wang explained the Chinese rationale: "Faced with severe challenges brought by reduced water resources and a severe drought that has affected a large portion of the country, China has started to consider diverting water from the Brahmaputra River, the watercourse that originates upstream from southwestern Tibet and finally enters India."

Prof. Wang Guangqian of the Chinese Academy of Sciences seems to say that China has no choice but to go for it.

Interestingly, Wang Guangqian, a scientist of the Chinese Academy of Sciences Engineering has the backing of Li Ruihuan, a former member of the Standing Committee of the CCP's Politburo and former Chairman of the Chinese People's Political Consultative Conference. Many in the PLA as well as the mega dam companies are also behind the project.

Wang Guangqian speaks of the newly proposed route: "Brahmaputra waters are expected to be rerouted to Xinjiang along the Qinghai-Tibet Railway and the Hexi Corridor—part of the Northern Silk Road located in Gansu Province".

Wang admitted: "We thought this would be a plan 50 years later", adding that presently Chinese experts and governmental officials are still studying the feasibility and possible impacts of different proposals.

THE OPENING OF METOK COUNTY

There is a big difference between 2006 and today: with the opening of the tunnel to Metok (Motuo in Mandarin), the Chinese engineers now have the possibility to start the mega power plant which could provide the necessary energy to the diversion scheme, planned a few hundred kilometres upstream the Brahmaputra.

On January 5, 2011, *The China Daily* reported that construction workers successfully blasted through the last section of mountain leading to Metok County on December 15: "The explosion ended an era of isolation for the region".

The newspaper quoted Weng Mengyong, former Vice Minister of Transport: "The 3,310-meter-long Galongla Tunnel, built at an altitude of 3,750 meters, is a crucial part of the Metok Highway. The 'extremely complex' geological and meteorological conditions made highway construction work arduous and difficult".

He further added: "Metok with a population of 11, 000 is China's last county with no highway link. Bad weather, like snow and rain, make the narrow paths to the county impassable for nine months of the year, and it takes more than 10 hours to get out of the mountains on foot. The Galongla Tunnel is the key sector of the project. Once completed, it will cut 24 km from the original rugged mountain road. The 117-km highway, linking Metok and Bome counties, will shorten the travel time."

Zhou Haitao, a government official who worked in Metok for five years said: "It was a life-threatening adventure every time I climbed through the mountains of Metok".

The China Daily gave more details: "Metok County, in Nyingchi Prefecture of the Tibet Autonomous Region, has the nickname 'plateau island'. The 3,400-square-kms county enjoys vertical climatic phenomenon with an environment that changes from icy mountain slopes to tropical rainforests, which brings a basic agriculture economy to the region. But poor transportation conditions make it difficult to get agricultural products out of the county".

The Metok-Bome Highway project was approved by the State Council in October 2008 with an investment of $ 144 million from the Central Government. The project included 29 bridges and 227 culverts and took 36 months to complete.

He Xianzhi, a member of the team who worked on the tunnel recounted: "We'd spent six years investigating the area to collect information about geological disasters and possible hazards".

The article stated: "the inaccessibility makes it one of the most untouched places in the world. The charm of an expedition to Metok lies in the very challenge of reaching this amazing place on foot".

The tunnel could open the way to the construction of mega power plant in this region which is, let us not forget, very close from the McMahon Line.

MORE DETAILS ON THE PROJECT

Most of the available information on the diversion project comes from an article by Zhang Ke, a reporter at *China Business News* published on the website *chinadialogue.com*[28].

Wang Guangqian admitted that his proposal, called the Major Western Route, has been inspired by the work of Gao Kai: "Everybody gets really excited when they hear about it".

Today, China has less and less water and is looking at ways to get it. Scientists can look to two possible directions, the sea (Bobai Sea) or the mountains (Tibetan Plateau).

Wang quoted a survey by the Cold and Arid Regions Environmental and Engineering Institute: "Since the 1980s, the quantity of water flowing from the Yellow River above the city of Lanzhou, in north-western China, has fallen by an average of 13% a year. In 2002, it dropped to 46%."

Further, figures from the Chinese Academy of Sciences show that "rivers on the Qinghai-Tibet and Yunnan-Guizhou plateaus, including the Yarlung Tsangpo, Salween and Mekong, carry between 637 billion cubic metres and 810 billion cubic metres of water out of China each year".

What disturbs some Chinese engineers is that most of it flows on to India and Southeast Asia—where they become the Brahmaputra, Salween and Mekong.

The diversion project envisaged by Wang (and Gao Kai) could move up to Northwestern China, some 200 billion cubic metres of water a year—the equivalent of four Yellow Rivers.

Wang explained that water usage has tremendously increased due to social and economic development on the lower reaches of the Yangtze River and Yellow River. Climate change and desertification are other factors, making water issues so crucial.

Zhang Ke, the reporter at *China Business News* who went in depth into the issue said that Guo Kai told him that the idea came to him in as early as 1990: why not take 200 billion cubic metres of water every year from the Yarlung Tsangpo and divert them into the Yellow River. Guo argued that his project "would not only ease water shortages in the north of China, but also transform desert landscapes, increase farmland, provide power and create jobs". At that time (in 1997), he estimated the cost of the project at $ 35 billion.

According to Li Ling, author of *Tibet's Water Will Save China*, the Institute of Advanced Technology at the Chinese Academy of Sciences is using supercomputers and data modelling to simulate the Major Western Route and evaluate its feasibility. Wang Guangqian himself works with the South-North Water Transfer office to prepare a feasibility study of his proposal.

Li admitted that "an initial simulation of the proposal has already been produced in Shenzhen, but limitations in the data used to create it means it cannot be made public."

This lack of data is probably one of the weaknesses of the project. But Li is convinced that it is doable: "If you can successfully build a railway between 4,500 metres and 5,072 metres above sea level, building the Major Western Route at 3,588 metres to 3,366 metres is not going to be a problem", he says. The cost remains the main issue, along with the strategic implications.

In 2006, the Chinese government pretended that 'a few mad men' were thinking of this pharaonic project, but if these few 'mad men' (supported by a former Politburo Standing Committee member) are able to use the super computers of the Chinese Academy of Sciences for their calculations, they may not be that mad.

In the meantime, the then Indian Foreign Minister S.M. Krishna said that the Indian government "has sought a report on the matter from its mission in Beijing. We are trying to get more details both from the government and our mission and then depending upon the report that we get, we will be able to make an assessment and take appropriate diplomatic steps."

Let us hope that 'appropriate' steps will be taken.

TWO IMPORTANT FACTORS

Two important factors have to be understood.

One, hydropower lobbies have a financial interest in 'concretizing' the project as soon as possible. Recently, an article in *The Financial Times* announced that "China's Three Gorges Project Corporation has proposed a $15bn hydropower scheme to Pakistan to dam the Indus river valley at several points, in a project aimed at controlling floods and tackling electricity shortages."

Dams, whether in India, Pakistan or Tibet, mean big business and the large Chinese corporations will continue to lobby hard to get the projects through.

The second crucial factor is the cost-benefit perspective. The Chinese leadership is very down-to-earth, rational. A person who worked on the issue told me: "If the price of transferring water is cheaper than conservation or getting water from the sea, China will go ahead."

THE BOHAI DIVERSION PROJECT

The diversion of the Brahmaputra is in competition with another diversion: to take water from the Bohai Sea, the innermost gulf of the Yellow Sea on the coast of Northeastern China and push it to Xinjiang.

The Chinese press reported that on November 5, 2010, the Xinjiang People's Government Development Research Center and Institute of Western and Eastern Economy sponsored a summit in Wushi on The Plan for the Diversion of Sea Water to Western China. Over 120 experts from throughout China gathered to discuss the water issue that has impeded Xinjiang's development: "Huo Youguang, a professor at Xian Transportation University, along with Chen Changli, a professor at China University of Geosciences, came up with the basic idea of diverting seawater from the Bohai Sea to Xinjiang. They believe that such a diversion project can thoroughly improve the deteriorating environmental conditions of north and northwest China." Later, the Development and Reform Commission [Planning Commission] of Inner Mongolia and Liaoning province had approved the project and that five construction sites related to the project had become operational. He was later denied.

On November 17, 2010, *Xinhua* published a news item: *Experts: Water diversion from Bohai to Xinjiang unfeasible*. Water resources scientists and experts asserted: "A proposal to divert water from the Bohai Sea on China's eastern coast to Xinjiang Uygur Autonomous Region in the far west to fight deserts and sandstorms is 'unfeasible' and an 'illusion'."

Xinhua quoted Shi Yulin, an academician at the Chinese Academy of Engineering and a research fellow at the Institute of Geographic Sciences and Natural Resources Research of the Chinese Academy of Sciences, who said: "the salt contained in the huge amount of diverted sea water could further encrust the saline land in Xinjiang."

While Li Zechun, an academician at Chinese Academy of Engineering, and former director of National Climate Center, explained that "the sea water could not produce sufficient vapor to create enough rainfall to affect the climate in northwestern regions."

Another scientist, Ning Yuan, former Deputy Director and Research Fellow of the South-North Water Diversion Project Commission (SNWDPC), working under the State Council, added that the Bohai Sea was 5,000 kms away from Xinjiang, five times the distance of the South-North Water Diversion from Danjiangkou, in central Hubei Province to Beijing and therefore too far.

WILL IT HAPPEN?

A similar discussion is probably taking place for the Great Western Diversion. There is no doubt that in the end, it will be a political decision, though today some scientists and bureaucrats say it is 'impossible', while others believe, we can do it. The fact remains that China today badly needs water:

1. To stop the desertification in Xinjiang, Gansu and Inner Mongolia.
2. To have the Yellow River running at full volume of water again.
3. To feed its people.

If such grandiose and seemingly unrealizable projects are even thought of, it is because the situation is quite desperate and nobody is able to foresee any 'realizable' solution.

And Beijing should look again into the disastrous performance of the Three Gorges Dam before taking a hurried decision.

One of the issues is that the Eastern and Central Water Diversions are running into serious technical and human difficulties.

On June 1, 2011 *The New York Times (Plan for China's Water Crisis Spurs Concern)* reported: "A chronic drought is ravaging farmland. The Gobi Desert is inching south. The Yellow River, the so-called birthplace of Chinese civilization, is so polluted it can no longer supply drinking water. The rapid growth of megacities—22 million people in Beijing and 12 million in Tianjin alone — has drained underground aquifers that took millenniums to fill."

The project is facing several problems: the construction has been seriously delayed (very unusual phenomenon in China). The costs have overshot the estimates and last, but not the least, waters are reaching their destination polluted. *The New York Times* continued: "Overseers of the eastern route, which is being built alongside an ancient waterway for barges called the Grand Canal, have found that the drinking water to be brought to Tianjin from the Yangtze is so polluted that 426 sewage treatment plants have to be built; water pollution control on the route takes up 44 per cent of the $5 billion investment, according to Xinhua, the official news agency."

The problems may be different for the Great Western Diversion, but the delay of the Eastern and Central parts is certainly an issue to consider for the 'deciders'.

When it makes its calculations, Beijing will also have to take into account the cost of a serious conflict with India. The price of water may then become exorbitant.

THE ARUNACHAL AND HIMACHAL FLOODS

It is important to cite here an event which occurred in June 2000. It illustrates, on a reduced scale, what could happen if the Tsangpo project is completed some day. Recently the breach of a natural dam in Tibet led to severe floods and left over a hundred people dead or missing in Arunachal Pradesh. It is not difficult to understand that areas downstream in Arunachal or Assam are extremely vulnerable to what takes place upstream in Tibet.[29] At the time of the incident, *Rediff.com* reported: "Although news of floods in distant north-east may not be hot for Delhi, the flash floods that hit the border state of Arunachal Pradesh in June has made officials at the Central Water Commission and the Ministry of Water Resources sit up and take notice. As officials pore over the technical data, a new dimension that the Chinese Army in Tibet, as part of an experiment, may have deliberately blasted the dam has been added to the already hazy picture."

According to Nabam Rebia, member of Parliament from Arunachal Pradesh, puzzled by the nature of the floods and the equally mysterious response of China, the Government of India's remote sensing agency hired a Canadian satellite to take a close look at the scene of the breach. Top officials who confirmed this said, "All the technical details and pictures from the area are with us now and confirm that a breach had taken place on a dam on the river Tsangpo leading to flash floods in the north-eastern region. According to the official, who had seen the technical data, the flash flood occurred because of a breach in a dam located in an area pinpointed as latitude 30.15 degrees north by 94.50 degrees east, which falls in China controlled Tibet."

A few weeks later, a similar mishap took place on the other end of the Himalayas. *The Tribune* in Chandigarh reported this strange event[30]: "Even three days after the disaster, the mystery of the flashfloods in the Sutlej, which wreaked havoc along its 200-kms length in the state, remains unresolved." It added: "Experts are at a loss to understand where the huge mass of water came from."

Imagine a 50-ft high wall of water descending into the gorges of Kinnaur in Himachal Pradesh! In a few hours, more than 100 persons died, 120 km of a strategic highway (Chini sector) was washed away and 98 bridges were destroyed.[31] The details of this incident were similar to the Arunachal Pradesh one.

A detailed study carried out a few months later by the ISRO scientists confirmed that the release of excess water accumulated in the Sutlej and the Siang river [the Tsangpo] basins in Tibet had led to the flooding. Nearly a year later, the weekly *India Today* commented[32]:

> While the satellite images remain classified, officials of the Ministry of Water Resources indicate that these pictures show the presence of huge water bodies or lakes upstream in Sutlej and Siang river basins before the flash floods took place. However, these lakes disappeared soon after the disaster struck Indian territory. This probably means that the Chinese had breached these water bodies as a result of which lakhs of cusecs of water were released into the Sutlej and Siang river basins.

It is not difficult to imagine what could 'naturally' (or less naturally) happen if a large structure is constructed north of the McMahon line during a time of conflict.

THE SOLUTION: A WATER TREATY WITH INDIA

The only solution seems to lie in bringing the matter to the negotiating table. If a river-water Treaty could be signed between India and Pakistan in the early sixties, why can not a similar agreement be made between China, India and Bangladesh, in order to assure a decent life for all in the region?

Further there is a Convention on the Law of the Non-Navigational Uses of International Watercourses adopted by the UN in 1997 (though not yet an international law, because not ratified by enough nations). It could serve as a model for bilateral or multilateral treaties/conventions with China.

But is Beijing interested?

ENDNOTES

1. *The Independent* (October 1, 2001), "New Projects to Balance China's Resources", by Zhao Qinghua.
2. The railway line to Lhasa became operational in July 2006.
3. See White Paper on food production on the People's Daily website: http://english.peopledaily.com.cn/whitepaper.html
4. Brown Lester R., *Who will Feed China?*, (New York: Worldwatch Institute, 1995).
5. For full article: "China's Water Shortage could Shake World Food Security", by Lester R. Brown and Brian Halweil, see website: http://www.worldwatch.org/bookstore/
6. Once finished the man-made rivers will carry 12.6 trillion gallons of water a year—which according to some studies are enough to fill New York City's taps for a quarter century.
7. *China's Tibet*, November 1997.
8. Or Tsangpo.
9. *Tibet World News* (May 4, 1994), "China Claims Tibetan Canyon is Largest".
10. In English: The Diamond Sow.
11. The World Commission on Large Dams, Dams and Development: A New Framework for Decision Making, p. 3.
12. According to their website: "The concept of the Global Infrastructure Fund (GIF) was announced in December 1977 by a study task force led by the late Mr. Masaki Nakajima, who then was president of Mitsubishi Research Institute, Inc. of Japan. The GIF concept is that the development of infrastructure on a global scale should be promoted to realize sustainable development so that all humankind can enjoy a better quality of life in a restored living sphere and a better environment." Well, such huge project would have been extremely unsustainable.
13. Or Great Bend.
14. China finally signed the CTBT in September 1996 but never ratified the Treaty which means that Beijing is still keeping a door open for using PNEs.
15. This writer contributed an article on the subject in *The Pioneer*, New Delhi, China and the River network (13 February 2003).
16. *Outlook*, New Delhi (18 June 1997).

17. *Tibet 2000—Environment & Development Issues*, (Dharamsala, DIIR, 2000).
18. It should be remembered here that the U turn of the Tsangpo is very close to the Indian border of Arunachal Pradesh (no more 10-15 km as the crow flies) and that China claims the Indian state as its own.
19. *The Telegraph*, London (October 22, 2000), "China Planning Nuclear Blasts to Build Giant Hydro Project", by Damien Mcelroy in Beijing.
20. Ibid.
21. The Dalai Lama who was a 15-year adolescent in 1950, later remembered: "It was like an artillery barrage—which is what we assumed to be the cause of both the tremors and the noise: a test of some sorts being carried out by the Tibetan army…Some people reported seeing a strange red glow in the skies in the direction from which the noise came…." See *The Dalai Lama, Freedom in Exile* (London: Hodder & Stoughton, 1990).
22. Ford Robert, *Captured in Tibet* (New York: Oxford University Press, 1990), p. 94.
23. *Selected Works of Jawaharlal Nehru* (Second Series), Vol. 15, Part II, (New Delhi: Jawaharlal Nehru Memorial Fund, 1993), p. 166.
24. Chinese province of Eastern Turkistan.
25. Though it is not enough documented.
26. *Tibet 2000*, op. cit.
27. See, http://www.2point6billion.com/news/2011/06/08/china-to-consider-diverting-the-brahmaputra-river-9430.html
28. See: http://www.chinadialogue.net/article/show/single/en/4349.
29. See also the following articles: "Breach in Tibet Dam Caused Arunachal Floods", *The Times of India* (July 8, 2000); "India Blames Flash Floods on Chinese Dam", *Agence France Presse* (July 10, 2000); "Arunachal Floods—Dam Breach in Tibet, China 'hushed' it up", *The Indian Express* (July 10, 2000).
30. *The Tribune* (4 August 2000), "Flood Started in Tibet?".
31. This writer personally witnessed the extensive damage while traveling Spiti valley a few days after the incident.
32. *India Today* (25 June 2001), "Made in China".

14

Socio-Economic Changes in Tibet

P.K. Gautam[1]

ABSTRACT

Socio-economic changes in Tibet have led to marginalisation of the locals. Besides Hanisation and loss of Tibetan culture and religion, socio-economic changes also adversely impact Tibet's ecology—which is a global common. The ecology of Tibet had a symbiotic relation with the traditional lives of nomads. The current policies of their sedantarisation are fraught with danger. This paper evaluates recent changes in China, Tibet and India. In the end, it suggests some matters for consideration by the parties concerned.

INTRODUCTION

There are problems with measuring everything in terms of gross domestic product (GDP). According to *News from China*, Tibet recorded double digit GDP growth of 12.2 per cent for the last 18 years.[2] The May 2011 issue further informs that China would invest 26 billion Yuan in Tibet in 2011 on major projects such as the Lhasa-Shigatse section of the Qinghai - Tibet Railways, the Qinghai-Tibet Plateau power grid interconnection project, and

Laohuzui hydro- electric project of 11th plan by 2011.[3] It asks the question—who has benefited from Chinese Tibet policy? It then answers that the 5th Forum on Work in Tibet Conference of 2010 had more favourable policies. Hanisation is not true, according to the Report. It argues that there are 95 per cent Tibetans of which 96 per cent are farmers and herders. The 14th Dalai Lama is lying, according to the Report.[4]

However, from a study of secondary literature including field work by scholars in Tibet, discussion with Indian and international scholars and Tibetans in exile, a totally different picture emerges.

Although it may be true that the CCP has spent a great deal of money in Tibet, this has not necessarily gone to the Tibetans. China has taken away more than it has given. It gives to itself, in the sense that the recipients are mostly Han Chinese. [5] The most balanced findings are perhaps of the noted anthropologist Melvyn C. Goldstein and his co-authors. Field work from 2006 to 2009 with Puchung Wangdui a Research Scientist from the Tibetan Academy of Social Science Lhasa shows that it is unclear if people's first orientation fulfils Beijing's broader political objective and the standard of living is improving. They point out that there are other deep-seated issues that concern Tibet, such as: (a) Restrictions on monks and monasteries, (b) Language and (c) Large number of non-Tibetan migrant workers.[6] Their policy prescription is that "current decision makers in Beijing apparently believe that it is enough, but we suggest that it is too early to say whether this belief is correct or just wishful thinking".[7]

Thus, in the first instance socio-economic changes are foremost issues of data, evidence, facts and perceptions. Visiting Chinese scholars ask if I have seen the Dalai Lama or have been to Tibet. To which I reply that it is irrelevant. Though as a child I was taken by elders in my family to see the Dalai Lama soon after his escape in 1959 to Mussoorie—what is important today are his deeds and charisma. Among Indians there is an inherent respect for him. This may well be an Asian value which we need to preserve. The answer to their next challenge on whether I have visited Tibet is also irrelevant. Max Müller never visited India and yet was an Indologist. Nirad C. Chaudhury had not been to England when he wrote the masterpiece *A Passage to England.*

With this background, this essay will analyse the socio economic changes in Tibet which lead to the marginalisation of locals. Besides Hanisation and loss of Tibetan culture and religion, it will also show how socio-economic change adversely impact Tibet—which is a global common. The ecology of Tibet had symbiotic relations with the traditional lives of nomads. It is argued further (along with many other writers[8]) that current policies of their sedantarisation are fraught with danger. There is then an evaluation of the changes in China, Tibet and India. In the end, this paper suggests some matters for consideration by the PRC and Tibetan officials and scholars.

MARGINALISATION OF TIBETANS IN TIBET

As Wang Shiyang explains, the Tibetans are poorly equipped to respond to and take advantage of opportunities.[9] This is due to a complex set of factors, political, social, cultural and environmental. In Tibetan-majority areas, only 20 per cent of the business is controlled by Tibetans. Buddhist society is monastery-centred and agriculture-animal husbandry based. The emphasis is on karma, which shuns material gains. In China's Western Development Programme in Tibet since 1999, though living standards have improved, this has happened more in urban than rural areas. Non-Tibetans, who are numerous, are attracted to urban Tibet. Besides, fluency in Chinese language is a passport for success. The net result is that the locals continue to be marginalized.[10]

TIBET AS A REGIONAL COMMON

The ecology of Tibet is crucial.[11] Scientific knowledge is now challenging the earlier (and wrong) assumption of traditional lifestyles as practiced by Tibetans as backward, irrational and unsustainable.[12] The Qinghai–Tibet Plateau is a global ecosystem—like the Amazon rainforest or the two Poles. Hanization of Tibet and the resultant population growth, infrastructure development and economic policies and river diversion and dams above all, go against the limited carrying capacity and fragility of the region. Autonomous also implies that the model of development is congruent with Nature, according to the Buddhist tradition as obtained in Tibet. One need not be a Buddhist to understand this. In the present situation this does not seem to be happening.

NOMADS

Tibetan nomads, who are now completely sidelined in terms of development, are reported to have been the first ones to notice changes in the land and weather.[13] Climate change and warming will spell disaster as so much is dependent on sustainable land use and respect for the environment. Desertification of open grassland and pastures, loss of biodiversity and overexploitation by way of resource extraction as in the case of water, deforestation and minerals, etc. are emerging as the new challenges to the environment. The Tibetans have pleaded with the Chinese government to rethink its development and environmental policies, be it settling of nomads, fencing of grasslands, reforestation, infrastructure development, and urbanisation.[14] In contrast to the economic policies of the PRC, the Tibetan government in exile would prefer to have real autonomy for preserving its religion, culture, traditions and way of life which are so closely linked to its ecology. The Central Tibetan Administration (CTA) has strong reservations about the wisdom of China's current development plans for the plateau as well as gaps in policy and implementation.[15]

GRASSLAND, PASTURES AND NOMADIC LIFE

The grassland ecosystem of the Tibetan plateau is in rapid decline due to economic development and increased population of non Tibetans. Under the dual influence of natural and human factors (like climate change), a large expanse of the Tibetan Plateau region is seriously degraded.[16] Perhaps the most salient and long term impact may well be due to the fact that they have been forced to a sedentary existence. The chief economic wealth of Tibet lies in its nomadic trade and cattle breeding. Nomad trade takes two forms. First is animal produce like sheep skins, wool, meat, milk and butter. The second is the use of pack animals as draft such as yaks, dzos (cross breeds), goats and sheep for trade. The Russian Tibetologist, Roerich, once said—deprive Tibet of its cattle breeding region and the country would starve.[17] Michel Zhao and Orville Schell argue convincingly for the need to preserve the health of glaciers, grasslands and the nomadic way of life, in a very delicately balanced ecology.[18]

However, if massive Hanisation continues then even the rural areas will be dominated by Han Chinese and it is unlikely that they will take to nomadism in the traditional sense. It needs to be appreciated that traditional Tibetan pastoralists had a fine balance with grasslands. Han Chinese herders instead have more and more yaks, goats, sheep and horses etc. Due to overexploitation by the Han with the wrong policies, degradation has set in.[19] Massive conversion of grasslands into farming plots and settled agriculture will change the ecosystem which for centuries has provided sustenance to the sparsely populated, high altitude environmentally fragile plateau. And in a fundamental way this, in turn, will destroy all cultural and religious practices which evolved to preserve this region for short term economic and agricultural gains. This may lead to an unmitigated environmental collapse. This will also impact South Asia and Southeast Asia as it depends on the water tower and a stable ecosystem there.

CTA sums up the problem by arguing that the desertification of Tibetan grasslands is due to mismanagement and forced settlements of nomads.[20] Tibetan nomads and their livestock play an important role as best stewards of grasslands. The Tibetan nomads are being removed from their ancestral pasturelands to concrete buildings with no alternative sources of livelihood, on grounds that they cause deterioration of the grasslands. Yet, contrary to Beijing's claims, recent scientific investigations conducted in Amdo region have proved that grazing eventually helps to rejuvenate the grasses. [21] It further elaborates on the ecological degradation:

> On the rangeland decades of compulsory overstocking in the 1960s and 1970s set off a process of degradation which turns the carbon rich living turf black, exposed to gales and blizzards which are becoming more extreme. Rangeland degradation is now so widespread that plants, usually able to store most of their biomass and their carbon below the ground, below the teeth of the grazers, away from the biting wind, now die. Quickly the high alpine meadow turns black; the soil whipped away by gale and all that is left is bare earth, with little likelihood of recolonisation by life for centuries.[22]

ASSAULT ON RELIGION AND CULTURE

WHY FLEE?

Had the Chinese policies been in tune with the religion and culture of the Tibetans, it would not have created socio - economic miseries. Why do Tibetans flee and escape from Tibet in spite of harsh conditions in crossing the border and reaching India? One of the important factors that pull them is that true religious, spiritual and cultural education is denied in Tibet. Kharat in a field trip in 1999 noted that every month hundreds of new refugees enter India, some register, some do not. Four types were classified by him:

(a)Those who fled Tibet due to torture and atrocity.

(b)Monks and nuns to take religious education about Buddhism in India since this is prohibited in China.

(c)The pilgrimage population which comes here just to get the blessings of the Dalai Lama and intends to return.

(d)The youngsters who come to India for the purpose of a good moral education as they do not get the opportunity in China. [23]

Matters have lately become worse. The spontaneous uprising of March 2008 not only in TAR, but in ethnic Tibetan areas has made a deep impact on the international community. It shows how GDP by itself is insufficient to know the feeling of the people. Policies such as government's role in reincarnation have all the potential to boomerang. But the phenomenon which will have the strongest and most profound impact on the world consciousness is the act of self immolation. Destruction of the self to get a message across to the world is a subject which I cover later.

The Cyberspace is also being used menacingly. In China posts on the web on Tibet, democracy, religion and politics in general tend to be taken down by 30,000 public censors within a day or two of publication.[24] In 2009 Canadian researchers uncovered 'Ghostnet'. This programme had the capability to remotely turn on a computer's camera and microphone without alerting the user and export the images and sound silently back to servers in China. Top targets of the programme were offices related to non governmental organisations working on the Tibetan issue.[25]

WHAT ARE THE CHANGES IN SOCIO ECONOMIC CONDITIONS IN CHINA AND TIBET?

I—CHINA

Both positive and negative changes are happening. While the new rich are a minority, consumerism with nationalism may be a strong force in the increasing urban and middle class population of China. But more important is the Chinese peoples' understanding of their own selves. *Wolf Totem* is a very popular novel in today's China.[26] People from difficult regions where resources are not plentiful had waged war for resources. Jiang Rong in *Wolf Totem* forces one to rethink China's past where the assumption that Han Chinese are culturally superior to their barbarian neighbours stands on its head. Instead he advocates that China should rethink its past by combining the Han agricultural lifestyle (sheep culture), with more heroic 'wolf' culture of nomads of Mongolia. The author portray Han as weak and lacking in respect for nature, good at growing crops and constructing buildings, but poor fighters. The only times when they have become a big strong power is when they have had an injection of blood through invasion by northern nomads, the Mongols and Manchus who created great empires.[27]

Another change is that of religion. In a pictorial album of Tibetans in exile, Chinese Han monks have been photographed in pious postures beautifully in having a *darshan* of the Dalai Lama.[28] Religion thus can not be taken lightly.[29] Even the protest over language policies according to media reports has had an impact. China was to reconsider the existing language policy of Mandarin only.[30] In the change of Chinese leadership there are some indications that a new approach may be adopted by the Chinese in dealing with the Tibetans. [31]

II—Chinese (Hans and Huis) in Tibet

Probably these are an unhappy lot. First they are not accustomed to high altitudes the way Tibetans are. However, for economic reasons (making good profits) they stay on. They will never be able to match the skills of Tibetan nomadic and agricultural methods.

III—Tibetans in TAR

This is a period of great turmoil and confusion. From the religious point of view they are told that the Dalai Lama in exile is not to be believed. There are two 11th Panchen Lamas—one missing (selected by the Dalai Lama) and the one selected by the Chinese who became CPPCC national Committee Member on February 28, 2010. He was elevated to the Standing Committee of the CPPCC in March 2013. Government now interferes in religion like appointments of monks, reincarnation and education.

If media reports are authentic then a ray of hope exists. Na Ceng, a Tibetan adviser to the Chinese People's Political Consultative Conference (CPPCC) during the annual session of National People's Congress (NPC) in March 2011 had mentioned the need for preservation of culture and heritage. On tourism he suggested monasteries and temples should not be reduced to tourist sites. Rather they only should be for cultural development and not a place to do business.[32]

According to CTA, in TAR 70 per cent of business including taxi services are owned and operated by Han Chinese, 50 per cent of top Party members of TAR are Chinese officials and 40 per cent of Tibetan graduates are unemployed. [33]

IV—Tibetans outside TAR in Ethnic Tibet

They may be better off than Tibetans in TAR. But protest in monasteries throws an unclear picture. The Kirti monastery in Sichuan province witnessed unrest on account of monks' re-education programme. Events in 2011 started getting media attention and began to be noticed, when there was a standoff at Kirit monastery and monks are known to have self-immolated for their religious beliefs. As on November 2012 from 2009 about 86 Tibetans not in TAR but mostly in ethnic Tibet areas have immolated themselves. According to Dr. Lobsang Sangay, Sikyong

(Democratically Elected Political Leader of Tibet) Central Tibetan Administration in a lecture at the Jawaharlal Nehru University on 29 November 2012 outlined the factors responsible for the self immolation are occupation, repression, denial of cultural and religious freedom. The demands of the self-immolators are the return of the Dalai Lama to Tibet and religious and cultural freedom of Tibetans.

V—Tibetans in Exile

On the question of resilience and as the most successful refugee group, Thubten Samphel, former Secretary General of the Department of Information and International Relations for the Tibetan Government-in-Exile quotes[34] Dagmar Bernstorff and Fredrich - Naumann Foundation director Hubertus von Welck. In their chapter they have identified three major reasons for resilience.[35] The three are: the ability of individual Tibetans to survive and sustain themselves economically; secondly, the education system created in exile; and thirdly, the fact that the Dalai Lama has introduced democracy to his people and is turning over political power to a directly democratically elected leader, the current Kalon Tripa.

There is a conflict over democratisation. Separating spiritual and temporal power is the only way. India needs to facilitate that. The "strike hard" campaign impacts Tibetans in TAR and ethnic Tibet. Exiles need to be sensitive to this. Any belligerence or violence as is being thought of or being mentioned in the discourse will only make the lives of Tibetans under Chinese control miserable. How the Tibetans outside relate to Tibetans inside is for the Tibetans to decide. Some refugee establishments have become urbanised and property value has skyrocketed. Rather to the locals, the refugees may appear to be richer, and this could lead to local problems. The seniors may need to guide the younger generation on this perception management. The society's support (domestic) is a driver for a country's foreign relations policies.

It must be appreciated that the Tibetan refugees have done some very serious thinking on the issue of preserving their culture and identity.[36]

Overall, about 85 per cent refugees are in South Asia and 15 per cent outside South Asia. Among the refugees, there is a demographic youth bulge. After the first phase of Rehabilitation from 1959 to 1980 and the second phase from 1980 to 2000 (Development Phase), they are now in the third phase, aptly called the revitalization phase. Today the focus is on sustainable development, counter-disintegration and resisting 'diasporaisation'. Many young Tibetans refugees are now pursuing higher studies. This will make them capable of global interaction in a changed world. However one issue which to me is a problem is the supply side of monks and ensuring the continuation of the institution of monks and their training as volunteers. The rapid urbanisation and spread of communication technologies does not provide for a secluded monastic environment. Much more thinking and action is required on these issues. Possibly a smaller number of monks may take to this way of life and retaining the oral *guru-shishya* tradition will be extremely important. Both secular and religious knowledge and wisdom needs to be incorporated. Here non-Tibetans or those closer to the region may get into monkhood. Fortunately Tibetan Buddhism is no longer considered as a proselytizing religion. Rather, the esoteric traditions and wisdom are being rediscovered by scientists at the global level. Thus the international community is now closely interfaced with the concern of preservation of the people and land of Tibet. The discourse has gone beyond just sovereignty.

POLICY SUGGESTIONS

PRC and Tibetan Official Serving in the Government in TAR

(a) The revival of livelihoods derived from pastures will have two consequences. First the grassland ecosystem will become central and will help in maintaining the delicate balance of the ecosystem as in the past. The second is that thriving local trade will economically benefit the indigenous people. Thus attention to insights, knowledge and skills of nomads and pastoralists need to be understood in a scientific manner.

(b) Do not blame the environmental degradation of the plateau on nomads, but also take into account climate change.[37] Recall how incorrect polices (which no one expected to be a curse in the future) during the Great Leap Forward devastated the environment.

TIBET-CHINA DIALOGUE

The dialogue process must continue. There are many voices even in China that suggest that the best time to negotiate is when the 14th Dalai Lama is present. The democratization thus is a good step and institutions need to be built over time. Buddhism has survived for centuries and will do so. Do not let go of the principles of Karuna.

LEARNING FROM GENE SHARP AND SAMDHONG RINPOCHE

The Tibetan Youth Congress (TYC) and others must now take the advice of the former Kalon Tripa. The learned former Kalon Tripa Samdhong Rinpoche has done some deep thinking on the issues of non-violence. Out of the six kinds of principled non violence types theorised by Gene Sharp[38], he feels that Satyagrah is the closest to Tibet's commitment to non-violent action and is the most perfect form of non-violent resistance.[39] We feel that TYC will not deviate from this in future. The DIIR accordingly has brought out a timely publication tilted *Introduction to The Nature and Achievement of the Middle-Way Policy* (2010) which explains the issue of the importance of the middle path.

GUESTS AND HOSTS RELATIONS

Guests

Most refugees and hosts are no longer of the first generation. It is natural that with changing time their attitude and concerns will change. Locals may not see the macro picture and this may create problems. More of local level interaction is needed with focus on perception management.

Hosts

At grass root level there is a need to get governance in order, without inspector Raj attitude and corruption. Procedures for Registration Certificates (RC), and Identity Certificates (IC) and local movement must be streamlined. A lot depends on regular dialogue between the local police, administration and civil society. Guests should not feel that they are being unduly harassed. Officials at these levels can do wonders by proper motivation and education for this unique problem. Trust of yesteryears is the key.

At a philosophical level we may ask what have we done for Tibet after Padmasambhav and Atisa? Hosts including policy elites should not get complacent or arrogant by just getting used to salutations by the guests (like "We are your *chelas*" and "thank you India"). Both state and society of the host country need to play a constructive role. Further, most Tibetologists of international stature are Europeans or North Americans. Soon even China may have more scholars. Even at the National Defence Academy Tibetan language has been done away with. Fresh thinking on its study must be done. Besides the lack of knowledge of Tibetan, we also do not know Sanskrit the way Prof. Samdhong Rinpoche or Prof. Ngawang Samten do (in one sense they are now the Gurus). Knowledge of Sanskrit is vital to understand Tibetan Buddhism/ language and also to recover our lost ancient scriptures by translation back to Sanskrit. Exiled Tibetans are helping in giving back this lost heritage. Tibetan-language versions of Indian literature, chiefly Buddhist, have been preserved in two great collections - similar to *Sruti* and *Smriti* of ancient India called *Kanjur* (bka' 'gyur—the commandments of Buddha) and *Tanjur* (bstan'gyur- doctrinal teaching given by subsequent teachers). The Indian *Nitisastras* in Tibetan have been preserved in the *Tanjur* collection. Most ancient texts including the *sutras* of *Arthasastra* of Kautilya and other works are in Sanskrit. Many lost Buddhist works from India were preserved in Tibet including Chanakya.[40] Some of these works are in the process of being re-translated back into Sanskrit from Tibetan at Central Institute of Higher Tibetan Studies at Sarnath.[41]

There is thus a need to create a pool of young Indian scholars with job security who possess language and related skills. This human resource will also work at the upcoming Nalanda International University and other multidisciplinary institutes.

INDIA-CHINA DIALOGUE

Tibet is the pivot in India-China relations. India may need to balance the positive in its trade relations and cooperation on ecological issues with its concerns over China's treatment of its minorities and destruction of a culture and ecology. Although the ecology of Tibet is important, the top priority is the issue of the fate of the Tibetan people.

Environment matters. Treating Tibet as a global common is an important issue. India should continue its diplomacy for the environmental protection of Tibet. The Buddhist nature of Tibetan ecology must be preserved with traditional ecological knowledge (TEK). As both India and China are together in BASIC (Brazil, South Africa, India and China) grouping on climate change negotiations, the problem of Tibet also need to be mutually identified—which to a great extent is on land use, land use change and forestry (LULUCF) and grasslands.

With hindsight, many strategists feel that had Tibet been independent, issues such as diversion of waters would not have arisen. Many Tibetans in India point to the heavy defence expenditure being incurred for the militarized border. But one cannot undo historical events. It is now the people to people dialogue that is important. The Indian state should allow opening up of traditional border trading routes to help the Himalayan communities to prosper, Bumla being one so that Tsosa can be visited by people from Tawang.

CONCLUSION

India needs to nurture Tibetan Buddhism and its soft power for a better future of Tibetans both in China and outside. It has a global responsibility to protect both the Tibetan people's culture and religion as well as Tibet's ecology. This needs to be pursued via its soft power and the patience of Tibetans informed by the four sublime states of *Brahmavihar-metta* (loving kindness), *karuna* (compassion), *mudita* (sympathetic joy), and *upekha* (equanimity).

Box (as referred to in footnote 29)

RELIGION IN CHINA

China recognises five religions—Islam, Taoism, Catholicism, Protestantism and Buddhism. There are more Buddhists than Communist Party Workers. One estimate by the CTA is that Buddhists may be about 300 million in number. There are about 20 million Muslims—the bulk of them in Xinjiang. Status of Buddhism and Christianity is:

BUDDHISM

Like the Dalai Lama's effort to create interest and fascination with himself, his cause, and his religion around the world, something similar is happening in China. Tom Grunfeld writes that "There is a similar phenomenon going on in China, where the government's attention to Tibet has resulted in a different sort of fad; an infatuation with things Tibetan, at times portraying Tibetans as 'noble savages' with curious ways. Tibetan traditional medicine has become very popular, while young Chinese are 'dropping out' by leading 'hippie lives' in Lhasa." (A. Tom Grunfeld, "Tibet and the United States, in Barry Sautman and June Teufel Dreyer (ed.), *Contemporary Tibet,* New York, M.E. Sharpe, Inc, 2006.)

Anant Krishnan ("In Search of an Identity", *The Hindu*, August 29, 2010) observes that in new China's cities millions of young people are turning to Buddhism to make sense of their country's rapid transformation while in the far West, minority communities are searching for ways to preserve their culture against the pressure of development. He reports that there are an estimated 100 million (300 million according to some estimates) followers of Buddhist faith in an officially atheist China.

Karma matters. The exemplary role of monks as first responders in quake recovery of the Sichuan earthquake of March 2008 also is reported to have impressed the Chinese people via media reports, though they were soon told to leave when state apparatus reached the location later.

CHRISTIANITY

It needs to be remembered that the 19th century episode of Taiping rebellion is linked to Christianity. Hong Xiuquan thought himself as being the younger brother of Jesus Christ. His mission was to get rid of Confucianism in China—the inward looking philosophy which saw competition, trade and industriousness as pernicious foreign imports. Taiping Tianguo (that is how Hong Xiuquan was known in China) led the Taiping Rebellion. The Qing emperor defeated that movement by 1871. It is estimated that from 1850 to 1864, 20 million died in central and South China. This indicates that history tells us that religion does have a complex role in China and can not be dismissed. Another key information is that Sun Yat Sen and Chang Kai-shek were Christians.

Now again, Christianity is spreading. Christians probably outnumber Communist Party Members. According to D. Aikman's *The Beijing Factor*, it is estimated that there may be 75 to 110 million Protestants and 20 million Catholics. In total, there could be 130 million Christians in China. In other words, there are more practicing Christians than in Europe. It is possible that within three decades, Christians will constitute between 20 and 30 per cent of Chinese population (See Niall Ferguson, *Civilization: the West and the Rest*, London, Allen Lane/Penguin, 2011, pp. 277-88)

ENDNOTES

1. I acknowledge my research at IDSA in facilitating the writing of this paper.
2. "Tibet Today", *News from China*, January 2011.
3. "Tibet Today", *News from China*, May 2011.
4. Ibid.
5. Andrew Martin Fischer, "The Political Economy of Boomerang Aid in China's Tibet", *China Perspective*, No. 2009/3, pp. 38-53.
6. Melvyn C. Goldstein, Geoff Childs and Punchung Wangdui, "Beijing's People First" Development Initiative for the Tibetan Autonomous Region's Rural Sector: A Case Study from Shingatse Area", *The China Journal*, No. 63, January 2010, pp. 57-75.
7. Ibid.
8. See Tibet 2003: State of the Environment, White Paper, Central Tibetan Administration, Dharamshala, 2003, Michael Zhao and Orville Schell, "Tibet: Plateau in Peril", *World Policy Journal*, Vol. XXV. No. 3, Fall 2008, pp. 171-80, "Editorial", *Green Tibet*, Annual Newsletter 2009, Environment and Development Desk, Department of Information and International Relations (DIIR) of the Central Tibetan Administration, Dharamsala, India, p. 2, *Tibet: A Human Development and Environment Report*, 2007, EDD, Department of Information and International Relations, CTA, Dharamshala, India, p. 1; Bertie J. Wedell, "Corralling the nomads", *Himalsouthasia*, October-November 2010, pp. 45-47, Tsering Tsomo, "Vanishing nomads of Tibetan grasslands", *Border Affairs*, October-December 2010, pp. 27-32, Jonathan Mirsky, "Will There Be a 'Duel' Dalai Lama?", in book review of *Tragedy in Crimson: How the Dalai Lama Conquered the World but Lost the Battle with China* by Tim Johnson, National Books, *The New York Review of Books*, Vol. LVIII, No. 9, May 26, 2011, pp. 35-36.
9. Wang Shiyan, "Policy Impact on Tibetan Market Participation", *Asian Ethnicity*, 10(1), February 2009, pp. 1-18.
10. Ibid.
11. P.K. Gautam, "Climate Change and Environmental Degradation in Tibet: Implications for Environmental Security in South Asia", *Strategic Analysis*, Vol. 34, No. 5, September 2010, pp. 744-55.
12. Katherine Morton, "Climate Change and Security at the Third Pole", *Contemporary International Relations*, Vol. 21, No. 3, May/June 2011, pp. 34-55

13. Michel Zhao and Orville Schell, "Tibet: Plateau in Peril", *World Policy Journal*, Fall, pp. 171-80.
14. Tibet 2003: State of the Environment, White Paper, Central Tibetan Administration, Dharamshala, 2003.
15. Tibet 2003: State of the Environment, White Paper Central Tibetan Administration, Dharamshala, July 2003, p. 8. Other publications of Environment and Development Desk being *China's Train, Tibet's Tragedy*, 2009 and *Green Tibet*, Annual Newsletter 2008.
16. *China's Train, Tibet's Tragedy, 2009*, Environment and Development Desk, Department of Information and International Relations (DIIR), Central Tibetan Administration, Dharamshala, India, pp. 48-49.
17. As quoted by Wim van Spengen, *Tibetan Borders: A Geohistoric Analysis of Trade and Traders*, London and New York, Keegan Paul International, 2000, pp. 98-102.
18. Michael Zhao and Orville Schell, "Tibet : Plateau in Peril", *World Policy Journal*, Vol. XXV. No. 3, Fall 2008, pp. 171-80
19. I am thankful to Professor B.G. Verghese in pointing this out during his lecture at the United Service Institution of India, New Delhi on 21April 2010 on the occasion of Major General Samir Sinha Memorial Lecture on "Water Conflict—The Looming Threat.
20. "Editorial", *Green Tibet*, Annual Newsletter 2009, Environment and Development Desk, Department of Information and International Relations (DIIR) of the Central Tibetan Administration, Dharamsala, India, p. 2.
21. Ibid., p. 3.
22. "Report", *Green Tibet*, Annual Newsletter 2009, Environment and Development Desk, Department of Information and International Relations (DIIR) of the Central Tibetan Administration, Dharamsala, India, p. 13. Also see *Tibet: A Human Development and Environment Report*, 2007, EDD, Department of Information and International Relations, CTA, Dharamshala, India.
23. Rajesh S. Kharat, *Tibetan Refugees in India*, New Delhi, Kaveri Books, 2003, p. 63.
24. Alexander Klimburg, "Mobilising Cyber Power", *Survival*, Vol. 53, No. 1, February-March 2011, pp. 44-45.

25. Richard A. Clarke and Robert K. Knake, *Cyber War: The Next Threat to National Security and What to Do About It*, New York, Harper Collins, 2010, p. 59.
26. *Jiang Rong*, translated by Howard Goldblatt, Wolf Totem, originally published in China as *Lang Tuteng* (2004), London, Penguin Books, 2009.
27. As quoted by Christopher R. Hughes, "Current Cultural Politics in China: What Makes the Chinese Tick?", *Asian Affairs*, Vol. XL, No.1, March 2009, pp. 63-76. I thank Isabel Hilton, author of *The Search for the Panchen Lama* (2000) in leading me to the English version. According to her it aroused very mixed feelings as some read it as a neo-fascist text. Isabel Hilton saw the book more as a long apology for what Han Chinese had done to Mongolia. She recalls that when she met the author, he said that when he urged his compatriots to be more like wolves, he meant that they were too docile in the face of authoritarian leaders, which is rather the opposite of what he was being accused of. Internet correspondence with Isabel Hilton of January 17, 2011.
28. Raghu Rai (photographs) and Jane Perkins (text), *Tibet in Exile*, New Delhi, Penguin Studio, 2010, pp. 100-01.
29. Overview given in box at the end of the chapter.
30. Ananth Krishnan, "China to Reconsider Language Policy", *The Hindu*, October 24, 2010. It needs to be pointed out that in no way the rich heritage of Chinese language is being questioned. Rather even in various institutes of learning at Dharamsala, knowledge of Chinese is considered important. Many ancient Buddhist scripts now lost in India may only be available in Chinese besides Tibetan.
31. Earlier the 14th Dalai Lama's representatives had resigned citing a hardening Chinese position. The Communist Party of China (CPC) has appointed a new head of the United Front Work Department, the leading organization in charge of Tibet policy and talks with the Dalai Lama under Ling Jihua. See Ananth Krishnan, "What China's Transition Means for India", *The Hindu*, December 3, 2012.
32. Ananth Krishnan, "China Hints at New Development Approach", *The Hindu*, March 14, 2011.
33. Dr. Lobsang Sangay, Sikyong (Democratically Elected Political Leader of Tibet), Central Tibetan Administration, unpublished

lecture "Middle-Way Approach", Awareness Programme at the Jawaharlal Nehru University, New Delhi on 29 November 2012.

34. Thubten Samphel, "Maintaining Vitality in Exile: The Tibetan Refugees in South Asia", *Harvard International Review*, Vol. XXXI, No. 3, Fall 2009, pp. 60-63.
35. Dagmar Bernstorff and Hubertus Von Welck, "Introduction" and Gerlad Schmitz, "Tibet's Position in International Law" in Dagmar Bernstorff and Hubertus Von Welck (eds.), *Exile as Challenge: The Tibetan Diaspora*, Hyderabad, Orient Longman, 2003, pp. 1-8.
36. Unpublished proceedings of a two day seminar on 'Tibetan Diaspora in India: Experiences and Challenges', March 8-9, 2012 organised by Department of Sociology, Christ University, Bangalore and Central Tibetan Administration (office of South Zone Coordinator).
37. Bertie J. Wedell, "Corralling the Nomads", *Himalsouthasia*, October-November 2010, pp. 45-47.
38. Gene Sharp, *Gandhi as Political Strategist*, Boston: Porter Sargent, 1979. The six major types are non resistance, active reconciliation, moral resistance, selective non- violence, Satyagraha and non-violent revolution. The Arab Spring revolution which began in early 2011 is also informed by Gene Sharp's work on Gandhi.
39. Samdhong Rinpoche, "Education for Non- Violence", in Dagmar Bernstorff and Hubertus von Welck (eds.), *Exile as Challenge: the Tibetan Diaspora*, Hyderabad, Orient Longman, 2003, pp. 454-470.
40. Suniti Kumar Pathak, *The Indian Nitisastras in Tibet*, Delhi, Motilal Banarsidass, 1974.
41. The Rare Buddhist Texts Research Unit at Central Institute of Higher Tibetan Studies, Saranth, Varanasi is now making good progress in this project. Unfortunately not many Indian scholars have interest and competence in Tibetan, Newari, and Buddhist Sanskrit. It is urged that Indian universities should make good provision for Buddhist studies including the study of languages like Pali, Sanskrit, Tibetan and Chinese. See S.S. Bahulkar, "Contribution of India Scholars to Buddhist Tantric Studies", *Dhih*, Journal of Rare Buddhist Texts Research Unit, No. 45, 2008, Central Institute of Higher Tibetan Studies, Saranth, Varanasi, pp. 17-38.

15

Human Rights in Tibet Today

Sonam Sangmo

INTRODUCTION

The current human rights situation in Tibet is grim. Tibetans live in an all-encompassing atmosphere of fear, control and intimidation, resulting in a massive rights and norm violations in all forms and in all spheres of life. The government of the People's Republic of China (PRC) has stepped up state repression and has hardened its position on Tibet and His Holiness the Dalai Lama. Instead of addressing the core issues of Tibet, the PRC government has consistently rejected all allegations of human rights abuses in Tibet. The PRC either frames the Tibet problem as an "internal affair" or claims that Tibetan rights are fully protected under law and that their "benevolent" rule in Tibet has brought prosperity.

The PRC's Tibet policy is fundamentally based on "grasping with both hands", deepening economic development and increasing political restrictions. The recurring political protests in Tibet before 2008 and the widespread protests that overwhelmed the whole of Tibet since March 2008 encompassing all strata of Tibetan society are clear indicators of China's failed Tibet policies. The historic protests of 2008 have been answered by China's brutal crackdown against the Tibetan protestors, information blackout and subsequent closure of Tibet to the outside world.

The protests were a response to a hardening of China's Tibet policies. Despite guarantees of regional autonomy in the PRC's Constitution and their National Regional Autonomy Law, there is an absence of a Tibetan voice and of participation in the political processes and policy formulation in Tibet. Beijing's top-down approach to nationality issues disregards the distinctiveness and strength of Tibetan culture and spirit. The manner in which the PRC dealt with the 2008 Tibet unrest has been "deflective". Either there is no Tibet problem or all the problems of instability are attributed to the Dalai Lama. This denial mechanism constrains China from addressing the core challenges that confront the Tibet issue. China's lack of genuine will and interest in the Sino-Tibetan dialogue, especially amongst the PRC's hardliners, is now made more apparent from the current dialogue stalemate and their uncompromising position. The vilification campaign against His Holiness the Dalai Lama has been intensified in all forms and manner, thereby exposing their failure to understand his important role and leadership in the Tibetan psyche and in the Tibetan issue.

Chinese scholars corroborate the failure of PRC's Tibet policy. Gongmeng (Open Constitution Initiative), a Beijing-based lawyer's organization and think tank, posted a daring online report on 12 May 2009. While acknowledging China's Tibet policy as a failure, the report states, "we deeply sensed the popular discontent and anger behind the incidents [of the 2008 protests] and the complexity of their social roots". The report says that the protests happened "under stress by a society and people to the various changes that have been taking place in their lives over the past few decades".

The Final Document of the 2009 Sino-Tibetan Conference 'Finding Common Ground' held in Geneva makes the scathing observation, "The root cause of the Tibetan issue is not a conflict between the Chinese people and the Tibetan people, but rather the autocratic rule of the PRC in Tibet and its cultural genocide in Tibet. And that Tibetan culture, religion, language and way of life are on the verge of extinction. That the Tibetan people have been deprived of their fundamental human rights, including the rights to national self-determination, political participation and religious belief".

On 15th July 2010, Qin Gang, spokesperson for the Chinese Ministry of Foreign Affairs, said "Facts speak louder than words..... Tibet's economy and social undertakings have continued to advance and human rights for Tibetans are fully guaranteed and people from different ethnic groups are leading a secure happy life." However, the human rights situation in Tibet is at its worst at present. It is as if a death sentence has been passed on Tibet. Internationally, the PRC is engaged in dictatorial politics and bullying tactics in their dealings with other nations over Tibet and His Holiness the Dalai Lama.

At the domestic level, Beijing has enforced iron-fisted measures to pre-empt protests whereby arrest, sentencing, detention and imprisonment of Tibetans have become routine. Yet the Tibetans defiantly protest against China's control and restrictive measures in different ways. The consequences of protests are always death sentence, life imprisonment, and inhuman torture.

After the riots and crackdown in Tibet, the pressure on the public security apparatus to fulfil the leadership's wishes was intense. Fear over the possibility of more peaceful protest coupled with sensitive dates like March 10, October 1 and June 4 as well as during the visits of top Western leaders to China has made the PRC feel compelled to deploy heavy military force in Lhasa and other parts of the region.

SPATE OF SELF-IMMOLATION PROTESTS

In the absence of space for conventional forms of protest, Tibetans have begun resorting to self-immolation in the last few years. Since 2009, till date over a hundred Tibetans are known to have self-immolated. 76 of them have died on the spot or shortly thereafter. The whereabouts and condition of 14 of the surviving self-immolators are unknown. All self-immolators called for "freedom in Tibet" and for the "return of His Holiness the Dalai Lama to Tibet." The Chinese authorities have responded to these self-immolations with further repressive policies and dismissing them as "acts of terrorism incited by the 'Dalai clique'".

In her first ever statement on self-immolation protests by Tibetans released on 2 November 2012, Navi Pillay, the United Nations High Commissioner for Human Rights urged the Chinese authorities to promptly address the long-standing grievances that have led Tibetans to take desperate form of self-immolation protest. She said she was disturbed by "continuing allegations of violence against Tibetans seeking to exercise their fundamental human rights of freedom of expression, association and religion", and emphasized the "reports of detentions and disappearances, of excessive use of forces against peaceful demonstration, and curbs on cultural rights of Tibetans."

Amnesty International and Human Rights Watch have called upon the Chinese authorities to address the underlying grievances of Tibetans by namely carrying out a comprehensive review of the human rights situation across the Tibetan Plateau. Such an initiative would be undertaken with the aim of ending legal and policy restrictions that breach human rights in the region.

TIBETAN DEATHS, DETENTIONS AND DISAPPEARANCES

Since March 2008, the Central Tibetan Administration (CTA) estimates the death of over 230 Tibetans, with detailed information available on 156 Tibetans, sentencing of nearly 539 Tibetans, arrest and detention of over 6907 Tibetans, disappearance of over 990 Tibetans and of nearly 1,294 injured Tibetans. If comprehensive information were available, the actual figure would be much higher.

The known estimate of over 230 Tibetan deaths have occurred due to indiscriminate firing by Chinese security forces during protests, severe beatings and torture during arrest, detention and interrogations that either leave the detainees infirm or permanently injured. Many die because of the suffering inflicted. Insurmountable repression and suppression drives the Tibetans to commit suicide. Several deaths were caused due to starvation in the initial phase of the March 2008 protests, when major monasteries were sealed off and closed for days together.

According to information received from Tibet, two monks from Amdo region at different times have committed suicide under different circumstances. Tashi Sangpo, 28, from Gyulgho in Golog in Amdo Province, plunged into Machu River, after he was subjected to torture at a detention centre following seizure of political pamphlets and the Tibetan national flag from his room on 21 March 2008. 40-year-old Shedup from a monastery in Malho in Amdo Province, committed suicide for fear of arrest and torture by the Chinese police. Shedup was earlier arrested for his involvement in a protest in Rebgong in 2008 and endured torture and beatings in custody. After his release from prison, his name again appeared on the wanted list issued by Chinese authorities, which compelled him to take this extreme step.

Pema Tsepak, 24, from Dzogang in Chamdo died on 23 January 2009 after succumbing to his injuries from beatings by the Chinese police. He had on 20 January 2009 carried a banner reading "Independence for Tibet" along with this brother Thargyal, 23 and Thinlay Ngodrup, 24. Chinese security forces had also beaten a Tibetan monk, Phuntsok, from Drango Monastery,

Kardze in Eastern Tibet to death on 25 March 2009 for urging local Tibetans to boycott farming.

Rare footage obtained by the Central Tibetan Administration (CTA) from Tibet exposes Chinese brutality and disproportionate use of force on Tibetans. A young Tibetan named Tendar died on 19 June 2008 after sustaining severe beatings and torture by Chinese police during his detention. Tendar had tried to save a Tibetan monk who was being beaten by Chinese police on 14 March 2008 while he was on his way to work at China Mobile Company in Lhasa. The footage not only shows the severe wounds on Tendar's body but also the heavy presence of China's paramilitary forces in Tibet and indiscriminate beatings of Tibetan protestors[1].

CIVIL DISOBEDIENCE MOVEMENT

In an interesting development since 2009, the Tibetans inside Tibet are employing various methods of high-level non-violent resistance strategies to express their discontent with China's policies in Tibet and suppression of peaceful protests.

Tibetans boycotted the celebration of Tibetan New Year as a sign of mourning for Tibetans who have died or been detained. They began observing Lhak-kar (Lit. "Good Wednesday", astrologically an auspicious day of His Holiness the Dalai Lama) on every Wednesday through prayer offerings and other welfare activities in honour of His Holiness the Dalai Lama. Especially in Kardze regions, the Tibetan farmers refused to farm in opposition against prevailing government policies. Nearly 100 monks of Lutsang Monastery in Mangra County, located a few hours from Rebgong, held a candlelight vigil on the eve of the Tibetan New Year. A monk named Tapey from Amdo attempted self-immolation to protest China's harsh control on religion and to express support for His Holiness the Dalai Lama.

DEATH PENALTY AND LIFE TERM

China's National Human Rights Action Plan for 2009-2010 says that the death penalty shall be "strictly controlled and prudently applied". In the context of Tibet, Lhasa Intermediate People's Court had sentenced two Tibetans—Lobsang Gyaltsen and Loyak—on 8 April 2009 on charges of "arson cases that reportedly left seven people dead and five shops burnt to the ground in Lhasa" in March 2008. According to confirmed information, on 20 October 2009, they have been executed. Two other Tibetans, Tenzin Phuntsok and Kangtsuk, have been given suspended death sentences with a two-year reprieve. Dawa Sangpo, aged around 30-40, is sentenced to life imprisonment.

China's Xinhua news agency reported on 21 April 2009 that the Lhasa Intermediate People's Court issued a suspended death sentence to 21- year-old Penkyi. Another girl named Penkyi, aged 23, is sentenced to life. Chime Lhanzom, 20, was given a 10 year sentence. It should be noted that the Chinese authorities had released no information on how and when the sentences were delivered nor any details of the defendants and their arguments.

The Kardze Intermediate People's Court on 17 November 2009 issued a suspended death sentence to Pema Yeshi, 28, from Thangkyi in Kardze in Eastern Tibet. He was allegedly charged with "inciting separatism" and "disturbing social order" and is currently known to be kept in Dartsedo detention centre in Eastern Tibet.

On 25 May 2010, the Lhasa Intermediate People's Court sentenced Sonam Tsering, 23, to death with two years reprieve. Sonam Tsering, from Rachap in Kardze in Eastern Tibet was sentenced on the charge of rioting and inciting the public to riot on 14 March 2008.

Ten Tibetans currently face life terms—Wangdue also known as Ngawang Songtsen, Ngawang Yiknyen also known as Passang,

Sonam Tsering, Gyurmey Dhondup, 28, Kalbha also known as Karma, 23, Tsultrim Gyatso, 37, Sonam Gonpo, 24, and includes both Dawa Sangpo and Penkyi from the preceding paragraphs.

FREEDOM OF RELIGIOUS BELIEF AND PRACTICE

The appointment of Zhang Qingli as the Communist Party Secretary of the "TAR" on 26 May 2006 ushered in a period of harsh and restrictive policies. Within a month of his appointment, Zhang Qingli intensified the "patriotic re-education" campaign, called for a "fight to the death in the struggle against the Dalai clique" and described His Holiness the Dalai Lama as "the biggest obstacle hindering Tibetan Buddhism from establishing normal Buddhist order". During the 2008 protests in Tibet, he even called His Holiness "a wolf in a monk's robe, a devil with a human face, and the heart of a beast".

Given that the monks and nuns constitute the majority of the Tibetans involved in political protests, the Chinese authorities view them with suspicion and punish them with expulsion from monasteries or by subjecting them to arrest and detention, frequently subjecting them to cruel and degrading treatment. Official limits were imposed on the monastic populace. Members of the clergy are vetted through the process of "patriotic re-education" campaign, institutionalization of administrative bodies in the monasteries with the Democratic Management Committee (DMC) and the anti-Dalai Lama campaign.

Zhang Qingli called on the provincial Party and government officials to widen the patriotic education campaign to include a broader population, and to intensify the 'rectification' and restricting of each monastery or nunnery from the Democratic Management Committee (DMC). Work teams have been appointed to re-educate the monks and nuns on the religious beliefs as prescribed by the Chinese government. To do this, work-teams require monks and nuns to sign five political pledges, in which they are forced to denounce the Dalai Lama, oppose Tibetan independence and recognise the Chinese government. To refuse means possible arrest or expulsion, coupled with harsh repression.

In July 2007, the State Religious Affair Bureau passed the so-called Order No. 5, a set of "management measures for the reincarnation of Living Buddhas in Tibetan Buddhism." This indicates a harder and more vigorous approach in controlling the religious activities of the Tibetan people and the monastic communities in particular. The Order No. 5 claims that the Chinese government has the ultimate authority on selection and installation of reincarnating Lamas. This decision by the Chinese Communist Party to arrogate to itself the right to recognise and install Tibetans' spiritual leaders will never be accepted by the Tibetan people. This is clearly reflected in the story of the reincarnation of Panchen Lama.

In May 1995 His Holiness the Dalai Lama recognised a six-year-old boy, Gedhun Chokeyi Nyima as the authentic reincarnation of the tenth Panchen Lama who had passed away under mysterious circumstances in Shigatse in 1989. Immediately, the Chinese authorities took away the six-year-old boy and his family to Beijing where they are still under detention. In November 1995, the Chinese authorities appointed another boy, Gyaltsen Norbu, as the Panchen Lama. The Tibetan people's hostility to this Chinese action is made clear by the fact that the Chinese appointed Panchen Lama is not able to live and study in Tashi Lhunpo monastery, the principal seat of the Panchen Lamas of Tibet, because of the continued hostility of the monks of the monastery. In July and August 2011, the Chinese authorities tried to have their Panchen Lama stay and study in the monastery of Labrang, Tashikyil in North-Eastern Tibet. The local Tibetans and the monks of the monsatery made it very clear that the Chinese Panchen Lama is not welcome at Labrang, Tashikyil monastery.

FREEDOM OF EXPRESSION AND OPINION

In Tibet and China, all opinions and viewpoints that contradict the official Chinese position on the issue of Tibet are considered "subversive", and any information which directly or indirectly concerns the governance, policies and activities of the PRC are viewed as "state secrets". China's arbitrary detention, sentencing and subsequent imprisonment of Tibetans solely on account of their peaceful and legitimate protests against the Chinese government violate key rights promised in China's domestic law as well as their obligations under international laws, and, of course, under the 17-point Agreement.

There has been a vibrant literary and cultural resurgence in Tibet since spring 2008 when protests against government policy and in support of the Dalai Lama swept across the plateau. Writers, using printed material and the Internet, who are often fluent in Chinese as well as Tibetan, in Xining and other areas of Amdo have been at the forefront. Singers and educators have also been involved in this cultural resurgence, which is grounded in a strong sense of Tibetan identity.

For the first time since the end of the Cultural Revolution in 1976, singers, artists and writers have been the target of a drive against Tibetan culture in which almost any expression of Tibetan identity not validated by the state can be branded 'splittist'.

A recent trend indicates a deepening crackdown on brave Tibetan intellectuals, writers, bloggers, film-makers, environmentalists and artists who express their true feelings and aspirations in a highly repressive atmosphere. There are cases of more than 100 Tibetans, including writers, involved in the arts and public sphere who are either in prison, have 'disappeared' or have faced torture or harassment due to expression of their views.

Tashi Rabten, a young Tibetan writer and university student, (pen-name Te'urang), the editor of a banned literary magazine on the 2008 protests in Tibet and author of a new collection of work called "Written in Blood", disappeared around 26 July 2009, and is now known to be reportedly detained. One of the most notable arrests related to freedom of expression is that of Paljor Norbu, 81 years old, who was arrested and secretly sentenced to 7 years on the charge of printing prohibited materials.

Dhondup Wangchen, 35, a Tibetan film-maker was arrested on 26th of March 2008 for making the film 'Leaving Fear Behind in Tibet', which documents the lives of Tibetans under China's rule, views about His Holiness the Dalai Lama and the Beijing Olympics. On 28 December 2009, he was sentenced to a 6-year prison term on the charge of "inciting separatism" and "espionage" and he was reportedly suffering from hepatitis B, for which he has been denied adequate medical treatment.

Tashi Dhondup, 30-year-old, a popular Tibetan singer from Admo was arrested on 3 December 2009 on the charge of composing 'subversive songs' with 'counter-revolutionary content' in his music album 'Torture Without Trace'. On 5 January 2010, the Chinese authorities sentenced him to 15 months 'reform through labour.'

Karma Samdrup, 42, is a prominent Tibetan environmental philanthropist, and one of China's leading collectors of Tibetan art. On 3 January 2010, Karma Samdrup was arrested from his home in Kham in Eastern Tibet on the charge of buying artefacts from a looted tomb in 1998. However, according to reliable information, his arrest was made following his attempt to defend his two younger brothers who are in jail since August 2009. According to Human Rights Watch, "Karma Samdrup's case showed serious and repeated violations of China's own criminal procedure law".

RIGHT TO FREEDOM OF LANGUAGE

Article 4 in the PRC constitution states that, "All ethnic groups in the People's Republic of China are equal. The state protects the lawful rights and interests of the minority ethnic groups and upholds and develops a relationship of equality, unity and mutual assistance among all of China's ethnic groups. All ethnic groups have the freedom to use and develop their own spoken and written languages and to preserve or reform their own folkways and customs".

On 12 October 2010, the Provincial Communist Party and the Amdo Provincial Government held a meeting on education during which a new policy to replace Tibetan by Chinese as the medium of instruction was launched. The new regulation requires that all the lessons and textbooks should be in Chinese in primary schools by 2015 except Tibetan and English language classes. The proposed regulation in the educational system is a clear violation of the Tibetan people's freedom to preserve and use their own language. Language is the life blood of Tibetan culture and civilization. In October 2010, thousands of Tibetan students in Rebkong and Chabcha of Amdo in North Eastern region of Tibet took to the street to protest the new regulation imposed by the Amdo Provincial government.

A petition by more than 300 teachers and students from Amdo in North Eastern Tibet expresses their view that while learning Chinese is essential for students in Tibet today, the main language medium for teaching should remain Tibetan. The letter was written by teachers from elementary and middle schools from the area, and also signed by students, following a conference held in Rebkong in North East Tibet from October 11-16, 2010, before the protests. It states that the Tibetan mother tongue is the most familiar tool for analyzing problems and expressing ideas, and therefore it should be the most effective tool for study in their lives at school. Using the mother tongue as the language of instruction for nationality elementary and middle school students does not imply a weakening of the Chinese language.

CONCLUSION

It is clear that Tibet's human rights condition is deteriorating amidst a dramatic increase in Chinese repression and information clampdown. The cycle of self-immolations in Tibet reflect the situation is at a critical stage and demonstrate the need for China to heed the aspirations of Tibetans. The information that is presented here is a tiny part of the actual scale and degree of human rights violations inside Tibet.

The PRC has been blatantly engaged in a propaganda offensive that fools neither the outsiders nor the Tibetans themselves. The 2008 protests in Tibet were therefore, something that was only waiting to happen. So long as the Tibet issue remains unresolved with the dialogue impasse, virtual martial law situation inside Tibet and dim prospects for change in China's Tibet policies, it will remain a challenge for the PRC government to ensure genuine stability in the region.

ENDNOTES

1. The web link for the footage is available at http://footage.tibetanbridges.com and its related information at http://www.tibet.net/en/index.php?id=89&articletype=press&rmenuid=morepress&tab=2.

Climate Change in Tibet and Asia

Tenzin Norbu

THE SIGNIFICANCE OF THE TIBETAN PLATEAU

Tibet, referred to as 'The Third Pole' and 'The Water Tower of Asia' reflects the significance of its snow capped mountains and its alpine grasslands. Since time immemorial, the plateau holds the Hindu Kush-Himalayan Ice Sheet, considered as the largest mass of ice outside the two poles. Its plateau contains more than 45,000 glaciers covering an area of 105,000 kms^2. Encompassing an area of about 2.5 million square kilometres, or about one-third the area of the continental United States, the Tibetan Plateau is the largest and highest region on Earth. With an average elevation of 4,500 metres above sea level, the Tibetan Plateau stretches for almost 3,000 kilometres from west to east and 1,500 kilometres from south to north. The Plateau is ringed by high mountains—the Himalayas to the south, the Karakorum in the west and the Kunlun across the north (Figure 1). One can just learn by looking at its map to figure out how the Tibetan Plateau dominates the geography of Asia (D.J. Miller, 2009).

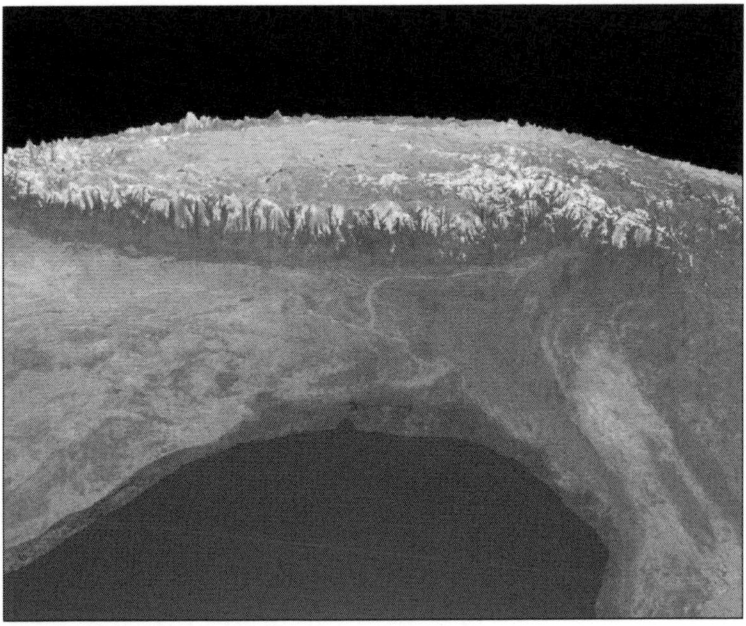

Fig. 1. Tibetan Plateau (*Image courtesy: NASA & D. J. Miller*).

GLACIERS AND RIVERS

Glacial runoff from these regions feeds the largest rivers in Asia, including Yarlung Tsangpo (Brahmaputra), Drichu (Yangtze), Machu (Yellow), Zachu (Mekong), Macha Khabab (Ganges) and Sengye Khabab (Indus River) and more. Referred to as 'The Water Tower of Asia', the Tibetan Plateau is the head region to major rivers that flow into India, Bangladesh, China, Nepal, Pakistan, Thailand, Burma and Vietnam (Figure 2). For China alone, 30 per cent of its fresh water supply is met from the rivers flowing from Tibet. For many generations, this Plateau has met the basic necessities to sustain life and flourishing human civilizations beyond its vast border. From the plains of Pakistan and India to the rice paddies of southern Vietnam, from the great Tonlesap lake of

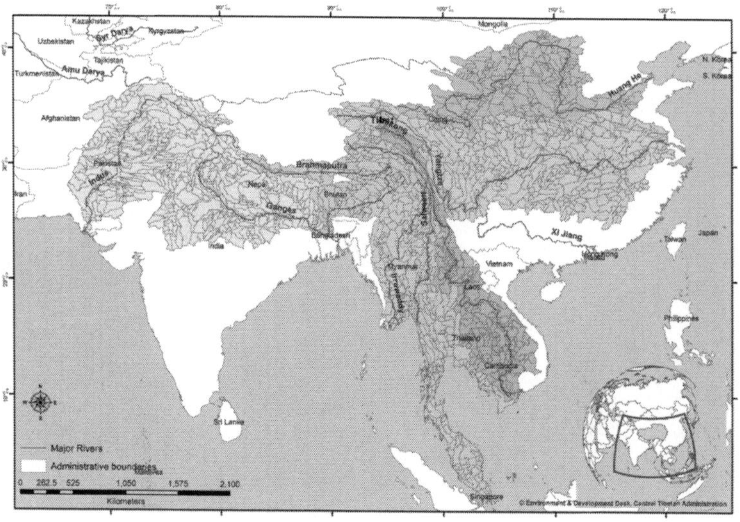

DRAINAGE BASIN OF MAJOR RIVERS ORIGINATING FROM TIBET

Fig. 2. Water Tower of Asia. Source: EDD/ DIIR.

Cambodia to the North China plain, these rivers bring life and joy to millions of peoples (EDD, 2008).

There is little doubt that melting glaciers of the Tibetan Plateau provide a key source of water in the summer months; as much as 70 per cent of the summer flow in the Ganges and 30–50 per cent of the flow in other major rivers. The glacier-fed rivers originating from the Tibetan Plateau make up the largest river run-off from any single location in the world. Perhaps the most critical region in which the melting glaciers will negatively affect water supply *(in the next few decades)* will be China and parts of Asia, including India and Bangladesh.

Zachu or Mekong River, originating from Mount Thangla, is the bloodline for the Mekong-region countries. This river flows from Central Tibet through Yunnan Province in China and then flowing through Laos, Thailand, Cambodia and finally ending its journey in Vietnam. This river directly supports

Fig. 3a. Permafrost degradation (Tibet). Mass-movement feature, possibly an active-layer detachment slide, developed during summer of 1996 on the south side of the Kunlun Pass (Tibet).

Fig. 3b. Permafrost degradation (Tibet). Retrogressive flow on the slope of Tanggula Mountain of the Tibet Plateau.

approximately 70 million people along its basin from fishermen to farmers.

PERMAFROST LAYERS AS CARBON STORE

The presence or absence of the permafrost layer entails major variations in the soil's physical structure, determining, to a large extent, the hydrological and nutritional status of the soil, which in turn, is pivotal in determining the vegetative coverage, plant community structure and productivity. Unlike the ones that are widespread in the Arctic and boreal regions of the Northern Hemisphere, the permafrost prevailing on the Tibetan Plateau (1.3 to 1.6 million kms^2) are alpine permafrost. The alpine permafrost on the Tibetan Plateau stores about 12,300 million tonnes of Carbon. A study conducted at the source region of the Yellow River indicated that a significant amount of methane is trapped in the permafrost layer of that region (EDD, 2009).

ALPINE GRASSLANDS AND MEADOWS AS CARBON SINK

Tibet's rangeland *(Tib: Jhangthang)*, from the Northern Plateau of upper Tibet to the extreme eastern edge of the plateau, with an average altitude of 4000 to 5000 meters, covers approximately 70 per cent of the total area of Tibet. The types of rangeland vary from alpine meadows and mountain scrub to mountain sparse wood and mountain desert, which helps sustain domestic herds and nurture a wide variety of wildlife species.

These rangelands and its cold alpine grassland soils are the major carbon sink and house a greater organic carbon pool. During the growing season, the alpine meadows appear to absorb or take up CO_2 at the rate of 1840 – 3050 $mg/m^3/day$. Studies showed that total Soil Organic Carbon storage *(sampled from the top 1 meter soil)* in the alpine grasslands of the Tibetan Plateau was estimated about 7400 Million tonnes of Carbon.

Fig. 4a. (Thailand). Stranded fishing boats in Mekong River in Mukdahan province. Image, courtesy: Ploysi, 2011.

Fig. 4b. (Thailand). Reduced flow of Mekong river Nakhon Panam. Image, courtesy: Ploysi, 2011.

For many generations, pastoralism on these rangelands has been the best and the only option to live successfully. Over time, Tibetan pastoral nomads have skillfully introduced domestic herds and maintained an extraordinary biodiversity of grasses and sedges, enabling human life to flourish at the Third pole.

WETLANDS AND WETLAND AREAS AS CARBON SEQUESTERS

Statistics of the natural wetlands *(excluding lakes and floodplains)* area by geographic regions in China revealed that the Tibetan Highland holds over 51 per cent of total natural wetlands. These wetlands are dominated by Salt Marsh, Peat land and Freshwater Marsh. These wetlands tend to trap carbon-rich sediments from watershed sources.

The Wetlands in Tibet play a major role in regulating the flow of rivers and also are the major carbon stores. They act like a sponge, absorbing water during the summer when the water is in excess and releasing it in the winter when the runoff is short.

CLIMATE CHANGE IMPACTS IN TIBET AND ASIA

Critical components to Tibet's ecosystem are undergoing major transformations due to climate change. For instance, it has led to the receding of Tibet's glaciers, shrinking and disappearance of thousands of lakes, drying of wetlands, thawing of permafrost, and reduced flow regimes in many rivers.

Abnormal weather conditions due to climate change such as non-sequential rainfall, delayed in milking season, reduced growth of cattle, etc., has made subsistence farming and herding more unpredictable, thus impacting the livelihoods of a majority of Tibetans. These days, on the plateau, the spring thaw is starting earlier and the permafrost is melting away before the growing plants can access the water. This affects not only the crops but also the native vegetation of Tibet, especially in wetlands and other low lying areas. The loss of wetland, in turn, threatens the migratory birds used to Tibetan stopovers (EDD-COP15).

Julia Klein (2005) mentioned in her studies that 'climate warming is an unusual environmental problem since the primary greenhouse gas emitters driving these changes can be far removed (*due to the large spatial disconnect between drivers and recipients*) from the most vulnerable recipients of the climate change effects'. This rise in temperature has also increased the rate of evapo-transpiration from the rivers and watershed areas intensifying the desertification process. According to Immerzel (2008), 'Eco-payment' for the Tibetan farmers could become a viable solution in order to protect the downstream areas from possible water crisis.

At present, the plateau is undergoing a multifaceted environmental degradation; the melting of glaciers, non-sequential thawing of permafrost, drying up of wetlands and vast desertification of grasslands leading to the failure to absorb atmospheric carbon. These carbon pools would soon disintegrate in due course of time, resulting in further emissions of greenhouse gases and the vicious cycle continues further. The immediate impact of climate change is on those herders and farmers, who did nothing to cause it in the first place. The Chinese National Climate Change Assessment Report (2007) revealed that China's average annual temperature could increase between 1.3-2.1 degrees by 2020 and as much as 3.3 degrees by 2050. It is predicted that precipitation in three of the seven major rivers will drop by 30 per cent in the second half of the century leading to a 37 per cent decline in wheat, rice, and corn yields. Major cities in coastal areas will face serious challenges due to rising sea levels, and extreme weather patterns are likely to increase.

GLACIAL MELTDOWN AND PERMAFROST DEGRADATION

According to Jane Qiu (2008), 82 per cent of the Tibetan Glaciers have already retreated in the past half century. In the past 40 years, Tibet's glaciers have shrunk by 6,600 sq km (*as of year 2006*). It is estimated that they are currently melting at a rate of 7 per cent per year. A separate study by a NASA scientist (2010) revealed that 20 per cent of Tibetan glaciers have retreated in the past 40 years and if the current trend continues, more than 60 per cent of the existing glaciers could be gone in the next 40 years.

The formation of glacial lakes as a result of the rapid melting of glaciers on the higher reaches of the mountain ranges continues to pose a serious threat to downstream countries, especially Nepal and Bhutan. The International Centre for Integrated Mountain Development (ICIMOD) has identified some 8,790 glacial lakes in parts of the Hindu-Kush and the Himalayas out of which, the organization has confirmed 204 glacial lakes as 'likely to burst'. Greenpeace reported that Imja glacier in Nepal is retreating at nearly 10 metres per year. Other reports show that the average temperature in Nepal has increased by 1.5 Celsius since 1975. Scientists from Nepal's ICIMOD said the lake is growing by just under 50 meters per year and is in danger of bursting its banks—a 31 metre-high dam of rocks and stones—and flooding nearby villages and trekking routes. They predicted that more than 7,500 people would be affected by the floods, including tourists hiking along the popular Everest Base Camp route. A recent BBC news report mentioned that the ethnic community residing in Nepal's western province (Halji village) is threatened by a glacial lake on the mountain overlooking their village.

Studies have also shown that glacial melting and thawing of permafrost in the Tibetan Plateau will lead to a large-scale release of greenhouse gases in the atmosphere and bring further changes in the already warming climate. The permafrost layers and the seasonally frozen soils on the Tibetan Plateau are well preserved over a long period of time by low winter air temperatures. Its seasonal thawing and refreezing have also played a vital role in balancing the delicate alpine vegetations, until now. With the significant increase in the cold season average temperature, the permafrost layers and seasonally frozen grounds are slowly degrading, leading to increased microbial decomposition of previously frozen organic carbon. Slope failures are often seen on the Tibetan Plateau due to permafrost degradation. Permafrost degradation has changed the regime of water retention and regulation by producing more runoff in areas of permafrost, leading to more evaporation. It has also prolonged the thawing period significantly leading to many interconnected ecological changes and technological worries. Locally, this degradation would result in the gradual desertification of grasslands, resulting to higher surface albedo and increased ground temperature.

Human interference is also largely responsible for the degradation of permafrost layer on the Tibetan Plateau. H. Jin *et al.* (2008) in their study along the Siling Lhasa Highway (SLH) corridor have found that the heat accumulation under the asphalt road bases resulted in increased thaw depths too great to be frozen and, consequently, resulting in the transformation of vertically connected permafrost into disconnected phase. They indicated that the ground temperature at the shallow depths in transition and quasi-stable permafrost zone have been increasing noticeably, as a result leading to the shrinkage of permafrost boundaries. Some other researchers have pointed out that approximately 30 per cent of the SLH has to be repaired every year due to damage cause by frost action.

Recent studies showed that permafrost thawing in many regions of the Tibetan Plateau is influencing both hydrological regimes and vegetation, as well as engineered structures. Such thawing of permafrost leads to the formation of thaw slumps, slope failure and in the process will inject lots of trapped carbon gases into the atmosphere. Examples of surface degradation associated with the thawing of ice-rich permafrost on the Tibetan Plateau are shown in (Figures 3 a and b).

The condition of permafrost degradation in some areas of the Tibetan Plateau was such that the active layers were oversaturated by water either as a result of glacial runoff or rainfall during the thawing season.

INFLUENCE ON ASIAN MONSOON PATTERN

The plateau's seasonal heating during summer and spring plays the principal role in determining the large-scale air circulation in summer. Heating over the Tibetan Plateau tends to generate a surface cyclonic circulation and upper-atmosphere anti-cyclonic circulation which results in the appearance of a large air motion in the eastern side of the plateau. As long ago as 1884, an English meteorologist working in India had the inspired idea that the snows of Tibet and the Indian monsoon are causally connected. Henry Francis Blanford, in the pages of Proceedings of the Royal Society, in London, proposed that the greater the snow cover in the land of snows, the later the Indian monsoon wets the parched earth on India. Conversely, he suggested, the less the winter snows in Tibet, the earlier the snowmelt, and the earlier the monsoon. During summer, the Tibetan Plateau intensifies the pressure gradient between the South Asian landmass and the Indian Ocean leading to the flow of air and moisture from the sea (EDD-COP15).

According to many scientists and researchers, the ground freezing and thawing of the Tibetan Plateau have a significant influence on the atmospheric circulation. The rise in the soil moisture content (*due to active layer thawing*) increases the level of heat exchange between the atmosphere and ground surface. For instance, the onset of summer precipitation in Southern China and in the middle and lower basin of the Drichu *(Yangtze River)* are influenced by the spring thaw timing over the Tibetan Plateau. Consistent with that, the significance of spring snow depth over the Tibetan Plateau correlates with the amount of summer precipitation on the middle and lower basins of Drichu.

SHRINKING LAKES AND WETLANDS

There used to be thousands of lakes in Tibet. Most of these lakes have no outlet, and depends entirely on local streams and underground sources to maintain their water level. These lake levels are mainly controlled by the warming climate and human activities. Already a large number of these lakes in Tibet have disappeared. As per Xinhua News Agency, the wetlands on the Tibetan Plateau have shrunk more than 10 per cent in the last four decades, with wetlands at the Yangtze's origin contracting at an alarming 29 per cent.

The wetlands on the Tibetan Plateau are shrinking and drying, resulting in the subsequent release of carbon dioxide, *methane*[1] and *nitrogen dioxide*[2]. As such, this further adds up to the yearly greenhouse gas emission. Methane emissions from the wetlands during the thaw season were estimated to be 0.7 – 1.05 Million tonnes per year and the annual N_2O emission from the wetlands of Tibetan Plateau are estimated at 0.022 – 0.025 million tonnes. Adding up the total GHG emission of CO_2 (316.02 g CO_2/m^3), CH_4 and N_2O from Tibetan Plateau wetlands in a year (*irrespective of their atmospheric stability and in terms of CO_2 GWP*), it adds up to 68 million tonnes of CO_2.

LOSS OF CARBON SINKS FROM DEGRADED CRASSLANDS, ENDANGERING PASTORALISM

Pastoralism on the Tibetan Plateau is an 'adaptation to a cold environment at elevations above the limit of cultivation'. For centuries, the Tibetan nomads and herders have successfully maintained a sustainable and mobile lifestyle, travelling from winter to summer pasture lands and autumn to spring pasture lands. The grasslands on the Tibetan Plateau represent one of the last remaining agro-pastoral regions in the world. The Plateau itself is covered in almost 70 per cent of these precious grasslands. The pasture lands are made habitable through the co-existence of the Tibetan people and their yaks. Through their efforts, they have maintained the sustainable use of this area for many centuries. China's introduction of different grassland policies over the years threatened the sustainability of this delicate environmental balance. The new policies restrict the flexibility and mobility of the nomads (*which is the main ingredient in the nomadic pastoral production)* and there are attempts to blame their livestock for overgrazing the grasslands (EDD-COP15).

These days, many researchers and rangeland specialists are arguing the applicability of these new policies, and how much these have actually benefited or affected them. Recent scientific findings (Julia *et al,* 2007; Tony Lovell and Bruce Ward, 2009) give us more information about the regeneration of the grasslands and the vital role of grazers in replenishing the grasslands. In their studies, they revealed that grazing actually helps in regenerating the grasslands by improving the soil Carbon/Nitrogen ratio and extending the growing season. Even some Chinese researchers have blamed the degradation of these grasslands on many factors such as permafrost degradation, irrational human disturbance (*mining, road construction, conversion of grassland to cropland, gold mining, overgrazing, etc.*) and climate warming.

WATER AVAILABILITY AND MANAGEMENT

The International Centre for Integrated Mountain Development (ICIMOD) has revealed alarming details on the sustainability of the Himalayan ecology. According to their findings, the current trend of melting glaciers suggests that the Ganges, Indus, Brahmaputra and other rivers across the northern Indian plains could most likely become seasonal rivers in the near future. The tension on water availability is further raised by the rate at which the PRC is commissioning dam projects on those rivers that flow from Tibet. The Chinese dam-building frenzy is leading to widespread suspicion as to whether these dams could be an initial step in enhancing its ambitious water transfer projects. Some experts believe that the current railway network linking Beijing and Lhasa would further enhance the need for transportation of technical staff and inventories to initiate this water diversion project. After many years of denial, the Chinese side finally accepted that it was building a HPP (*Hydropower Plant; 510 megawatts*) on the upper reaches of Yarlung Tsangpo at Zangmu, at Lhoka prefecture in Tibet. No doubt, the PRC was quick in responding that the current HPP is a run-of-the-river project. But that too requires some storing of water to fill the reservoir. But that is not the end, six more dams are on the drawing board along the Yarlung Tsangpo and no clear information is flowing out of Tibet as to how and when they will initiate the other projects.

According to a report published by the IDSA (2010), water demand in India will grow to almost 1.5 trillion m^3 by 2030, principally driven by population growth and the domestic need for agriculture. And with no proportional increase in water availability and an ever increasing demand, a water crisis is imminent. Water being international, indispensable, and emotive, it can serve as a cornerstone for confidence building and a potential entry point for peace.

China has built over 87,000 hydro dams, more than any other country in the world. Besides performing various functions, the issue of dam safety has always been treated as a sensitive subject. Now, incidents at a number of dams and reservoirs have cast doubt on the quality of these projects, but they are rarely reported to the general public (Lu and Shen, 2011).

Zhang Boting, secretary of the China Society for Hydropower Engineering, told reporters that the 12th Five Year Plan called for hydropower development to be prioritized. For various reasons, two thirds of the hydropower projects detailed in the 11th Five Year Plan had not been completed and would be revived in the 12th Five Year Plan *(China Tibet News, 2011).*

On March 5, 2011 former Premier Wen Jiabao presented his "government work report" during China's annual parliamentary session in Beijing, revealing the key goals of the country's 12th Five Year Plan (2011-2015). Apart from other grand visions to cut energy and carbon intensity, China also aims to boost the proportion of non-fossil fuels in primary energy consumption to 11.4 per cent. After the Japanese nuclear tragedy and the subsequent freezing of further approvals of nuclear projects in China *(at least for a few years)*, this statement is in fact a green signal for the dam construction companies to invest more on the Tibetan rivers and to meet its energy target *(please refer to Box1. for more information).*

Meng Si, the managing editor of China dialogue's Beijing office mentioned that Chinese Environmental NGOs believe that hydropower projects could bring economic development, but not necessarily to the benefit of local people. They believe that today's insufficiently transparent policy-making mechanisms are maximizing the interests of the hydropower industry, officials and a small number of experts, while driving ecological destruction, affecting local livelihoods and increasing the risk of geological disasters.

The damming activities along the upstream of Zachu/ Mekong have significantly affected the flow volume of the river. So far, the PRC has in total 21 HPP either built, under construction or under active consideration in Tibet alone (Tashi, 2011). The users downstream are turning their frustration on the Chinese government whose damming projects on the upstream Mekong River have greatly affected their lifestyles. Figures 4a and 4b reveal the current state of the Mekong River in Mukdahan Province and at Nakhon Panam in Thailand. The livelihoods of the local fishermen and many other communities from Cambodia are threatened by the reduced flow of the river but their concerned voices are blanketed by the aid their government receives from PRC.

For China, Tibet's rivers are proving to be rich resources for hydro electric and geo-political power as its mineral wealth. But frenzied dam construction projected until 2020 means that a prehistoric irrigation system that dates back 30 to 40 million years is coming to an end (*Huffington Post*, August 2011).

Growing industrialization, population growth, and increasing levels of consumption are placing heavy demands on water resources, which provide vital support for the subsistence livelihoods of millions of people. According to a report by the International Water Management Institute "the capacity of India and China to efficiently manage water resources, especially on a regional basis, is likely to be one of the key determinants of future global food security (K. Morton, 2008).

CONCLUSION AND RECOMMENDATIONS

The Tibetan Plateau is the land bridge connecting South Asia with East Asia. If India continues its habitual stance of viewing events in Tibet as if in some far-off place, it will fail to engage with the rapid changes outlined above, all of which directly impact India and its long term sustainability.

As Jane Qiu quoted an excerpt in her article from Veerabhadran Ramanathan (*an atmospheric scientist*), "Our understanding of global climate change would be incomplete without taking into consideration what's happening to the Tibetan plateau".

The very survival of almost 2 billion people depends on the water resources originating from the Tibetan Plateau. The impact on Tibet's landscape and its natural resources due to climate warming will threaten not only the future food security of many nations but also its developments. If Tibet's grasslands are maintained and improved, through a combination of nomadic work and state/donor finance, they will form a part of the solution to a global problem. This is a far better alternative than excluding nomads, and will enable grasslands to recapture carbon while also sustaining human livelihoods.

India can and should take a proactive role in mitigating the environmental effects of China's development policies in Tibet, so as to preserve the benefits and environmental services which Tibet provides to India.

While India has shown proper concern for the downstream impacts of dams on the river systems shared by both China and India, we need to recognize that China now has plans for radical change which will impact well beyond security of water supply.

Much effort is needed on the ground in Tibet to restore wetlands, adapt farm and pastureland, and preserve forests before the impact of climate change makes it more difficult to save ecosystems. Through state and people working together, desertification may also be reversed. The fate of future developments and social security of the lower riparian countries depends on how well the resources are managed in Tibet.

ENDNOTES

1. CH_4 (Methane): 21 times more Global Warming Potential (GWP) than Carbon dioxide.
2. N_2O (Nitrogen dioxide): 310 times more GWP than Carbon dioxide.

REFERENCES

BBC news report, "Himalaya Village Caught Between Culture and Nature", 24 August 2011, Navin Singh Khadia. http://www.bbc.co.uk/news/science-environment-14620091

China Daily, "China's Vital Wetlands Shrinking Due to Climate Change", http://www.chinadaily.com.cn/china/2007-07/17/content_ 5437231.htm

Chinatibetnews.com, "Three Rivers Area: 25 Cascade Hydropower Stations to be Built", http://www.tibet3.com/news/content/2011-01/18/content_439558.htm

China Dialogue, http://www.chinadialogue.net

Clifford Coonan, "Global warming: Tibet's Lofty Glaciers Melt Away", *The Independent*, 17 November, 2006. http://www.independent.co.uk/environment/climate-change/global-warming-tibets-lofty-glaciers-melt-away-424651.html

D.J. Miller, "Why Tibet Matters Now, Part 1", *China Dialogue*, http://www.chinadialogue.net.

Environment and Development Desk, *Tibet: A Human Development and Environment Report*, Published by DIIR, Central Tibetan Administration, Dharamsala, HP, India, ISBN 81-86627-68-5, (2008).

Environment and Development Desk, *The Impacts of Climate Change on the Tibetan Plateau: A Synthesis of Recent Science and Tibetan Research*, Published by Central Tibetan Administration, Dharamsala, HP, India, 2009, ISBN# 978-81-86627-92-1.

EDD-COP15 Briefing papers, Environment and Development Desk, DIIR, Central Tibetan Administration, Dharamsala, HP, India. Available online, http://tibet/en/index.php?id=361&rmenuid=11

Huffington Post; Catriona Luke, "China Will Have Mastery of Asia's Water Tap by 2020", http://www.huffingtonpost.co.uk/catriona-luke/china-will-have-mastery-o_b_917158.html

Hui-jun Jin, Qi-hao Yu, Shao-ling Wang and Lan-zhi Lü, "Changes in Permafrost Environments Along the Qinghai–Tibet Engineering Corridor Induced by Anthropogenic Activities and Climate Warming", *Cold Regions Science and Technology* 53 (2008) 317-33.

Henry F. Blanford, "On the Connexion of the Himalaya Snowfall with Dry Winds and Seasons of Drought in India", *Proceedings of the Royal Society of London*, Vol. 37 (1884), pp. 3-22.

IDSA, Institute for Defence Studies and Analyses, New Delhi, "Water Security For India: The External Dynamics," *IDSA Task Force Report*, September, 2010, ISBN # 81-86019-83-9.

Jane Qiu, China; "The Third Pole: Climate Change is Coming Fast and Furious to the Tibetan Plateau", *Nature News*, published online July 23, (2008).

Julia A. Klein, John Harte and Xin-Quan Zhao, "Experimental Warming, Not Grazing, Decreases Rangeland Quality on the Tibetan Plateau", *Ecological Applications*, 17-2, (2007).

—, *TRIN-GYI-PHO-NYA: Tibet's Environment & Development Digest*, Tibet Justice Center, January, Vol. 2, No. 6 (2005).

Katherine Morton, "China and Environmental Security in the Age of Consequences", *Asia-Pacific Review* 15(2), (2008).

Lu Zongshu and Shen Nianzu, "Dams Gone Wrong: Is Danger Lurking in China's Dams?", August 24, 2011. http://journal.probeinternational.org/2011/08/24/dams-gone-wrong-is-danger-lurking-in-china%E2%80%99s-dams/

Meng Si, "Hydropowers Green Excuse", China Dialogue, http://www.chinadialogue.net.

NASA, Jordan Camp, "Melting Glaciers of Tibet", Climate Change Research at NASA - Goddard Space Flight Center, 2010.

People's Republic of China, Ministry of Science and Technology, "National Climate Change Report" (Beijing, 2007).

Tashi Tsering; "Hydropower Projects on Drichu (Yangtze), Zachu (Mekong) and Gyalmo Ngulchu (Salween)", Tuesday, February 16, 2010. http://tibetanplateau.blogspot.com/2010/02/dams-on-upper-reaches-of-yangtze-mekong.html.

Tenzin Norbu and Chokyi, "Climate Change on the Roof of the World", Global Convention on Climate Security and Eco-Investors Forum, S.M. Convention Centre, Palampur (HP), India.12-14 June 2009, pp. 123-24.

Tenzin Norbu, Chokyi and Dhondup Dolma, Chokyi, "Climate Change and its Impacts on the Tibetan Plateau", National Conference on Climate Change in the Himalaya, 17th November 2009, New Delhi.

The Impacts of Climate Change on the Tibetan Plateau: A Synthesis of Recent Science and Tibetan Research, Published by Environment and Development Desk, DIIR/ CTA, 2009, ISBN# 978-81-86627-92-1.

Tony Lovell and Bruce Ward, "Regenerating Grasslands", (2009), http://www.guardian.co.uk/environment/2009/jul/13/manchester-report-grasslands.

Walter Immerzeel, Jetse Stoorvogel and John Antle, "Can Payments for Ecosystem Services Secure the Water Tower of Tibet?" *Agricultural Systems* 96 (2008), pp. 52-63.

Xinhua News, 'Scientists Pinpoint Sources of Four Major International Rivers', http://news.xinhuanet.com/english2010/china/2011-08/22/c_131067137.htm.

Time for Transforming India's Policy on Tibet

Lalit Mansingh

As India enters the 65th year of its existence as a sovereign nation, it is time to take a pause to reflect on the policies of the past, to revisit our triumphs, our failures and to reflect on challenges met and opportunities lost.

The macro picture that emerges is of great success. Following a traumatic and violent partition, and burdened with a colonial economy drained by 200 years of exploitation, India in 1947 faced an uncertain future. In contrast, the India of 2011 boasts a strong demographically young society and a $4 trillion economy set on the path of irreversible growth. It is taken for granted that India will be a major player in the new global balance of power.

And yet, as we celebrate success, we need to introspect and identify the areas where we missed the mark. If I am asked to name

Valedictory address delivered at VIF's seminar held in September 2011 [updated].

a single issue on which India failed to measure up to its challenges I will, without hesitation, say it was Tibet. The Tibet issue is a perfect illustration of Murphy's Law: if something can go wrong, it will! Many will question this conclusion as wisdom by hindsight. Yes it is. And such wisdom by hindsight is important because it ensures that the errors of judgment of the past will not be repeated.

WHAT WENT WRONG WITH INDIA'S TIBET POLICY?

So what went wrong with our Tibet policy? Ten points, according to me:-

1. India's assumption that China was interested in larger issues like joining India in creating an Asian renaissance turned out to be entirely erroneous.
2. Under a policy described by former Foreign Secretary Jagat Mehta as "unilateral friendliness" with China, India naively believed the false assurances of the Chinese leaders that the Chinese maps of our northern borders were cartographic errors. This would be rectified soon. They were never corrected.
3. Equally naively India believed the Chinese assurances regarding the safety of the Dalai Lama and the welfare of the Tibetan People. This was never carried out.
4. In subsequent negotiations with China on the border issue, we were wrong in taking a rigid, legalistic posture and asserting territorial claims for which there was insufficient evidence. The jury is still out, however, on the assertion of those scholars who maintain that our claims were not entirely founded on empirical evidence.
5. The Tibetan issue reflects a major systemic failure in Indian policy-making. There were voices within the cabinet that were urging caution in dealing with China—amongst them two Home Ministers; Sardar Patel and Pandit Govind

Ballabh Pant and Finance Minister Morarji Desai. Their advice was ignored. India's national interests would have been better protected if Pandit Nehru had taken his cabinet colleagues to his meeting with Chou En Lai in April 1960. Also ignored was the professional advice of the Foreign Service establishment, including Sir G.S. Bajpai, then Secretary General in the MEA and younger Foreign Service officers like Sumal Sinha, V.V. Paranjpe, P.K. Banerjee and Arvind Deo who incidentally served as India's Consul General in Lhasa. Sadly, the Prime Minister relied on a group of political appointees like Sardar K.M. Panikkar and Mr. Raghavan, who failed in offering their independent assessment of what was happening in Tibet to the P.M. Panikkar in fact was informed in advance of the Chinese plans to quote unquote "liberate" Tibet but did not apparently report this for fear that it would affect India's ambitions to play a mediating role in the Korean war.

6. India failed to demand reciprocity before accepting the Chinese demands to support its "One China" policy and its sovereignty over Tibet and Taiwan. Had reciprocity been applied in the beginning, China might have refrained from questioning India's sovereignty in J&K and Arunachal Pradesh.
7. The Chinese have been relentlessly pursuing their goal of integrating Tibet with mainland China by rail, road and air. In their eyes, they have every right to do so. India, in contrast has lagged behind in integrating its border areas adjoining Tibet.
8. There is growing evidence to suggest that China is seriously proceeding to construct a series of dams on the Brahmaputra or the Yarlung - Tsangpo. This will have catastrophic consequences on the North East of India and

Bangladesh. India's concerns on this issue have been muted and ineffective.

9. The frantic pace of development activities in Tibet is having its effects on the environment, with consequences not only for Tibet, but the entire South Asian region and parts of Southeast Asia. It will affect the glaciers, the rivers which supply water to the region and the seismic safety of the fragile Himalayan eco- system. I am not aware if this has been seriously discussed by India, either bilaterally or internationality.
10. And finally, the conclusion is inescapable that we have failed the people of Tibet time and again, in their greatest hour of need. India was a silent witness to the brutal takeover of Tibet, the systematic suppression of the cultural and religious rights of the Tibetans, the savage attacks on Buddhist monks and nuns, the pillaging and destruction of their monasteries and the demographic manipulation under which Tibetans may well became a minority in their own homeland.

In 1950, when PLA troops entered Lhasa, not only did India do nothing, it dissuaded the UN and other countries that were willing to come to the rescue of the Tibetans.

In 1951, when the so-called 17-point agreement was forced on the hapless government of the Dalai Lama, India did not protest.

In 1954, India signed an agreement with China under which it surrendered all its rights and responsibilities in Tibet and withdrew its garrisons from Yatung and Shigatse. That the 1954 agreement was signed in the name of the Buddhist principles of the Pancha Shila made it a tragic mockery of the Tibetan people.

Let me make one point clear. If there was a failure of India's Tibet policy, it was a bipartisan failure. Every government of India, whether led by the Congress or the BJP, has been complicit in evading India's historical responsibilities in Tibet. The formulation of the 1954 agreement has been repeated as a mantra in joint statements issued during Mr. Rajiv Gandhi's visit to China in 1988, Mr. A.B. Vajyapee's visit in 2003, and during the Indian visits of Wen Jiabao and Hu Jintao in 2005 and 2006.

It is worth noting that the standard formulation on Tibet was absent, for the first time, in the joint statement issued after Wen Jiabao's visit during December 2010.

If this is a signal of change in our China policy, it is to be welcomed.

CAN ANYTHING BE DONE?

If, as our scholars conclude, India has irrevocably surrendered its 'Tibet Card' and formally accepted Chinese sovereignty over Tibet, is there nothing that can be done for the Tibetan people by India or the international Community?

I am not so pessimistic. There is a growing body of opinion that in a global and interdependent world, the concept of state sovereignty is no longer absolute. The talk is increasingly about a "responsible sovereignty" or "shared sovereignty". No state in the world today can claim the absolute, sovereign right to deny basic human rights and freedom to its own citizens. In extreme circumstances, and subject to transparent and credible safeguards, the international community can also exercise the Responsibility to Protect (R2P) to affected groups.

Admittedly, this is still a grey area in international law but this is increasingly acceptable internationally. I am not suggesting that the R2P should be applied to the Tibetans in China. It is nevertheless a useful reminder to China that, as a great nation and civilization, it must act as a responsible global citizen and show sensitivity to the rights of the Tibetan people.

Secondly, India has never hesitated to express concern over the plight of people who happen to be the citizens of another state. Mahatma Gandhi wrote letters to President Roosevelt about the status of Blacks in America. India took the leadership in opposing Apartheid in South Africa. India continues to voice its anxiety about the treatment of the Tamil citizens in Sri Lanka. These are but a few examples.

A NEW OPPORTUNITY FOR INDIA

India must seize the opportunity that has opened up today to review and recalibrate its policy on Tibet. The decision of the Dalai Lama to abdicate his political responsibilities and hand them over to a democratically elected 'Kalon Tripa' is a momentous development in the history of Tibet. It reflects the profound wisdom and foresight of the Dalai Lama.

Felicitations are due to the new Kalon Tripa, Dr. Lobsang Sangay. I have followed his articles, speeches and interviews with great interest and admiration. It is also fortunate that the Tibetans today have in addition to their supreme spiritual guide, the Dalai Lama, two young leaders from the next generation: the 17th Karmapa and the Kalon Tripa, Dr. Lobsang Sangay.

Let me conclude by offering a few suggestions for the action India needs to take as a part of a bold new policy on Tibet.

1. Removal of restrictions on the activities and movements of the Dalai Lama and the Karmapa. All directives in place must be withdrawn which require political leaders and senior officials not to be seen in public with the Dalai Lama and the Karmapa. It is an affront to India's sovereignty that such restrictions are in force to accommodate the wishes of another country. The Dalai Lama and the Karmapa deserve our deepest respect as internationally acclaimed spiritual leaders.

   There should also be an end to the suspicions and reservations that a section of our establishment has against the Dalai Lama and the Karmapa. There were powerful voices in the Indian establishment in the 1950s and 1960s that the Dalai Lama should be sent back to Tibet. There are segments of our establishment today that are keen to accord the same treatment to the Karmapa. I am pleased that the Ministry of External Affairs prevailed in offering asylum to the Karmapa when he turned up in Dharamsala a decade ago. I am convinced that it was the right thing to do.

2. India must identify completely with efforts to preserve Tibetan culture and Tibetan Buddhism. When Buddhism was virtually wiped out from India, the land of its origin, the Tibetans undertook to nurture this rich heritage over the centuries. The time has come for India to reciprocate this gesture.

   I hope that the Dalai Lama can be persuaded to take the leadership in bringing the scattered schools of Buddhism in India under a common umbrella. On a personal note, as a Vice President of the Maha Bodhi Society of India, I am keen on seeing this success.

   I would also like to see the Dalai Lama being closely associated with the Nalanda University Project. It is hard to appreciate that he is being kept at arm's length fearing the reactions of another country.

3. It is time to remove the refugee tag from the Tibetans who have opted to make India their home. Those who are inclined to be Indian citizens must be granted citizenship without going through harassing procedures.

   Tibetans must be given the same privileges as the citizens of Nepal and Bhutan.

   Young Tibetans of Indian origin should be encouraged to form Indo-Tibet friendship societies or associations which will promote the awareness of Tibet among the Indian public.

4. Reciprocity must be the guiding principle hereafter in India's response to Chinese demands on the status of Tibet.
5. India must not hesitate to express concern over the violation of the human, cultural and religious rights of the Tibetan people, not only in the Tibetan Autonomous Region, but in other states with significant Tibetan populations.
   This should not be seen as a challenge to China's sovereignty but as a part of India's continuing advocacy of the rights of vulnerable communities across the world.
6. India must publicly and vehemently oppose the construction of dams on the Brahmaputra / Yarlung Tsangpo which would divert its waters away from India and Bangladesh. This should be taken up by India both bilaterally and at appropriate global forums.
7. India must be equally firm in expressing concern over the ecological damage caused by the unrestricted development projects in Tibet. It is the source of 10 major rivers and numerous glaciers which provide sustenance to two million people in Asia.
   I am pleased that the Kalon Tripa, Dr. Lobsang Sangay has appealed to the world to recognize the historic role of the Tibetan people as the guardians of the environment of the Tibetan Plateau.

CONCLUSION

In conclusion, let me recall to you a statement made by Pundit Nehru in the Indian Parliament on 27 April 1959. He declared that India's policy on Tibet was guided by three elements: (1) India's national security (2) friendship with China, and (3) Autonomy of Tibet under Chinese suzerainty.

We may blame Pundit Nehru for errors of judgement on Tibet, but his triple formulations is as valid today as it was five decades ago. Friendship with China is a desired goal but it cannot be allowed to override our concerns for Indian security or Tibetan autonomy.

Appendices

Appendix I

CONVENTION BETWEEN GREAT BRITAIN AND THIBET (1904) [385]
(Signed at Lhasa, 7 September, 1904)

Whereas doubts and difficulties have arisen as to the meaning and validity of the Anglo-Chinese Convention of 1890, and the Trade Regulations of 1893, and as to the liabilities of the Thibetan Government under these Agreements; and whereas recent occurrences have tended towards a disturbance of the relations of friendship and good understanding which have existed between the British Government and the Government of Thibet; and whereas it is desirable to restore peace and amicable relations, and to resolve and determine the doubts and difficulties as aforesaid, the said Governments have resolved to conclude a Convention with these objects, and the following Articles have been agreed upon by Colonel F.E. Young-husband, C.I.E., in virtue of full powers vested in him by His Britannic Majesty's Government and on behalf of that said Government, and Lo-Sang Gyal-Tsen, the Gaden Ti-Rimpoche, and the Representatives of the Council of the three monasteries, Sera, Drepung, and Gaden, and of the ecclesiastical and lay officials of the National Assembly on behalf of the Government of Thibet.

I. The Government of Thibet engages to respect the Anglo-Chinese Convention of 1890 and to recognize the frontier between Sikkim and Thibet, as defined in Article I of the said Convention, and to erect boundary pillars accordingly.

II. The Thibetan Government undertakes to open forthwith trade marts to which all British and Thibetan subjects shall have free right of access at Gyangtse and Gartok, as well as at Yatung.

The Regulations applicable to the trade mart at Yatung, under the Anglo-Chinese Agreement of 1893, shall, subject to such amendments as may hereafter be agreed upon by common consent between the British and Thibetan Governments, apply to the marts above mentioned.

In addition to establishing trade marts at the places mentioned, the Thibetan Government undertakes to place no restrictions on the trade by existing routes, and to consider the question of establishing fresh trade marts under similar conditions if development of trade requires it.

III. The question of the amendment of the Regulations of 1893 is reserved for separate consideration, and the Thibetan Government undertakes to appoint fully authorized Delegates to negotiate with the Representatives of the British Government as to the details of the amendments required.

IV. The Thibetan Government undertakes to levy no dues of any kind other than those provided for in the tariff to be mutually agreed upon.

V. The Thibetan Government undertakes to keep the roads to Gyangtse and Gartok from the frontier clear of all obstruction and in a state of repair suited to the needs of the trade, and to establish at Yatung, Gyangtse, and Gartok, and at each of the other trade marts that may hereafter be established, a Thibetan

Agent, who shall receive from the British Agent appointed to watch over British trade at the marts in question any letter which the latter may desire to send to the Thibetan or to the Chinese authorities. The Thibetan Agent shall also be responsible for the due delivery of such communications and for the transmission of replies.

VI. As an indemnity to the British Government for the expense incurred in the dispatch of armed troops to Lhasa, to exact reparation for breaches of Treaty obligations and for the insults offered to and attacks upon the British Commissioner and his following and escort, the Thibetan Government engages to pay a sum of 500,0001.—equivalent to 75 lakhs of rupees—to the British Government.

The indemnity shall be payable at such places as the British Government may from time to time, after due notice, indicate, whether in Thibet or in the British districts of Darjeeling or Jalpaiguri, in seventy-five annual installments of 1ýÿlakh of rupees each, on the 1st January in each year, beginning from the 1st January, 1906.

VII. As security for the payment of the above-mentioned indemnity and for the fulfillment of the provisions relative to trade marts specified in ArticlesýÿII, III, IV andýÿV, the British Government shall continue to occupy the Chumbi Valley until the indemnity has been paid, and until the trade marts have been effectively opened for three years, whichever date may be the later.

VIII. The Thibetan Government agrees to raze all forts and fortifications and remove all armaments which might impede the course of free com-munication between the British frontier and the towns of Gyangtse and Lhassa.

IX. The Government of Thibet engages that, without the previous consent of the British Government.

a. No portion of Thibetan territory shall be ceded, sold, leased, mortgaged or otherwise given for occupation, to any foreign Power;
b. No such Power shall be permitted to intervene in Thibetan affairs;
c. No Representatives or Agents of any foreign Power shall be admitted to Thibet;
d. No concessions for railways, roads, telegraphs, mining or other rights, shall be granted to any foreign Power, or the subject of any foreign Power. In the event of consent to such concessions being granted, similar or equivalent concessions shall be granted to the British Government;
e. No Thibetan revenues, whether in kind or in cash, shall be pledged or assigned to any foreign Power, or to the subject of any foreign Power.

X. In witness whereof the negotiators have signed the same, and affixed thereunto the seals of their arms.

Done in quintuplicate at Lhassa, this 7th day of September, in the year of our Lord 1904, corresponding with the Thibetan date, the 27th of the 7th month of the Wood Dragon year.

(Seal of Dalai Lama, affixed by the Ga-den Ti-Rimpoche)
(Seal of Thibet Frontier Commission)
(Seal of British Commissioner)
(Seal of Council)
(Seal of the Dre-pung Monastery)
(Seal of Se-ra Monastery)
(Seal of Ga-den Monastery)
(Seal of National Assembly)
F.E. Younghusband, Colonel,
British Commissioner

In proceeding to the signature of the Convention, dated this day, the Representatives of Great Britain and Thibet declare that the English text shall be binding.

(Seal of Dalai Lama, affixed by the Ga-den Ti-Rimpoche)
(Seal of Thibet Frontier Commission)
(Seal of British Commissioner)
(Seal of Council)
(Seal of Dre-pung Monastery)
(Seal of Se-ra Monastery)
(Seal of Ga-den Monastery)
(Seal of National Assembly)
F.E. Younghusband, Colonel,
British Commissioner
Ampthill,
Viceroy and Governor-General of India

This Convention was ratified by the Viceroy and Governor-General of India in Council at Simla on the llth day of November, AD 1904.

S.M. Fraser
Secretary to the Government of India
(Foreign Department)

Declaration Signed by his Excellency the Viceroy
and Governor-General of India on the 11 November, 1904,
and Appended to the Ratified Convention
of 7 September, 1904

His Excellency the Viceroy and Governor-General of India, having ratified the Convention which was concluded at Lhassa on 7th September, 1904, by Colonel Younghusband, C.I.E., British Commissioner for Thibet Frontier Matters, on behalf of His Britannic Majesty's Government; and by Lo-Sang Gyal-Tsen, the Ga-den Ti-Rimpoche, and the Representatives of the Council, of the three Monasteries Sera, Dre,pung, and Ga-den, and of the ecclesiastical and lay officials of the National Assembly, on behalf of the Government of Thibet, is pleased to direct as an act of grace that the sum of money which the Thibetan Government have bound themselves under the terms of Article VI of the said Convention to pay to His Majesty's Government as an indemnity for the expenses incurred by the latter in connection with the dispatch of armed forces to Lhassa be reduced from 75,00,000 rupees to 25,00,000 rupees; and to declare that the British occupation of the Chumbi valley shall cease after the due payment of three annual installments of the said indemnity as fixed by the said Article: Provided, however, that the trade marts as stipulated in Article][p.I of the Convention shall have been effectively opened for three years as provided in Article VI of the Convention; and that, in the meantime, the Thibetans shall have faithfully complied with the terms of the said Convention in all other respects.

Ampthill,
Viceroy and Governor-General of India

---

1. Source for 7 September document: B.F.S.P., 1904-1905, Vol. 98, pp. 148-151.
2. (Source for 11 November document: Crown-copyright document, FO 405/179, Confidential Memorandum Respecting Negotiations for Regulations for Trade between India and Thibet, 31 December 1907, Appendix I. Crown-copyright documents in the India Office Records and the Public Record Office reproduced and/or transcribed in this publication appear by permission of the Controller of Her Majesty's Stationery Office.
   Reproduced from M.C. van Walt van Praag's, *Status of Tibet: History, Rights and Prospects in International Law*. With permission of the author.

Appendix II

CONVENTION BETWEEN GREAT BRITAIN AND CHINA RESPECTING TIBET (1906) [389]
(Signed at Peking, 27 April 1906)
(Ratified at London, 23 July 1906)

Whereas His Majesty the King of Great Britain and Ireland and of the British Dominions beyond the Seas, Emperor of India, and His Majesty the Emperor of China are sincerely desirous to maintain and perpetuate the relations of friendship and good understanding which now exist between their respective Empires;

And whereas the refusal of Tibet to recognize the validity of or to carry into full effect the provisions of the Anglo-Chinese Conventions of March 17, 1890 and Regulations of December 5, 1893 placed the British Government under the necessity of taking steps to secure their rights and interests under the said Convention and Regulations;

And whereas a Convention of ten Articles was signed at Lhasa on September 7, 1904 on behalf of Great Britain and Tibet, and was ratified by the Viceroy and Governor-General of India on behalf of Great Britain on November 11, 1904, a declaration on behalf of

Great Britain modifying its terms under certain conditions being appended thereto;

His Britannic Majesty and His Majesty the Emperor of China have resolved to conclude a Convention on this subject and have for this purpose named Plenipotentiaries, that is to say—His Majesty the King of Great Britain and Ireland: Sir Ernest Mason Satow, Knight Grand Cross of the Most Distinguished Order of Saint Michael and Saint George, His said Majesty's Envoy Extraordinary and Minister Plenipotentiary to His Majesty the Emperor of China; And His Majesty the Emperor of China: His Excellency Tong Shoa-yi, His said Majesty's High Commissioner Plenipo-tentiary and a Vice-President of the Board of Foreign Affairs—who having communicated to each other their respective full powers and finding them to be in good and true form have agreed upon and concluded the following Convention in six Articles.

I. The Convention concluded on September 7, 1904 by Great Britain and Tibet, the texts of which in English and Chinese are attached to the present Convention as an annex, is hereby confirmed, subject to the modification stated in the declaration appended thereto, and both of the High Contracting Parties engage to take at all times such steps as may be necessary to secure the due fulfillment of the terms specified therein.

II. The Government of Great Britain engages not to annex Tibetan territory or to interfere in the administration of Tibet. The Government of China also undertakes not to permit any other foreign State to interfere with the territory or internal administration of Tibet.

III. The Concessions which are mentioned in Article IX (d) of the Convention concluded on September 7, 1904 by Great Britain and Tibet are denied to any State or to the subject of any State other than China, but it has been arranged with China that at the trade marts specified in Article II of the aforesaid Convention Great Britain shall be entitled to lay down telegraph lines connecting with India.

IV. The provisions of the Anglo-Chinese Convention of 1890 and Regulations of 1893 shall, subject to the terms of this present Convention and annex thereto, remain in full force.

V. The English and Chinese texts of the present Convention have been carefully compared and found to correspond but in the event of there being any difference of meaning between them the English text shall be authoritative.

VI. This Convention shall be ratified by the Sovereigns of both countries and ratifications shall be exchanged at London within three months after the date of signature by the Plenipotentiaries of both Powers.

In token whereof the respective Plenipotentiaries have signed and sealed this Convention, four copies in English and four in Chinese.

Done at Peking this twenty-seventh day of April, one thousand nine hundred and six, being the fourth day of the fourth month of the thirty-second year of the reign of Kuang-hsu.

(L.S.) Ernest Satow
(Signature and Seal
of the Chinese Plenipotentiary)

Exchange of Notes Between Great Britain and China Respecting the Non-Employment of Foreigners in Tibet, Peking, April 27, 1906

Tong Shoa-yi to Sir E. Satow

Your Excellency,

With reference to the Convention relating to Tibet which was signed to-day by your Excellency and myself on behalf of our respective Governments, I have the honour to declare formally that the Government of China undertakes not to employ any one not a Chinese subject and not of Chinese nationality in any capacity whatsoever in Tibet.

I avail, & c.

Tong Shoa-yi

Sir E. Satow to Tong Shoa-yi

Your Excellency,

I have the honor to acknowledge the receipt of your Excellency's note of this day's date, in which you declare formally, with reference to the Convention relating to Tibet which was signed today by your Excellency and myself on behalf of our respective Governments, that the Government of China undertakes not to employ any one not a Chinese subject and not of Chinese nationality in any capacity whatsoever in Tibet.

I avail, & c.

Ernest Satow

Appendix III

CONVENTION BETWEEN GREAT BRITAIN AND RUSSIA (1907) [391]

(Signed at St. Petersburg on the 18th (31st) August 1907)

His Majesty the King of the United Kingdom of Great Britain and Ireland and of the British Dominions beyond the Seas, Emperor of India, and His Majesty the Emperor of All the Russias, animated by the sincere desire to settle by mutual agreement different questions concerning the interests of their States on the Continent of Asia, have determined to conclude Agreements destined to prevent all cause of misunderstanding between Great Britain and Russia in regard to the questions referred to, and have nominated for this purpose their respective Plenipotentiaries, to wit:

His Majesty the King of the United Kingdom of Great Britain and Ireland and of the British Dominions beyond the Seas, Emperor of India, the Right Honorable Sir Arthur Nicolson, His Majesty's Ambassador Ex-traordinary and Plenipotentiary to His Majesty the Emperor of All the Russias;

His Majesty the Emperor of All the Russias, the Master of his Court Alexander Iswolsky, Minister for Foreign Affairs;

Who, having communicated to each other their full powers, found in good and due form, have agreed on the following.

Arrangement Concerning Thibet

The Governments of Great Britain and Russia recognizing the suzerain rights of China in Thibet, and considering the fact that Great Britain, by reason of her geographical position, has a special interest in the maintenance of the status quo in the external relations of Thibet, have made the following arrangement.

Article I. The two High Contracting Parties engage to respect the territorial integrity of Thibet and to abstain from all interference in the internal administration.

Article II. In conformity with the admitted principle of the suzerainty of China over Thibet, Great Britain and Russia engage not to enter into negotiations with Thibet except through the intermediary of the Chinese Government. This engagement does not exclude the direct relations between British Commercial Agents and the Thibetan authorities provided for in Article V of the Convention between Great Britain and Thibet of the 7th September 1904, and confirmed by the Convention between Great Britain and China of the 27th April 1906; nor does it modify the engagements entered into by Great Britain and China in Article I of the said Convention of 1906.

It is dearly understood that Buddhists, subjects of Great Britain or of Russia, may enter into direct relations on strictly religious matters with the Dalai Lama and the other representatives of Buddhism in Thibet; the Governments of Great Britain and Russia engage, as far as they are concerned, not to allow those relations to infringe the stipulations of the present arrangement.

Article III. The British and Russian Governments respectively engage not to send Representatives to Lhassa.

Article IV. The two High Contracting Parties engage neither to seek nor to obtain, whether for themselves or their subjects, any

Concessions for railways, roads, telegraphs, and mines, or other rights in Thibet.

Article V. The two Governments agree that no part of the revenues of Thibet, whether in kind or in cash, shall be pledged or assigned to Great Britain or Russia or to any of their subjects.

Annex to the Arrangement Between Great Britain and Russia Concerning Thibet

Great Britain reaffirms the declaration, signed by His Excellency the Viceroy and Governor-General of India and appended to the ratification of the Convention of the 7th September 1904, to the effect that the occupation of the Chumbi Valley by British forces shall cease after the payment of three annual installments of the indemnity of 25,00,000 rupees, provided that the trade marts mentioned in Article VII of that Convention have been effectively opened for three years, and that in the meantime the Thibetan authorities have faithfully complied in all respects with the terms of the said Convention of 1904. It is clearly understood that if the occupation of the Chumbi Valley by the British forces has, for any reason, not been terminated at the time anticipated in the above Declaration, the British and Russian Governments will enter upon a friendly exchange of views on this subject.

The present Convention shall be ratified, and the ratifications exchanged at St. Petersburgh as soon as possible.

In witness whereof the respective Plenipotentiaries have signed the present Convention and affixed thereto their seals.

Done in duplicate at St. Petersburgh, the 18th (31st) of August, 1907.

---

1. Source: C.A. Bell, *Tibet: Past and Present* (1924; rpt. Oxford, 1968), pp. 289-291. Reprinted by permission.

2. Reproduced from M.C. van Walt van Praag's, *Status of Tibet: History, Rights and Prospects in International Law.* With permission of the author.

Appendix IV

TREATY OF FRIENDSHIP AND ALLIANCE BETWEEN THE GOVERNMENT OF MONGOLIA AND TIBET AT URGA (1913) [397]
29 December 1912 (11 January 1913)
(*translation of the Tibetan text*)

Mongolia and Thibet, having freed themselves from the dynasty of the Manchus and separated from China, have formed their own independent States, and, having in view that both States from time immemorial have professed one and the same religion, with a view to strengthening their historic and mutual friendship the Minister for Foreign Affairs, Nikta Biliktu Da-Lama Rabdan, and the Assistant Minister, General and Manlai baatyr beiseh Damdinsurun, as plenipotentiaries of the Government of the ruler of the Mongol people, and gudjir tsanshib kanchen-Lubsan-Agvan, donir Agvan Choinzin, director of the Bank Ishichjamtso, and the clerk Gendun Galsan, as plenipotentiaries of the Dalai Lama, the ruler of Thibet,'have made the following agreement.

Article 1. The ruler of Thibet, Dalai Lama, approves and recognizes the formation of an independent Mongol State, and the proclamation, in the year of the pig and the ninth day of the eleventh month, of Chjebzun Damba Lama of the yellow faith as ruler of the country.

Article 2. The ruler of the Mongol people, Chjebzun Damba Lama, approves and recognizes the formation of an independent (Thibetan) State and the proclamation of the Dalai Lama as ruler of Thibet.

Article 3. Both States will work by joint consideration for the well-being of the Buddhist faith.

Article 4. Both States, Mongolia and Thibet, from now and for all time will afford each other assistance against external and internal dangers.

Article 5. Each State within its own territory will afford assistance to the subjects of the other travelling officially or privately on affairs of religion or State.

Article 6. Both States, Mongolia and Thibet, as formerly, will carry on a reciprocal trade in the products of their respective countries in wares, cattle, &c., and will also open industrial establishments.

Article 7. From now the granting of credit to anyone will be permitted only with the knowledge and sanction of official institutions. Without such sanction Government institutions will not consider claims.

As regards contracts made previous to the conclusion of the present treaty, where serious loss is being incurred through the inability of the two parties to come to terms, such debts may be recovered by (Government) institutions, but in no case shall the debt concern "shabinars" or "khoshuns."

Article 8. Should it prove necessary to supplement the articles of the present treaty, the Mongolian and Thibetan Governments must appoint special delegates, who will conclude such agreements as the conditions of the time shall demand.

Article 9. The present treaty shall come into force from the date of its signature.

Plenipotentiaries from the Mongolian Government for the conclusion of the treaty: Nikta Biliktu Da-Lama Rabdan, Minister for Foreign Affairs; and General and Manlai baatyr beiseh Damdinsurun, Assistant Minister.

Plenipotentiaries from the Dalai Lama, the ruler of Thibet, for the conclusion of the treaty: Gudjir tsanshib kanchen Lubsan-Agvan, Choinzin, the Director of the Bank of Thibet Ishichjamtsa, and the clerk, Gendun--Galsan.

Signed (by Mongol reckoning) in the fourth day of the twelfth month of the second year of the "Raised by the Many," and by Thibetan reckoning on the same day and month of the year of the "water-mouse."

---

1. Source: FO 535/16, No. 88, Inclosure 1, 1913.
Reproduced from M. C. van Walt van Praag's Status of Tibet: History, Rights and Prospects in International Law. With permission of the author.

Appendix V

MEMORANDUM OF BRITISH FOREIGN SECRETARY TO CHINESE FOREIGN MINISTER (EDEN MEMORANDUM)
5th August 1943

Personal
Dear Dr. Soong,

When you visited me on the 26th July, you spoke of Tibet and enquired as to our attitude.

I have the pleasure in sending you the accompanying informal memorandum which I trust will serve to clear this matter up

(signed) Anthony Eden

His Excellency,
Dr. T.V. Soong.
TIBET

Since the Chinese Revolution of 1911, when Chinese forces were withdrawn from Tibet, Tibet has enjoyed de facto independence. She has ever since regarded herself as in practice completely autonomous and has opposed Chinese attempts to reassert control.

Since 1911, repeated attempts have been made to bring about an accord between China and Tibet. It seemed likely that agreement could be found on the basis that Tibet should be autonomous under the nominal suzerainty of China, and this was the basis of the draft tripartite (Chinese-Tibetan-British) convention of 1914 which was initialled by the Chinese representative by was not ratified by the Chinese Government. The rock on which the convention and subsequent attempts to reach an understanding were wrecked was not the question of autonomy (which was expressly admitted by China) but was the question of the boundary between China and Tibet, since the Chinese Government claimed sovereignty over areas which the Tibetan Government claimed belonged to their autonomous jurisdiction.

The boundary question, however, remained insuperable and, since the delay in reaching agreement was hampering the development of more normal relations between India and Tibet, eventually in 1921 the Secretary of State for Foreign Affairs (Lord Curzon) informed the then Chinese Minister (Dr. Wellington Koo) that the British Government did not feel justified in withholding any longer their recognition of the status of Tibet as an autonomous State under the suzerainty of China, and intended dealing on this basis with Tibet in the future.

This is the principle which has since guided the attitude of the British Government towards Tibet. They have always been prepared to recognize Chinese suzerainty over Tibet but only on the understanding that Tibet is regarded as autonomous. Neither the British Government nor the Government of India have any territorial ambitions in Tibet but they are interested in the maintenance of friendly relations with, and in the preservation of peaceful conditions in an area which is coterminous with the North-

East frontiers of India. They would welcome any amicable arrangements which the Chinese Government might be disposed to make with Tibet whereby the latter recognized Chinese suzerainty in return for an agreed frontier and an undertaking to recognise Tibetan autonomy and they would gladly offer any help desired by both parties to this end.

FO 371-93001

---

1. Source: Goldstein, Melvyn; A *History of Modern Tibet, 1913-1951*; University of California Press; 1989; pp. 400-2. Also available via Google Books.

Appendix VI

SINO-TIBETAN AGREEMENT OF 1951
17 POINT AGREEMENT 23rd May 1951

1. The Tibetan people shall unite and drive out imperialist aggressive force from Tibet; the Tibetan people shall return to the big family of the Motherland – the People's Republic of China.
2. The local government of Tibet shall actively assist the PLA to enter Tibet and consolidate the national defences.
3. In accordance with the policy towards nationalities laid down in the Common Programme of the CPPCC, the Tibetan people have the right of exercising national regional autonomy under the unified leadership of the CPG.
4. 'The central authorities will not alter the existing political system in Tibet. The central authorities also will not alter the established status, functions and the power of the Dalai Lama. Officials of various ranks shall hold office as usual.
5. The established status, functions and powers of the Panchen Ngerhtehni shall be maintained.

6. By the established status, functions and powers of the Dalai Lama and of the Panchen Ngoerhtehni are meant the status, functions and powers of the thirteenth Dalai Lama and of the Panchen Ngoerhtehni when they were friendly and amicable relations with each other.
7. The policy of freedom of religious belief laid down in the Common Programme of the CPCC shall be carried out. The religious beliefs, customs and habits of the Tibetan people shall be respected and lama monasteries shall be protected. The central authorities will not effect a change in the income of the monasteries.
8. Tibetan troops shall be reorganised step by step into the PLA and become a part of the national defence force of the CPR.
9. The spoken and written language and school education of the Tibetan nationality shall be developed step by step in accordance with the actual condition in Tibet.
10. Tibetan agriculture, livestock raising, industry and commerce shall be developed step by step and the people's livelihood shall be improved step by step in accordance with the actual condition in Tibet.
11. In matters related to various reforms in Tibet, there will be no compulsion on the part of the central authorities. The local government of Tibet should carry out reforms of its own accord, and when the people raise demands for reform; they shall be settled by means of consultation with the leading personal of Tibet.
12. In so far as former pro-Kuomintang officials resolutely sever relations with imperialist and the Kuomintang and do not engage in sabotage or resistance, they may continue to hold office irrespective of their past.
13. The PLA entering Tibet shall abide by all the above-mentioned policies and shall also be fair in all buying and

selling and shall not arbitrarily take a needle or thread from the people.

14. The CPG shall have centralised handling of all external affairs of the area of Tibet; and there will be peaceful Co-existence with neighbouring countries and establishment and development of fair commercial and trading relations with them on basis of equality, mutual benefit and mutual respect for territory and sovereignty.
15. In order to ensure the implementation of this agreement, the CPG shall set up a Military and Administrative Committee and a Military Area HQ in Tibet. And-apart from the personnel sent there by the CPG- shall absorb as many local Tibetan personnel as possible to take part in the work. Local Tibetan personnel taking part in the Military and Administrative Committee may include patriotic elements from the local government of Tibet, various districts and various principle monasteries; the name-list shall be set forth after consultation between the representatives designed by the CPG and various quarters concerned and shall be submitted to the CPG for appointment.
16. Funds needed by the Military and Administrative Committee, the Military Area HQ and the PLA entering Tibet shall be provided by the CPG. The local government of Tibet should assist the PLA in the purchase and transport of food, fodder and other daily necessities.
17. This agreement shall come into force immediately after signature and seal are fixed on it.

Signed and sealed by delegates of the CPG with full powers:

Chief Delegate- Li Wei –Han (Chairman of commission of Nationalities Affairs); Delegate- Chang Ching-Wu, Chang Kuo-hua, Sun Chib-yuan, Delegates with full powers of the local government of Tibet: Chief Delegate- Kaloon Ngabou Ngawang Jigme (Ngabo Shape); Delegate- Dazasak Khemey Sonam Wangdi, Khentrung Thupten Tenthar, Khenchung Thupten Lekmuun, Rimshi Samposey Tenzin Thundup. Peking 23rd May 1951.

Soon after his arrival in Tezpur, India, His Holiness the Dalai Lama issued a statement on 18th April 1959, explaining that the 17-Point Agreement was signed under duress and that the Chinese government had deliberately violated the terms of the Agreement. Thus from that day onwards, he declared that the agreement would be considered null and void, and he would strive for restoration of Tibet's independence –Thuten Kesang

Appendix VII

RESOLUTION 1723 (XVI)
20 December 1961

The General Assembly,

Recalling its resolution 1353 (XIV) of 21 October 1959 on the question of Tibet,

Gravely concerned at the continuation of events in Tibet, including the violation of the fundamental human rights of the Tibetan people and the suppression of the distinctive cultural and religious life which they have traditionally enjoyed,

Noting with deep anxiety the severe hardships which these events have inflicted on the Tibetan people, as evidenced by the large-scale exodus of Tibetan refugees to the neighboring countries,

Considering that these events violate fundamental human rights and freedoms set out in the Charter of the United Nations and the Universal Declaration of Human Rights, including the principle of self-determination of peoples and nations, and have the deplorable effect of increasing international tension and embittering relations between peoples,

1. *Reaffirms its conviction* that respect for the principles of the Charter of the United Nations and of the Universal Declaration of Human Rights is essential for the evolution of a peaceful world order based on the rule of law;
2. *Solemnly renews* its call for the cessation of practices which deprive the Tibetan people of their fundamental human rights and freedoms, including their right to self-determination;
3. *Expresses the hope* that the Member States will make all possible efforts, as appropriate, towards achieving the purposes of the present resolution.

Appendix VIII

UN RESOLUTION 2079

El Salvador, Ireland, Malaysia, Malta, Nicaragua, Philippines, and Thailand requested 3rd consideration of "The Question of Tibet" in the UN General Assembly. Resolution 2079 (XX) was adopted by the General Assembly by a vote of 43 to 26, with 22 abstentions.

18 December 1965

The General Assembly,

Bearing in mind the principles relating to human rights and fundamental freedoms set forth in the Charter of the United Nations and proclaimed in the Universal Declaration of Human Rights,

Reaffirming its resolutions 1353 (XIV) of 21 October 1959 and 1723 (XVI) of 20 December 1961 on the question of Tibet,

Gravely concerned at the continued violation of the fundamental rights and freedoms of the people of Tibet and the continued suppression of their distinctive cultural and religious life, as evidenced by the exodus of refugees to the neighbouring countries,

Deplores the continued violation of the fundamental rights and freedoms of the people of Tibet;

Reaffirms that respect for the principles of the Charter of the United Nations and of the Universal Declaration of Human Rights is essential for the evolution of a peaceful world order based on the rule of law;

Declares its conviction that the violation of human rights and fundamental freedoms in Tibet and the suppression of the distinctive cultural and religious life of its people increase international tension and embitter relations between peoples;

Solemnly renews its call for the cessation of all practices which deprive the Tibetan people of the human rights and fundamental freedoms which they have always enjoyed;

Appeals to all States to use their best endeavors to achieve the purposes of the present resolution.

Remarks by India on the United Nations General Assembly, Resolution 2079 (XX)

Remarks made in the United Nations General Assembly - 20th Session - 1394th Plenary Meeting. New York. UN Doc. A/PV.1394

AGENDA ITEM 91: QUESTION OF TIBET

1. Mr. Zakaria (India): As representatives are aware, for the past fifteen years the question of Tibet has been, from time to time, under the consideration of the United Nations. It was first raised here in 1950 at the fifth session of the General Assembly, but it could not be placed on the agenda. In fact, my country opposed its inclusion at that time because we were assured by China that it was anxious to settle the problem by peaceful means. However, instead of improving, the situation in Tibet began to worsen, and since then the question has come up several times before the General Assembly of the United Nations.

Our delegation participated in the discussion at the fourteenth session, in 1959, and although we abstained from voting we made it clear that, because of our close historical, cultural and religious ties with the Tibetans, we could not but be deeply moved and affected by what was happening in that region. I've hoped against hope that wiser counsel would prevail among the Chinese and that there would be an end to the sufferings of the people of Tibet.

2. However, the passage of time has completely belied our hopes. As the days pass, the situation becomes worse and cries out for the attention of all mankind. As we know, ever since Tibet came under the strangle-hold of China, the Tibetans have been subjected to a continuous and increasing ruthlessness which has few parallels in the annals of the world. In the name of introducing "democratic reforms" and of fighting a "counter-revolution", the Chinese have indulged in the worst kind of genocide and the suppression of a minority race.

3. To begin with, we in India were hopeful that, as contacts between the Chinese and the Tibetans under the changed set-up became closer and more intimate, a more harmonious relationship would emerge. In fact, in 1956, as a result of his long talks with Mr. Chou En-lai, the Chinese Premier, my late Prime Minister, Jawaharlal Nehru, felt confident that a mutually agreeable adjustment between the two peoples would be established. Even the Dalai Lama expressed a similar hope to our late Prime Minister, but, as subsequent events have proved, the Chinese never believed in living up to their assurances. They promised autonomy to Tibet and the safeguarding of its cultural and religious heritage and traditions but, as

the International Commission of Jurists in its June 1959 report on Tibet has emphasized, they attempted, on the contrary, "to destroy the national, ethnical, racial and religious group of Tibetans as such by killing members of the group and by causing serious bodily and mental harm to members of the group."[1]

4. The world is aware that it was in protest against the oppression and enslavement of Tibet that the Dalai Lama, who is held in the highest esteem by all Tibetans and, indeed, respected as a spiritual leader by all Indians, fled from Lhasa and took asylum in India. Today there are thousands of Tibetan refugees in my country-approximately 50,000-who have left their hearths and homes and fled from their country to join their leader and seek refuge in India. The flight of these refugees still continues, for the Chinese have transformed Tibet into a vast military camp, where the indigenous Tibetans are made to live like hewers of wood and drawers of water.
5. Although the relationship between Tibet and India is centuries old and has flourished all through the ages in all its manifestations, whether religious, cultural or economic, we have always taken care not to make that relationship a political problem. In recent years, despite the fact that the Dalai Lama and thousands of his Tibetan followers have come to our land, and despite the fact that China has turned Tibet itself into a base for aggression against our northern borders, we have not exploited the situation. Undoubtedly, our national sentiments are now and again aroused as a result of the atrocities and cruelties committed by the Chinese against Tibetans, but we have exercised the greatest caution, for we believe that what should concern all of us is the much larger human problem, namely, the

plight of these good and innocent people who are being victimized merely because they are different, ethnically and culturally, from the Chinese.

6. Here I feel that it would not be out of place to put before this Assembly the following facts which stand out stubbornly and irrefutably in connexion with Chinese policy in Tibet: i.The autonomy guaranteed in the Sino-Tibetan Agreement of 1951 has from the beginning remained a dead letter; ii.Through increasing application of military force, the Chinese have in fact obliterated the autonomous character of Tibet; iii. There has been arbitrary confiscation of properties belonging to monasteries and individuals and Tibetan Government institutions; iv. Freedom of religion is denied to the Tibetans, and Buddhism is being suppressed, together with the system of priests, monasteries, shrines and monuments v. The Tibetans are allowed no freedom of information or expression; vi. There has also been carried out a systematic policy of killing, imprisonment and deportation of those Tibetans who have been active in their opposition to Chinese rule; vii. The Chinese have forcibly transferred large numbers of Tibetan children to China in order to denationalize them, to indoctrinate them in Chinese ideology and to make them forget their own Tibetan religion, culture and way of life; and viii. There has also been a large-scale attempt to bring Han Chinese into Tibet, and thereby make Tibet Chinese and overwhelm the indigenous people with a more numerous Chinese population.
7. These atrocities, carried out ruthlessly, with utter disregard for Tibetan sentiments and aspirations, and in complete violation of universally recognized human rights, add up

to a frightful programme of the suppression of a whole people. It surpasses anything that colonialists have done in the past to the peoples whom they ruled and enslaved. That is why the United Nations General Assembly took note of the situation in Tibet and passed two resolutions, one in 1959 and the other in 1961, deploring the denial of these human rights to the people of Tibet by the Chinese Government and appealing to it to restore those rights to the Tibetan people. But all such pleas have fallen on deaf ears.

8. Is this situation not a challenge to human conscience? Can we - dedicated as we are here to the Charter of the United Nations and the Universal Declaration of Human Rights - remain mute spectators to the ghastly tragedy that is being enacted by a ruthless and oppressive régime in Tibet? In a recent appeal to the Secretary-General of the United Nations and to the Member States [see A/6081], the Dalai Lama, who has been a model of restraint, serenity and, indeed, of humanity, has warned the Organization that the Chinese, if unchecked, would "resort to still more brutal means of exterminating the Tibetan race". There is no limit to the hardships that the Tibetan people are suffering. Even their supply of food is restricted and controlled by the Chinese, who first feed their military forces in Tibet, and then whatever remains is given to the indigenous Tibetans. My delegation naturally feels concerned about the terrible deterioration in the situation in Tibet. On 17 December 1964, for instance, the Dalai Lama was formally deprived of his position as Chairman of the Preparatory Committee for the Autonomous Region of Tibet and denounced as "an incorrigible running dog of imperialism and foreign reactionaries"; this was immediately followed

by the deposition on 30 December 1964 of the Panchen Lama, whom the Chinese tried assiduously to take under their wing, and by his condemnation as a leader of the "clique of reactionary serf owners".

9. Thus the Chinese have severed the remaining political links between Tibet and its two politico- religious structures, and have given a final blow to what they fondly used to call, in the past, "the special status of Tibet".
10. Moreover, the campaign to dispossess Tibetan peasants of their land and to distribute, their properties is also being accelerated with the definition of what precisely constitutes feudal elements being expanded, from time to time, to cover a wider and wider range of peasants. In fact, these so-called land reforms are being used by the Chinese Government to advance its own political purpose and to turn the Tibetan peasants into slaves of its system. The naked truth-which all of us must face - is that the Chinese Government is determined to obliterate the Tibetan people; but surely no people can remain for long suppressed. I have faith in the world community. I believe it will be able to help restore to the Tibetans all the freedoms which we have enshrined, with such dedication, in the Universal Declaration of Human Rights.
11. For our part, we assure the United Nations that - as in the past - we shall continue to give all facilities to the Tibetan refugees, and do our best to alleviate their sufferings and hardships. The Dalai Lama has been living in India for some years now, and is carrying on his religious and humanitarian activities without any restrictions from us. We shall continue to give the Dalai Lama and his simple and peace- loving people these facilities and all our hospitality.

12. It is for these reasons that we support, fully and wholeheartedly, the cause of the people of Tibet. Our hearts go out to them in their miserable plight and in the terrible suppression that they are suffering at the hands of the Government of the People's Republic of China. Although that régime has given us, and continues to give us, provocations, we have refused to use the Tibetan refugees as pawns in our conflict with China. We do not believe that the sufferings of one people should be made a weapon in the armoury of another.
13. Finally, may I express the fervent hope, on behalf of the United Nations, that there will soon be an end to the reign of misery and oppression in Tibet, and that the people of Tibet will be able to share with us all those human rights that all of us, in different lands, are so fortunate as to possess and enjoy.
14. My delegation will therefore vote in favour of the draft resolution in document [A/L. 473], and I commend the same to this Assembly.

---

1. *The Question of Tibet and the Rule of Law* (Geneva, International Commission of Jurists, 1959).

Appendix IX

CASES OF SELF-IMMOLATION

1. **Thupten Ngodup,** 60, Ex-soldier. 27 Apr 1998, Jantar Mantar, New Delhi, India.
2. **Lhakpa Tsering,** President of RTYC Bangalore. 23 Nov 2006, Mumbai, India.
3. **Tapey,** 20, Monk. 27 Feb 2009, Ngaba Town, Amdo Ngaba (Ngaba TAP, SIC).
4. **Lobsang Phuntsok,** 21, Monk. 16 Mar 2011, Ngaba Town, Amdo Ngaba (Ngaba TAP, SIC).
5. **Tsewang Norbu,** 29, Monk. 18 Aug 2011, Kham Tawu (Kandze TAP, SIC).
6. **Lobsang Kelsang,** 18, Monk. 26 Sep 2011, Ngaba Town, Amdo Ngaba (Ngaba TAP, SIC).
7. **Lobsang Könchok,** 18, Monk. 26 Sep 2011, Ngaba Town, Amdo Ngaba (Ngaba TAP, SIC).
8. **Kelsang Wangchuk,** 17, Monk. 3 Oct 2011, Ngaba Town, Amdo Ngaba (Ngaba TAP, SIC).
9. **Choephel,** 19, Former Monk. 7 Oct 2011, Ngaba Town, Amdo Ngaba (Ngaba TAP, SIC).
10. **Khaying,** 18, Former Monk. 7 Oct 2011, Ngaba Town, Amdo Ngaba (Ngaba TAP, SIC).

11. **Norbu Dramdul,** 19, Former Monk. 15 Oct **2011,** Ngaba Town, Amdo Ngaba (Ngaba TAP, SIC).
12. **Tenzin Wangmo,** 20, Nun of Mame Dechen Chokhorling Nunnery. 17 Oct 2011, Ngaba Town, Amdo Ngaba (Ngaba TAP, SIC).
13. **Dawa Tsering,** 38, Monk. 25 Oct 2011, Kham Kandze (Kandze TAP, SIC).
14. **Palden Choetso,** 35, Nun. 3 Nov 2011, Kham Tawu (Kandze TAP, SIC).
15. **Sherab Tsedor,** 25. 4 Nov 2011, Chinese Embassy, New Delhi, India.
16. **Bhutuk,** 45. 10 Nov 2011, Boudhanath, Kathmandu, Nepal.
17. **Tenzin Phuntsok,** 41, Former monk. 1 Dec 2011, Karma, Kham Chamdo (Chamdo Prefecture, TAR).
18. **Lobsang Tsultrim,** 22, Former monk. 6 Jan 2012, Ngaba Town, Amdo Ngaba (Ngaba TAP, SIC).
19. **Tenyi,** 18, Former Monk. 6 Jan 2012, Ngaba Town, Amdo Ngaba (Ngaba TAP, SIC).
20. **Sobha Tulku,** 42, Tulku. 8 Jan 2012, Amdo Darlak (Golok, QIN).
21. **Lobsang Jamyang,** 21, Member of an association for the promotion of Tibetan language. 14 Jan 2012, Ngaba Town, Amdo Ngaba (Ngaba TAP, SIC).
22. **Rigzin Dorje,** 19, Former Monk. 8 Feb 2012, Ngaba Town, Amdo Ngaba (Ngaba TAP, SIC).
23. **Sonam Rabyang,** 37, Monk. 9 Feb 2012, Kham Thrindu (Jyekundo, QIN).
24. **Tenzin Choedron,** 18, Nun. 11 Feb 2012, Ngaba Town, Amdo Ngaba (Ngaba TAP, SIC).
25. **Lobsang Gyatso,** 19, Monk. 13 Feb 2012, Ngaba Town, Amdo Ngaba (Ngaba TAP, SIC).
26. **Dhamchoe Sangpo,** 38, Monk. 17 Feb 2012, Sengge, Amdo Themchen (Tsonub MTAP, QIN).
27. **Nangdrol,** 18, Layman. 19 Feb 2012, Amdo Dzamthang (Ngaba TAP, SIC).
28. **Tsering Kyi,** 19, Student. 3 Mar 2012, Amdo Machu (Kanlho TAP, GAN).

29. **Rinchen,** 30, Pastoralist, widowed mother of four. 4 Mar 2012, Ngaba Town, Amdo Ngaba (Ngaba TAP, SIC).
30. **Dorjee,** 18. 5 Mar 2012, Charo, Amdo Ngaba (Ngaba TAP, SIC).
31. **Gepey,** 18, Monk. 10 Mar 2012, Ngaba Town, Amdo Ngaba (Ngaba TAP, SIC).
32. **Jamyang Palden,** 34, Monk. 14 Mar 2012, Rongwo Gönchen, Amdo Rebkong (Malho TAP, QIN).
33. **Lobsang Tsultrim,** 20, Monk. 16 Mar 2012,Ngaba Town, Amdo Ngaba (Ngaba TAP, SIC).
34. **Sonam Dhargye,** 43, Farmer. 17 Mar 2012, Rongwo Gyelthang, Amdo Rebkong (Malho TAP QIN).
35. **Jamphel Yeshi,** 27. 26 Mar 2012, Jantar Mantar, New Delhi, India.
36. **Lobsang Sherab,** 20. 28 Mar 2012, Charo, Amdo Ngaba (Ngaba TAP, SIC).
37. **Chime Palden,** 21, Monk. 30 Mar 2012, Gyalrong Barkham (Ngaba TAP, SIC).
38. **Tenpa Dhargye,** 22, Monk. 30 Mar 2012, Gyalrong Barkham (Ngaba TAP, SIC).
39. **Tulku Thupten Nyendak,** 45, Monk. 6 Apr 2012, Lhagang, Kham Dartsedo (Kandze TAP, SIC).
40. **Ani Atse,** 23, Nun. 6 Apr 2012, Lhagang, Kham Dartsedo (Kandze TAP, SIC).
41. **Choephak Kyap,** 25. 19 Apr 2012, Amdo Dzamthang (Ngaba TAP, SIC).
42. **Sonam,** 24. 19 Apr 2012, Amdo Dzamthang (Ngaba TAP, SIC).
43. **Dorje Tseten,** 19. 27 May 2012, Lhasa, Central Tibet Lhasa Municipality (Lhasa, TAR).
44. **Dargye,** 25. 27 May 2012, Lhasa, Central Tibet Lhasa Municipality (Lhasa, TAR).
45. **Rikyo,** 33, Mother of three. 30 May 2012, Amdo Dzamthang (Ngaba TAP, SIC).
46. **Tamdrin Thar,** 64, Nomad. 15 Jun 2012, Markethang, Amdo Chentsa (Malho TAP, QIN).
47. **Tenzin Khedup,** 24, Former monk. 20 Jun 2012, Dzatö, Kham Thrindu (Jyekundo TAP, QIN).

48. **Ngawang Norphel,** 22, Former monk. 20 Jun 2012, Dzatö, Kham Thrindu (Jyekundo TAP, QIN).
49. **Dickyi Choezom,** 40, Mother of two. 27 Jun 2012, Dhondupling monastery, Kham Jyekundo (Jyekundo TAP, QIN).
50. **Tsewang Dorje,** 22. 7 Jul 2012, Damchukha, Central Tibet Damshung (Lhasa, TAR).
51. **Lobsang Lozin,** 18, Monk. 17 Jul 2012, Gyalrong Barkham (Ngaba TAP, SIC).
52. **Lobsang Tsultrim,** 21. Monk. 7 Aug 2012, Ngaba Town, Amdo Ngaba (Ngaba TAP, SIC).
53. **Dolkar Kyi,** 26, Mother of two. 8 Aug 2012, Amdo Tsö (Kanlho TAP, GAN).
54. **Choepa,** 24. 10 Aug 2012, Me'uruma, Amdo Ngaba (Ngaba TAP, SIC).
55. **Lungtok,** 20. Monk. 13 Aug 2012, Ngaba Town, Amdo Ngaba (Ngaba TAP, SIC).
56. **Tashi,** 21. Layman. 13 Aug 2012, Ngaba Town, Amdo Ngaba (Ngaba TAP, SIC).
57. **Lobsang Kelsang,** 18. Monk. 27 Aug 2012, Ngaba Town, Amdo Ngaba (Ngaba TAP, SIC).
58. **Damchoe,** 17. Nomad. 27 Aug 2012, Ngaba Town, Amdo Ngaba (Ngaba TAP, SIC).
59. **Yangdrung,** 27. 29 Sept 2012, Dzatö, Kham Thrindu (Jyekundo TAP, QIN).
60. **Gudrub,** 43. 4 Oct 2012, Nakchu Town, Kham (Nakchu Prefecture, TAR).
61. **Sangye Gyatso,** 27, Farmer. 6 Oct 2012, Amdo Tsö (Kanlho TAP, GAN).
62. **Tamdrin Dorje,** 52. 13 Oct 2012, Amdo Tsö (Kanlho TAP, GAN).
63. **Lhamo Kyab,** 27. 20 Oct 2012, Bora, Amdo Sangchu (Kanlho TAP, GAN).
64. **Dhondup,** 61, Nomad. 22 Oct 2012, Labrang Tashikhyil, Amdo Sangchu (Kanlho TAP, GAN).
65. **Dorje Rinchen,** 58, Nomad. 23 Oct 2012, Amdo Sangchu (Kanlho TAP, GAN).
66. **Tsepo,** 20. 25 Oct 2012, Nakrok Phampa, Kham Driru (Nakchu Prefecture, TAR).

67. **Tenzin,** 25. 25 Oct 2012, Nakrok Phampa, Kham Driru (Nakchu Prefecture, TAR).
68. **Lhamo Tseten,** 24. 26 Oct 2012, Amchok, Amdo Sangchu (Kanlho TAP, GAN).
69. **Thubwang Kyab,** 23, Nomad. 26 Oct 2012, Sangkhok, Amdo Sangchu (Kanlho TAP, GAN).
70. **Dorje Lhundrub,** 25, Farmer. 4 Nov 2012, Amdo Rebkong (Malho TAP, QIN).
71. **Dorje,** 15, Monk. 7 Nov 2012, Gomang, Amdo Ngaba (Ngaba TAP, SIC).
72. **Samdrub,** 16, Monk. 7 Nov 2012, Gomang, Amdo Ngaba (Ngaba TAP, SIC).
73. **Dorje Kyab,** 16, Monk. 7 Nov 2012, Gomang, Amdo Ngaba (Ngaba TAP, SIC).
74. **Tamdrin Tso,** 23, Mother. 7 Nov 2012, Amdo Rebkong (Malho TAP, QIN).
75. **Tsegye,** 27. 7 Nov 2012, Benkar, Kham Driru (Nakchu Prefecture, TAR).
76. **Kelsang Jinpa,** 18, Nomad. 8 Nov 2012,Amdo Rebkong (Malho TAP, QIN).
77. **Gonpo Tsering,** 18, Artist. 10 Nov 2012, Lushö, Tsö City (Kanlho TAP, GAN).
78. **Nyingkar Tashi,** 24. 12 Nov 2012, Dowa, Amdo Rebkong (Malho TAP, QIN).
79. **Nyingchak Bhum,** 16.12 Nov 2012, Dowa, Amdo Rebkong (Malho TAP, QIN).
80. **Tangzin Drolma,** 23.15 Nov 2012, Tsenmo, Amdo Rebkong (Malho TAP, QIN).
81. **Khambum Gyal,** 18. 15 Nov 2012, Gyawo Luchu, Amdo Rebkong (Malho TAP, QIN).
82. **Chakmo Kyi,** 26, Mother. 17 Nov 2012, Amdo Rebkong (Malho TAP, QIN).
83. **Sangdak Tsering,** 24, Nomad. 17 Nov 2012, Dokarmo, Amdo Tsekhok (Malho TAP, QIN).
84. **Wangchen Norbu,** 25. 19 Nov 2012, Kangtsa, Amdo Yadzi (Tsoshar TAP, QIN).

85. **Tsering Dhondub,** 34. 20 Nov 2012, Amchok, Amdo Sangchu (Kanlho TAP, GAN).
86. **Lumbum Gyal,** 18. 22 Nov 2012, Dowa, Amdo Rebkong (Malho TAP, QIN).
87. **Tamdrin Kyab,** 23. 22 Nov 2012, Amdo Luchu (Kanlho TAP, GAN).
88. **Tamdrin Dorje,** 29. 24 Nov 2012, Dokarmo, Amdo Tsekhok (Malho TAP, QIN).
89. **Sangye Dolma.** 17, Nun. 25 Nov 2012, Dokarmo, Amdo Tsekhok (Malho TAP, QIN).
90. **Wangyal,** 20. 26 Nov 2012, Amdo Serthar (Kandze TAP, SIC).
91. **Konchok Tsering,** 18, Nomad. 26 Nov 2012, Amchok, Amdo Sangchu (Kanlho TAP, GAN).
92. **Gonpo Tsering,** 24. 26 Nov 2012, Amdo Luchu (Kanlho TAP, GAN).
93. **Kelsang Kyab,** 24, Nomad. 27 Nov 2012, Kyangtsa, Amdo Dzoge (Ngaba TAP, SIC).
94. **Sangye Tashi,** 18. 27 Nov 2012, Sangkhok, Amdo Sangchu (Kanlho TAP, GAN).
95. **Wande Khar,** 21. 28 Nov 2012, Dzöge, Amdo Tsö (Kanlho, GAN).
96. **Tsering Tashi,** 31. 29 Nov 2012, Samtsa, Amdo Luchu (Kanlho TAP, GAN).
97. **Konchok Kyab,** 29. 30 Nov 2012, Shakdom, Amdo Dzöge (Ngaba TAP, SIC).

List of Contributors

Lobsang Sangay

Sikyong Dr. Lobsang Sangay was born in 1968 in a village in Darjeeling, West Bengal and completed his schooling from Central School for Tibetans (CST) in Sonada and Darjeeling and graduated in English Literature and Bachelor in Law from Delhi University, 1991/1994 respectively. In 2004 he was awarded Doctorate in Law from Harvard Law School.

In 2007, he was selected as one of the 24 Young Leaders of Asia by the Asia Society and in 2011 he was democratically elected as the Kalon Tripa (Executive Head of the Tibetan Cabinet) by the Tibetan diaspora and he took oath of office on August 08, 2011. Dr. Sangay is the first elected Tibetan leader who has been bestowed with all the political authority exercised by His Holiness the Dalai Lama.

Penpa Tsering

Mr. Penpa Tsering was born in 1967 at Bylakupee, India. He studied in Central School for Tibetans, Bylakuppe and later graduated with Economics Major from Madras Christian College, Chennai. In 2001, he worked as the Executive Director of Tibetan Parliamentary and Research Policy Centre (TPPRC) in New Delhi for seven years.

In 2008, he was sworn in as the speaker of the 14th Tibetan Parliament-in-exile.

In 2011, he got re-elected to the Fifteenth Tibetan Parliament-in-Exile and again sworn in as the Speaker. He was earlier elected to the twelfth, thirteenth and fourteenth Tibetan Parliament-in-Exile.

Abanti Bhattacharya

Dr. Abanti Bhattacharya is currently Associate Professor at the Department of East Asian Studies, University of Delhi. She teaches courses on China's foreign policy, India-China relations, East Asian international relations and Chinese nationalism. Prior to joining the University of Delhi, Dr. Bhattacharya was an Associate Fellow at the Institute for Defence Studies and Analyses, New Delhi (2002 to 2009) where her research was primarily on Chinese nationalism, minority politics and China's foreign policy. At the IDSA, Dr. Bhattacharya was also a member of the editorial board for the IDSA journal, *Strategic Analysis*, and part of many specialized projects on China, including those from the MEA and the DRDO. She had been part of the Government Exchange Programme and got Chinese language training from Fudan University, Shanghai. She has published extensively in national and international journals including *Issues and Studies*, *Asia-Pacific Review*, *East Asia*, *Journal of East Asian Affairs* among others.

Chok Tsering

Mr. Chok Tsering is currently a part time Research Associate cum Programme Coordinator at the Foundation for Non-violent Alternatives, New Delhi. He is doing his M.Phil. in Central Asian Studies from JNU, New Delhi. Prior to joining FNVA, he worked at Institute of Peace and Conflict Studies, New Delhi as a research intern with China Research Programme.

P.P. Shukla

Amb. Prabhat Prakash Shukla is the Joint Director, Vivekananda International Foundation (VIF). He was born on 29 March 1951 in New Delhi, where he also went to school and university. A good academic student, he finished his school and college education with honours, and finished his masters at the well-known Delhi School of Economics. Following his Masters, he joined the Indian Foreign Service in 1974. During a career spanning 37 years, he served in Moscow, Brussels, London and Kathmandu, among other places. He served in Delhi twice, including as the Diplomatic Adviser to the Prime Minister from 1996 to 2000. He has recently retired as Ambassador of India to Moscow and has settled in New Delhi.

Geshe Ngawang Samten

Prof. Samten is the Vice-Chancellor of Central University of Tibetan Studies, Sarnath, Varanasi. He came to India along with his parents after the Chinese occupation of Tibet in 1959. He had his monastic education at Gaden Shartse Monastery at Mundgod in Karnataka. He obtained Geshe Dhorampa and later Geshe Lharampa degree, equivalent to Ph.D. degree in the modern system.

He has been an outstanding scholar in Tibetan and Sanskrit languages and has great translation skills. He is also actively engaged in Hindi translations of Buddhist texts in Sanskrit and Tibetan. He is credited with important publications, such as a critical edition of *Abhidhammattha Samgaho*, a critical edition of Sanskrit and Tibetan versions of the *Pindidrita* and the *Pancakrama* of Nagarjuna, and recently, *The Ocean of Reasoning*, an annotated English translation of the commentary on Nagarjuna's *Mulamadhyamaka Karika* by the Tibetan master thinker Tson-Kha-Pa, published by Oxford University Press. *The Ocean of Reasoning* is acclaimed far and wide. Professor Samten has been on numerous academic bodies and expert committees of University Grants Commission of India; Ministries, Government of India, and as a member on the boards of several Institutes in USA, Canada, Thailand, France and Austria. In 2009, he has been awarded *Padma Shri* by the President of India for his distinguished services in the fields of education and literature.

Ajit Doval

Mr. Ajit Doval, KC is the Director, Vivekananda International Foundation (VIF). He retired as Director, Intelligence Bureau (IB) in 2005. Mr Doval, a highly decorated Kerala cadre IPS officer, whose expertise range from Northeast insurgency, Punjab insurgency, Kashmir separatism to terrorism. He is a much sought after commentator on internal security issues as well as national and international security and strategic affairs both in electronic and print media.

C.D. Sahay

Mr. C.D. Sahay is the Former Secretary (Research and Analysis Wing), Cabinet Secretariat. He joined the Indian Police Service in 1967 and moved to Delhi in 1975 to join the Research and Analysis Wing, India's external Intelligence setup. He rose to head the organisation from 2003 till superannuation in 2005. He has decades of experience in dealing with national security issues and international terrorism. Mr Sahay spends a great deal of time in delivering lectures on these subjects at various training institutions in India.

Bhavna Singh

Ms. Bhavna Singh is Senior Research Officer at the Institute of Peace and Conflict Studies (IPCS), New Delhi and a Doctoral candidate at the Chinese division in the Centre of East Asian Studies, Jawaharlal Nehru University (JNU), New Delhi. Her work focuses on Chinese nationalism and China's foreign policy with regards to the US, Japan and South Asia. She is particularly interested in separatist and sub-national tendencies in the regions of Xinjiang, Tibet, Taiwan and Inner Mongolia. She is the author of the book *China's Discursive Nationalism: Contending in Softer Realms* (Pentagon Press: 2012) and has written for several esteemed journals.

N.C. Vij

General (Retd.) Nirmal Chander Vij, PVSM, UYSM, AVSM was the Vice Chairman of the newly constituted National Disaster Management Authority (NDMA) from 28 Sep 2005 to 28 Sep 2010, with the status of a Cabinet Minister. Gen. Vij had retired from the Indian Army, as the 21st Chief of Army Staff on 31 Jan 2005, after 43 years of distinguished service to the nation.

Earlier he was the Director General of Military Operations (DGMO) during the Kargil War wherein the Country won a historic battle. Gen. Vij also had the distinction of commanding two Corps, including a Strike Corps on the Western Borders and a Corps deployed in Active Counter Insurgency Operations in the North East. He was also Army Commander of Southern Command during his distinguished career in the armed forces.

Rahul K. Bhonsle

Brig. (Retd.) Rahul K. Bhonsle is an army veteran with over three decades active service. He is an independent consultant on research in defence and security issues in South Asia. He has written a number of books on defence and security issues.

Madhu Bhalla

Prof. Madhu Bhalla is currently professor at the Department of East Asian Studies, Delhi University. She has an M.A. and Ph.D. from Queen's University, Canada. Before joining Delhi University in 2005 she taught at the Jawaharlal Nehru University, New Delhi, Queens' University, Canada and Trent University, Canada. Her teaching and research interests lie in the areas of Chinese security and foreign policy, the political economy of China, United States' foreign policy and international relations theory. She has published many scholarly papers in these areas and contributed several book chapters to edited volumes. Prof. Madhu Bhalla has held a visiting fellowship at the Fudan University, Shanghai and has been a visiting scholar at the University of Sichuan at Chengdu. She serves on the advisory bodies of four of the newly instituted China and Asian studies centres across the country.

Madhuri Santanam Sondhi

Ms. Madhuri Santanam Sondhi, writer and researcher, has been Executive President, M.L. Sondhi Institute for Asia-Pacific Affairs since 2004. Her books include *Modernity, Morality and the Mahatma, Martin Buber & Basanta Kumar Mallik: Towards Inter-Civilizational Dialogue and Peace* and (with Mary M. Walker) *Ecology Culture and Philosophy.* From 1962 onwards she has continuously advocated freedom and respect for human rights in Tibet. She presented Evidence on Indian Activities in Support of Tibetan Freedom and the Case for Tibetan Freedom at the Session on Tibet of the Permanent People's Tribunal, Strasbourg (1992).

Thubten Samphel

Mr. Thubten Samphel is the Director of the Tibet Policy Institute, a think tank of the Central Tibetan Administration. Before this he was the secretary of the Department of Information and International Relations of the Central Tibetan Administration. He is the author of *Falling Through the Roof*, a work of fiction. He writes extensively on Tibet for publications and online news services in India and abroad.

Sujit Dutta

Prof. Sujit Dutta is Professor in Conflict Analysis and holds the M.K. Gandhi Chair at the Nelson Mandela Centre for Peace and Conflict Resolution at the Jamia Millia Islamia, a central university in New Delhi. He was till 2009, Senior Fellow and Head of the East Asian Studies Programme at the Institute for Defence Studies and Analyses (IDSA).

His major areas of research and studies have been: Chinese politics, foreign and security policies, India-China relations, India's foreign and security policy, and Asian regionalism. Prof. Dutta has published a large number of research papers and chapters in books, and has edited the book *India and the World: Strategic Thought—the Formative Years.* He edited the country's leading strategic studies and international affairs journal, *Strategic Analysis*, published by Routledge, between 2005 and 2008.

Prof. Dutta was a member of India-China Eminent Persons' Group (2001-2005), Council for Security Cooperation in the Asia Pacific Working Group on Confidence Building Measures (1994-1999), and other high-level bodies devoted to international peace and security building. He was a Senior Fellow at the prestigious United States Institute of Peace, Washington D.C.

Vijay Kranti

Mr. Vijay Kranti is a senior media professional with wide experience in Print Media, TV, Radio, Photography, Media Education and Corporate Communications. During past four decades he has been on the staff of some leading media groups which include India Today, BBC TV, Aaj Tak TV, Zee News TV, Deutsche Welle (German Radio) and Radio Voice of America. He also has wide experience in media teaching and corporate communications. As a journalist, his main subject of specialization is Tibet and China. For past 40 years he has been tracking and writing on Tibetan situation and political developments in India-China relations. He is a keen observer of His Holiness the Dalai Lama's non-violent struggle for the freedom and human rights of his country Tibet.

Mr. Vijay Kranti has eight books to his credit in English and Hindi. These include *Dalai Lama Speaks*, his famous coffee table book on Dalai Lama, and his Hindi Style Book for Discovery Channel. He is the founder editor of *Tibbat Desh*, the first and only Hindi news monthly magazine on Tibet since 1979. He received the coveted K.K. Birla Foundation Fellowship in journalism for his work on Tibet.

Claude Arpi

Born in 1949 in Angoulême, France, Mr. Claude Arpi studied dental surgery in Bordeaux University. After graduating as a Dental Surgeon in June 1974, he decided to come to India. He is the author of *The Fate of Tibet* (Har Anand Publications, 1999), *Tibet, le pays sacrifié*(Calmann-Lévy, Paris, 2000), *And Dark Shall be the Night: The Karma of Tibet* (Editions Auroville Press International, 2001), *La politique française de Nehru : 1947-1954* (Pavilions Series, Auroville 2002), *Cachemire, le paradis perdu* (Editions Philippe Picquier, France, 2004), *Born in Sin: The Panchsheel Agreement* (Mittal Publications, New Delhi, 2004), *India and Her Neighbourhood: A French Observers' Views* (Har Anand, Delhi, 2005), *Tibet: The Lost Frontier* (Lancers Publishers) and *The Negotiations that Never Were: Dharamsala and Beijing* (Lancer Publishers). More recently, he published *1962: The McMahon Saga* (Lancer Publishers).

He regularly writes on Tibet, China, India and Indo-French relations for *Rediff.com, Sify.com, The Pioneer, The Statesman, DNA* and other Indian publications. He is member of the Editorial Board of the *Indian Defence Review.*

P.K. Gautam

Col. (Retd.) P.K. Gautam joined IDSA in 2005. He has over 29 years of military service and is a veteran of 1971 war in Bangladesh and Operation Meghdoot (Siachen). He has a number of publications on environment, military matters and non traditional security and has authored "Climate Change and Environmental Degradation in Tibet: Implications for Environmental Security in South Asia", *Strategic Analysis*, Vol.34, No.5, September 2010 and *Tibet and India's Security: Himalayan Region, Refugees and Sino-Indian Relations* co-authored with Dr. Jagannath Panda and Dr. Zakir Hussain, May 2012 (IDSA Task Force Report). He is now researching on Kautilya's *Arthasastra.*

Sonam Sangmo

Ms. Sonam Sangmo was born and raised in India and has never seen her country Tibet. She did her schooling from Tibetan Children's Village School, Dharamsala and graduated in English Literature from Delhi University. From the year 2006 to 2011 she worked as the Tibet Support Groups Liaison Officer in Department of Information and International Relations, Central Tibetan Administration (CTA), Dharamsala. At present she is working as the Tibetan Settlement Officer in Darjeeling, which is a Unit of Department of Home, CTA, Dharamsala.

Tenzin Norbu

Mr. Tenzin Norbu, was born in Dharamshala and did his schooling from TCV school, graduated in MS. Environmental Technology from Asian Institute of Technology, Bangkok. He has worked as a senior research associate in the Environmental Engineering Program at AIT, Bangkok. He joined Central Tibetan Administration, Dharamsala in the year 2008 and has been since then serving as a researcher and Director of the Environment and Development Desk at the Department of Information and International Relations.